Market Restraints in the Retail Drug Industry

Industrial Research Unit
Department of Industry
Wharton School of Finance and Commerce
University of Pennsylvania

Industrial Research Unit Study No. 43

The Industrial Research Unit is the business and labor market research arm of the Industry Department of the Wharton School of Finance and Commerce. Founded after World War I as a separate Wharton School Department, the Industrial Research Unit has a long record of publication and research in the labor market, productivity, union relations, and business report fields. Major Industrial Research Unit Studies are published as research projects are completed.

OTHER RECENT INDUSTRIAL RESEARCH UNIT STUDIES

Gladys L. Palmer, *et al., The Reluctant Job Changer.*   No. 40

George M. Parks, *The Economics of Carpeting and Resilient Flooring: An Evaluation and Comparison.*   No. 41

Michael H. Moskow, *Teachers and Unions: The Applicability of Collective Bargaining to Public Education.*   No. 42

Herbert R. Northrup and Gordon R. Storholm, *Restrictive Labor Practices in the Supermarket Industry.*   No. 44

F. MARION FLETCHER

Market Restraints
in the
Retail Drug Industry

University of Pennsylvania Press · Philadelphia · 1967

Copyright © 1967 by the TRUSTEES OF THE UNIVERSITY OF PENNSYLVANIA
Library of Congress Catalog Card Number 67-26218
7561
Manufactured in the United States of America

To Linda

Preface

Occupational and business licensing are complex. There appears to be considerable overlap in the laws within a given state, partly because licensing is carried out at city and county levels, as well as by the state. Another reason for the complexity is the varying purposes for licensing: to obtain revenue, to regulate businesses, and to protect local businesses from incursions by organizations in other states.

One possible—and very dangerous—result of business licensing, completely overlooked by the U.S. Justice Department, is the curtailment of competition if licenses are withheld from qualified establishments. Competition can be further reduced if the rules and regulations promulgated by the licensing agency restrict legitimate business practices to insulate one group of businessmen from the competitive effect of other businesses in the same field.

Because of its inherent affinity with the public interest, probably no other industry is so closely regulated as the drug industry. The regulation runs the full gamut of political subdivisions—federal, state, and local. The supervision also extends from a drug's inception to its retail sale. At one extreme, regulation begins with the federal government prescribing how and to what extent new drugs shall be tested. At the opposite end of the spectrum, the retail level, governmental regulations specify which person may actually make the sale and which business may carry drugs for retail sale.

That most of the total drug industry regulation is essential cannot be questioned. It is the established obligation of the various levels of government to prevent dangerous and inefficacious drugs from being offered to consumers and to require a truthful description of the effects of a drug—both to cure illnesses and to cause new ones (side effects).

There remains, however, the question of at what point public health protection ends and restrictive trade practices begin. There is such a thing as monopoly creation by over-protection of health. Where such over-protection results in marketing practices which are at odds with the well-accepted precept that there should be a minimum of trade barriers in industry, special privilege for a few is substituted for the protection of the public health. This study revolves about the public health *vis-a-vis* the trade barriers question.

Many people have contributed to this study. It would be impossible to name them all, and some prefer to remain anonymous. A note of special thanks, however, is to be accorded to the secretaries of state boards of pharmacy and the executives of the retail drug industry with whom I visited. In addition, generous help was given by several trade and professional organizations. Among these are the American Pharmaceutical Association, National Association of Boards of Pharmacy, National Association of Chain Drug Stores, National Association of Retail Druggists, and The Proprietary Association.

Several professors at the University of Pennsylvania read the entire manuscript and made many helpful criticisms. These professors are Dr. Cornelius W. Gillam, Dr. Almarin Phillips, and Dr. Ross A. Webber.

Dr. Herbert R. Northrup, Chairman of the Department of Industry, has also given invaluable assistance. In addition to a research grant made available through his efforts, Dr. Northrup supervised the study from its inception and in that capacity suggested several improvements during the preparation of the final manuscript.

Mrs. Aileen Cummings and Miss Mary McCutcheon performed skillfully, diligently, and patiently as typists under trying circumstances. I am especially appreciative of Miss McCutcheon's efforts during the final prepublication phase. In addition, Mrs. Marjorie C. Denison and Miss Elsa Klemp of the Industrial Research Unit disposed of the final editorial details with their usual efficiency.

The contributions of my wife to this study are incalculable. In addition to her housewifely duties and her obligations as Assistant Professor of Insurance at the Wharton School, she has given distinguished service as an unpaid research assistant, as a demanding editor, and as a sympathizing encourager. Her efforts hastened the completion of the study by several months, and I am grateful for all she has done and all she is.

If, despite all the assistance I have been fortunate enough to receive, any errors and omissions remain, they are my own.

Philadelphia   F. MARION FLETCHER
February 1, 1967

Foreword

Barriers to competition in the marketplace are frequent subjects of scholarly works and equally frequent targets of governmental action. Generally, however, both the subjects studied and the actions taken by government involve the attempts of large enterprises to control the price or the market for a product or group of products. Little attention has been devoted either by scholars or by government activists to the debilitation of competition by small business or professional groups. Likewise, business and occupational licensing practices have not been studied in any detail, nor do they seem to have been the target of significant governmental investigations or actions.

The significance of Dr. F. Marion Fletcher's study and the basic reason why it is being published for the Industrial Research Unit is that it focuses attention on the restrictions on competition by a group of small businessmen and by a profession, acting with the overt assistance of governmental bodies. The extent to which these practices exist in other industries is not known, but the information uncovered by Dr. Fletcher suggests that it would be fruitful for scholars to examine several other industries, utilizing the same format which Dr. Fletcher has developed. It may well be that impediments to competition in many other industries are as substantial as they are in the retail drug field.

This book represents a revision and updating of Dr. Fletcher's University of Pennsylvania dissertation. Members of the Dissertation Committee included Drs. Cornelius W. Gillam, Professor of Business Law; Almarin Phillips, Professor of Economics and Law; Ross A. Webber, Assistant Professor of Industry; and the undersigned. The Committee unanimously recommended publication of the work. Dr. Fletcher's researches were supported by funds provided by the Industrial Research Unit from grants and sales of publications. It is hoped that its publication will encourage other studies in this general area.

Philadelphia
February 15, 1967

HERBERT R. NORTHRUP, *Chairman*
Department of Industry

Contents

PART II: RESTRICTIONS ON THE SALE OF
PROPRIETARY DRUGS

PART III: RESTRICTIVE PHARMACY LAWS AND
RESULTING LITIGATION

PART IV: RESULTS AND IMPLICATIONS OF
RESTRICTIONISM

List of Tables and Figures

PART ONE

Introduction

CHAPTER ONE

Introduction

One of the almost inviolable guarantees under law is the right to engage in any lawful occupation or to initiate any legal business enterprise. Any abridgement of this right by any party must clearly be related to the public health, safety, or welfare. Certain occupations and business establishments have been deemed essential to the public health, safety, or welfare. In these cases unrestricted entry is injurious to the public health. For example, an individual may not simply open an office and start practicing medicine or law. It is in the best interests of the populace to restrict entrants to persons who can demonstrate their competence in these fields. By the device of licensing those persons, the state is thus protector of the public, and, in a sense, guarantor of the proficiency of those permitted to practice in such fields.

In recent years the states have come to require licensure of a large number of occupations. Mandatory licensure creates an occupational licensing board for each vocation for which licensure is required. In many instances, the place of business, as well as the practitioner, must be licensed. This book is mainly a study of one of these two-function occupational licensing boards—the board of pharmacy.

Retail drug outlets and pharmacists, the professionals most closely associated with drug outlets, have, in the past half-century, come to be recognized as being worthy of inclusion in that group requiring licensing for public health purposes. There are limits, however, beyond which states may not go. States, through their licensing agencies, are obligated to license all who meet the qualifications imposed. Further, there must be an equal administration of the applicable laws—standards must be the same for all applicants. Similarly, rules promulgated by the licensing bodies must be uniformly enforced and must be designed to protect the public health. Regulations which exclude legitimate applicants or which place unreasonable restraints upon the conduct of the business are not allowed—economic questions may not be stated in terms of public health.

Nevertheless, there have been complaints that some state boards of pharmacy have refused to grant licenses to pharmacies for economic reasons—particularly those to be located in general merchandise stores or supermarkets. Moreover, it is claimed that rules and regulations have been adopted that impair operations of some drug outlets without a corresponding benefit to public health, but with a benefit to independent retail druggists and conventional drugstores.

As a result, this study was conceived to investigate the allegations of entry barriers and restraint of trade in the retail drug industry.

The results of this study have vindicated those who have complained of restrictions. As the research progressed, it became evident that the restrictions were too numerous, too uniform, and too clearly discriminatory to be anything but economic weapons directed toward those who would disrupt the status quo of retail drug distribution.

Adam Smith understood the situation:

Merchants . . . draw to themselves the greatest share of the public consideration. . . . As their thoughts . . . are commonly exercised rather about the interest of their own particular branch of business, than about that of the society, their judgment, even when given with the greatest candour (which it has not been upon every occasion), is much more to be depended upon with regard to the former of those two objects, than with regard to the latter. . . . The interest of the dealers . . . in any particular branch of trade . . . is always in some respects different from, and even opposite to, that of the public. To widen the market and to narrow the competition, is always the interest of the dealers. To widen the market may frequently be agreeable enough to the interest of the public; but to narrow the competition must always be against it, and can serve only to enable the dealers, by raising their profits above what they naturally would be, to levy, for their own benefit, an absurd tax upon the rest of their fellow-citizens. The proposal of any new law or regulation of commerce which comes from this order, ought always to be listened to with great precaution, and ought never to be adopted till after having been long and carefully examined, not only with the most scrupulous, but with the most suspicious attention. It comes from an order of men, whose interest is never exactly the same with that of the public, who have generally an interest to deceive and even to oppress the public, and who accordingly have, upon many occasions, both deceived and oppressed it.[1]

Some merchants have not changed since Adam Smith's day. There are still attempts to "narrow the competition" and to impose "an absurd

[1] Adam Smith, *The Wealth of Nations*, ed. Edwin Cannan (New York: Random House, n.d.), p. 250.

levy" upon the public.[2] The necessity of licensing pharmacists and drugstores has provided one such vehicle for accomplishment of these restrictionist goals.

After it had been established that entry barriers and operating restrictions *do* exist in the retail drug industry, the research objectives were formulated. They were: (1) to gain an understanding (apart from Adam Smith's perceptive observation) of why restrictionism has become *de rigueur* in the retail drug industry, (2) to discover the mechanisms by which this restrictionism is perpetuated, (3) to analyze state pharmacy rules, regulations, and laws in order to determine which ones are genuinely concerned with public health and which ones are designed to promote the economic interests of independent owners, (4) to list the various types of entry barriers and operating restraints so that their prevalence may be demonstrated, (5) to explain the economic and managerial consequences of the restrictions, and (6) to develop recommendations that would reduce current restrictions and guard against a future resurgence of similar or other restrictions.

Scope of the Study

This study is limited to an analysis of free market restrictions in the retail drug industry, which industry, for the purposes of this study, is defined as those retail outlets offering prescription and/or over-the-counter drugs for sale to the public. Accordingly, hospital pharmacies for in-patients and/or out-patients are excluded. Similarly, arrangements for supplying drugs to the indigent receive no attention. Chapter 2 explains and defines the firms considered to be in the retail drug industry.

A second limitation is the retailer-retailer nature of the analysis; i.e., barriers that some drug retailers erect against other drug retailers or would-be drug retailers. Problems of a similar vein can occur between retailers and wholesalers, between retailers and manufacturers, and between wholesalers and manufacturers. This study does not cover such interlevel distribution constraints, mainly because the problems appear to be rather minor.

This book does, however, attempt to present an accurate picture of the regulatory climate of the retail drug industry of the fifty states and the District of Columbia. Naturally, the jurisdictions with a record

---

[2] This is not an implication that large business enterprises possess superior business morals, but it is an assertion that small businessmen have no *better* morals than the executives of large corporations, for as Professor Weintraub has said, "monopoly pricing is a matter not of motive but rather of opportunity." See Sidney Weintraub, *Intermediate Price Theory* (Philadelphia: Chilton Books, 1964), p. 173.

of unfriendliness to corporate drug retailers have been given special emphasis. The analysis is concerned with state laws and regulations since the federal government has largely left the sphere of retail drug distribution to the states.

Some Terminological Difficulties

Part of the regulatory difficulties that have arisen in the retail drug industry is due to disagreements over the meaning of various words commonly used in the industry. Even the word "drug" does not denote the same products in all states. In this book, "drug" means a substance useful in treating illnesses and diseases in man and/or other animals.

All drugs fall into one of two categories: prescription or nonprescription. There is no classification problem with respect to whether or not a drug is a prescription drug. The Food and Drug Administration (FDA) decides which drugs are to be dispensed only on prescription and which are not. For a particular drug or a "combination of ingredients" medication, prescription status depends on (1) whether the drug is intended to treat an illness that may readily be diagnosed by the sufferer himself and (2) whether the drug is safe to take without medical supervision.

An example of the self-diagnosis requirement is a drug for treatment of heart disease. A person cannot readily detect a heart ailment himself. Therefore, it is a prescription item even if it is safe to take without medical supervision.

Several factors are considered by FDA in determining whether a drug is safe to use without instructions from a physician. These are (1) toxicity, (2) addicting qualities, (3) method of use (e.g., injection), (4) collateral measures required for use (e.g., other drugs to be used in conjunction), and (5) any other potentiality for harmful effect.

New drugs are frequently placed on prescription until some experience has been gained to gauge their safety. When antihistamines were new, they were prescription items. Now, many are not. At any given time, however, every drug (or combination) is in one classification or the other, even though FDA does reclassify drugs from time to time.

Prescription drugs are sometimes referred to as "legend" drugs. The term is derived from the "legend" that appears on all packages of prescription drugs: "Caution: Federal law prohibits dispensing without prescription." Nonprescription drugs also have another name—"over-the-counter" drugs. Such a term is used because FDA has authorized the drugs to be sold "over-the-counter," that is, without a prescription.

Nonprescription drugs have several additional appelations. These terms, however, are intended to be subclassifications rather than just another term to use in lieu of nonprescription. These subgroups are (1) patented medicines, (2) patent and proprietary medications, (3) ethical proprietaries, and for want of better language (4) other nonprescription medicines. Patented medicines are those registered with the U.S. Patent Office by virtue of some secret process or ingredient that merits a patent, just as inventions are patented. This term is largely meaningless, since it is frequently misused to indicate nonprescription drugs in general. Considerable litigation has been initiated over the meaning of patent proprietary medicines. Chapter 6 explores the various definitions offered.

Although the meaning and application of proprietary medicines are open to question, there appears to be substantial agreement that an ethical proprietary is a proprietary that is not advertised to the public. Naturally enough, the "other" category is what is left after the other three categories have been eliminated. Again, it is not certain, from laws and litigation, which drugs are in this category.

Finally, two other terms are used in connection with nonprescription drugs. These are "home remedies" and "drugs for self-medication." It seems that these terms are synonymous with each other and with nonprescription or proprietary and patent drugs as a group. It is not clear, however, that this is the case.

To avoid the terminological maze just described, the discussion will seek to use the terms "prescription" and "nonprescription" wherever possible, except in those chapters dealing with litigation arising from the failure of the legislatures to define the classes (if any) of nonprescription drugs.

Outline of the Study

This study is divided into four main parts. Part I is introductory in nature, and consists of the chapters necessary to provide a background for the rest of the study. Several important topics are included in the three remaining introductory chapters. These are (1) the growth of pharmaceutical associations and their influence on the early legislation in the field, (2) the rise of pharmacy as a profession, (3) a structural analysis of the retail drug industry, (4) the qualifications and selection of boards of pharmacy, and (5) several illustrations of the prevailing restrictionist attitude among pharmacists.

Part II is concerned with the efforts of pharmacists to prevent proprietary medicines (Anacin, Alka-Seltzer, etc.) from being sold in grocery stores and other nondrug outlets. This section contains two chapters and is mainly a recitation of the opposing arguments and court decisions. Also included are some comments regarding the legislative inactivity (even though the courts have asked for guidelines) and the propriety of proprietary sales restrictions.

Part III is a compilation, discussion, analysis, and trend indicator of the many free market restrictions to be found in state pharmacy laws and rules and regulations of state boards of pharmacy. The primary aim of these five chapters is to demonstrate that the rules are, in fact, restrictive and not measures designed to protect the public health.

The three chapters of Part IV indicate the effects of allowing the restrictions to exist and offers certain generalized conclusions to be drawn from the substantive chapters. Also, the final chapter suggests several devices to reduce present restrictions and to minimize their occurrence in the future.

CHAPTER TWO

The Development of the Retail Drug Industry

The purpose of this chapter is to depict the changes that have occurred in the retail drug industry from its inception to the present. Three major topics will be considered: the origins and development of the profession of pharmacy, the emergence of mass merchandisers, and the current structural distribution patterns of the industry.

Although the origin of a profession is not necessarily a structural element in the evolution of an industry, pharmacists are so essential to the retail drug business that a structural analysis of the industry would be of little value without an understanding of how the profession of pharmacy has evolved.

Origin of Pharmacy as a Profession

It is impractical to attempt to designate a specific date at which a vocation ceases to be a trade and becomes a profession. Part of the difficulty stems from the evolutionary process itself—the key change that initiates professional status is often hidden and combined with other shifts in the activities within a given field of endeavor. Another source of confusion is the lack of a generally accepted definition of the term profession. Thus, there are no uniformly accepted objective criteria against which an occupation can be measured to ascertain its professional status.

In an attempt to assess the professional status of pharmacy, several indicators of professionalism are analyzed in the following section. These guidelines are (1) organizations for pharmacists, (2) state licensure requirements, and (3) educational attainment. Further, a professional rating scale is suggested to determine the stature of pharma-

cists on a percentile basis as compared to other occupations. Two additional criteria to which some attention is given are (1) utilization
of acquired skills and knowledge and (2) strength of the service motive
(professional) as compared to the profit motive (commercial).

FORMATION OF ASSOCIATIONS

Pharmacists, along with the vast majority of other Americans, are
oriented toward association membership. For this reason, it cannot
be said that the existence of occupational organizations in a particular
field denotes a profession. Nevertheless, the age, goals, and authority
of such organizations do provide information regarding the degree of
professionalism in the particular job category. Thus, to aid in ascertain-
ing whether a degree of professionalism can be attributed to pharmaceutical activities, it is worthwhile to note with respect to pharmacists'
organizations the ages of the various groups, how they came into existence, their legislative influence, and the degree to which they control
the attitudes and actions of practicing pharmacists.

Local Associations.[1] The first advocates of professional stature for
pharmacists were physicians in Philadelphia. This was a logical development since the University of Pennsylvania's medical school, in Philadelphia, was the first one established in the United States and a distinct
separation of medicine and pharmacy had been endorsed by the institution since its formation. The advocacy was given additional weight
by the fact that Philadelphia was one of the country's major cultural
and scientific centers.

To further this pronounced philosophy, J. Redman Coxe, professor
of medicine at the University, proposed in March 1820, that the school
confer an honorary degree of Master of Pharmacy on all Philadelphia
pharmacists who had become proficient in their profession. Sixteen
prominent local pharmacists signed the proposal, midst the howls of
a large group of other local merchants who called themselves
pharmacists.[2]

In the closing sentence of his proposal, Dr. Coxe remarked that
he could see no other way to achieve the professional progress he visual-
ized for pharmacists, since there were no local pharmaceutical associations—such as those in the United Kingdom—to aid in advancing the
field. To offset this argument, the dissenting druggists immediately
organized an association called the College of Apothecaries. Despite

[1] Edward Kremers and George Urdang, *History of Pharmacy*, Revised by Glenn
Sonnedecker (3rd ed.; Philadelphia: J. B. Lippincott Co., 1963), pp. 171–172, 175–177.
[2] This association evidently was later merged with the present educational institution, The Philadelphia College of Pharmacy and Science. *Proceedings of the National
Association of Boards of Pharmacy* (Chicago, 1961), p. 96.

this action, the University of Pennsylvania adopted Dr. Coxe's suggestion and conferred the honorary degree of Master of Pharmacy on sixteen Philadelphia pharmacists.

The Philadelphia College of Pharmacy, as the College of Apothecaries came to be called, was very active from its inception. It published a pharmaceutical journal designed both to keep pharmacists informed on developments in their specialty and to supply them with lists of standard formulas for English patent medicines and other compounds issued by physicians.

Since it was so active, the Philadelphia College of Pharmacy influenced the formation of other local associations. Most of the organizations listed below patterned their constitutions, bylaws, and activities after the Philadelphia group:

1823   Massachusetts College of Pharmacy (Boston)
1829   College of Pharmacy of the City and County of New York
1840   Maryland College of Pharmacy
1859   Chicago College of Pharmacy
1864   St. Louis College of Pharmacy

The Chicago society was organized by the American Pharmaceutical Association that had been founded in 1852. For the other associations, a major impetus to organize was provided by the attempts of medical practitioners to secure legislation that would give them authority to regulate all branches of medicine, including pharmacy. Hence, it was not the ideal of professionalism, but fear of domination by physicians that prompted the growth of most of these early alliances. And, rather than being advocates of controlling legislation, the pharmacists were opposed to it, as were most Americans during that era.

American Pharmaceutical Association.[3] The primary force which led to the birth of the American Pharmaceutical Association (APhA) was the inferior condition of the United States drug market in the late 1840's. New York physicians and pharmacists became aware of adulteration and substitution of drugs—supplied at that time mainly by the English. A complaint to the Britishers brought back the reply that the drugs were as good as the prices the Americans would pay.

Outraged physicians and pharmacists from all over the country signed petitions urging Congress to pass a law requiring inspection of imported drugs. Congress complied, but the results were disappointing since the inspectors authorized by the legislation were appointed on the basis of political affiliation rather than their knowledge of drugs.

[3] *Ibid.*, p. 182.

At this point a physician, who was also a member of the New York College of Pharmacy, proposed (at the request of the New York pharmacy group) to the American Medical Association (AMA) that an attempt be made to persuade drug inspectors to adopt certain inspection standards to be specified by AMA. But AMA was doubtful that the proposal was representative of pharmacists as a whole. As a result, the New York society invited its sister associations to form a national body which could speak for all pharmacists in the matter of drug adulteration and standards for drug inspectors.

The Philadelphia College of Pharmacy was of the opinion that a broader professional basis was needed for a new national organization than just the narrow problem of drug adulteration. Coming to the 1851 New York "Convention of Pharmaceutists and Druggists" with these definite views, the Philadelphians were able to obtain unanimous approval of a resolution recommending:

that a Convention be called, consisting of three Delegates from each incorporated and unincorporated Pharmaceutical Societies, to meet at Philadelphia, on the first Wednesday in October, 1852, when all the important questions bearing on the Profession may be considered, and measures adopted for the organization of a National Association to meet every year.[4]

From this meeting was born APhA.

State Associations. Although the avoidance of medical influence was not as important as in the formation of local societies, it was sometimes the force behind the emergence of state pharmaceutical societies. In New Jersey, for instance, it was not until the Medical Society of New Jersey had taken steps to force legislative control on "all dispensers of medicine" that the New Jersey Pharmaceutical Association was formed (1870) "to establish the relation between . . . [pharmacists] and physicians, and the people at large, under just principles . . ."[5]

Similarly, an 1871 resolution of the State Medical Association of Mississippi asked:

that the druggists, pharmacists, and chemists of the state of Mississippi be requested to call a convention at an early day, and organize a State Pharmaceutical Association, to meet annually at the same time and place that the Medical Association does, and cooperate with it in any and all measures of mutual interest and importance.[6]

A month later the Mississippi Pharmaceutical Association was founded.

---

[4] As quoted in *Ibid.*, p. 183.

[5] D. L. Cowen, "The New Jersey Pharmaceutical Association," *New Jersey Journal of Pharmacy*, Vol. 18, No. 12 (Dec. 1945), pp. 16–17.

[6] Kremers and Urdang, *op. cit.*, p. 180.

   Despite the activity just cited, many of the state associations are
the children of APhA, having been formed in the same year that
APhA held its annual convention in the respective states. Moreover,
the fact that more than half of the state groups were established in
the decade beginning in 1880 (see Table 2-1) suggests that there was
a nationwide wave of interest by pharmacists in organizing the
societies.

TABLE 2-1: Organization Dates of State Pharmaceutical Associations[a]

Date Formed	State	Date Formed	State
1. 1852	District of Columbia[b]	26. 1881	Alabama
2. 1867	Maine[c]	27. 1882	Virginia
3. 1869	California	28. 1882	Louisiana
4. 1870	New Jersey	29. 1882	Indiana
5. 1870	West Virginia[d]	30. 1882	Massachusetts
6. 1870	Vermont	31. 1882	Nebraska
7. 1871	Mississippi[e]	32. 1883	Maryland
8. 1873	Tennessee[f]	33. 1883	Minnesota
9. 1874	New Hampshire	34. 1883	Arkansas
10. 1874	Michigan[g]	35. 1885	North Dakota
11. 1874	Rhode Island	36. 1886	South Dakota
12. 1875	Georgia	37. 1887	Delaware
13. 1876	South Carolina	38. 1887	Florida[h]
14. 1876	Connecticut	39. 1887	Idaho[i]
15. 1877	Kentucky	40. 1890	Washington
16. 1878	Pennsylvania	41. 1890	Oregon
17. 1879	Texas	42. 1890	Oklahoma[j]
18. 1879	New York	43. 1890	Colorado
19. 1879	Ohio	44. 1891	Montana
20. 1879	Missouri	45. 1892	Utah
21. 1880	Iowa	46. 1893	New Mexico
22. 1880	Kansas	47. 1910	Arizona
23. 1880	Wisconsin	48. 1915	Wyoming
24. 1880	North Carolina	49. 1932	Nevada
25. 1880	Illinois		

   Source: Edward Kremers and George Urdang, *History of Pharmacy*, Revised by
Glenn Sonnedecker (3rd ed.; Philadelphia: J. B. Lippincott Co., 1963), p. 379. Reprinted by permission of the publisher.
   [a] Information unavailable for Alaska and Hawaii.
   [b] Data received in unsigned letter from District of Columbia Pharmaceutical
Association, March 18, 1966.
   [c] Reorganized in 1890.   [g] Reorganized in 1883.
   [d] Reorganized in 1881, 1906.   [h] Reorganized in 1904.
   [e] Reorganized in 1883, 1891, 1902.   [i] Reorganized in 1905.
   [f] Reorganized in 1886.   [j] At that time Oklahoma territory.

For a substantial period of time following their birth, the associations were concerned primarily with the commercial aspects of pharmacy. This has ostensibly changed:

[Originally the programs of the state pharmaceutical associations] . . . tended to be dominated by commercial concerns. But by . . . [1950], state associations in general were gaining wide support (partly by giving employee-pharmacists a status more nearly compatible with that of pharmacy owners), enlarging administrative facilities, and sharing more fully in the professional as well as the economic concerns of pharmacy.

Symptomatic of the change was the [movement of state societies to affiliate with their national body] . . . Whether or not this will become a general trend, . . . it appears that the incursions of crassly commercial interests after World War II failed to overwhelm the independent pharmacist and, indeed, gave him a new conviction that his professional heritage and prerogatives must be safeguarded cooperatively. In that cause, the American Pharmaceutical Association already had invested more than a century of consistent thought and endeavor. For, paradoxically, the Association was not erected on the foundation of an established professional pharmacy; rather, it had largely created American professional pharmacy.[7]

GROWTH OF LICENSURE REQUIREMENTS

Another indicator of the professionalism achieved by a job category is the requirement that the practitioner be licensed by the state to assure that only proficient persons engage in the occupation. Unfortunately, this is an inexact criterion. For example, plumbers, generally considered as nonprofessional workers, must be licensed, although clergymen, usually viewed as professional individuals, are not licensed. Despite this general inconsistency, it has been traditional in the health field to establish licensure requirements as various occupations evolved toward professional status—e.g., veterinarians, nurses, and physical therapists. Hence, it is important to note when the licensure of pharmacists became a well-established requirement.

Early Licensing Requirements.[8] As Table 2-2 illustrates, there was very little regulation of the practice of pharmacy prior to 1870. What little control there was existed primarily in specific cities. For example, New Orleans tried as early as 1804 to require pharmacists to register their diplomas with local officials or submit to a proficiency examination, but the effort was short-lived. An 1832 New York State law stipulated that pharmacists in New York City had to have a diploma from a college of pharmacy or submit to an examination before the county

---

[7] *Ibid.*, p. 181. Reprinted by permission of the publisher.
[8] *Ibid.*, p. 198.

TABLE 2-2: Dates of Passage of Local and State Pharmacy Laws

Local Enactments

Date	Local Jurisdiction	Date	Local Jurisdiction
1. 1832, 1871	New York City	9. 1873	St. Louis, Missouri
2. 1844	Adams County, Miss.	10. 1876	Milwaukee, Wisconsin
3. 1851	Louisville, Ky.	11. 1879	Kings County, N.Y.
4. 1866	Lycoming County, Pa.	12. 1884	Erie County, N.Y.
5. 1870	Baltimore, Md.	13. 1884	Other New York Counties
6. 1872	Philadelphia, Pa.	14. 1902	Md. Counties except Talbot
7. 1872	San Francisco, Calif.	15. 1906	Talbot County, Maryland
8. 1873	Cincinnati, Ohio		

State Enactments

Date	State	Date	State
1. 1808, 1816, 1872	Louisiana	26. 1886	Virginia
		27. 1886	Wyoming
2. 1817, 1876	South Carolina	28. 1887	Colorado
3. 1825, 1881	Georgia	29. 1887	Idaho
4. 1852, 1887	Alabama	30. 1887	Nebraska
5. 1869, 1900	New York	31. 1887	Pennsylvania
6. 1870	Rhode Island	32. 1889	New Mexico
7. 1872	Florida	33. 1889	Texas
8. 1874	Kentucky	34. 1890	South Dakota
9. 1875	New Hampshire	35. 1891	Arkansas
10. 1877	New Jersey	36. 1891	California
11. 1877	Maine	37. 1891	North Dakota
12. 1878	District of Columbia	38. 1891	Oklahoma
13. 1880	Iowa	39. 1891	Oregon
14. 1881	Connecticut	40. 1891	Washington
15. 1881	Illinois	41. 1892	Mississippi
16. 1881	North Carolina	42. 1892	Utah
17. 1881	Missouri	43. 1893	Tennessee
18. 1881	West Virginia	44. 1894	Vermont
19. 1882	Wisconsin	45. 1895	Montana
20. 1883	Delaware	46. 1899	Indiana
21. 1884	Ohio	47. 1901	Nevada
22. 1885	Kansas	48. 1903	Arizona
23. 1885	Massachusetts	49. 1903	Hawaii
24. 1885	Michigan	50. 1908	Maryland
25. 1885	Minnesota	51. 1913	Alaska

Source: Edward Kremers and George Urdang, *History of Pharmacy*, Revised by Glenn Sonnedecker (3rd ed.; Philadelphia: J. B. Lippincott Co., 1963), p. 380. Adapted by permission of the publisher.

medical society. In Kentucky the city charter of Louisville authorized the city council to establish a board of pharmacy and gave the board the power to require that all pharmacists be examined and licensed by it.

The dearth of pharmacy regulation is explained by one authority as a combination of American laissez faire ideology, frontier conditions, and lack of pharmacy schools. Although the first two reasons seem to be reasonable, it appears that the lack of pharmacy schools was a result of no regulation rather than the cause of it.

Another possibility for the lack of supervision was the relative unimportance of drug therapy in the nineteenth century. The potions available as remedies were limited and it could not have been too difficult for physicians, especially in rural areas, to supply medicines directly to their patients.

State Requirements.[9] Mandatory state licensure of pharmacists is a recent phenomenon, being less than one hundred years old in all states except Louisiana, South Carolina, Georgia, and Alabama. There is no suitable explanation as to why southern states pioneered in pharmacy regulatory legislation. Louisiana's leadership may have been due to the considerable European element in New Orleans that was probably less concerned about governmental interference in entrepreneurial affairs. Reasons for passage in the other three states remain a mystery.

Licensure laws of the remaining states were enacted at the insistence of APhA through the state pharmaceutical societies. Most of the state societies were, in fact, organized to agitate for pharmacy legislation. The campaign to enact the laws centered on the model law presented before an APhA committee in 1869.

The movement was not very successful at first. Many rural states initially resisted the pharmacist licensure drive since it would mean that drugs and medicines no longer could be purchased from general stores. From 1869 to 1879, only eight enactments occurred, for a total of twelve state pharmacy laws. But the efforts expended in the next two decades were extraordinarily productive so that by 1900, forty-five states (or territories which were to become states) and the District of Columbia had a pharmacy law on their legislative books. The five remaining states had enacted pharmacy laws by 1913.

EDUCATION OF PHARMACISTS

Even though all of the pharmacy laws have now been in effect some fifty years, the concept of pharmacy as a profession cannot be said to date from the passage of the various state statutes. According

[9] *Ibid.*, pp. 194–196.

to the generally accepted criterion of education as an indication of professional status, it is only within the last thirty years that pharmacy has achieved elevation to this classification.

The early state pharmacy legislation placed little emphasis on college education requisites. Generally, licensure requirements were graduation from high school, a certain number of years of experience, attained age of twenty-one, satisfactory moral character, and state and United States citizenship.

The recent development of mandatory graduation from a college of pharmacy is indicated by Table 2-3. Although by 1930 thirty-two states imposed state licensing requirements of graduation from a college of pharmacy, the requisite was not adopted by all states until 1956.

When states enacted the educational standard, they usually allowed existing registered pharmacists to continue in practice regardless of

TABLE 2-3: Year when Graduation from School of Pharmacy Became Mandatory for Licensure

Year Adopted	Jurisdiction	Year Adopted	Jurisdiction
1. 1905	New York	27. 1928	Florida
2. 1906	Pennsylvania	28. 1928	Louisiana
3. 1910	Rhode Island	29. 1929	Colorado
4. 1914	Washington	30. 1929	Kansas
5. 1915	Ohio	31. 1929	Minnesota
6. 1915	North Dakota	32. 1930	Idaho
7. 1917	Illinois	33. 1931	Maine
8. 1917	Iowa	34. 1933	South Dakota
9. 1918	South Carolina	35. 1934	Georgia
10. 1920	Indiana	36. 1934	Texas
11. 1920	Maryland	37. 1935	Arizona
12. 1920	New Jersey	38. 1935	New Mexico
13. 1921	Mississippi	39. 1936	Arkansas
14. 1922	North Carolina	40. 1936	Wyoming
15. 1922	Oregon	41. 1937	Missouri
16. 1922	Virginia	42. 1938	Michigan
17. 1923	Oklahoma	43. 1939	Montana
18. 1923	West Virginia	44. 1939	New Hampshire
19. 1924	Kentucky	45. 1941	Tennessee
20. 1925	Connecticut	46. 1942	Nebraska
21. 1927	Alabama	47. 1945	Hawaii
22. 1927	Delaware	48. 1948	Massachusetts
23. 1927	Utah	49. 1948	Nevada
24. 1927	Wisconsin	50. 1955	Alaska
25. 1928	California	51. 1956	Vermont
26. 1928	District of Columbia		

Source: *Proceedings of the National Association of Boards of Pharmacy* (Chicago, 1965), pp. 92–93.

their educational attainments. Annual attrition has practically eradicated this class of pharmacists. Nevertheless, another group of pharmacists that does not have a formal technical education is still present in the retail drug industry to some extent.

For an extensive period of time, the states registered "assistant pharmacists." These individuals received their training via a registered pharmacist, and, during the short absences of a registered pharmacist, could act in his capacity. At other times assistants filled prescriptions under a pharmacist's supervision. Eventually this subprofessional group was abolished[10] in order to deny prescription filling authority to all except registered pharmacists. The elimination of the assistant pharmacist was accomplished by changing the state laws (1) to proscribe registration of new assistant pharmacists and (2) to allow existing assistant pharmacists to become registered pharmacists if they could meet minimum experience requirements.

Assistant pharmacists continue to practice in some states, even though no new assistants are permitted to be registered. Table 4 lists the states that still have assistant pharmacists and the number in each state. Arkansas has the "practical druggist," which apparently corresponds to the assistant pharmacist classification. The number registered is not known.[11]

The total number of assistant pharmacists and registered pharmacists who were originally assistant pharmacists cannot be determined. Fourteen states have 1,107 active assistant pharmacists and 38,571 registered pharmacists[12] employed in retail stores; hence, assistant pharmacists constitute 2.8 percent of those permitted to fill prescriptions in these states. It is possible that if figures were available to allow the calculation of the ratio

$$\frac{\text{present assistants} + \text{registered pharmacists formerly assistants}}{\text{total registrants}},$$

[10] According to its statute, Mississippi still registers assistant pharmacists, but none were able to pass the examination in 1965. In addition, the 1966 recodification of the Alabama pharmacy law resurrected the title of assistant pharmacist, requiring that persons having worked fifteen consecutive years under the supervision of a registered pharmacist be registered as assistant pharmacists. Registered pharmacists opposed the provision but adquiesced since the issue had thwarted two previous attempts to recodify the pharmacy law. The president of the Alabama Board of Pharmacy pointed out that those eligible under the new law have been violating the old law, inasmuchas the old law did not permit unregistered individuals to fill prescriptions under the supervision of a registered pharmacist. "Alabama's New OK To Assistants Flayed," *Drug News Weekly*, November 21, 1966, p. 14.

[11] Interview with Mrs. Verna McHughes, Assistant to the Secretary of the Arkansas State Board of Pharmacy, January 4, 1966.

[12] Calculated from a chart included in *Proceedings of the National Association of Boards of Pharmacy* (Chicago, 1965), p. 71.

TABLE 2-4: Practicing Assistant Pharmacists—January 1, 1965

State	Number in Active Practice	State	Number in Active Practice
Colorado	59	Mississippi	57
Connecticut	24	New Jersey	1
Delaware	12	North Carolina	22
Illinois	400	North Dakota	0
Indiana	7	Ohio	21
Kansas	—	Oklahoma	195
Maine	88	Pennsylvania	134
Massachusetts	71	Texas	—
		Wisconsin	16

Source: *Proceedings of the National Association of Boards of Pharmancy* (Chicago, 1965), p. 81.

it would be found that about 5 percent of the prescription fillers are not college graduates. This figure gains further validity when it is remembered that there are still registered pharmacists practicing who were never assistant pharmacists and who were registered before college graduation became mandatory.

In addition to the college graduation licensing requirement, the number of years necessary for graduation is important. If the equivalent of the baccalaureate degree is considered to be the minimum scholastic attainment for a profession, pharmacy did not achieve professional rank educationally until about the middle of the 1931–1940 decade. As Table 2-5 shows, about one-third of the schools of pharmacy were on a three-year program in that interval. This was the period during which there was a general movement from the three-year program to a four-year course.

Beginning with first-year students of 1932, most schools of pharmacy added a year to their three-year degree programs to maintain accreditation. The accreditation requirements added still another year for 1961 enrollees, making a five-year degree granting program the standard. Since about 1936, then, educational requirement shave equalled or exceeded the minimum professional standards as previously defined.

The relatively recent adoption of the four-year program has resulted in a number of practicing registered pharmacists who do not hold the B.S. degree. If such individuals are considered nonprofessional and are grouped with assistant pharmacists and registered pharmacists who did not graduate from a college of pharmacy, possibly 10 percent

TABLE 2-5: Length of U.S. College of Pharmacy Programs

Dates	Average No. of 2-Year Programs	Average No. of 3-Year Programs	Average No. of 4-Year Programs	Average No. of 5-Year Programs	Total No. of Schools at End of Period
Before 1867	—	—	—	—	—
1867–1880	4.0	—	—	—	7
1881–1890	13.4	0.6	—	—	22
1891–1900	33.8	0.5	—	—	46
1901–1910	56.4	0.9	—	—	64
1911–1920	60.5	5.8	—	—	62
1921–1930	44.0	32.8	2.9	—	68
1931–1940	2.0	25.6	48.6	—	66
1941–1950	0.1	0.6	64.3	0.1	67
1951–1960	—	—	60.5	8.6	69[a]
1961[b]	—	—	—	68.0	68[a]

Compiled from: *Proceedings of the National Association of Boards of Pharmacy* (Chicago, 1961), pp. 85–99.

[a] Beginning in 1958, one college required six years for graduation. That college is not included in the averages or totals.

[b] Since 1961 some additional schools have switched to a six-year program.

of the total number of practicing pharmacists can be classified as "nonprofessional."[13]

Members of the drug industry would protest vigorously the assertion that pharmacists with two or three years of college training in pharmacy are nonprofessional. The writer would agree. The three-year courses were devoted almost exclusively to technical pharmaceutical study. The four- and five-year programs usually included additional nontechnical courses such as pharmacy administration and humanities.

On a strictly years-of-college basis, then, if 90 percent of the practicing pharmacists are four-year college graduates, the educational criterion of professionalism is met.

PRESENT PROFESSIONAL STATUS OF PHARMACISTS

Pharmacists appear to have a well-established right to call themselves professionals on the basis of existing pharmaceutical organizations, state licensure requirements, and educational attainments. An-

[13] In North Carolina, for example, according to the 1965 annual report of the Board of Pharmacy, there are 1,777 registered practicing pharmacists and 22 assistant pharmacists for a total of 1,799 registrants. Of the 1,777 registered pharmacists, 137 are nongraduates, 179 are graduates from a two-year college course in pharmacy, and 130 are graduates from a three-year course. Hence, 446 out of 1,777, or 25.1 percent may be said to be "nonprofessional." North Carolina Board of Pharmacy, *Eighty-Fourth Annual Report* (Chapel Hill: North Carolina Board of Pharmacy, 1965), pp. 11–12.

TABLE 2-6: Professional Status of Various Occupations

	Rating Factors and Weights				
	(0–40)	(0–30) Legal Respon- sibility	(0–20) Personal Relation- ships	(0–10) Ethical Relation- ships	
Occupation	Training				Total
Medic	40	30	20	5	95
Lawyer	40	30	10	5	85
Pharmacist[a]	40	30	10	5	85
Engineer	30	30	15	5	80
Soldier	30	30	20	—	80
Architect	30	15	15	5	65
Cleric	30	—	20	10	60
Teacher	30	—	10	10	50
Scientist	40	—	—	—	40
Banker	20	10	—	10	40
Journalist	20	5	10	—	35
Adman	10	5	5	—	20

Source: Joseph G. Wilson, "How Professional Is Engineering?," *Mechanical Engineering*, Vol. 86, No. 6 (June 1964), p. 19. Reprinted by permission of the publisher.
[a] This category not included in the source table.

other suggested method of ranking the professional status of occupations recently appeared in a professional engineering publication.

According to this measurement technique, the criteria and the weights to be assigned to each are:[14]

1. specialized training and experience 40%
2. professional legal responsibility 30%
3. professional personal relationships 20%
4. professional ethical relationships 10%.

Criteria (1) and (2) refer to topics previously discussed; that is, education and licensure. The third factor is a measure of the professional-client relationship and the fourth is supposed to indicate the professional bonds within the occupation.

Using the four rating factors and subjectively applying weights, the author of the article ranked the professional status of various occupations. The ratings are reproduced as Table 2-6. Strangely enough, the title "pharmacist" is absent from the listing. Disregarding the engineer-writer's possible myopia, his rating factors may be subjectively applied to pharmacists. The writer's subjective evaluation of the pharmacist is included as a part of Table 2-6.

[14] Joseph G. Wilson, "How Professional is Engineering?," *Mechanical Engineering*, Vol. 86, No. 6 (June 1964), p. 19.

According to the composite contained in Table 2-6, pharmacy ranks as one of the most professional of occupations. No special brief is made for the evaluation criteria outlined in Table 2-6 or for the nonobjective evaluations applied to pharmacists. But, as the subjective appraisal reveals, this writer concludes that pharmacy may properly be regarded as a profession, if the only criteria worthy of note are those listed in Table 2-6.

Two additional factors, however, should be considered in reaching a judgment as to whether a vocation is a profession. One of these factors is the degree to which professional skills are employed in the job environment. If, for example, a pharmacist (or physician or lawyer) is employed as a janitor, he is not a professional because he is not using the skills acquired by education.

A less harsh—but equally accurate—example is the time spent by pharmacists stocking shelves and selling hair tonic, shaving cream, cosmetics, magazines, and tobacco. Such activities do not require professional knowledge and persons spending a large proportion of the day performing such nonprofessional functions cannot be described as professionals.

This is precisely the job content of a substantial number of pharmacists, especially in those stores where the volume of prescriptions filled and related activities (such as sorting and stocking drugs in the prescription department) are insufficient to fill the pharmacist's working hours. For owner pharmacists there is even less professional work, since they must fulfill entrepreneurial and managerial roles even if the prescription volume is sufficient to fill a normal work day. In such cases, the owner will probably hire other pharmacists to perform the professional functions. At least 60 percent of the practicing pharmacists may be called nonprofessionals in that managerial or clerical duties consume a majority of the hours spent at work.[15]

The second additional determinant of an occupation's professional status is the strength of the service motive as opposed to the profit motive. If mercantilism holds sway, the professional ethic of service first, profit second, is not being adhered to and the practitioner, regardless of his specialty, has weakened his professional standing. Judgment on this criterion is to be reserved until the performance of pharmacists in economic areas has been discussed.

For the present, it can be said that pharmacy *can be* a profession if pharmacists perform as professionals. Left unanswered is whether pharmacists exhibit that performance. Such a judgment must be re-

[15] For a critical analysis of the extent of a typical pharmacist's nonprofessional activities, see E. B. Weiss, "Is the Traditional Pharmacist as Dead as the Dodo?," *Advertising Age*, April 8, 1963, pp. 100, 102.

served until the activities pursued by pharmacists are described and analyzed. Subsequent chapters thus will shed light on the strength and pervasiveness of the service motive as compared to the profit motive.

Emergence of Chain Drugstores

In contrast to the development of and changes in the professional concept of pharmacists, the retail drug industry itself did not experience a series of small evolutionary changes. Pharmacy as an occupation was continuously and gradually modified through ever more rigorous education and state registration requirements. On the other hand, neighborhood pharmacies were the dominant type of retail drug outlet for a long period of time until suddenly chain drugstores appeared.

TABLE 2-7: Early Drugstore Chains

Date Founded	Name	Location
1850	Schlegal Drug Stores	Davenport, Iowa
1852	Meyer Brothers Company	Fort Wayne, Indiana
1879	T. P. Taylor & Company	Louisville, Kentucky
1879	Jacobs Pharmacy Company	Atlanta, Georgia
1883	Read Drug & Chemical Co.	Baltimore, Maryland
1884	Marshall Drug Co.	Cleveland, Ohio
1885	Skillern's Drug Stores	Dallas, Texas
1889	Cunningham Drug Stores	Detroit, Michigan
1890	Bartell Drug Company	Seattle, Washington
1892	Owl Drug Company	San Francisco, Calif.
1898	Eckerd Drug Stores	Erie, Pa.
1899	Standard Drug Stores	Cleveland, Ohio
1907	Louis K. Liggett Co.	New York City

Source: Godfrey M. Lebhar, *Chain Stores in America, 1859–1962* (3rd ed.; New York: Chain Store Publishing Corp., 1963), pp. 43–44.

Chain drugstores can be traced as far back as the middle of the nineteenth century, but their impact upon the economy in general and upon the retail drug industry in particular is of more recent history. Chain stores in other fields, such as food markets and department stores, achieved prominence long before chain drugstores.

Some of the oldest chain drugstores are listed in Table 2-7 which indicates that there were a number of drugstore chains operating by 1900. Their total number of outlets, however, was small. It is doubtful that all the chain drugstores combined had a total of seventy-five stores in operation by 1900.[16]

[16] Godfrey M. Lebhar, *Chain Stores in America, 1859–1962* (3rd ed.; New York: Chain Store Publishing Corp., 1963), pp. 43–44.

Within the next ten years, the presence of the drug chains began to be acknowledged by their competitors and the consuming public. This was a period of general chain development, but drugstore chains attracted attention quite early in this growth era because they quickly adopted the aggressive merchandising techniques of the cut-rate drug establishments already functioning and added other original retailing schemes.[17] It is interesting to note that ruthless price-cutting and the sale of nonpharmaceutical merchandise was a well-established practice long before the establishment of chain drugstores.[18]

PRIMARY REASONS FOR THE CHAIN MOVEMENT

Price Competition. A major stimulus to the organization of chain drugstores was the intense price competition among drug enterprises during the latter 1800's. Owners cast about desperately for some device to relieve the pressure. One solution was the formation of chains.[19] Incorporating the stores into one unit banded them closely together so that maximum advantage could be obtained from advertising and quantity discounts given by wholesalers and manufacturers. Moreover, price-cutting as a merchandising technique could be more effectively utilized when coupled with bulk buying.

Another factor prompting combination, also related to low prices, was the necessity of having several outlets to generate a profitable volume of sales. Since per unit profit was low in most drug enterprises, the adoption of some sort of cooperative venture was natural since it offered the possibility of a larger total profit through increased sales, and an extra profit from quantity purchases.

Changing Manufacturing Methods. During the Civil War, American pharmaceutical manufacturers developed for the first time a firm position as suppliers of drugs. Previously, European producers had dominated the market since the imported items were often better in quality and lower in price than domestically produced drugs. The goods secured from the Continent were compounded by the pharmacists into various remedies. With the advent of the internal hostilities, imports were restricted and demand expanded because of war-induced needs. Domestic manufacturers not only filled the pharmaceutical requirements, but did so with compounded drugs. By the close of the war the American industry was strong and efficient. The local producers continued to flourish after the return to peaceful conditions since drug-

---

[17] *Ibid.*, pp. 52–53.
[18] Kremers and Urdang, *op. cit.*, pp. 266–268.
[19] Another remedy was the creation of cooperatives.

gists found it more advantageous to buy their compounds than to mix them.

Hence, every pharmacist no longer needed to be a part-time drug manufacturer with sufficient equipment to perform compounding functions. The expansion path for chains was eased by this elimination of the need for extensive knowledge in blending medicinal remedies and the now dispensable investment in compounding equipment.

Advantages of Corporate Ownership. Some of the advantages of corporate organization furthered the chain movement. Among the more significant influences were:

1. limited liability (stockholders can lose no more than their corporate investment)

2. ease in raising capital

3. perpetual life of the firm

4. possibility of attracting superior management.

These factors probably were, at best, contributory rather than decisive in the decision to incorporate.

Mass Merchandising Techniques. There is little doubt that the intriguing idea of mass distribution played the major role in the development of drug chain stores. The activity generated by the adoption of the chain concept in the food and general merchandise areas created an irresistible impulse for entrepreneurs to try the approach in the drug field. The mass merchandising principles of the day came to be known as the "Rosenwald Creed," named for a member of Sears, Roebuck and Company's management. The fundamentals were:

1. Sell for less by buying for less. Buy for less through the instrumentality of mass buying and cash buying. *But maintain the quality.*
2. Sell for less by cutting the cost of sales. Reduce to the absolute practical minimum the expense of moving goods from producers to consumers. *But maintain the quality.*
3. Make less profit on each individual item and increase your aggregate profit by selling more items. *But maintain the quality.*[20]

OPPOSITION OF INDEPENDENTS

Chains of all types enjoyed phenomenal growth between 1920 and 1930. During that interval the number of stores for a selected group of twenty chains increased from 9,912 to 37,524. Actual total growth among all such establishments was much higher. The Federal Trade Commission estimated that in 1920 there was a total of 50,000 chain outlets. The exact aggregate number in 1920 is not so significant as

[20] Julius Rosenwald as quoted in Lebhar, *op. cit.*, pp. 47–48.

the specific figures for the twenty selected chains. Their number of outlets more than quadrupled during the ten years following 1920. The statistics for the two drug chains included in the group of twenty are even more impressive. From 31 outlets in 1920, Walgreen Company and Peoples Drug Stores, Inc. expanded to 557 units by 1930—an 1,800 percent increase.[21] From these statistics it is not hard to understand why independent retail druggists began to seek methods for halting the growth of chains and/or their cut-rate pricing methods.

The opposition by independents first took the form of court action against price reductions of patent and proprietary medicines since price-maintenance agreements on these items were legal. The suits against the early drug discounters were based on the allegation that selling at amounts below those printed on the products constituted an infringement of the plaintiffs' copyrights and/or patents. Several lower court contests were won by the independents, but the U.S. Supreme Court, in 1911, declared such agreements unenforceable except for true patents and copyrights.[22]

From the time of the 1911 decision, the independents urged upon Congress the passage of price-maintenance legislations. Several bills were introduced but not one was ever enacted. It was not until there were forty-two state laws that Congress passed a federal fair trade enabling act.

Structure of the Retail Drug Industry[23]

The preceding pages have discussed the professional and structural metamorphoses that the retail drug industry has experienced. The description is incomplete without an explanation of the present structural arrangement of the industry because such a categorization of the various types of retail drug outlets serves as an aid in understanding the motivations of the different groups that represent the diverse segments of the retail drug industry. Also, by indicating the growing strength of some classes and the erosion of the competitive position of others, some understanding can be gained of the purpose of the various free market restrictions in the retail drug industry.

A number of classification schemes, each with certain merits, can be adopted for the retail drug industry. The major organizing devices that seem most appropriate for this study are (1) classification by the nature of goods sold and (2) classification by form of ownership.

[21] *Ibid.*, p. 56.

[22] *Dr. Miles Medical Co.* v. *John D. Park & Sons Co.*, 220 U.S. 373 (1911).

[23] The ideas in this section are, for the most part, a synthesis of conversations with various members in the retail drug industry. The bibliography lists the persons interviewed.

CLASSIFICATION OF RETAIL DRUG OUTLETS
BY TYPE OF MERCHANDISE SOLD

A division of retail drugstores by type of merchandise sold results in two major groupings—those outlets that specialize in the sale of health items and those that carry a large line of nonhealth merchandise in addition to health-related goods. That these two groupings are so readily identifiable reflects a basic conflict of philosophy within the ranks of pharmacists. One faction insists that the sale of general merchandise is nonprofessional, while others contend that offering nonhealth commodities for purchase does not detract from the stature of pharmacists.

Sale of Health and Nonhealth Items. The argument advanced in favor of drugstores marketing general merchandise is that a pharmacist can concurrently be both a professional and a businessman.[24] Physicians are often cited as an example of the compatibility of the two areas of interest.

Community Pharmacy—The most prevalent of general merchandisers, in terms of numbers, is the community or neighborhood pharmacy. This group comprises the vast majority of NARD supporters. NARD membership is not limited to pharmacists—it is restricted to proprietors of retail durgstores and very small chain organizations. NARD, then, is an amalgam of pharmacists and merchants. Nevertheless, most neighborhood drugstore owners are pharmacists.

The community pharmacy generally has a rather confined trading area. The "corner drugstore" serves only those who live nearby, as a general rule. It is located adjacent to urban or suburban residential areas, as opposed to a shopping center or downtown location. These outlets can be characterized as low volume, high-markup firms that depend on the loyalty of local residents (not price structure) to keep the business prospering. In justification of these establishments, it must be said that the stores usually offer many services not available elsewhere, including charge accounts, free delivery service, and the maintenance of the drug expenditure records of their patrons for income tax purposes.

Although specific statistical evidence is difficult to isolate, the number of neighborhood pharmacies appears to be declining. For example, from the figures in Table 2-8 it can be ascertained that stores with an annual volume of under $100,000 declined about 23 percent in number and 17 percent in sales volume during the 1958–1963 period. During this same period the number of drugstores fell by 1,051 (2.1

[24] The National Association of Retail Druggists (NARD) is a strong advocate this view.

TABLE 2-8: Drugstore Statistics

Number of Drugstores[a] by Volume Group

	Number		% of Total No. of Drugstores		Sales (millions)		% of Total Sales	
Annual Sales	1958	1963	1958	1963	1958	1963	1958	1963
$1,000,000 and over	247	506	0.5	1.0	1004	767	16.0	9.8
500,000–999,000	941	1515	1.9	3.1	—	1009	—	12.8
300,000–499,000	2173	3264	4.4	6.8	813	1222	13.0	15.6
100,000–299,000	18381	21673	37.4	45.1	2975	3622	47.4	46.1
50,000– 99,000	15378	13408	31.3	27.9	1126	1000	17.9	12.7
30,000– 49,000	6526	4451	13.3	9.3	261	178	4.2	2.3
Under 30,000	5485	3223	11.2	6.8	97	57	1.5	0.7
Total	49131	48080	100.0	100.0	6275	7855	100.0	100.0

Number of Drugstores[a] by Number of Employees

Number of Employees	Number of Drugstores			Percent of Total No. of Drugstores		
	1948	1958	1963	1948	1958	1963
None	5763	4744	2456	12.3	9.7	5.1
1	5258	4337	5123	11.2	8.8	10.7
2	6178	5403	5218	13.2	11.0	10.9
3	6043	6032	5913	12.9	12.3	12.3
4 or 5	8959	9161	8862	19.1	18.6	18.4
6 or 7	5700	6177	6302	12.1	12.6	13.1
8 or 9	2504	3990	4184	5.3	8.1	8.7
10 to 14	} 4972	4729	5066	} 9.7	9.6	10.5
15 to 19		1996	2260		4.1	4.7
20 to 49	1749	2323	2460	3.7	4.7	5.1
50 to 99	206	214	177	0.4	0.4	0.4
100 or more	23	25	29	0.1	0.1	0.1
Total	47355	49131	48080	100.0	100.0	100.0

percent) while sales were expanding by 1.58 billion (25.2 percent). Interviews with board of pharmacy secretaries revealed that the decreasing number of stores was due to the closing of small one-man operations and the opening of a relatively small number of large-volume stores, with most of the larger stores being opened by conventional chain drugstore corporations and discounters. It is not surprising, as the small retailers see their friends collapsing under the pressure of economic change, that there is a clamor for action to halt and reverse the trend via fair trade and free market restrictions.

TABLE 2-8 (*Continued*)

Number of Drugstores[a] by Stores Per Company[b]

Stores Per Company	Number of Stores		% of Total No. of Stores		% of Total Drugstore Sales	
	1958	1963	1958	1963	1958	1963
1	44650	42278	86.8	84.0	70.8	66.6
2	2433	2785	4.7	5.5	5.5	5.3
3	614	790	1.2	1.6	1.7	2.0
4 or 5	485	517	1.0	1.0	1.8	1.6
6 to 10	549	523	1.1	1.0	2.2	2.0
11 to 25	581	609	1.1	1.2	4.3	—
26 to 50	466	625	0.9	1.3	} 3.9	8.7
51 to 100	217	592	0.4	1.2		2.7
over 100	1453	1599	2.8	3.2	9.8	11.1
Total	49131	48080	100.0	100.0	100.0	100.0

Number of Drugstores[a] by Legal Form of Organization

Form of Organization	Number of Stores		% of Total No. of Stores		% of Total Drugstore Sales	
	1958	1963	1958	1963	1958	1963
Proprietorships	29425	24844	59.9	51.7	40.0	31.5
Partnerships	8807	7173	17.9	14.9	18.5	13.0
Corporations	10826	15969	22.0	33.2	41.3	55.4
Other Legal Forms	73	94	0.2	0.2	0.2	0.1
Total	49131	48080	100.0	100.0	100.0	100.0

Source: U.S. Census of Business, 1963, *Retail Trade: Sales Size, BC63-RS2*, Vol. I, pp. 12–13, 37–38, 54, 256, 268. Percentages are calculated.

[a] Drugstores in business for entire year.

[b] According to *Chain Store Age*, the government figures are understated. *The 1963 Directory of Chain Drugstores*, published by a *Chain Store Age* affiliate, lists 2,614 more multi-unit stores than does the government. A similar discrepancy (1,761) exists for 1958. The disagreement seems to stem from definitional factors. For example, the *Directory* would define as one chain three stores operating under three separate corporate names if controlled by the same person. On the other hand, the Census Bureau would define the three stores as three single units. See *Chain Store Age—Drug Executives Edition*, February 1966.

Metropolitan Drugstore—Drugstores in downtown locations generally are high volume stores. A significant portion of this volume is derived from fountain sales—the proximity of office buildings induces a brisk lunch and coffee-break trade in addition to the small (cost per item) drug sundry business. As is to be suspected, the prescription department sales are determined partly by how many physicians practice nearby.

Metropolitan drugstores may be owned and managed by a pharmacist, merchant, or corporate executives. It is difficult to ascertain which group dominates. There has been, in the past, a tendency for chains to seek downtown locations, but a considerable number of merchant-pharmacists are there, too. The outlets have been injured by the general decay of downtown areas and by the popularity of shopping centers.

Suburban Drugstore—The immense growth of shopping centers in the past few years has given rise to a new type of drugstore—the shopping center drugstore. These stores are much larger than metropolitan drugstores and carry a broader line of merchandise. As is true of metropolitan stores, the suburban enterprises have every conceivable type of owner. Chains, however, clearly predominate in this area. For various reasons, they are more able to obtain leases in shopping centers than their independent counterparts.

Sale of Health Items Only. Many pharmacists believe that the sale of general merchandise is degrading and unprofessional. This is a recurring theme in statements made by Dr. William S. Apple, Executive Director of the American Pharmaceutical Association (APhA).[25] Hence, there are a number of pharmacies that specialize in selling prescription drugs and related health products.

Apothecary[26]—An apothecary, as the term is defined in the drug field, is a retail outlet in which 60 percent or more of the store's annual sales are health items—e.g., prescriptions, cough drops, headache remedies, laxatives, bedpans, cotton swabs, surgical supports, and related items. In practice, apothecaries sell almost no general merchandise.

Pharmacist-proprietors have a virtual monopoly in this field, primarily as a result of being the philosophical opposite of others engaged in the retail drug industry. Apothecaries are not as concerned about volume of sales as are others in the drug trade. Moreover, there is less emphasis on self-service than in other outlets. Proprietaries, patents, and health aids are apt to be displayed in glass cases and serviced by a pharmacist. The "drugstore atmosphere" is not present.

Very few apothecaries are found in residential areas or shopping centers. For the most part they are concentrated near medical complexes, office buildings where many physicians are congregated, and dense population centers such as large apartment building areas. In

---

[25] "Anti-Chain Pattern Emerges from Talks by Apple; He Hits 'Traffic' Use of Rxs," *American Druggist*, April 30, 1962, pp. 5–6.

[26] Physician-owned pharmacies are a special case. See Chapter 7 for a discussion of these outlets.

such locations, there is a sufficient amount of exclusively drug trade to economically justify an apothecary's presence.

Pharmaceutical Center—As one pharmacist expressed it, a pharmaceutical center is a pharmacy that looks like a bank. To be more accurate, this type of outlet is a refinement of the apothecary. Not many pharmaceutical centers exist—it is a new concept, introduced in 1965 by McKesson & Robbins, Inc., a drug manufacturer and wholesaler.

When a customer (in the trade literature, a patient) goes into a pharmaceutical center, he enters an attractively appointed waiting room with paneled walls (upon which there are no drug displays) and a number of what appear to be bank tellers' windows. He proceeds with his prescription or request to one of the windows and is asked to be seated while his order or prescription is being readied. While waiting, the customer can listen to soft music, read a magazine, or examine pictures hanging on the walls. When the order is ready, the purchaser is paged, receives his merchandise and pays a receptionist—not the pharmacist.

This arrangement, to many pharmacists, is the ultimate in professionalism. It must also be impressive to the layman. Even though some pharmaceutical centers are being opened, the concept is too new and too untried to attempt to judge what the public reaction will be to this new type of service. It should also be noted that although chains have not been overly enthusiastic about apothecaries or pharmaceutical centers, they are, nevertheless, prepared to move in that direction if it appears that consumer preferences are shifting toward those types of outlets.

Department of a Store—The drug section of a store may physically resemble a pharmacy. The distinctive characteristics are: (1) drug department sales are usually dependent on traffic generated by other departments in the firm, (2) items sold in the drug area do not compete with goods offered in other portions of the business, and (3) the pharmacists generally are employees rather than owners of the operation.

One popular type of drug department is found in conventional department stores. Sometimes the pharmacist in this location owns the business—The Morgan Apothecary in the John Wanamaker center city Philadelphia department store is a good example. Frequently in these situations there is an agreement that the drugstore will not sell cosmetics and that the department store will not sell drug related items.

The two other types of drug departments are those found in food markets, and, more commonly, in general merchandise discount stores. In these outlets the drug section may be leased to an outside owner. The ordinary procedure is to lease the pharmacy areas to a drug chain rather than to an independent retailer. This approach seems to offer a greater assurance of success which is particularly important to general merchandise discounters and many have adopted the leased department technique. The theory behind the preference for contracting with a drug chain is that if the discounters are to relinquish managerial authority over one of their departments, they want control to be vested in an organization known to be competent.

As is to be expected, the installation of a drug department as part of a store is not based on an ideological motivation, but rather on a business decision made by the corporation owning the entire operation. Despite the lack of philosophical inducement, pharmacists employed in drug departments of a store can be considered more professional than their neighborhood counterparts. Unlike community pharmacists, drug department pharmacists spend most or all of their time filling prescriptions and do not have to include in their duties the task of selling general merchandise.

Mail Order Drugstores—Although many conventional drugstores function, to some extent, as mail order pharmacy houses, this categorization ordinarily is limited to those outlets whose sales are conducted primarily by mail. Because of state regulations, the mail order houses of any significance are located exclusively in the District of Columbia. Both the federal government and private enterprises make mail order drug sales and each serves special groups.

As they now exist, the major mail order drug firms sell mainly to retired individuals, teachers, and epileptics. These enterprises are more or less organs of associations devoted to advancing the interests of those groups of purchasers. The Veterans Administration (VA) also is in the mail order drug business. Veterans eligible for government medical care are directed to send certain prescriptions to regional VA dispensaries to be filled, although reimbursement will be made for some drugs bought locally.

CLASSIFICATION OF RETAIL DRUG OUTLETS
BY FORM OF OWNERSHIP

A few years ago, it would not have been too great a distortion to equate independent drug retailers with proprietorships and partnerships and to identify retail drug corporations with drug chains. The passage of time has blurred this simple relationship.

Proprietorship. Owning and managing a single drugstore is the usual definition of proprietorships that operate in the retail drug industry. Although the explanation is sufficiently accurate, there are multistore proprietorships, just as there are single store corporations. A person need not be a pharmacist to be a drugstore proprietor.[27] At one time merchant-owners were quite prevalent and many are still active. Evidence of past merchant influence is found in the NARD rule that membership in that association is limited to drugstore owners, not pharmacist-owners.

Today, it is rather difficult for a small nonpharmacist merchant to possess a pharmacy. The shortage of pharmacists has caused their salaries to rise to such a level[28] that it is difficult for a merchant to net enough profit from the business to support himself and to justify the risk of losing his capital investment in the enterprise. As a result, most proprietorships or single unit ownerships now are being established by pharmacists. The druggists may not reap a large return above their salaries, but the pleasure they derive from owning their own businesses apparently compensates for the low rate of return on their property.

Partnership. What has been noted about proprietorships similarly applies to partnerships. Nevertheless, there is the possibility that the co-owners (usually two) will expand their operations to two units so that each manages one store. This tendency, however, is counterbalanced by the need to employ two high-priced pharmacists if the growth occurs.

Corporate Ownership. Because of advantageous taxation provisions, capital-raising opportunities, economies of operation, and the attractiveness of limited liability, many varieties of drugstore corporations now exist and corporate retail pharmacies can no longer be classified exclusively as chain drugstores. One form is the close corporation. The stockholders may be a pharmacist and a member of his family or two or three pharmacists and their families. The primary object of adopting this legal form is to secure tax advantages and/or limited financial liability. If incorporations were made for expansion purposes, stock holdings generally would be distributed widely so as to acquire the capital needed for opening new units.

A close corporation may also be formed by physicians entering the drug business. This situation most frequently arises when doctors share a group or clinic practice, particularly if the purchase or construction of a new building in which they will be located is contemplated. The building is generally owned by the corporation, the corporation being responsible for amortization of the mortgage and building maintenance. By including a pharmacy in the new edifice, profits generated from that activity can be used to defray the mortgage and

---

[27] This is not true according to the pharmacy laws and/or regulations of some states.

[28] Some California pharmacists earn $6.60 per hour.

maintenance costs. The physicians can be reasonably sure that the pharmacy will be lucrative, assuming, of course, that it is patronized by their patients.

A third type of corporate entity is employed in the drug departments of supermarkets and discount houses. Typically, this section will be leased to a drug chain or operated as one of the discounter's (or food chain's) corporate divisions.

The final corporate form is the well-known chain drug corporation. In the past, these organizations were closely held and once a certain level of sales activity was achieved, a professional managerial staff was included in the activities, in addition to the founders and their immediate relatives. The trend now appears to be widespread public ownership of drug chains. Another recent trend is for food corporations to purchase a going drug concern (Jewel Tea Company and National Tea Company are examples) or organize a new enterprise (Kroger Company). In these instances, the drug chain is ordinarily a wholly owned subsidiary of the parent corporation.

Table 2-8 indicates that the corporate form of organization in the retail drug industry is increasingly and prosperously utilized. The most rapid growth is occurring in discount houses, food chain subsidiaries, and to a lesser extent, conventional chain drugstore corporations.

ATTITUDES AND STRUCTURE

Attitudes are more important than structure. Although it is quite helpful at times to compare corporations to proprietorships and sale of health items versus sale of general merchandise as well as health items, it is necessary to point out which category is under discussion in the aggregated structure; otherwise, the shadings of attitudes of the various associations in the retail drug field cannot be fully explained.

NARD represents those druggists who have the merchant-pharmacist attitude. It is correct to say that this attitude is predominant in the community pharmacy, but the same outlook can be found in many of the other type establishments.

APhA elucidates the professional pharmacist philosophy. Pharmacists with this value system either are or would like to be in apothecaries, pharmaceutical centers, or hospitals. The "or would like to be" is important. A large number of pharmacists in all of the various structural configurations, if they had their preference, and if APhA publications are to be believed, would change their status. Hence, their statements and motivations are colored by where they *want* to be, not by where they are.

The National Association of Chain Drug Stores (NACDS) is the organization of senior chain store executives, but it is the authoritative voice for more than those individuals. It expounds the chain store concept which is also the organization-pharmacists' attitude. Some of those pharmacists that are in the lower portion of the hierarchy have hopes of moving up the corporate ladder and/or have accepted chains as offering superior professional prospects as compared to the traditional neighborhood pharmacy. Also in this philosophical category are discount-affiliated chains or subsidiaries.

These comments have been appended to the discussion of structure to point out the limitations of attributing a particular attitude to a particular structure. It will be found that in some cases reference to structure is most appropriate, while at other times attitudes or a combination of attitudes and structure is the best basis of analysis.

CHAPTER THREE

Government Regulation of the Retail Drug Industry[1]

The extent and type of government regulation in any sphere is dependent upon those persons responsible for administration of the law as well as the provisions of the statutes. Too often in the regulatory arena, the psychology of the administrator is a more accurate guide to what is allowed than is the law. For this reason, an understanding of the backgrounds and philosophy of state regulatory officials (boards of pharmacy) is essential to a meaningful analysis of particular restrictive pharmacy laws and regulations.

To gain such an understanding, the following are necessary subjects for discussion: (1) division of pharmacy regulatory power between the states and the federal government, (2) location of the state board of pharmacy in the hierarchy of the state government, (3) qualifications that prospective members must meet to be eligible for appointment to the board, (4) the nomination process, and (5) the effect of the qualification requirements and appointment procedures on the composition of the board.

Governmental Locus of Regulation

The drug industry is extensively regulated at both the federal and state levels. Much of the supervision, especially at the federal level, is necessary—drugs are intimately connected with and crucial to the public health and welfare. The nature of the industry and the profes-

[1] Throughout this study reference will be made to various provisions of state pharmacy laws and regulations of the state boards of pharmacy. To avoid the vast number of footnotes necessary for statute and regulation citations, the relevant portions of the laws and regulations are included in Appendix I. The reader may refer to this appendix for the appropriate source and the exact wording of the various laws and regulations.

sions related to it are such that regulatory responsibility is divided between the states and the federal government.

FEDERAL REGULATION

The federal government has, necessarily, assumed jurisdiction over some aspects of drug industry supervision. Essentially, the federal government, through the Food and Drug Administration (FDA), regulates those facets of the industry that cannot practically be supervised by each state. The only exceptions to this philosophy are federal rules pertaining to the dispensing of narcotics and some other drugs and the maintenance of records concerning those drugs.

The primary duties of the FDA are to insure that (1) adequate sanitary and quality controls are observed in drug manufacture, (2) medications are safe for human use via prescription or over-the-counter distribution, (3) no useless drugs are marketed, and (4) advertising claims for drugs are verified by experimental results. The FDA and related agencies engage in other activities, but they are subordinate to the tasks just mentioned.

A major portion of federal authority and interest is concentrated on the manufacturers of drugs. Once the drugs are ready to be shipped to distributors, the FDA's interest in the product wanes, aside from the important matter of how prescription drugs are advertised to physicians and how nonprescription medications are publicized to the public. Supervision of the wholesale and retail distribution of drugs is almost entirely in the hands of the states.

NATURE OF STATE REGULATION

There are three essential features of state regulation that require clarification for a thorough understanding of the nature and activities of a board of pharmacy. These three areas are (1) the board's relationship to other regulatory bodies within the state, (2) the board of pharmacy's location in the governmental hierarchy, and (3) the focal point of board authority.

Relationship to Other State Regulatory Boards. State boards of pharmacy are not markedly different from other similar agencies such as the Board of Medical Examiners and so forth. That is to say, all boards (from barbers on up) are first and foremost occupational licensing bodies. The amount of legislatively-granted authority a board is given over the occupation it licenses varies, but all such regulatory entities are created to assure competency of those permitted to engage in a particular vocation.

The qualification and appointment criteria of the members of various boards are likely to be parallel, especially in closely related fields. Hence, criticism or praise of a particular occupational licensing agency is apt to be applicable to some, if not all similar organizations. For this reason, it should be constantly kept in mind that, because licensure is a state-sanctioned monopoly for a particular group of people, practices that have developed in pharmacy regulation may be present or forming in the supervision of other professions and vocations.

Location in Government Hierarchy. State licensing agencies are comparable to the independent regulatory agencies at the federal level. Both groups are not truly a part of any of the three branches of government (executive, legislative, or judicial).

The state licensing agencies are nominally a part of the executive branch, but administrators in this area, including the governor, exert very little control over the supervisory bodies. The only cause for removal of a member from a board is malfeasance in office, which prevents the governor from removing appointees if they endorse and execute policies with which he does not agree.

In a few states, all licensing boards have been grouped together to form a Department of Registration and Licensing, but this has had little effect so far as the exercise of executive control is concerned. The Director of such a department is little more than an administrator for the boards, helping them set up examination dates, keeping files, and so forth. He cannot hire or fire board members or their employees.

This type of centralized licensing department was originally proposed by the Council of State Governments. The concept was opposed by the American Pharmaceutical Association (APhA) on the basis that such a department would be a menace to self-rule by pharmacists.[2] There is no evidence, however, that the departments have had the prophesied effect. This is probably because the proposal that each board be composed of five individuals, including two public (nonprofessional) members, has not been adopted by any of the states.

The problems that the new coordinating department was supposed to solve are:

1. Relative lack of responsiveness by the individual boards to the wider public interest.
2. Absence of direct public representation, as a rule, in most agencies.
3. Restrictions on the governor's appointing power with respect to the membership of such boards.

[2] "Drive to Submerge Rx Boards in Non-Professional Bodies Menaces Pharmacy's Self-Rule, APhA Told," *American Druggist*, September 13, 1954, p. 2.

4. Excessive influence of professional and trade groups on the attitudes and activities of board members.[3]

This study will verify the contention that these problems exist with respect to state pharmacy boards.

Focal Point of Board Authority. Historically, state regulation has been concentrated on retail pharmacy outlets, to the exclusion of wholesale drug distribution and hospital drug use. Although boards of pharmacy have recently indicated interest in these neglected areas, the primary focus of supervisory activities is still on individual retail drugstores.

State regulation of retail drug outlets is vested in the state board of pharmacy (or its terminological equivalent). These boards enforce the state laws relating to the practice of pharmacy and, in addition, promulgate and enforce their own rules and regulations—a power granted by the state legislatures.

Most of the state laws do not contain provisions that are concerned with the minutiae of retail drugstore operations, but rather (1) require registered pharmacists to dispense drugs, (2) specify registration requisites, (3) establish certain standards, and (4) empower the pharmacy boards to adopt the detailed rules necessary for administering the other enactments. The boards also are generally responsible for securing compliance with state drug adulteration laws and for promulgation and enforcement of rules to govern the practice of retail pharmacy.

Of the pharmacy boards in the fifty-one jurisdictions under consideration in this study (the fifty states and the District of Columbia), all have the power to adopt and carry out rules and regulations "consistent with the law."

Six jurisdictions require their boards to consult with other state officials before board promulgations become effective. In the District of Columbia, proposed regulations must be approved by the District Commissioners. The Idaho and Massachusetts Boards must obtain the sanction of the state department of health. The Department of Registration and Education promulgates the pharmacy regulations in Illinois, but the rules are written by the Board. The Nebraska law is similar to that of Illinois—the Nebraska Board of Health, however, does the actual promulgation. The regents of the New York State Department of Education must approve the regulations proposed by that state's Board.

The remaining forty-four states permit the boards to enact regulations without the approval of other agencies, although a board (Missouri, for example) may consult the attorney general in some cases.

[3] *Ibid.*

Kentucky joined this group in May 1966. Prior to that time, the Kentucky Board did not have rule-making authority.

The pharmacy laws and rules of the various states give the boards a powerful weapon to force compliance with the provisions—license suspension and/or revocation. A pharmacist must be registered to practice his profession. Threat of revocation of his license is a menace to his livelihood, so he is apt to abide by the board's wishes. The same is true for a pharmacy, since it must be registered before it may open for business.

The use or abuse of a board's extraordinary power to a large extent determines the regulatory climate in a particular jurisdiction. Several states have similar laws and regulations, but the administration of these statutes varies. As a result there is a recognizable divergence in pharmacy regulation among the states that far exceeds differences in laws and rules. For example, fifteen states require that a pharmacist be the manager of a drugstore, but the Massachusetts law has generated more litigation over this issue than the statutes and regulations of all the other states combined.[4]

To partially explain how abuses of regulatory power may arise, it is necessary to review (1) the statutory qualifications for membership on a board of pharmacy and (2) the appointive process for boards of pharmacy.

Qualifications for Board of Pharmacy Appointment

Eligibility for appointment to a board of pharmacy is set forth in each state's pharmacy law. The several laws are not uniform, but they are quite similar in some respects. Table 3-1 lists the qualifications required in the states and the District of Columbia.

In order to be a board of pharmacy member, a person must be a registered pharmacist, except for one member in each of three states. In California, provision is made for one of the eight officials to be a "public" member, presumably a layman. The Idaho Board includes the Director of Health and the Pennsylvania law specifies the Superintendent of Public Instruction as an ex-officio member. There are no instances of nonpharmacist representation in the remaining forty-seven jurisdictions.

Besides the registered pharmacist requirement, thirty-nine jurisdictions demand that a pharmacist be licensed for a specific number of years before being eligible for appointment. The periods most frequently stated in the laws are five years (twenty-four jurisdictions)

---

[4] See Chapter 11.

TABLE 3-1: Qualifications for Board of Pharmacy Members

State	Min. No. of Years as a Registered Pharmacist	Must Be Actively Engaged in Retail Pharmacy	Person Connected with School of Pharmacy not Eligible for Appointment	Must Be Member of State Pharmaceutical Association
1. Alabama	10	x	x	x
2. Alaska	3	x		
3. Arizona	10			
4. Arkansas	5	x		x
5. California[a]				
6. Colorado	10	x		
7. Connecticut	10	x		
8. Delaware		x		
9. Dist. of Col.	5	x		
10. Florida	5	x		
11. Georgia	5	x		x
12. Hawaii	5	x		
13. Idaho[b]	5	x		
14. Illinois[c]	5	x		
15. Indiana		x	x	
16. Iowa	5	x	x	
17. Kansas	5	x		x
18. Kentucky	5	x		x
19. Louisiana	5	x	x	
20. Maine		x		x
21. Maryland	5	x[d]	x	x

TABLE 3-1 (*Continued*)

State	Min. No. of Years as a Registered Pharmacist	Must Be Actively Engaged in Retail Pharmacy	Person Connected with School of Pharmacy not Eligible for Appointment	Must Be Member of State Pharmaceutical Association
22. Massachusetts	10	x		
23. Michigan	10	x		
24. Minnesota	5	x		
25. Mississippi	5	x		
26. Missouri		x	x	
27. Montana	5	x		
28. Nebraska	5			
29. Nevada	10	x		
30. New Hampshire	10	x		
31. New Jersey	5	x	x	
32. New Mexico	8	x		x
33. New York	10			
34. North Carolina				x
35. North Dakota				
36. Ohio				
37. Oklahoma	5	x		x
38. Oregon	5	x		
39. Pennsylvania[e]	10	x		
40. Rhode Island	10	x		
41. South Carolina	3	x		x
42. South Dakota				x

TABLE 3-1 (Continued)

State	Min. No. of Years as a Registered Pharmacist	Must Be Actively Engaged in Retail Pharmacy	Person Connected with School of Pharmacy not Eligible for Appointment	Must Be Member of State Pharmaceutical Association
43. Tennessee	10	x		x
44. Texas	5	x	x	
45. Utah	5			
46. Vermont	5	x		
47. Virginia				x
48. Washington	5			
49. W. Virginia		x		
50. Wisconsin		x		
51. Wyoming	5	x	x	

Source: Appendix I.

ᵃ The eight-member California Board has one public member.

ᵇ The four-member Idaho Board includes the Director of Health.

ᶜ A faculty member of the College of Pharmacy of the University of Illinois sits on the Board.

ᵈ Four of the five members.

ᵉ The Superintendent of Public Instruction is an ex-officio member of the Board.

ᶠ The law includes the phrase "doing business." This could be construed to be an ownership requirement as a qualification.

ᵍ Optional for graduates of college of pharmacy.

and ten years (twelve states). Alaska and South Carolina specify three years and New Mexico sets an eight-year minimum.

Establishing a minimum number of years of registration might be acceptable in the abstract, but it does not appear to be of much practical merit. The board of pharmacy examines for pharmacy licensure, passes on pharmacy applications, renders judicial decisions on alleged law violations, and activates new legislation and regulations. The pharmacists' occupational experience that supposedly results from a specified period of registration does not supply on-the-job training in any of these functions.

At most, minimum registration requirements assure a certain maturity that otherwise might be absent. The question arises as to how much maturity is needed. An individual can be President of the United States at age thirty-five, but in those states that condition pharmacy board membership on a ten-year registration requirement, a person may not become a board member until age thirty-four (18 years of age at graduation from high school + 5 years of pharmaceutical education + 1 year of internship + 10 years of experience). An individual could be a governor, U.S. Representative, or U.S. Senator, but lack sufficient experience to be a member of a board of pharmacy.

Although the experience requirement is an annoyance,[5] the other qualifications for board of pharmacy membership are clearly discriminatory. This is especially noticeable in the forty jurisdictions whose laws state that a registered pharmacist must also be actively engaged in retail pharmacy activities to be appointed to the board of pharmacy. This effectively excludes pharmacists employed in other pharmaceutical activities—manufacturing, representing pharmaceutical manufacturers, hospital pharmacist, research, and teaching.[6]

Since the actions of boards of pharmacy affect these other occupational groups, they deserve board representation. In addition, their different areas of expertise can infuse the agency with beneficially divergent viewpoints. Even though retail pharmacists comprise some 80 percent of all pharmacists, to exclude the remainder is to encourage a parochial and one-sided view of all issues the boards must decide.

The general exclusion from board membership of pharmacists not engaged in retail pharmacy is augmented in nine states by specifically prohibiting pharmacists employed by colleges of pharmacy to participate in board activities. This is apparently a holdover from the days when the academicians of pharmacy—at that time the only druggists generally not engaged in retail endeavors—had to supplement their incomes by part-time work in a drugstore. Seemingly, the goal is to refuse pharmacy board membership to all whose primary field of interest is not retail pharmacy.[7]

The final eligibility requirement for board of pharmacy membership found in fourteen state laws compels a prospective official to be a member of the state pharmaceutical association. This requisite has absolutely no relationship to an individual's regulatory competency.

[5] The fact that all persons on the boards must be registered pharmacists (aside from the three noted exceptions) may be questioned. Self-regulation often means self-aggrandizement.
[6] Maryland allows one of its five-member Board to be engaged in other than retail pharmaceutical pursuits.
[7] Illinois takes the opposite position, specifically requiring a college of pharmacy faculty member to serve on the Board.

Such a statutory provision gives a state pharmaceutical association immense power over a board of pharmacy. If board members do not conform to the wishes of the association, they may be ousted from it and hence from the regulatory agency. More likely is the expulsion from the organization of members prior to their consideration for the board of pharmacy. If a member practices unprofessional conduct as defined by the association or espouses unapproved viewpoints, he can be removed from the membership roster and not ever be considered for appointment to the pharmacy board.

Appointment of Boards of Pharmacy

More important than qualifications is the selection process for pharmacy board members. The method of designating members from among those eligible determines, in large measure, the composition and composite character exhibited by the boards.

As Table 3-2 shows, the governor designates the board of pharmacy in forty-one states. The executive's power, however, is limited. In ten states, he *must* fill vacancies from a list supplied by the state pharmaceutical association.[8] Ordinarily, three to five names are supplied for each unoccupied position on the board. Such a procedure allows the association, in effect, to insure that board of pharmacy members endorse views held by the association.

In thirteen additional states, a list may be compiled, but the governor may select pharmacists other than those suggested by the association, provided the appointees meet the qualifications outlined in the law. It appears that most governors rarely exercise their option to designate board members other than those on the pharmaceutical association's list.

The infrequency of independent action by a chief executive is illustrated by the reaction to the reappointment of a board member in 1960 by New Jersey's Governor Robert B. Meyner without association approval. The New Jersey Pharmaceutical Association (NJPhA) submits three names to the governor after the candidates have been approved at the organization's annual winter meeting. Once a member has served a term on the board, the association's bylaws do not permit recommendation for reappointment. But the governor, for the first time in eighty-three years, ignored the NJPhA list and reappointed Meyer

[8] Although Oklahoma is one of these states, Governor Bellmon has, three consecutive times, refused to appoint from the list. The Oklahoma Pharmaceutical Association has successfully concluded a suit to determine the legality of Bellmon's most recent appointment. "Okla. Top Court Backs PhA; Voids Appointment to Board," *Drug News Weekly*, October 31, 1966, p. 8.

TABLE 3-2: Appointment of Boards of Pharmacy

State	Appointment by Governor			Appointment by Other Persons
	Without List	With List Supplied by Pharmaceutical Association		
		Optional	Mandatory	
1. Alabama			x	
2. Alaska	x			
3. Arizona		x		
4. Arkansas	x			
5. California	x			
6. Colorado	x			
7. Connecticut		x		
8. Delaware	x			
9. District of Columbia				District Commissioners
10. Florida		x		
11. Georgia				State Pharmaceutical Assn., confirmed by governor
12. Hawaii	x			
13. Idaho		x		
14. Illinois				Director of Dept. of Education and Registration[a]
15. Indiana	x			
16. Iowa			x	
17. Kansas			x	
18. Kentucky			x	
19. Louisiana	x			

TABLE 3-2 (*Continued*)

| State | Appointment by Governor | | | Appointment by Other Persons |
| | Without List | With List Supplied by Pharmaceutical Association | | |
		Optional	Mandatory	
20. Maine			x[b]	
21. Maryland			x	
22. Massachusetts	x			
23. Michigan	x			
24. Minnesota		x		
25. Mississippi			x[c]	
26. Missouri			x	
27. Montana			x	
28. Nebraska				Department of Health[d]
29. Nevada	x			
30. New Hampshire	x			
31. New Jersey		x		
32. New Mexico		x		
33. New York				Board of Regents of Dept. of Education
34. North Carolina				State Pharmaceutical Assn., confirmed by governor
35. North Dakota				State Pharmaceutical Assn., confirmed by governor
36. Ohio		x		
37. Oklahoma			x	

TABLE 3-2 (*Continued*)

| State | Appointment by Governor | | | Appointment by Other Persons |
| | Without List | With List Supplied by Pharmaceutical Association | | |
		Optional	Mandatory	
38. Oregon		x		
39. Pennsylvania		x		
40. Rhode Island				Director of Health, with governor's approval
41. South Carolina				State Pharmaceutical] Assn., confirmed by governor
42. South Dakota		x^e		
43. Tennessee		x		
44. Texas	x			
45. Utah				Director of Registration^f
46. Vermont	x			
47. Virginia		x		
48. Washington	x			
49. West Virginia	x			
50. Wisconsin	x			
51. Wyoming	x			

Source: Appendix I.

[a] The Director may use a list supplied by the Illinois Pharmaceutical Association.

[b] Mandatory unless the governor can show that all on the list are "manifestly incompetent."

[c] Four Board members shall be appointed by the governor from the list. The fifth member, to be Executive Secretary of the Board, shall be selected by the Mississippi Pharmaceutical Association and confirmed by the governor.

[d] Must use list supplied by state pharmaceutical association.

[e] One member of the Board must be the Secretary-Treasurer of the South Dakota Pharmaceutical Association, who shall also occupy the same position for the board.

[f] "Shall give due consideration to recommendations by" state pharmaceutical association.

Israel. Pharmacists were "surprised" at the governor's action and the move merited an article in the drug industry press.[9]

Other states in the optional classification are as habituated to the governor's using the list as is New Jersey, according to interviews with pharmacy board officials. The discretionary use of the list, therefore, is really an illusion. In at least three states (Minnesota, Ohio, Tennessee) other than New Jersey, the governor generally makes his appointments from among individuals suggested by the state pharmaceutical association.

Even in the eighteen states where the pharmacy statute does not refer to a list composed by the state pharmaceutical association, the governor may receive such a list and make his selection from among the names presented by the pharmaceutical organization. This is the case in Arkansas and Delaware. Probably the same practice occurs in several other states.

It would appear, then, that in jurisdictions where the governor ostensibly controls the designation of pharmacy board members, the state association has the real power of appointment by law and/or by custom.

Nine states (the District of Columbia Board is appointed by the District Commissioners) authorize persons other than the governor to determine the personnel of boards of pharmacy. In five of the states, appointment is by a department within the executive branch: Illinois, Director of Department of Education and Registration; Nebraska, Department of Health; New York, Board of Regents of Department of Education; Rhode Island, Director of Health; Utah, Director of Registration. The board of pharmacy is elected directly by the state pharmaceutical association in Georgia, North Carolina, North Dakota, and South Dakota. It eight of the nine states (the exception being New York) the appointments must be approved by the governor.

Effect of Qualification Requirements and Selection Procedures

From the analysis of the statutory qualification requirements and the formal and informal selection processes that apply to boards of pharmacy, the conclusion emerges that the agencies generally are controlled by state pharmaceutical associations. These organizations are, in turn, controlled by retail pharmacists, since they comprise such a large proportion of the pharmacist population.

[9] "N.J. Board Member Reappointed Without Association's Approval," *Drug Topics*, June 6, 1960, p. 10.

Within this retail pharmacist group, however, it is the independent owner segment that exerts the actual control over the actions and espoused philosophies of the state associations. This state of affairs exists for three reasons. One is that the economic issues that come within the domain of the boards of pharmacy are of utmost importance to owners. They are vitally interested in such items as sales tax allowances, trading stamps, and competitive threats to their position. For example, independent pharmacist entrepreneurs are acutely aware of the threat to their financial status that is created by chain and discount drugstore operations. The independents, accordingly, embrace legislative and regulatory policies that restrict the right of these types of outlets to enter the retail drug industry and limit the managerial prerogatives of chains and discounters. As the following chapters will illustrate, to combat the potentially detrimental competitive situation, pharmacy owners have supported statutory enactments such as those that require drugstores to be owned by registered pharmacists and those that prohibit the advertising of drug prices. Thus, independent pharmacy owners are highly motivated to join and to work with the association framework to insure that the right people (i.e., those who will further the owners' goals) sit on the boards of pharmacy.

A second reason for the dominance of retail owners over state pharmaceutical associations and hence state pharmacy boards is the failure of employee pharmacists to participate actively in association activities. This dormant attitude is not wholly the result of a lack of interest on the part of employees.[10] Rather, employee status itself is what hinders their greater participation in formulating the objectives of state pharmaceutical associations. An employee has neither the time nor the money to do much more than pay his dues and attend local meetings. Owners, on the other hand, can take part in regional, state, and national meetings with much greater ease. An owner's salary continues in his absence, whereas that of an employee generally does not.

The third factor that facilitates control of state pharmaceutical associations by independent drugstore owners is the membership status given to pharmacist drugstore owners, nonpharmacist drugstore owners, and pharmacists who are employed by drugstores. In some states all have equal status, but in other states employee pharmacists are relegated to second class membership or denied membership completely while nonpharmacist drugstore owners are accorded full membership priviledges along with pharmacist drugstore owners. Where state

[10] Many employee pharmacists do display a lack of interest in state pharmaceutical associations. Part of the disinterest is due to domination of the organizations by owners. See "voice of the druggist," the title of the letters to the editor column of *Drug Topics*, especially the issues of January 24, 1966 and March 7, 1966.

(and local) pharmaceutical associations condition full participation upon employer status rather than professional status, the associations' claim of being professional societies is just that—nothing more than a claim. Discriminatory membership requirements are not supported by most pharmacists. According to a survey of pharmacists, 81 percent favor full membership priviledges for employee pharmacists and 94 percent endorse elimination of the full membership priviledges enjoyed by nonpharmacist drugstore owners.[11]

Recently, the domination of state pharmacy boards by independent entrepreneurs has been attacked by two institutions that usually endorse opposing positions—management and unions. Carl W. Evans, President of Gray Drug Stores, speaking at the 1963 meeting of The American Pharmaceutical Association, said that the attempt by drugstore owners to monopolize the boards injures the entire profession. Mr. Evans noted that between 55 and 60 percent of Ohio pharmacists are employees, but that only one employee pharmacist is presently on the Ohio board. Moreover, that individual is only the second employee pharmacist Board member since 1884.[12]

A New York City pharmacy union also protested exclusive owner representation on the New York Board. The union members refused to send their pharmacist registration renewal fees to the agency to dramatize their demand for employee representation on the New York Board.

Kenneth Griswold, Secretary of the New York State Board of Pharmacy, said the union was laboring under a misconception in assuming that the purpose of the Board is to serve the profession. Griswold declared that the Board is an agency created to protect public health and for that reason

we must continue to recommend to the New York State Regents [of the Department of Education] pharmacy board candidates who, because of education, ability, experience, interest and personality are best fitted for service. [13]

Eventually, the union, which had been holding the fees in escrow, did forward them to the Board.[14]

[11] "81% Endorse Amendments For Non-Owner Pharmacists," *Drug Topics*, March 20, 1967, p. 19. The statistical validity of this poll is not known, but a survey of pharmacists' opinions on some topic is featured in every issue of *Drug Topics* and the results generally seem to accurately reflect current attitudes of pharmacists.
[12] "Urges Employee-Ph on State Boards," *Drug News Weekly*, May 15, 1963, p. 11.
[13] As quoted in " 'Board Serves Public, Not the Profession,' " *American Druggist*, March 1, 1965, p. 14.
[14] "Union Abandons Boycott of Rx Board," *American Druggist*, May 10, 1965, p. 27.

The logic that pharmacist owners have education, ability, experience, interest, and personality superior to that of pharmacist employees is very difficult to follow. And it is not at all certain that drugstore owners will serve the public interest better than employees—whose interest in the restrictive economic policies of the boards is sure to be much less than that of owners.

That independent drugstore owners dominate boards of pharmacy is rather well established. The total number of members of the state boards of pharmacy and the District of Columbia Board of Pharmacy is 264. Of this number, it appears that all except eleven are sole owners, partners, or shareholders in close corporations of drugstores or a full-time regulatory official whose job depends on the good will of the boards of pharmacy. The eleven nonowners are (1) the public member in California (required by law), (2) a faculty member of the College of Pharmacy of the University of Illinois in Illinois (the law requires a faculty member from an Illinois pharmacy school), (3) the state Director of Health in Idaho, (4) the dean of the College of Pharmacy of Fordham University[15] and the chief pharmacist of a county nursing home in New York, and (5) five employee pharmacists: District of Columbia (employed by Drug Fair, Inc.), Illinois (employed by Walgreen's), Nevada (employed by Hale Drug Stores), Ohio (employed by Gray Drug Stores), Texas (employed by Sommers Drug Stores), and Washington (employed by Thrifty Drug of Washington). In terms of percentages, only 4.2 percent of the board of pharmacy membership is not an owner or a full-time employee of the Board and sitting on the Board.[16]

The primary conclusion to be drawn from this chapter is that the state boards of pharmacy have a remarkable degree of autonomy within the state governments conbined with a considerable grant of power. Although these facts may be of interest to students of government, the significance for this study is to evaluate the uses to which the autonomy and authority are put in connection with the regulation of the retail drug industry.

The autonomy of the boards of pharmacy is greatly reduced (though their power is not) through their relationship with the state pharmaceutical associations. Because of the way state laws are drawn and because of the extra-legal precedents that have evolved, the state pharmaceutical associations, in effect, select the state boards of pharmacy.

[15] This appears to be contary to the New York law, which states that each board member must be a licensed pharmacist and must have "legally practiced as such for at least ten years" in New York. See Appendix I.

[16] Abstracted from a list of board of pharmacy members compiled by the National Pharmaceutical Council.

Such a procedure may result in direct benefits to the associations as organizational entities. There have been instances of the executive director of the association serving simultaneously as executive secretary of the board of pharmacy, thus easing the strain on the association treasury. Also, in a few states, the board of pharmacy remits to the association a part of the registration fees collected by the board. The legality of the latter practice is questionable.[17]

Apart from the institutional benefits accruing to the associations, the defacto selection of boards of pharmacy results in boards of pharmacy composed almost exclusively of the dominant group in the associations. In most cases the dominant group is independent retail drugstore owners. That this group dominates is indicated by the overwhelming majority of the group on the state boards of pharmacy.

Given that independent retail drugstore owners hold almost all the board of pharmacy positions, even an altruist would be impelled to surmise that the boards are likely to be sympathetic to the needs of their colleagues as compared to the needs of mass merchandising retail drug outlets, even so, the boards and especially the executive secretaries find it necessary to oppose the demands of the independent owners. The board-owner relationship is friendly, but the boards are not subsurvient to the associations or their owner groups.

Subsequent chapters indicate the issues and jurisdictions where the friendship places a burden on the public interest in order to preserve and enhance the position of the independent owner group.

[17] "Okla. Atty-Genl Rules That It Is Illegal For Boards To Give Part Of Renewal Fee To Assn," *American Druggist*, May 8, 1967, p. 30.

CHAPTER FOUR

The Philosophy of Restrictionism

One of the main efforts of this study is to identify the free market restrictions embodied in state pharmacy laws and in the rules and regulations of state boards of pharmacy. The purpose of this chapter is to illustrate that restrictionism is indeed a philosophy in that the idea is employed in many areas other than the prescription department of a drugstore.

Many examples of specific restrictive practices applicable to the retail drug field are cited in other portions of this study. This chapter focuses on restraining tactics that are broader in scope than those intended to control the operation of individual pharmacies and exclude certain entrepreneurs from the industry. The topics to be considered are fair trade legislation, conspiracies to fix prices, limitation of the supply of pharmacists, and opposition to mechanized dispensing of drugs in hospitals. Each of these subjects will show the pervasiveness of the restrictionist philosophy that is so firmly entrenched in the retail drug industry. From these discussions, certain impressions of the restrictionist philosophy will be mentioned.

Fair Trade Laws

The term "fair trade" is a euphemism for resale price maintenance, an arrangement that permits the manufacturer or distributor of a branded product to set a minimum retail price below which the retailer may not sell the product. The effect of fair trade legislation, by outlawing the sale of a good at a price under the recommended minimum for that commodity, is the eradication of price competition for branded goods. An analysis of the development and present status of price-maintenance legislation is helpful in establishing the relationship between fair trade laws and free market restrictions in the retail drug industry.[1]

[1] There is a vast literature pertaining to the merits of fair trade, experience

As indicated in Chapter 2, the U.S. Supreme Court did not, before the enactment of the fair trade laws in the 1930's, permit penalties to be imposed on retailers who adopted price-cutting techniques. Nevertheless, two methods of price maintenance were permitted: (1) Manufacturers could refuse to sell their products to discounters so long as the denials were not an attempt to enforce an illegal agreement to maintain a resale price.[2] (2) Producers could establish the prices at which their agents sold the goods, but there had to be a bona fide agency relationship; i.e., the agent did not take title to the merchandise and he acted solely on behalf of his principal.[3]

STATE FAIR TRADE LAWS

Following the rebuff by the Court and after several unsuccessful attempts to have Congress enact price maintenance laws, the protectionists turned to state legislation to seek relief. Foremost among those advocating fair trade principles is the National Association of Retail Druggists (NARD)—an organization composed largely of pharmacist-owners of drugstores. Although NARD is generally given credit for the successful enactment of state fair trade legislation, some notice should be given to the chain drugstores' position during this period.

Until the depression, chains were firmly opposed to fair trade statutes since up to that time the spectacular growth of these firms was largely a result of price-cutting activities applied to branded goods. This attitude quickly changed during the depression. Whereas in 1929 the average chain store's annual sales volume was $116,400 with a 3 percent net profit, by 1932 average sales had fallen to $90,398 with a net loss of 3 percent.

With this decline, price competition lost its appeal. The general feeling among chain store owners was that if discounting techniques did not draw a sufficient number of customers to create a profit, there was nothing to be said in favor of the practice. Hence, in 1932, Charles R. Walgreen publicly endorsed legalized price maintenance. His position was immediately and enthusiastically adopted by the presidents of Louis K. Liggett Company and Peoples Drug Stores. With the major

under the acts, effects of the statutes and so forth. Since this study does not delve into the many ramifications of fair trade, reference to the large body of work is not necessary. Lebhar and Wilcox are the two most important sources that deal with the enactment of state fair trade laws and the positions (pro or con) adopted by various trade and industry groups.

[2] *United States* v. *A. Schrader's Sons, Inc.*, 252 U.S. 85 (1920).

[3] *FTC* v. *Beech-Nut Packing Co.*, 257 U.S. 441 (1922).

chains as well as independent drugstores favoring price maintenance, the drive for enactment of fair trade laws was destined for success.[4]

California Fair Trade Law.[5] California was the first state to enact a fair trade law as a result of the united efforts of druggists. The statute exempted from Calfornia's antitrust act any contract between the buyer and seller of a branded product in which the buyer agreed to resell the product at or above the price named by the seller. The law was a failure since retailers who did not sign contracts could and did market goods at sums lower than those required in the agreements.

To make the enactment accomplish the desired result, it was amended to require even nonsigners to sell branded products at the stipulated price. Thus, as soon as one person had contracted to maintain the price of a good, the nonsigner clause in the amended law made the agreement binding on everyone marketing the commodity in the state. This amendment and the basic law were copied by other states.

The constitutionality of fair trade legislation, including the nonsigner clause, apparently was settled in 1936—both the basic law and the amended version were declared constitutional by the U.S. Supreme Court. The reasoning was that a manufacturer makes a substantial investment in good will by advertising his product. This good will, although an intangible, is the property of the manufacturer even after he has physically sold the product. Hence, price cutting, by damaging this proprietary good will, damages the manufacturer's property. The Court held that it is proper to legislate to prevent this damage.[6]

State Fair Trade Laws in Operation. States had been passing fair trade laws ever since California had shown the way in 1931. The *Old Dearborn* decision added such momentum to the trend, however, that by 1941, just ten years after the first enactment, all jurisdictions except the District of Columbia, Missouri, Texas, and Vermont had such laws on their statute books. The number of non-fair trade states was raised to four when Alaska entered the Union.

The rapid passage of the laws is an indication of the political power available to and used by the protectionists. Dr. Wilcox describes the process as follows:

The statutes legalizing resale price maintenance were whipped through the legislatures at breakneck speed. There is no record of hearings having been held in forty [of the forty-six] states. There is no transcript of hearings available in any state. The California law was supposed to contain

[4] Godfrey M. Lebhar, *Chain Stores in America, 1859–1962* (3rd ed.; New York: Chain Store Publishing Corp., 1958), pp. 113–114.
[5] Clair Wilcox, *Public Policies Toward Business* (2nd ed.; Homewood, Illinois: Richard D. Irwin, Inc., 1960), p. 379.
[6] *Old Dearborn Distrib. Co.* v. *Seagram-Distillers Corp.*, 299 U.S. 183 (1936).

a provision authorizing a producer to require "any dealer" to maintain a stipulated price. The text enacted, however, was garbled. Instead of "any dealer," it read "in delivery," so that the authorization made no sense. The care with which the laws were considered is indicated by the fact that this version was passed by the House and Senate and signed by the governor, not only in California, but also in Arizona, Iowa, Louisiana, New Jersey, New York, Pennsylvania, and Tennessee. The N.A.R.D. held the hoop and cracked the whip. The legislators and the executives obediently jumped.[7]

A similar sort of pressure was applied to manufacturers who were not particularly interested in signing price-maintenance contracts. When the manufacturer of Pepsodent toothpaste canceled its resale agreement in California, "Pepsodent went under the counter in practically every California drug store . . . and . . . clear across the country. . . . Rapidly, other brands which were carefully cultivating dealer good will by strict price stabilization . . . forged ahead. . . . Result: a few months later, Pepsodent returned to the fold and brought with it a check for $25,000 to help support the cause of fair trade laws . . ."[8]

Since the Pepsodent campaign was so successful, it appears that chain outlets were cooperating fully with independents in enforcing fair trade philosophy to the maximum extent possible.

FEDERAL FAIR TRADE LEGISLATION

Miller-Tydings Act. Although fair trade laws began to accomplish the desired results in intrastate transactions, the requirements had no effect on interstate shipments because the statutes were held to be a violation of federal antitrust laws. Since most branded goods did move across state lines, a federal law (the Miller-Tydings Act) exempting fair trade from prosecution under antitrust laws was proposed. This legislation, which was to amend the Sherman Antitrust Act, would allow interstate price-fixing contracts in those states having a fair trade law. The amendment was attached as a rider to a District of Columbia appropriation bill just before Congress adjourned in 1937. Although President Roosevelt voiced his objections, he signed the bill into law to avoid depriving the District of the revenue needed to finance its operations.[9]

---

[7] Wilcox, *op. cit.*, p. 381. Reprinted by permission of the publisher, Richard D. Irwin, Inc., 1960.

[8] "Resale Price-Fixing Under the Fair Trade Laws," *Business Week*, August 28, 1937, p. 38.

[9] Wilcox, *op. cit.*, p. 382.

Thereafter, the Fair Trade set-up was widely adopted by the manufacturers of branded lines, although it was favored in some fields more than in others. In the drug field, for instance, it became almost universal. That was because of the wide demand for it by distributors of all types—wholesalers, chains and independents. On the other hand, it made little headway in the grocery field, largely because the chains in that field were opposed to it on principle. They wanted no restriction whatever on their freedom to set their own retail prices.[10]

From 1937 to 1951 fair trade proved to be so legally sound that its most vigorous opponents came to view court action as futile. In 1951, however, the U.S. Supreme Court discovered a crack in the seemingly impregnable price-maintenance wall. The Court held that although resale agreements were federally sanctioned because of the Miller-Tydings Act, there was nothing in the law that bound nonsigners to respect minimum prices established by the contractual arrangements of others.[11] In effect, the Court was saying that the amendment to the Sherman Act did not include, either explicitly or implicitly, the nonsigner clause found in most state laws.

McGuire-Keogh Act. The *Schwegmann* decision precipitated price wars of such magnitude that they were headline news in the daily newspapers for several weeks. The fair traders capitalized on the interest by demanding that Congress restore the impregnability of fair trade by acting to plaster over the flaw located or created by the Supreme Court. Congress dutifully responded in 1952 with the McGuire Act.[12]

The McGuire Act was not the panacea its supporters had supposed. Fair trade fighters switched their tactics to attack the state price-maintenance laws on the basis of violation of other guarantees in the state constitutions. Almost at once the fair trade edifice began to crumble. Now, as Table 4-1 illustrates, the jurisdictions with viable fair trade laws number only twenty.

RECENT DEVELOPMENTS IN FAIR TRADE

The Masters Mail Order Case.[13] Even though fair trade laws are enforceable in nearly half of the states, the statutes have lost a substantial amount of their effectiveness. This is due, in part, to a 1957 court decision involving the General Electric Company and Masters Mail Order Company, a discounter based in the District of Columbia. The discounter had shipped GE appliances to New York buyers and had

---

[10] Lebhar, *op. cit.*, pp. 114–115.
[11] *Schwgemann Bros.* v. *Calvert Distillers Corp.*, 341 U.S. 384 (1951).
[12] Lebhar, *op. cit.*, p. 115.
[13] *General Elec. Co.* v. *Masters Mail Order Co.*, 355 U.S. 824 (1957).

TABLE 4-1: Status of State Fair Trade Laws

State	Status	State Code Reference	Case Source
1. Alabama	Entire Law Held Invalid	*Code of Alabama,* Title 57, c.2	*Bulova Watch Co.* v. *Zale Jewelry Co.,* 274 Ala. 270, 147 So. 2d 797 (1962).
2. Alaska	Law Never Enacted		
3. Arizona	Law Upheld	*Arizona Revised Statutes,* Title 44, art. 2	*General Electric Co.* v. *Telco Supply, Inc.,* 84 Ariz. 132, 325 P.2d 394 (1958).
4. Arkansas	Nonsigner Clause Held Invalid	*Arkansas Statutes, 1947,* Title 70, c.2	*Union Carbide & Carbon Corp.* v. *White River Distributors, Inc.,* 224 Ark. 558, 275 S.W. 2d 455 (1955).
5. California	Law Upheld	*West's Annotated California Codes,* Div. 7, c.3	*Glaser Bros.* v. *21st Sales Co.,* 36 Cal. Rptr. 379, 224 C.A.2d 197 (1964).
6. Colorado	Nonsigner Clause Held Invalid	*Colorado Revised Statutes, 1963,* c.55, art. 1	*Olin Mathieson Chemical Corp.* v. *Francis,* 134 Colo. 160, 301 P.2d 139 (1956).
7. Connecticut	Law Upheld	*Connecticut General Statutes Annotated,* Title 42, c.735	*Dorothy Gray, Ltd.* v. *Johnson Wholesale Perfume Co.,* 45 F. Supp. 744 (1942).
8. Delaware	Law Upheld	*Delaware Code Annotated* Title 6, c.19	*Klein* v. *National Pressure Cooker Co.,* 31 Del. Ch. 459, 64 A.2d 529 (1949).
9. District of Columbia	Law Never Enacted		
10. Florida	Nonsigner Clause Held Invalid	*Florida Statutes Annotated,* Title 31, c. 541	*Miles Laboratories* v. *Eckerd,* 73 So. 2d 680 (1954).
11. Georgia	Entire Law Held Invalid	*Code of Georgia Annotated,* Title 106, c.106-4	*Cox* v. *General Electric Co.,* 211 Ga. 286, 85 S.E.2d 514 (1955).
12. Hawaii[a]	Nonsigner Clause Held Invalid	*Revised Laws of Hawaii, 1955—1965 Supplement,* Title 24, c.205	*Johnson & Johnson, Inc.* v. *G.E.M. Sundries Co., Inc.,* 43 Hawaii 105, aff.283 F.2d 86 (1960).
13. Idaho	Law Not Tested	*Idaho Code,* Title 48, c.4	
14. Illinois	Law Upheld	*Smith-Hurd Illinois Annotated Statutes,* c.121½, s.189	*Old Dearborn Distributing Co.* v. *Seagram-Distillers Corp.,* 575 S.Ct. 139, 299 U.S. 183, 81 L.Ed. 109, A.L.R. 1476 (1936).
15. Indiana	Nonsigner Clause Held Invalid	*Burns Indiana Statutes Annotated,* Title 66, c.3	*Bissell Carpet Sweeper Co.* v. *Shane Co., Inc.,* 237 Ind. 188, 143 N.E.2d 415 (1957).

Table 4-1 (*Continued*)

State	Status	State Code Reference	Case Source
16. Iowa	Nonsigner Clause Held Invalid	*Iowa Code Annotated,* Title 23, c.550	*Iowa Pharmaceutical Assn.* v. *May's Drug Stores,* 229 Iowa 554, 294 N.W.756 (1940).
17. Kansas	Nonsigner Clause Held Invalid	*Kansas Statutes Annotated,* c.50 art. 3	*Quality Oil Co.* v. *DuPont & Co.,* 182 Kan.488, 322 P.2d 731 (1958).
18. Kentucky	Entire Law Held Invalid	*Baldwin's Kentucky Revised Statutes,* c.365, s.365,090	*General Electric Co.* v. *American Buyers Coop,* 316 S.W.2d 354 (1958).
19. Louisiana	Nonsigner Clause Held Invalid	*Louisiana Revised Statutes,* c.1, subpart c.	*Dr. G. H. Tichenor Antiseptic Co.* v. *Schwegmann Bros. Giant Super Markets,* 231 La. 51, 9050 2d 343 (1956).
20. Maine	Law Not Tested	*Maine Revised Statutes Annotated,* Title 10, c.203	
21. Maryland	Law Upheld	*Annotated Code of Maryland, 1957,* art. 83, s.102–s.110	*Home Utilities Co., Inc.* v. *Revere Copper Brass, Inc.,* 209 Md. 610, 122A.2d 109 (1956).
22. Massachusetts	Law Upheld	*Annotated Law of Massachusetts,* Title 15, c.93, s.14A–s.14c.	*DuPont & Co.* v. *Kaufman & Chernick, Inc.,* 337 Mass. 216, 148 N.E.2d 634; *Colgate-Palmolive Co.* v. *Elm Farm Foods Co.,* 337 Mass. 221, 148 N.E.2d 861 (1958).
23. Michigan	Nonsigner Clause Held Invalid	*Michigan Statutes Annotated,* c.178, s.19.321–s.19.324	*Arous Cameras, Inc.* v. *Hall of Distributors, Inc.,* 343 Mich. 54 (1955).
24. Minnesota	Nonsigner Clause Held Invalid	*Minnesota Statutes Annotated,* c.325, s.325.08–s.325.14	*Remington Arms Co.* v. *G.E.M. of St. Louis, Inc.,* 257 Minn. 562, 102 N.W.2d 528 (1960).
25. Mississippi	Law Upheld	*Mississippi Code 1942 Annotated,* Title 8, c.4, s.1108	*W. A. Schaeffer Pen Co.* v. *Barrett,* 209 Miss. 1, 45 So. 2d 833 (1950).
26. Missouri	Law Never Enacted		
27. Montana	Entire Law Held Invalid	*Revised Codes of Montana, 1947,* Title 85, c.2	*Union Carbide & Carbon Corp.* v. *Skaggs Drug Center, Inc.,* 139 Mont.15, 359 P.2d 644 (1961).
28. Nebraska	Repealed	Laws, 1959, c.280, s.1	
29. Nevada	Repealed	Laws, 1965, c.24	

TABLE 4-1 (*Continued*)

State	Status	State Code Reference	Case Source
30. New Hampshire	Law Upheld	*New Hampshire Revised Statutes Annotated, 1966*, c.358	*McIntire* v. *Borofsky*, 95 N.H. 174, 59 A.2d 471 (1948).
31. New Jersey	Law Upheld	*New Jersey Statutes Annotated*, Title 56, c.4	*Upjohn Co.* v. *Vineland Discount Health & Vitamin Center, Inc.*, 235 F. Supp. 191 (1964).
32. New Mexico	Nonsigner Clause Held Invalid	*New Mexico Statutes, 1953*, c.49, art.2	*Skaggs Drug Center, Inc.* v. *General Electric Co.*, 63 N.M. 215, 315 P.2d 967 (1957).
33. New York	Law Upheld	*McKinney's Consolidated Laws of New York Annotated*, c.25, art.24A	*Calvert Distilleries Corp.* v. *Stockman*, 26 F. Supp. 73 (1939).
34. North Carolina	Law Upheld	*General Laws of North Carolina*, c.66, art.10	*Parker Pen Co.* v. *Dart Drug Co.*, 202 F. Supp. 646 (1962).
35. North Dakota	Law Not Tested		
36. Ohio	Law Upheld	*Page's Ohio Revised Code Annotated*, Title 13, c.1333, s.1333.27–s.1333.34	*Hudson Distributors, Inc.* v. *Eli Lilli & Co.* and *Hudson Distributors, Inc.* v. *Upjohn Co.*, 386 U.S. 377 (1964).
37. Oklahoma	Nonsigner Clause Held Invalid	*Oklahoma Statutes Annotated*, Title 78, 5.41–5.44	*American Home Products Corp.* v. *Homsey*, 361 P.2d 297 (1961).
38. Oregon	Nonsigner Clause Held Invalid	*Oregon Revised Statutes*, Title 50, c.646, s.646.310–s.646.370	*General Electric Co.* v. *Wahle*, 296 P.2d 635 (1956).
39. Pennsylvania	Nonsigner Clause Held Invalid	*Pennsylvania Statutes Annotated*, Title 73, s.8	*Olin Mathieson Chemical Corp.* v. *White Cross Stores, Inc.*, 414 Pa.95, 199 A.2d 266 (1964).
40. Rhode Island	Law Upheld	*General Laws of Rhode Island, 1956*, c.12	*United States Time Corp.* v. *Ann & Hope Factory Outlet, Inc.*, 205 A.2d 125 (1964).
41. South Carolina	Entire Law Held Invalid	*Code of Laws of South Carolina, 1962*, c.2, art. 4	*Bulova Watch Co.* v. *Rogers-Kent, Inc.*, 181 F. Supp. 340 (1960).
42. South Dakota	Law Not Tested	*South Dakota Code of 1939*, Title 54, c.54.04	
43. Tennessee	Law Upheld	*Tennessee Code Annotated*, Title 69, c.2	*Plough, Inc.* v. *Hogue & Knot Super Market*, 211 Tenn. 480, 365 S.W.2d 884 (1963).
44. Texas	Law Never Enacted		

TABLE 4-1 (*Continued*)

State	Status	State Code Reference	Case Source
45. Utah	Entire Law Held Invalid	*Utah Code Annotated, 1953*, Title 13, c.4	*General Electric Co. v. Thrifty Sales, Inc.*, 5 Utah2d 326, 301 P.2d 741 (1956).
46. Vermont	Law Never Enacted		
47. Virginia	Law Upheld	*Code of Virginia, 1950*, Title 59, c.1.1	*Standard Drug Co., Inc. v. General Electric Co.*, 202 Va. 367, 117 S.E. 2d 289 (1960).
48. Washington	Nonsigner Clause Held Invalid	*Revised Code of Washington Annotated*, Title 19, c.19.89	*Remington Arms Co. v. Skaggs Drug Center, Inc.*, 345 P.2d 1085 (1959).
49. West Virginia	Nonsigner Clause Held Invalid	*West Virginia Code of 1961 Annotated*, c.47, art.11	*General Electric Co. v. A. Dandy Appliance Co.*, 134 W. Va. 491, 103 S.E. 2d 310 (1963).
50. Wisconsin	Law Upheld	*West's Wisconsin Statutes Annotated*, Title 14, c.133, s.133.25	*Schuster & Co. v. Steffes*, 237 Wis. 41, 295 N.W. 737 (1941).
51. Wyoming	Entire Law Held Invalid	*Wyoming Statutes, 1957*, Title 40, c.2	*Bulova Watch Co. v. Zale Jewelry Co. of Cheyenne*, 371 P.2d 409 (1962).

[a] Repealed in 1967. "Hawaii: Fair Trade End Triggers Price War," *Drugs News Weekly*, June 12, 1967, p. 4.

charged the purchasers a sum less than the fair trade minimum required by New York law. GE brought suit to enforce the payment of a consideration equal to the price-maintenance requisite. The case was eventually appealed by the mail order company to the Court of Appeals. This court ruled that the sales had been consummated in the District of Columbia and were not bound by New York law. The U.S. Supreme Court refused to review the lower court's decision. The ruling makes it possible for price cutters to avoid state fair trade laws by shipping goods in from states where price-maintenance statutes are not in force.

Parke, Davis & Co. Case.[14] A recent fair trade case has clarified the connection between a drug manufacturer's sales to drugstores and a drug manufacturer's sales to other institutions such as hospitals and clinics. Parke, Davis brought a standard fair trade suit against a drugstore. The plea asked for an injunction to prevent a drugstore from selling Parke, Davis products at prices below the fair trade minimum.

[14] *Parke, Davis & Co. v. Janel Sales Corp.*, 328 F.2d 105 (2d Cir.), *cert. denied* 379 U.S. 835 (1964).

The District Court for the Southern District of New York granted the injunction by Parke, Davis, but the defendant appealed. The defendant's main defense before the U.S. Second Circuit Court of Appeals was that Parke, Davis was not eligible for protection under the fair trade laws because Parke, Davis itself sold at retail (to hospitals, clinics, and veterinarians) below fair trade prices. As evidence of the retail nature of the rules, the defendant pointed out that Parke, Davis had paid New York sales tax on the items sold to nondrugstore purchasers.

The Circuit Court judges did not agree with the defendant's argument. The court said that payment of a sales tax was inadequate evidence of retail sales since Parke, Davis also paid sales tax on manufacturing equipment it rented. According to the court, the true test of a retail sale is whether the purchaser of an item is doing so to satisfy his or his family's personal needs. As a result, the circuit court upheld the district court's issuance of the injunction. The U.S. Supreme Court refused to hear the case.

Quality Stabilization. Even though retail drug outlets were little affected by the *Masters Mail Order* ruling, NARD immediately began to press again for federal fair trade legislation which was labeled the "Quality Stabilization Bill." It was introduced every year from 1958 through 1964, but to no avail. Finally, NARD leaders confessed that "political realities" made state enactments of the proposal more likely to succeed.[15]

The quality stabilization bill introduces the concept of "contract by notice." A federal version would require all states, whether they have a fair trade law or not, to abide by a price publicly announced by a manufacturer. There would be no formal contract, just the understanding that by accepting the goods of a manufacturer whose prices are marked on containers, the resale by a retailer has to be at or above the named price. Moreover, the new strategy avoids the tremulous legal ground of nonsigner clauses.

Ohio-Type Fair Trade Law. Three (North Dakota, Ohio, and Virginia) state fair trade laws have the new "contract by notice" feature. Although the drug industry press refers to "public notice" fair trade statutes as the Ohio-type, the law was first passed in Virginia. The provision as enacted by Virginia is:

The acceptance of a commodity for resale, after notice imparted by mail or attached to the commodity or containers thereof shall be prima facie evidence of actual notice of the terms of the contract. Acceptance for resale with actual notice shall be deemed to be assent to the terms of the 'contract.'[16]

[15] "Political Realities Require State-by-State Fight for Fair Trade, NARD Is Told," *American Druggist*, October 26, 1964, p. 13.

[16] *Va. Code of 1950*, tit. 59, c.1.1s.59.8.2 (1958).

Enactment in Ohio—The next state to endorse this measure was Ohio. Early in 1959 a war chest was collected to finance the campaign.[17] (The former Ohio fair trade law had been invalidated by the State Supreme Court the preceding year.) In May, the House of Representatives voted 123 to 4 in favor of the bill. In July, the Senate added its approval with a 31 to 2 vote.[18] Pharmacists were astounded when Governor DiSalle vetoed the bill. The Governor said:

I do not feel that the state may properly interfere with the operation of a free economy in a free enterprise system by using its police powers to attempt to halt the practice which, although unfair, is not necessarily contrary to law in that it infringes upon the health, safety or welfare of the general public.

Controls are justified in times of emergency when the public health, safety and welfare are threatened, but in day-to-day operation the fact that a business practice disadvantages some and benefits others does not necessarily warrant the state's interference.

We cannot advocate and speak lightly about a free enterprise system while, at the same time, we attempt to restrain competition . . .

Although I was tempted to let the court act upon this law, I felt that, inasmuch as there is a philosophical principle involved, as to where the state has a right to interfere and when it does not have the right, I could not in good conscience sign the legislation.

How many of those who urged enactment of the legislation would have done so if the purpose was to fix a maximum price instead of a minimum?[19]

In view of the original vote, it was a foregone conclusion that the veto would not stand. The Governor's action was overturned by a 112 to 6 vote in the House and by a 30 to 3 vote in the Senate.[20]

Litigation Under the New Law[21]—The "public notice" statute was quickly brought to the courts in Ohio. By August of 1960, one state district court had upheld the validity of the law and two others had declared the concept unconstitutional. The case that eventually brought the law before the U.S. Supreme Court was an action begun in the Ohio courts for a declaratory judgment. The action was instituted by Hudson Distributors, Inc., which owns Revco Drug Stores, a discount

[17] "Ohioins Seek Funds to Push Drive for New State Fair Trade Law," *American Druggist*, January 12, 1959, p. 20. The participation by the Ohio Pharmaceutical Association is indicated by the fact that James D. Cope, secretary of the Association was also chairman of the Fair Trade Committee.

[18] "F. T. Measure Clears Ohio Legislature," *American Druggist*, July 13, 1959, p. 9.

[19] As quoted in "Ohio Overrides Veto and Enacts Fair Trade Law," *Drug Topics*, August 3, 1959, p. 3. Used by permission of the publisher.

[20] *Ibid.*

[21] *Hudson Distrib., Inc.* v. *Eli Lilly & Co.*, 377 U.S. 386 (1964).

drug store chain headquartered in Cleveland. Eli Lilly and Co., a leading pharmaceutical manufacturer, cross-petitioned for enforcement of the new law.

The Ohio Court of Common Pleas for Cuyahoga County ruled that the law was in violation of the state constitution. The Court of Appeals for Cuyahoga County reversed the lower court, and the Supreme Court of Ohio sustained the appellate court's reversal. The U.S. Supreme Court settled the issue, at least temporarily, by ruling that the law was constitutional.

In the eight to one decision, delivered by Mr. Justice Goldberg, the Court saw as the basic question whether or not the McGuire Act condoned contract by notice. In forming their opinion, the Justices relied heavily on the Report of the House Committee on Interstate Commerce for the McGuire Act. The relevant portion of that Report states:

The primary purpose of the McGuire bill is to reaffirm the very same proposition which, in the committee's opinion, the Congress intended to enact into law when it passed the Miller-Tydings Act . . . , to the effect that the application and enforcement of State fair-trade laws—including the nonsigner provisions of such laws—with regard to interstate transactions shall not constitute a violation of the Federal Trade Commission Act or the Sherman Act. . . .
The end result of the Supreme Court decision [in *Schwegmann* v. *Calvert*, 341 U.S. 384, May 21, 1951] has been seriously to undermine the effectiveness of the Miller-Tydings Act and, in turn, of the fair-trade laws enacted by 45 states.
H.R. 5767, as amended, is designed to restore the effectiveness of those acts by making it abundantly clear that Congress means to let State fair-trade laws apply in their totality; that is with respect to nonsigners as well as signers.[22]

The forcefulness of the committee report—together with (1) the provision of the McGuire Act (Section 3) that permits a state to enforce resale price contracts on both signers and nonsigners and (2) the clear meaning of the Ohio law that contracts by notice were to be considered the same as conventional contracts—led the Court to conclude that the Ohio act was lawful.

The Court refused to rule on other issues postulated by Hudson, saying that these questions were still being heard in lower courts, so that a ruling by the Court at that time would be premature. Hence, it is entirely possible that other constitutional issues, such as the hori-

---

[22] H. R. Rep. No. 1437, 82nd Cong., 2d Sess. 1–2, as quoted in *id.* at 392. Emphasis supplied by the Court.

zontal price-fixing agreements alleged by Hudson, may invalidate the Ohio law or certain contracts entered into under the statute.

RELATIONSHIP BETWEEN FAIR TRADE LAWS
AND FREE MARKET RESTRICTIONS

Although fair trade legislation can be considered a free market restriction,[23] the discussion has not been presented with that idea in mind. Rather, the purpose of the synopsis is to suggest that there is a relationship between fair trade and all other free market restrictions in the retail drug industry. It is proposed that the cyclical fair trade successes generate the counter cyclical "other restrictions."

The rapidity with which fair trade laws cleared state legislatures demonstrates the political power of NARD and its supporters. The ease with which the federal acts were enacted similarly indicates that pharmacists are (or were) a potent political force. Although advocates of quality stabilization have been stymied at the federal level (for some reason that is not clear) it appears from the activities of recent Ohio and Virginia legislatures that there has been no waning of influence—at least on the state level.

Fair trade's circumscribed success has not been because of an erosion of political power. Rather, it is the several unfavorable rulings by the U.S. Supreme Court on the interstate aspects of the laws and the numerous reverses at the state supreme court level (see Table 4-1) that have been the roadblocks to price-maintenance enforcement. These cases and others involving restrictive procedures to be discussed later have led to a utilization of discounting practices that have resulted in a loss of nonprescription sales made by drugstores—especially neighborhood pharmacies. Since prescriptions are virtually a drugstore monopoly, the independents' share of these sales has not suffered, except where food chains and discount stores have entered the local prescription market.

The many free market restrictions that now exist in the retail drug industry seem to coincide with the fair trade enforcement problem that has existed since 1951. Observing their nondrug sales diminishing, independent druggists moved to protect their portion of total drug sales by a variety of devices. Their actions may have been more of an instinctive procedure than a conscious plan. Nevertheless, whatever the motivation, the legality of several of the pharmacists' techniques have

---

[23] For a defense of the fair trade mechanism see P.W.S. Andrews and Frank A. Friday, *Fair Trade: Resale Price Maintenance Re-examined* (New York: St. Martin's Press, 1961).

been and are being tested in court. One purpose of this study is to present the tactics adopted in the druggists' attempts to maintain their market position and the counteractions utilized by those seeking to enter the retail drug field.

If the thesis of interaction between fair trade laws and free market restrictions is correct, future events hinge upon the constitutional merits and legislative success of Ohio-type fair trade laws. If the new price-maintenance laws are declared valid, there will be less need for other types of restrictions. On the other hand, if the fair trade concept fails, restraints on entry and operating practices are apt to become more important.

FAIR TRADE AND RESTRICTIONISM

The long history of the fair trade struggle illustrates the deep-seated desire of pharmacists for protection from competition. It is true that all of the support for price maintenance has not come from the retail drug industry. It is also true that the acknowledged leader in the fight for fair trade laws is NARD, an organization composed of pharmacists and merchants that own retail drugstores. The persistent activity of NARD and the financial support given to it for price maintenance advocacy are indicative of the importance of restrictionism to members of the retail drug industry.

As has previously been indicated, chain drug organizations have not been adverse to fair trade legislation. Nevertheless, according to sentiments expressed in interviews and in some court decisions listed in Table 4-1, a minority of chain executives do feel that price maintenance legislation has been detrimental to the industry. The contention is that fair trade provisions have maintained prices at a sufficiently high level to encourage others to enter merchandising fields that once were the preserve of drugstores. This argument is advanced by some to account for the movement of supermarkets into the vending of health and beauty aids as an important adjunct to food sales.

The viewpoint opposing fair trade that is found in some chain organizations generally is a function of the size of the firm. Large concerns emphasize sales volume as well as price mark-up, but small retailers often are not expansion-minded and place more emphasis on per item profit than on volume of sales. This difference in marketing procedure explains in large measure why independents tend to be restrictionists and chains generally are inclined to be free traders. Both groups apparently follow a philosophy that they perceive to be in their best interests.

Price Conspiracy Prosecutions

The most visible result of a restrictionist policy is an agreement to sell at uniform prices. Beginning in 1960, the U.S. Justice Department filed complaints against several state pharmaceutical associations, charging them with the action, and specifically alleging a conspiracy to fix the prices of prescription drugs—products not protected by fair trade provisions. The defense adopted by the associations gives an insight into the restrictionist attitudes of many pharmaceutical association members.

THE CALIFORNIA CASE

Although the California lawsuit was not the first to be filed by the Justice Department it was the price-fixing test case. Once a precedent was established by the California litigation the cases in other states were disposed of rather easily.

The California action began with a federal grand jury investigation of prescription drug prices in northern California. After hearing several witnesses and learning of a pricing schedule printed and distributed by the Northern California Pharmaceutical Association,[24] the grand jury returned a criminal indictment against that organization and the pharmacist who devised the pricing system. Later, the U.S. Justice Department filed a civil complaint in the same action.[25]

The Criminal Indictment.[26] The defendants were charged with engaging in a conspiracy to fix retail drug prices, a practice that is illegal under the Sherman Antitrust Act. The Justice Department claimed that the defendants and their co-conspirators had combined and contrived to (1) establish and maintain uniform prices for prescription drugs in northern California, (2) adopt a prescription pricing schedule formulated by Donald K. Hedgpeth, a pharmacist, (3) publish and distribute the pricing schedule to members of the Northern California Pharmaceutical Association, (4) revise the pricing schedules from time to time, and (5) urge and induce members of the association and

[24] "U.S. Grand Jury Probes Calif. Rx Prices," *American Druggist,* December 12, 1960, pp. 9–10.
[25] "Will More U.S. Price Conspiracy Cases . . . Follow Indictment of Calif. Rx Men?," *American Druggist,* January 9, 1961, pp. 8–9. It is standard practice for the Justice Department to file both a civil and criminal complaint in such cases. A criminal conviction allows the collection of damages from the defendants and a civil action permits injunctive relief of the illegal practices (Wilcox, *op. cit.,* pp. 110–114).
[26] *Indictment, United States* v. *Northern Cal. Pharmaceutical Ass'n,* Criminal No. 37653, D. No. Cal.

county pharmactutical association members to formulate uniform retail prices via the Hedgpeth pricing schedule.

The indictment explained that these actions had resulted in (1) suppression or elimination of price competition in prescription drugs, (2) increased prices for prescription drugs, and (3) the charging of high, arbitrary, and noncompetitive fees for prescription drugs in northern California.

APhA-NARD Activity.[27] Soon after the grand jury returned the indictment, representatives of the American Pharmaceutical Association (APhA) and NARD met to draft a plan for supporting the defendants in the antitrust action. Sensing that there would be a great deal of publicity for the sponsoring organization, NARD suggested that funds for the defense be drawn proportionately from the operating income of the two groups. APhA countered with a proposal that the legal costs be financed by a fund raising drive within the ranks of the pharmacy profession—a tactic that would enhance APhA's status and gain new members, perhaps at the expense of NARD.

NARD rejected this plan and approached the defendant Northern California Pharmaceutical Association with an offer to retain the most competent antitrust lawyer available at no expense to the California organization. The association refused and instead appealed to APhA for financial assistance. APhA responded with a fund-raising campaign that, among other things, urged members to solicit nonmembers to join APhA so that the fight—in the words of the organization—to "save the profession" could be adequately financed.

The attempt to amass defense resources and APhA's contention that the California case could be won because pharmacy as a profession is exempt from antitrust legislation brought vituperative comment from NARD in the pages of its journal. The retail druggists' association attacked the financial campaign as a membership gimmick for APhA. With this assault, the long-standing schism between the two pharmaceutical organizations[28] was brought into the open again.

U.S. District Court. When the case against the California association was brought to trial, the defense presented three arguments:

1. Pharmacy is a profession and therefore antitrust law does not apply to it.

---

[27] "Professional Status Doesn't Exempt Rx Men from Antitrust Law, NARD Says," *American Druggist*, May 29, 1961, pp. 5–7; "Key Charges-and Answers," *American Druggist*, May 29, 1961, p. 6.

[28] This refers to the merchant philosophy of NARD as opposed to the professional philosophy of APhA as mentioned in Chapter 2. Implicit in the disagreement is the institutional need for competing organizations to attempt to gain preeminence over their competitors.

2. Filling and selling prescriptions is not an interstate act and therefore the antitrust law does not apply to those actions.
3. There was no conspiracy to fix prices.[29]

In his statement to the jury, and in response to the defendants' allegations, Judge Goodman made the following points:

1. Whether pharmacy is a profession has no bearing on the case. For this reason testimony along that line was excluded from the trial.
2. The government has proved that the retail distribution of prescription drugs is a form of interstate commerce, but this conclusion is a personal opinion and jurors need not be bound by it.
3. "The only question in this case . . . is . . . whether or not [defendants and co-conspirators] . . . entered into an agreement to provide for the fixing and making of uniform prices . . . [for prescription drugs]."[30]

The jury returned a verdict finding the defendants guilty of price collusion.

After the decision was handed down, Arthur B. Hanson, a defense attorney, said that the professional status of pharmacy was at stake. For anyone to say otherwise, "either venality, cupidity or senility must be involved—perhaps all three." Hanson also voiced several complaints in connection with the case. First, the assurance of the assignment judge that a day or so would be allowed to settle procedural matters after the trial started, but before jury impanelment began was not fulfilled. (The delay was not granted because there had already been a two-week postponement in beginning the litigation due to Judge Goodman's illness.) Also, according to the attorney, conversations with Judge Goodman indicated that he was biased against the defendants. As a result, "It was not easy to get up every day for a period of three trial weeks and go into the courtroom knowing that he who controlled your destiny in that courtroom was one hundred percent opposed to your position." Finally, Judge Goodman's "instructions to the jury did everything except direct a verdict."[31]

APhA also had several grievances concerning the trial. Among them were (1) the fine imposed was "a gross miscarriage of justice," (2) Judge Goodman handled the case improperly by not allowing testi-

[29] Robert P. Fischelis, "What Are We Defending?," *American Druggist,* September 4, 1961, pp. 11–13.
[30] As quoted in "What Judge Louis E. Goodman Told Jury Before It Found Defendants Guilty," *American Druggist,* July 10, 1961, pp. 8–9.
[31] Arthur B. Hanson, "Antitrust Looks at Profession of Pharmacy," *Journal of the American Pharmaceutical Association,* Vol. NS1, No. 11 (Nov. 1961), p. 681.

mony on the concept of professionalism, and (3) the Justice Department's lawyer made inflammatory statements to the jury. In contrast to these views, NARD said the judgment vindicated its earlier statement that professionalism is not an antitrust defense. It also accused the defense lawyer of bungling the case.[32]

U.S. Court of Appeals. The defendants appealed the adverse decision to the U.S. Court of Appeals. The judges of that tribunal, William E. Orr, Frederick A. Hamley, and Charles M. Merrill, seemed to be particularly interested in the interstate commerce aspects of the case and the evidence concerning professionalism that Judge Goodman had not allowed to be heard.

To the defendants' claim that the allegedly illegal activities listed in the indictment were merely reasonable regulation of the profession, the higher court said:

In short, there is no defense to *price-fixing* on the ground that it is reasonable or that it is being done by professionals. Appellants' "professional" status *per se* will not protect them . . .
. . .

Appellants' attempt to show the need for supervision of the pharmaceutical price structure might make a case for the regulation of drug prices *by law*. But here . . . there is no showing that existing legislation in this field authorizes price-fixing in any form. And far from suggesting that public regulation be instituted, appellants suggest that they should be permitted to carry on that regulation with no public overseer. It is precisely such use of uncontrolled private economic and quasi-political power in the market place which the Sherman Act condemns. . . .

We do not decide that every action of professionals is within the reach of the Sherman Act. We do decide that an agreement among professionals to fix prices is.[33]

The appellate court then unanimously concluded that the lower court's jury and presiding justice had acted properly. "Overwhelming" evidence supported the government's contention that there was a conspiracy to fix the prices of goods moving in interstate commerce. The U.S. Supreme Court refused to hear an appeal from the decision of the U.S. Circuit Court of Appeals.[34]

The Civil Indictment. The civil action entered in the California case was settled by consent decree on April 9, 1963. The following fall, a petition for modification or clarification of the consent decree was requested by the Social Welfare Committee of the California Pharmaceutical Association. The Committee wished to discuss price schedules

---

[32] "U.S. Asks Early Trials in Civil Rx Price Cases to Capitalize on 'Criminal' Win," *American Druggist*, July 10, 1961, pp. 5–6.

[33] *Northern Cal. Pharmaceutical Ass'n* v. *United States*, 306 F.2d 379 (9th Cir.), *cert. denied*, 371 U.S. 852 (1963).

[34] 306 F.2d at 385–386.

for welfare payments with the Department of General Welfare of the State of California, but some members of the Committee were also members of the Northern California Pharmaceutical Association which had agreed not to discuss prices with one another. Judge Sweigert denied the plea, saying that legitimate activities should be no cause for concern and that no deviation from the decree would be permitted to allow pharmacists to confer with one another on price structures.[35]

THE UTAH CASE[36]

The allegations and defense in the litigation the Justice Department initiated against the Utah Pharmaceutical Association were very similar to the ones appearing in the California criminal action. One difference, however, was that Judge Christensen allowed a great deal of testimony concerning professionalism. The judge also rebuked the government's lawyers for trying to suppress that testimony.

Nevertheless, the decision handed down by the Utah court (civil complaint) was similar to the jury charge and appellate ruling in the California criminal case. In the Utah justice's view, the four questions to be settled were:

1. Does the restraint of trade constitute the restriction of interstate commerce within the purview of Section 1 of the Sherman Act?
2. Does the fact that the filling of a prescription is a professional act exempt the Utah Pharmaceutical Association from the reach of the Sherman Act?
3. Has the defendant conspired to fix the prices of prescription drugs?
4. If there has been a conspiracy, is it a reasonable restraint of trade acceptable under the Sherman Act or is it a violation of the Act?

The bench ruled against the defendant on all four areas of dispute. Regarding the question of professional immunity, the court said:

The fact that a pharmacist in filling a prescription is engaged in the practice of a learned profession does not immunize the defendant from this application of Section 1 of the Sherman Act.

Defendant seeks to state that issue in the form of two mutually exclusive alternatives: Is the dispensing of prescriptions a learned profession, or is

[35] *United States* v. *Northern Cal. Pharmaceutical Ass'n*, 235 F. Supp. 378 (D. No. Cal. 1964).

[36] *United States* v. *Utah Pharmaceutical Ass'n*, 201 F. Supp. 29 (D. Utah), *aff'd per curium*, 371 U.S. 24 (1962).

it the retail sales of a commodity in commerce? But the mere circumstance that goods in commerce are treated or handled by, or otherwise connected with, a learned profession does not remove the goods, themselves, nor transactions affecting them, from the applicability of the Sherman Act.[37]

The Judge then explained his reasoning behind the ruling on the other questions and concluded that no penalties (fines) were to be imposed, but the Utah Pharmaceutical Association was to be prohibited from engaging in price-fixing activities in the future. An appeal of the decision to the U.S. Supreme Court failed. The Court would not review the case.

THE ARIZONA AND IDAHO CASES

These litigations involve alleged antitrust violations similar to those in the California and Utah lawsuits. The Arizona case had been filed before the California suit, but was held in abeyance until the California case was settled. The Arizona litigation was unusual since two local pharmaceutical associations (those of Maricopa County and the city of Tucson) were named as defendants along with the Arizona Pharmaceutical Association. Both of these cases were settled by consent decree after the U.S. Supreme Court turned down the appeals presented by the defendants in the Utah and California actions.[38]

SUMMARY OF PRICE CONSPIRACY CASES

Two major defenses by the pharmaceutical associations charged with price-fixing conspiracy emphasize the restrictonist philosophy of druggists. The first defense declared that pharmacy is a profession and as such is immune from the antitrust law. Hence, pharmacists may combine and conspire to fix prices or engage in any other type of restrictive activity.

The other defense raised contended that even if pharmacists did come within the limits of the Sherman Act, they should be adjudged innocent because their tactics were reasonable restraints. The actions were justifiable since some regulation of prescription prices was needed and the state associations were the proper bodies for effecting such supervision.

The courts, of course, did not agree with these arguments, but the interesting point is the degree of reliance placed on the defenses by persons writing for pharmaceutical publications. It appeared to those authors that the arguments were eminently reasonable and ones with

[37] 201 F. Supp. at 32.
[38] "U.S. Closes Idaho Case Via Consent," *Drug Topics*, May 6, 1963, p. 3; Mildred Scott, "Arizona's Anti Trust Complaint," *The Arizona Pharmacist*, Vol. 43, No. 1 (Jan. 1963), p. 6.

which any impartial court would agree. This is further substantiation of the belief that pharmacists, by and large, are philosophically inclined toward restrictionism.

The Brewer Drug Distribution System[39]

The Brewer system is a mechanical drug issuing device, the purpose of which is to provide control over drugs distributed in hospitals. In several states, pharmacists have vehemently opposed the introduction of the Brewer machines. The need for better drug control in medical institutions and the unreality of pharmacist enmity to the Brewer system is made clearer by an explanation of the historical nature of hospital drug dispensing techniques.

In the early days of hospital pharmacy, all drugs were kept at a central pharmacy, usually in the basement of the hospital. When drugs were needed, a nurse went to the hospital pharmacy, obtained the medication, returned to the patient, and administered the drug. At that time, the practice was acceptable because drug therapy was not very important and hence trips to the pharmacy were relatively infrequent.

As the use of drugs intensified, individual requisitions from the central pharmacy became more frequent and also more impractical. To solve the logistical problem, there developed the practice of stocking commonly used drugs at the various nursing stations in a hospital. Now, when a physician writes the prescribed medication on a patient's chart, a nurse interprets the doctor's instructions, selects the appropriate drug from the "floor stock" (as it came to be known) and administers the medication at the times and in the strengths specified by the physician.

The only drugs not on floor stock are those with a short shelf life, those used infrequently, and those requiring compounding. Ordinarily, these exceptions constitute less than 20 percent of the volume of drugs administered. Nearly every hospital in the United States utilizes the floor stock system as its drug distribution pattern.

In the late 1950's a group of Philadelphia pharmacists began to work on a method to control the procurement of drugs from the floor stock of a hospital. The result was the Brewer[40] system. This work

---

[39] Except as otherwise noted, the information in this section was received from interviews with H. M. Trowern, Jr., Vice President, Brewer Pharmacal Engineering Corporation, on November 19, 1965; May 26, 1966; and June 10, 1966.

[40] The Brewer title derives from the name of the owner of a pharmaceutical manufacturing company. Mr. Brewer helped the inventors contact people in the office machine business who could assist in the further development of the pharmacists' idea.

coincided with the growing realization of hospital pharmacists that they had relinquished virtually all supervision over hospital drug dispensing and were no longer being given the opportunity to practice the skills for which they had been trained.

The main component of the Brewer system is a vending-type machine that issues ninety-six different drugs. A system of keys and nameplates are inserted into the machine before it can be loaded and before a nurse can remove items from it. The keys and nameplates are arranged so that only a pharmacist, if it is desired, may stock the machine. When the nurse withdraws drugs from the device, a record is printed internally to show who withdrew the item and the amount and strength of the drug withdrawn. At the same time, the patient's name is printed on a label to be affixed to the package (the drug has previously been prepackaged and labeled by the pharmacy) to assure that each patient receives his correct medication.

This system seems to offer a high degree of drug security. By checking machine records against physician's orders it can be ascertained whether unauthorized drugs have been removed and, if so, by whom. In addition, there are cost savings since the inventory at floor stations is reduced (thus preventing drugs from becoming outdated) and since drug pilferage is eliminated.

Those who have utilized the system have nothing but praise for it. Among the advantages of the machines, according to the hospitals that have adopted them, are efficiency of equipment usage, control over drug distribution, significant reduction of medication errors, and adequate checks to avoid mistakes. Included in these categories are time savings to nurses and pharmacists, a high proportion (95 percent) of prescriptions filled from the machines, and a remarkable reduction in the amount of purchase of some drugs. The decrease in drug use (one hospital reported that its purchases of aspirin had dropped to 20 percent of the former number bought and purchases of quarter-grain phenobarbital had decreased to 30 percent of the former figure) is probably because of the anti-pilfering feature of the machines.[41]

Despite testimonials from satisfied users, retail pharmacists—through the state boards of pharmacy—have consistently opposed the Brewer system. Brewer, however, delays its response to the complaints until they become a formal hearing before a state agency or until the attorney general is asked to rule on the legality of the use of the system.

[41] Letter from Robert L. Evans, M.D., Director of Medical Education and Services, York Hospital, York, Pennsylvania to Floyd N. Heffron, Executive Secretary, California State Board of Pharmacy, dated March 30, 1962; "Hospital Pharmacy Chief Praises Brewer System," *Drug Topics*, January 10, 1966, p. 28.

Brewer (on the assumption that the equipment is legal) usually installs its machines without seeking the approval of the board of pharmacy or state health department. If there is some objection voiced after the machines are installed, the appropriate state agency asks the attorney general for an opinion or holds a hearing to determine the legality of the use of the machines. Hearings have been held in ten states and there have been three attorney general rulings (Delaware, Georgia, Kentucky). Brewer appears at the hearings or before the attorney general and states its case. Although at the conclusion of all hearings the Brewer system has been ruled legal, all attorney general opinions concerning the use of the machines were adverse. The Delaware opinion, however, was reversed when the attorney general learned how the pharmacies of hospitals ordinarily are operated. The Kentucky decision was reversed by court action.[42]

Brewer machines are presently operating in thirty-three states and the District of Columbia. In about ten of the thirty-three states where Brewer now operates, opposition had to be overcome before the machines were allowed to operate on a permanent basis. No attempt has been made to place Brewer machines in six (Alaska, Hawaii, Idaho, Iowa, North Dakota, and Wyoming) of the remaining seventeen states. Attempted placements in Georgia (unfavorable attorney general opinion) were unsuccessful. Brewer probably will institute litigation in Georgia soon to remedy this situation. No Kentucky hospitals have decided to use the Brewer machines. Utah and Louisiana outlawed the Brewer system long before entry was contemplated and no efforts have been made to penetrate these states. Brewer has no machines in use in the remaining seven states (Arkansas, Nebraska, New Mexico, Oregon, South Dakota, Vermont, and West Virginia) because no hospitals in these states have wished to use the Brewer machines.

Board of pharmacy opposition to the Brewer system is enlightening, in view of the fact that the boards have generally ignored or overlooked certain acts associated with hospital floor stocks that, according to state pharmacy laws, should be performed only by pharmacists. These actions include (1) the supposedly illegal practice of nurses interpreting physicians' prescriptions and (2) the selecting of drugs from floor stock by nurses.

Perhaps retail pharmacists visualize the dispensing devices next being installed in air terminals and supermarkets. Whatever the underlying motive, the purpose of prohibiting the use of the Brewer system is to maintain conventional drug handling procedures to the exclusion of new and improved methods that might induce a saving of pharma-

[42] *Brewer Pharmacal Eng'r Corp.* v. *Kentucky Bd. of Pharmacy*, Franklin County Cir. Ct. Ky., October 18, 1965.

cists' time. Strangely enough, those most affected by the devices, hospital pharmacists, have overcome their initial reluctance to the use of the Brewer units. They apparently are cognizant of the urgent need for improved hospital drug handling procedures.

Limitation of Supply of Pharmacists

Restrictionism has reached full flower when the number of entrants into a profession is controlled. As far as can be determined, this has not yet occurred in the field of pharmacy, even though the formal education requirement for pharmacists was stretched to five years in 1960. Together with the one-year mandatory internship, student pharmacists must wait six years before they are qualified to become registered pharmacists. Whether such a lengthy program of instruction is necessary is beyond the scope of this study. Nevertheless, it should be noted that many have objected that such time-consuming programs are driving away prospective pharmacists. Although there is no evidence to suggest that the pharmacy program was lengthened to reduce the number of graduating pharmacists, a total six-year requirement for community pharmacy dispensing seems excessive, when compared to the eight-year physician education requirement.

One prominent pharmacy spokesman, Mr. Lee E. Eiler, President of the American College of Apothecaries, has advocated that the number of students entering pharmacy schools be limited. In Eiler's view, the proclaimed shortage of pharmacists does not exist. Rather, there is an oversupply of drugstores. "There are simply not enough prescriptions written . . . to support the number of pharmacies now operating."[43]

These remarks, made in a speech given at Wayne State University, were interpreted by many as endorsing the closing of several thousand drugstores and there were several disagreements with this point of view. Eiler, in a later speech, clarified his position by stating that according to statistical evidence, the number of prescriptions written in a year would permit an average of only twenty prescriptions per day per store, too few to support the number of professional (drugs only) shops corresponding to the number of drugstores now operating.

Eiler contended that to fulfill the ideal of professionalism, it becomes necessary to raise the number of prescriptions filled per store by reducing the number of outlets and the number of pharmacists over the long run. A number of proposals were outlined to reduce

[43] As quoted in " 'Limit Students to Assure Jobs for All,' " *American Druggist,* March 18, 1963, p. 21.

the alleged oversupply of drugstores and druggists: (1) limit pharmacy ownership to pharmacists, (2) use a ratio of pharmacies to population to determine the number of stores to be registered, and (3) "make sure that the number of students entering and graduating from our colleges of pharmacy do [sic] not exceed the number required to maintain both themselves and adequate pharmaceutical service to the public."[44]

Most of the leaders in the drug business strongly disagree with the contention that there are too many pharmacists. Personal interviews support the recurring articles in the trade press lamenting the *shortage* of pharmacists. To overcome the shortage, drug manufacturers and drug retailers actively engage in promotional efforts to interest more high school students in a career in pharmacy. The propagandazing is reinforced by offering a surprising number of scholarships through professional and trade association grants to schools of pharmacy, as well as substantial scholarship gifts by individual companies.

The prevailing industry view that a much larger annual number of new pharmacists is needed does not agree with the projections of the Health Manpower Statistics Branch of the U.S. Public Health Service. The head of the agency, Miss Maryland Y. Pennell, feels that the trend toward larger drugstores and the greater use of pharmacist assistants and helpers will mute the demand for more pharmacists. By 1975, a net increase of only 6,000 pharmacists will be adequate. The current projected graduation of 38,000 students and the expected 32,000 attritions from the current pharmacist population over the 1966–1975 decade will supply the net growth of 6,000.[45]

Regardless of which is correct, it is hardly necessary or desirable to establish a maximum quota for the schools of pharmacy. Market forces are capable of equating demand and supply. If a shortage of pharmacists exists and persists, ever more attractive scholarships and salaries will swell the pharmacist student body; if a surplus occurs, the withdrawal of scholarships and the stagnation of salaries will effectively limit the number of graduates.

Impressions on the Philosophy of Restrictionism

The philosophy of restrictionism, as embodied in fair trade legislation, price fixing of prescription drugs, opposition to technological improvement, and the suggestion that the supply of pharmacists be lim-

[44] Lee E. Eiler, "Pharmacy, by Pharmacists, in Pharmacies," *The Kentucky Pharmacist*, Vol. 26, No. 7 (July 1963), pp. 10–11, 17. Speech delivered in Arlington, Virginia before the Virginia Pharmaceutical Association, June 24, 1963.

[45] " 'There Is No Shortage of Pharmacists,' " *American Druggist*, May 22, 1967, p. 19.

ited, seems to be deeply embedded in the minds of a large number of pharmacists.[46] These examples indicate that this value structure is of long standing, is pervasive, and is currently accepted.

The antitrust cases are a particularly good illustration of the philosophy in operation. The pricing schedules were composed and adopted openly—unlike those resulting from the typical price conspiracy. The pharmacists sincerely believed it was their right to fix prices and the schedules were published and freely distributed. No serious attempt was made to keep these agreements secret, and when they were declared illegal, pharmacy leaders took the rebuke as a direct attack on the profession of pharmacy itself.

A possible explanation for this belief in restrictionism is the traditional reliance on state legislatures (i.e., fairtrade laws) and state boards of pharmacy as protectors as well as regulators. It may be that pharmacists rely upon boards of pharmacy for guidance and regard other jurisdictions as interlopers. In such a case, there would be a tendency to overlook the social implications of broad economic questions that extend beyond the scope of the boards of pharmacy.

A second probable reason for the restrictionist position of pharmacists is that their specialized training in some way promotes this feeling. The source of such views, however, aside from a course in "professionalism," would be difficult to locate in the curriculum of colleges of pharmacy.

Thus, the restrictionist philosophy of pharmacists seems to be attributable to a combination of professional orientation, economic self-interest, and a belief in the inherent merit of restrictionism.

---

[46] It should be pointed out that this refers primarily to independent drugstore owners, the dominant group in pharmaceutical associations. Since the largely unaffiliated employee pharmacists have no spokesmen, their views are unknown.

PART TWO

Restrictions on the Sale of Proprietary Drugs

CHAPTER FIVE

Issues Involved in the Sales Restriction Controversy

For about the past twenty years, there has been heated discussion and litigation concerning the types of stores in which nonprescription drugs should be sold. Two diverse views exist. The proponents of one position insist that some or all over-the-counter items are potentially dangerous and should be sold only in drugstores under the supervision of a pharmacist. The individuals who are advocates of this distribution system contend that the public health is endangered by the indiscriminate sale of nonprescription products such as those intended to alleviate headaches, constipation, simple colds, and indigestion. The opponents of this limited outlet concept scoff at the supposition that the sale of products such as Anacin, Ex-Lax, Dristan, and Pepto-Bismol by supermarkets and discount houses is more detrimental to the public health than similar sales by drugstores.

The purpose of this chapter is to assess the arguments advanced by those favoring restrictions on the types of stores authorized to merchandise nonprescription drugs and by those protesting the proposed restraints. The assessment will be in the form of a conclusion following the presentation of (1) the views of the opposing parties, (2) some of their legislative proposals, and (3) the views of some outside parties.

Limited Distribution of Nonprescription Drugs: Pro and Con

Those who would restrict the sale of nonprescription drugs to drugstores are primarily pharmacists.[1] Not all druggists favor this restraint, nevertheless, the majority of those who endorse the system are pharmacists. The restrictionists' position is voiced by local pharmaceutical publications and by spokesmen such as the American Pharmaceutical Association (APhA), National Association of Retail Druggists (NARD), state pharmaceutical associations, and some state boards of pharmacy. APhA and NARD provide little more than moral support. The main

---

[1] The pharmacists in agreement with sales limitations generally are independent drugstore owners. The chain operations have not endorsed any position as an organizational entity.

burden of proprietary sales restriction devolves to independent drugstore owners and state pharmaceutical associations.

Opposing the views held by pharmacists are state retail grocers associations, general retail associations, labor unions, farm organizations, and The Proprietary Association.[2] In most states, the brunt of the struggle to preserve free distribution of proprietary drugs is borne by the state grocers associations. The Proprietary Association serves mainly in an advisory capacity to the grocers associations—limiting its role to technical assistance, alerting grocers to pending restrictionist bills and occasionally entering a litigation concerning sales restrictions.

Although several reasons for restricting nonprescription drug sales to pharmacies will be mentioned, all (except the economic argument) are variations of the basic theme mentioned previously: all types of drugs and medicines are potentially dangerous and their sale should be strictly regulated in the interest of public health.

CONTINUUM OF DANGEROUS DRUGS

One of the most convincing reasons advanced for the restriction of nonprescription drug sales is that there is an almost infinite range of risk involved in taking drugs.[3] Near the completely safe end of the risk spectrum are such nonprescription drugs as bicarbonate of soda and aspirin. Verging on the lethal terminus are such prescription drugs as strychnine and experimental cancer drugs. According to this line of reasoning, the arbitrary dichotomization of drugs into prescription (potentially dangerous) and nonprescription (supposedly not hazardous) categories is not realistic. Drugs that fall close to the line separating the two types could be misclassified because of the difficulty of achieving a precise measure of drug toxicity. Figure 5-1 illustrates this concept of a continuum of drug dangerousness.

In addition to the inherent inaccuracy of toxicity classifications themselves, proponents of restriction argue that the effective lethality of a nonprescription drug sold on an unsupervised basis may be in-

---

[2] The Proprietary Association was formed as a trade association a few years after the end of the Civil War. During the period of hostilities between the states, the federal government imposed excise taxes on all "patent" medicines as a revenue raising measure. Upon cessation of the war, however, Congress neglected to repeal the tax. The companies affected by the levy organized a trade association to appeal to Congress to remove the tax. The persuasive efforts were so successful that the patent-proprietary manufacturers decided to give their spokesmen permanent status as The Proprietary Association ("A Brief Look at the History of The Proprietary Association," mimeographed sheets distributed by The Proprietary Association).

[3] Interview with Paul G. Grussing, Secretary, Minnesota State Board of Pharmacy, January 10, 1966.

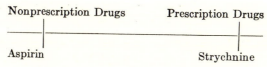

Fig. 5-1.—Continuum of Drug Toxicity

creased by a consumer (1) taking medicine that is not needed, (2) masking serious symptoms of an unknown or unidentified illness by taking safe drugs, (3) ingesting the right drug at the wrong time, and (4) taking a too large dosage. All these possibilities result in a situation where the dividing line between toxic and nontoxic drugs is constantly shifting. These problems, say the "continuum school" proponents, could be largely eliminated by requiring a pharmacist to supervise the sale of potentially detrimental articles.

Opponents of the continuum theory maintain that any validity that the concept might have is negated by the existence and actions of FDA. It is asserted that in addition to the general federal regulatory activities, it is the specific duty of the FDA to prevent unsafe drugs from being included in over-the-counter (OTC) sales. If the FDA is performing as it should, there can and will be a clear delineation between (1) drugs that are potentially harmful and which are kept on prescription status where they cannot be used indiscriminately, and (2) drugs that are not harmful and can be sold without restriction. The continuum of drugs is thus eliminated. According to this argument the FDA's success in distinguishing between dangerous and harmless drugs is based on four areas: toxicity tests, labeling requirements, treatment of drugs that are not clearly safe or unsafe, and ability to self-diagnose.

One part of the FDA's responsibilities is to ascertain the toxicity of drugs. If a drug can have adverse effects—not necessarily fatal—when taken in too large dosages or too frequently, the FDA will not release the drug for nonprescription sale. If, for example, twice the normal dosage can produce adverse effects, the drug will not be released for nonprescription sale. On the other hand, a drug that does not produce adverse effects until twenty times the normal dosage is taken at one time, the drug will get OTC status. This also applies to drugs that are not specifically dangerous, but which can cause habituation or addiction if used for any length of time. If such drugs are removed from the open market, the ones released by the FDA for general sale should be considered safe.

In addition to guarding against toxicity, the FDA is very particular about the directions for use and other appropriate cautions that accompany the sale of nonprescription medicinal remedies. The FDA has to approve the label on a new drug's container before the good can enter any distribution channel. Depending on the particular product, the label would warn against giving the drug to children, note that a physician should be consulted if symptoms persist, detail that persons with certain chronic ailments should not take the drug, and warn that certain symptoms indicate a serious illness in which case a physician should be consulted immediately and use of the drug be discontinued.

The label must also contain directions adequate to make the drug safe for a person to take if he reads and understands them. If the drug cannot be made safe for consumption by directions for usage, the FDA will require the drug to be sold only on prescription.

In cases where there is some doubt as to whether a drug should have nonprescription status, the FDA will initially require that it be sold only under a prescription until reliable experience concerning the effects of the drug has been compiled. If the drug is not virtually impervious to misuse, from either the labeling or toxicity standpoint, the FDA is reluctant to release the product for general sale.

ALL DRUGS POTENTIALLY HARMFUL

Some restrictionists do not subscribe to the theory that certain drugs are dangerous and others are not. These persons contend that any drug, if utilized improperly, is fatal; thus, there are no safe drugs since all medications are susceptible to incorrect use. The annual number of deaths of children caused from aspirin overdosage is cited as evidence that even the most innocuous drug can be lethal.

Statistics collected by the federal government substantiate this claim.[4] In 1965, for example, 16,328 children under five years of age accidently ingested aspirin. Of this number, 11,308 required hospitalization. In 1964, aspirin and salicylates caused the death of 125 children under five years of age. Further, the number of aspirin poisonings reported for children under five has almost doubled since 1962 (8,779 to 16,328). The large increase is probably due to a greater number of hospitals now reporting (97 in 1965) accidental poisonings than in 1962 (73).

Antirestrictionists, however, point out that the number of aspirin and salicylate caused deaths in the under five age group has remained fairly constant (144 in 1960, 128 in 1961, 122 in 1962, 140 in 1963, 125 in 1964) while total population in the age group has been expanding. Moreover, deaths from ingestions of nondrug items (234 in 1960, 249 in 1961, 231 in 1962, 236 in 1963, 196 in 1964) are also rather

[4] *National Clearinghouse for Poison Control Centers Bulletin,* May–June 1966, pp. 1–10. Published by the Public Health Service of the Department of Health, Education, and Welfare.

high,[5] and there are no restrictions as to where the products may be sold.

Supporters of the nonrestrictive sales viewpoint also contend that where a nonprescription drug (aspirin or otherwise) is sold has little bearing upon how the drug will be used. Once the purchase is consummated, the seller is no longer of consequence with respect to misuse of the drug. Regardless of where it is purchased, from the time a product is in a buyer's possession, he alone has control over the ingestion of the drug.

It is true that some children die each year from the excessive consumption of aspirin, but those deaths are mainly the result of carelessness of drug storage in the home rather than an inherent danger associated with the place of purchase of the drug. All other things being equal, the same deaths would occur whether the aspirin was purchased in a supermarket or a pharmacy.

Proponents of the unrestricted sale of nonprescription drugs cite the results of a survey of aspirin-caused deaths that occurred from August 1956 to February 1957 as being illustrative of the validity of their view. Of 69 deaths caused by aspirin consumption during that period, 45 were associated with drugstore sales, 19 cases involved sales made by nondrug outlets, and the source of supply could not be determined for the 5 remaining cases. Hence, the antirestrictionists conclude that the source of sale does not prevent misuse of nonprescription drugs.[6]

Pharmacists reply to this argument by pointing out that if items such as aspirin were sold by a pharmacist, he could impress upon the purchaser the dangers inherent in the use of drugs and such tragic happenings could be avoided. The same survey demonstrated, however, that in 17 of the 45 deaths corresponding to drugstore sales, the purchase had been supervised by a pharmacist.[7] Whether warnings were issued by the pharmacists at the time of the sale is not known, but if not, the pharmacists either were derelict in their duty or did not think the aspirin sufficiently dangerous to require cautioning comments. Either way, the deaths were not prevented.

PHARMACIST HAS EXPERT KNOWLEDGE

Another base for some restrictionists' attitude is the professional aspect of pharmacy. According to this theory, it is preposterous to presume that it is immaterial whether a nonprescription item is sold

[5] *Ibid.*

[6] "P. A. Plans "To Get Better Acquainted,'" *American Druggist,* June 3, 1957, pp. 9–10.

[7] *Ibid.*

in a supermarket or in a drugstore. Supermarkets hire clerks that generally are unskilled in pharmaceutical matters whereas drugstores employ individuals (pharmacists) who have been intensively trained in the composition and effects of drugs. Thus, it is certain that a pharmacist has the ability to protect and guide the public in the purchase and use of dangerous (i.e., all) drugs. On the other hand, nonprescription drug outlets do not employ persons with similar skills and therefore cannot provide such advice. To assert that the degree of public health protection is the same in both cases is, to the advocates of this philosophy, poor reasoning.

The contention, then, is that by requiring all medications to be sold only in drugstores, a source of pharmaceutical knowledge is constantly available to the public and questions that a nonprescription drug buyer might have about a product can be answered. In this way, the public health is protected, an achievement that is not obtained if drug sales are permitted in other outlets that do not employ the services of a pharmacist.

Advocates of free distribution of nonprescription drugs do not dispute that pharmacists are drug experts, but the antirestrictionists do question whether a pharmacist is able to give advice beyond what is printed on the label. To do so would probably make the pharmacist liable if some injury were to occur from taking the medicine. About all the pharmacist can do is read the label to the purchaser.

LABELING IS INEFFECTIVE

Restrictionists claim that just reading the label to the purchaser is very important because many people do not read and/or understand what the labels say. The opponents of the restrictionists say that most people do read and understand instructions and warnings on labels. There is no evidence to suggest which argument is correct. There are indications, however, that pharmacists frequently do not even participate in the sale of nonprescription medicines, much less give oral warnings. In several of the cases discussed in the next chapter—although not specifically mentioned there—it was shown that, in most cases, nonprescription drug sales in drugstores were made by clerks with no more training than supermarket clerks.

INGREDIENT CONCEPT

Another argument used by restrictionists relates to the constituent drugs used in some over-the-counter medicines. Some ingredients, if used in greater strength, acquire prescription status. These drugs, say the restrictionists, are obviously very dangerous and should not be sold except under the supervision of a pharmacist. Two classes of such drugs are barbiturates and some antihistamines.

The antirestrictionists note, however, that FDA is alert to possible abuses and side effects. Phenobarbital, for example, in amounts up to one-fourth grain may be sold without a prescription. But, the phenobarbital must be combined with other ingredients and in such a way that the feeling of well-being associated with phenobarbital is damped out. As a result, several pills containing a small amount of the drug cannot give the same effect of one larger pill consisting of pure phenobarbital.

FDA has placed similar controls on antihistamines used in decongestants that may cause drowsiness as an undesirable side effect. If one of these drugs is used in a compound, the compound must also contain sufficient caffein (or other stimulant) to counteract any drowsiness that might be produced by the antihistamine. Even so, the labels of such a preparation carry warnings concerning possible drowsiness.

Bromine is a drug contained in some proprietaries, which is lethal if taken in large doses. Restrictionists would limit the sale of such products to drugstores on the theory that a person could kill himself with a sufficiently large overdose. Other persons claim that only a mental defective or emotionally disturbed individual would consume at one time the 50 or 60 doses necessary to reach the danger point. Advocates of free distribution contend this is analogous to children consuming large quantities of aspirin.

RECALLS

Recalls in the drug industry are not quite the same as in the auto industry. Drug manufacturers seek out and destroy bad batches of drugs that have already entered distribution channels. The most common reason for recalls is impurities or contaminants in a particular batch of drugs. Since all drugstores are registered, recalls for prescription drugs can quickly and efficiently be directed to the proper persons. According to those who would limit the sale of *all* drugs to drugstores, this ease of recall should be extended to nonprescription drugs.

In the proprietary field, however, recalls are rare, possibly because such products enjoy huge production runs and as a result avoid the danger of contaminating lots by switching products on the production line.

CONTRAINDICATIONS

Sometimes, a person taking a prescription drug should not take certain nonprescription drugs. To do so neutralizes the effect of the prescription drug or makes the person more ill than he already is. By limiting all drugs to drugstores, say the restrictionists, the pharmacist could warn a person purchasing a proprietary under those circumstances. Four implicit and invalid assumptions are present in this line of reasoning, according to the antirestrictionists: (1) people purchase all their drug needs at one drugstore, (2) the pharmacist who sold the prescription will be on duty when the person arrives to make his proprietary purchase, (3) the pharmacist will remember the customer, and (4) the physician neglected to warn his patient about contraindications.

THE ECONOMIC ARGUMENT

Another reason advanced in favor of the philosophy of restricting the types of outlets permitted to merchandise drug items is the economic argument. Prior to World War II, the retail distribution of drugs was dominated by drugstores.[8] It was not until the late 1940's that Anacin and similar items accelerated their exodus from pharmacies to food store shelves. In some states the movement has been delayed and/or muted by court actions, but in general there has been a massive shift of nonprescription drug sales from pharmacies to supermarkets. Druggists have not been unaware of the increase in nonprescription medicinal sales achieved by nondrug outlets; nor have the pharmacists been passive. Several attempts were made in the late 1950's to have statutes enacted that would outlaw nondrugstore sale of drugs, but the efforts were to no avail.[9]

The proposed legislation has had an underlying economic motive in addition to the stated public health argument. One favorite point is that supermarkets are expanding their sales at the expense of druggists, a tactic which is unfair competition. The contention is that grocery stores should sell food and not infringe upon the rightful sales of drugstores.[10]

The other aspect of the economic argument asserts that if drugstores are deprived of nonprescription sales, the resulting lower volume will force many of the firms from the market. In turn, the public health

[8] This was the result of marketing decisions by nonprescription drug manufacturers and/or food retailers, not legal compulsion.

[9] "Supers Buck 3 State Sales Hems Bills," *American Druggist*, March 9, 1959, p. 19; "Strengthening of Sales Restrictions Is Listed as Top 1959 Legislative Goal," *American Druggist*, January 12, 1959, pp. 5–7; "Penna. Assn. Urges Federal Law to Limit Drugs to Pharmacies," *American Druggist*, July 29, 1957, p. 10; "NARD Votes to Work for Federal Law Restricting Sale of Drugs to Pharmacies," *American Druggist*, October 20, 1958, pp. 5, 7.

[10] "Friends of the Grocers," *The Brooklyn Pharmacist*, April 1965, p. 4.

will be endangered because a shortage of prescription service outlets will be created. This reasoning is based, of course, upon the premise that the total market for nonprescription drugs cannot be enlarged by merchandising methods so that every sale made by a supermarket is one less for a drugstore.[11]

The opposite point of view is taken by supermarkets and proprietary manufacturers. Food stores feel that they should continue to be allowed to sell the products so long as they are safe; the items are profitable to the stores and a convenience to shoppers. The drug manufacturers wish to keep the freedom to expand to as many outlets as possible so as to maximize sales. It is also argued that there is no noticeable shortage of drugstores and that no such shortage is likely.

Regardless of which side of the economic argument one chooses, there is ample evidence that drug sales are expanding on a per capita basis and that there is a substantial amount to be gained or lost. Before World War II, per capita shipments of drugs ranged from $2.00 to $2.50 annually. Since 1939, shipments have more than quintupled, rising from $2.49 to $15.12 (1963) per capita. The greater part of the $12.63 increase ($9.66) is attributable to prescription drugs, but the per capita use of proprietary drugs also increased ($2.97).[12] Given the extraordinary stability in the number of retail drug outlets, druggists should have experienced a sharp rise in revenue from *both* prescription and over-the-counter drugs.

Drugstores, however, did not receive the full benefit of increased per capita expenditure for proprietaries—as statistics for five groups of proprietary drugs reveal. In 1952, drugstore sales of (1) noneffervescent aspirin salicylates, (2) aspirin, (3) effervescent aspirin salicylates, (4) laxative tablets, pills, gums, and lozenges, and (5) cough and cold medicines, salves and ointments totaled $111,446,000 or 56.4 percent of all sales of such items. By 1962, the drugstore sales of the products had risen to $174,115,300, but the market share claimed by drugstores had declined to 42.6 percent. During the same interval nondrugstore outlets increased sales of the same products from $86,344,100 to $234,449,800 (a 173.5 percent increase) and in so doing, raised their market share from 43.6 percent to 57.4 percent.[13]

The nondrug outlets lured business by discounting. Chains attempted to retain proprietary sales by resorting to similar tactics. Therefore,

---

[11] "The Debate on Restrictive Sales," *American Druggist*, September 22, 1958, p. 9.

[12] Jules Bachman, "Economics of Proprietary Drugs," *Annals of the New York Academy of Sciences*, Vol. 120, Art. 2 (July 14, 1965), pp. 881–882.

[13] H. George Mandel, "Therapeutic Range and Extent of Use of Home Remedies," *Annals of the New York Academy of Sciences*, Vol. 120, Art. 2 (July 14, 1965), p. 910. Statistics cited are calculated from data on referenced page.

the relative sales decline was probably higher in independent drugstores than statistics indicate. As a result, independents sought protective legislation and encouraged boards of pharmacy to institute legal actions to halt the flight of proprietary sales from drugstores to supermarkets.

Other Sales Restriction Views

CONFERENCE ON HOME MEDICATION AND THE PUBLIC WELFARE

In 1965 the New York Academy of Sciences conducted a symposium on home medication. It was attended by an impressive array of persons representing many different groups who gave papers and participated in panel discussions. At the close of the meeting, the conference chairman, Chester S. Keefer, a physician on the faculty of Harvard University Medical School, summarized the proceedings and presented the conclusions that he felt were justified from the discussions. These conclusions are:

1. Home medication is useful and satisfies a public need and demand and renders a public service.
2. Such medicines are safe and effective within the limitations of the beneficial claims made for them.
3. The products' labeling, directions for use, warnings about their misuse, as well as advertising, are controlled and regulated both by law and voluntarily by the drug industry. In this way the public interest is protected.
4. Home medications, when used wisely and in accordance with the directions and information provided by the manufacturer, are not only useful but contribute to the health of the American public and to the public welfare.[14]

U.S. JUSTICE DEPARTMENT

The federal government, as personified by Congress, has never taken a definite position on restricted drug sales. It, however, can be inferred—from existing federal legislation and from the remarks of Congressman Kenneth A. Roberts at the conference just discussed—that the federal government is not inclined to restrict the sale of nonprescription drugs.

Although Congress is silent on the subject of limiting the type of outlets that distribute nonprescription drugs, the Justice Department

[14] Chester S. Keefer, "Summary and Conclusions," *Annals of the New York Academy of Sciences,* Vol. 120, Art. 2 (July 14, 1965), p. 1005.

has voiced its opinion on the matter. The department was asked to state its view of certain provisions of a proposed revision of the District of Columbia pharmacy act. In commenting on the clause that would have restricted the sale of most nonprescription drugs to drugstores, a Justice Department spokesman said:

> Our comments are confined to those provisions . . . which in our view restrain competition and free enterprise in the marketing of drug products in the District of Columbia and which have not been proved necessary . . . to the protection of the public health and safety. . . .
> . . . Under the provision which permits only pharmacists to sell drugs requiring a cautionary statement, drug stores in the District of Columbia would obtain a monopoly in the sale of most pre-packaged, nonprescription drugs, including, for example, such a necessary household item as aspirin. Preventing supermarkets and related stores from selling such products would substantially lessen competition, and unduly inconvenience the consumer by limiting market access. Courts in several states have viewed the health justification for such a measure as a sham.[15]

The Justice Department then cited the *Loblaw* case and the *Safeway* decision to verify that the courts are opposed to restricting nonprescription drug sales.[16]

Legislative Proposals of Advocates and Opponents of Sales Restrictions

As is to be expected, the restrictive sales controversy has generated considerable ill-will between the parties involved. The opposing positions of the two sides seem to have been crystallized at the 1955 meetings of two of the organizations concerned with the question. At the American Pharmaceutical Association meeting, "pharmacy leaders made clear their intention to fight, 'tooth and nail,' any move to relax state laws that restrict the sale of drugs to drugstores."[17] The Proprietary Association, at its meeting held three weeks later, declared that it would "fight for the right of packaged medicine manufacturers to sell their drugs in nondrug outlets."[18]

The following year, a resolution was introduced to eject The Proprietary Association from the APhA's House of Delegates, the policymak-

---

[15] Letter from Lawrence E. Walsh, Deputy Attorney General to John L. McMillan, Chairman, House of Representatives District of Columbia Committee, dated May 3, 1960.

[16] See Chapter 6 for a discussion of these cases.

[17] " 'We'll Continue to Fight Restrictions'," *American Druggist*, June 6, 1955, p. 7.

[18] *Ibid.*

ing body of the APhA, but the move was defeated.[19] Various attempts were made to effect a compromise between the two organizations. The National Drug Trade Conference (NDTC)[20] endeavored to act as a mediator, but all its efforts met with failure.[21]

The antagonism between APhA and the Proprietary Association reached a peak during APhA's 1958 annual meeting. For the second time it was proposed that The Proprietary Association be expelled from the APhA House of Delegates, a position held by the proprietary group since 1923. This time the movement was successful. The text of the resolution read:

Whereas the Proprietary Association has demonstrated its refusal to conform with the aims and objects of the American Pharmaceutical Association, be it resolved that representation of the Proprietary Association in the APhA House of Delegates be terminated.[22]

The resolution did not have the desired effect immediately, but the Proprietary Association, since 1965, has not sent an official representative to APhA meetings.

PROPOSAL OF APhA[23]

The opposite positions of APhA and The Proprietary Association are reflected in their legislative proposals. The extent to which the APhA would restrict sales outlets of nonprescription drugs is indicated by its advocacy of four classes of drugs to replace the two classes (prescription and nonprescription) now used by FDA. According to APhA the four classes required are:

[19] "NABP Calls on All Rx Boards to Submit Lists of Drugs that Should Be Allowed in Non-Drug Stores," *American Druggist*, April 23, 1956, p. 6.

[20] NDTC is a body whose purpose is to promote the interests of the drug industry as a whole. Its members are the American Association of Colleges of Pharmacy, American Pharmaceutical Association, Federal Wholesale Druggists Association, National Association of Boards of Pharmacy, National Association of Chain Drug Stores, National Association of Retail Druggists, National Wholesale Druggists Association, Pharmaceutical Manufacturers Association, and The Proprietary Association. The function of NDTC is hampered by its self-imposed rule that unanimous assent is necessary before it can take any action on a matter.

[21] Various issues of *American Druggist* report these activities: "Speed Drive for Drug Sales Compromise," December 20, 1954, pp. 13–15; "NABP Calls on All Rx Boards to Submit Lists of Drugs that Should Be Allowed in Non-Drug Stores," April 23, 1956, pp. 5–7, 9; "P.A. Sees Hope for Accord on Sales Ban," May 21, 1956, pp. 13–14; "Restrictive Sales Solution Is Proposed," December 17, 1956, pp. 9–10; "P.A. Plans 'To Get Better Acquainted,'" June 3, 1957, pp. 9–10; "NDTC Will Try to List Non-Rx Drugs that Should Be Sold Only in Pharmacies," December 16, 1957, pp. 5–6, 8; and "Experts Find No Clean-Cut Way to Solve Restrictive Sales Issue," September 22, 1958, pp. 8, 10–11.

[22] As quoted in "Restrictive Sales Issue Explodes at APhA Confab; Resolution Asks End of P.A.'s Delegate Status," *American Druggist*, May 5, 1958, p. 5.

[23] "Four Drug Classes Are Needed," *APhA Newsletter*, March 28, 1964, p. 2.

1. Drugs to be dispensed only by prescription and renewable at the prescriber's direction only.
2. Drugs to be initially obtained by prescription only, but renewable at the pharmacist's discretion.
3. Drugs to be dispensed by the pharmacist at the request of the patient.
4. Drugs to be directly available to the public without professional direction or control.

Present federal law embodies, essentially, categories (1) and (4). Creation of the two new classes would result in a large number of what are now nonprescription drugs being placed exclusively in drugstores. This is in keeping with the APhA philosophy that many nonprescription drugs should only be sold in pharmacies by pharmacists.

Another proposal advocated by the restrictionists is a three-class concept advocated by the National Association of Retail Druggists (NARD) and some local and state pharmaceutical associations. The three-class plan envisions retention of the two categories now in force and would add a third class of drugs by dividing nonprescription drugs into two groups, one salable anywhere and the other salable only in drugstores. APhA would accept the three-class proposal if the "drugstore only" category is by law salable only by a pharmacist. NARD wants any drugstore employee to be able to sell the third class of drugs.

To convince FDA that a third class of drugs is needed, *American Druggist* suggested that pharmacists keep diaries of advice given to patrons on nonprescription drugs. In New Jersey, the Essex County Pharmaceutical Society adopted the idea and 105 of the 325 drugstores in the county kept diaries for the month of March 1967. The journals were then presented to Dr. James L. Goddard, head of FDA. A total of 932 "incidents" were reported. That is, pharmacists gave advice 932 times in connection with nonprescription drugs. In 634 cases (67.9 percent) patrons were advised to see their physician, 122 (13.1 percent) were advised not to take the medication requested because of possible contra-indications, 86 (9.2 percent) needed explanation of dosage or usage, 22 (2.4 percent) were informed of possible side-effects, 10 (1.1 percent) could not read English, and, presumably there were 58 (6.3 percent) miscellaneous conversations.

In 236 (25.3 percent) of the 932 cases sales were made and in 276 (29.6 percent) cases the pharmacist refused to sell the patron any nonprescription drug. A sale was evidently in order in some cases in addition to the advice to see a physician.[24]

The figures of 932 incidents by 105-pharmacies in 31 days seem impressive, but further analysis reduces the importance of the numbers

[24] "Goddard Gets N. J. Diaries; Looks At Pharmacy's Future," *American Druggist*, June 5, 1967, pp. 13–14, 16.

and raises some questions. Assume that the 105 pharmacies were open 25 days during March; a reasonable assumption since almost all drugstores are open six days a week, and since some are open seven days a week. Given the figures reported and the 25 days open assumption, each pharmacy had, on the average, only 0.35 incidents per day:

$$\text{incidents per day per pharmacy} = \frac{932}{(105)(25)} = 0.35$$

Stated another way, there were only two instances of advice each week at each pharmacy. Now the question becomes clear: how many nonprescription drug sales were there without the benefit of a pharmacist's advice? It stands to reason that the drugstores had *many* more than two nonprescription drug sales each week, and it follows that the pharmacists failed to advise nonprescription drug buyers in the vast majority of the cases.

PROPOSAL OF THE PROPRIETARY ASSOCIATION

The Proprietary Association's counter proposal to the APhA's suggestion would limit to drugstores the sale of all trademarked nonprescription drugs that are not advertised directly to the public (i.e., ethical proprietaries). Advertised items could be sold by any retailer. Prescription drugs, of course, would be dispensed only by pharmacists.

Legislation of this type has been enacted in a few states.[25] Nevertheless, this line of action is viewed by The Proprietary Association as a compromise. The Association contends that, with few exceptions, any item approved by the FDA for over-the-counter sale should be available in any outlet. The organization is willing, however,—not from a health basis, but from an economic basis—to agree to the exclusive sale by pharmacists of those nonprescription drugs where no effort is made by the manufacturer to achieve distribution in nondrug outlets.[26]

Summary and Conclusion

Restrictionists produce a formidable list of reasons why nonprescription drugs should be sold only by drugstores. These reasons are explained away by those favoring unlimited distribution. Aside from the economic argument—which is a political question—the rebuttals of the antirestrictionists appear to be well founded.

[25] Colorado (1959), Florida (1961), Iowa (1957), North Dakota (1959), Tennessee (1961), Alabama (1966), Georgia (1967), and New Hampshire (1967).
[26] Interview with James D. Cope, Executive Vice President (then Secretary), The Proprietary Association, November 3, 1966.

One group of restrictionists contends that because of the drug toxicity continuum, an arbitrary division of drugs into only two categories results in dangerous drugs being given nonprescription status. The antirestrictionists say that FDA's authority and actions disrupt the continuum by placing all questionable drugs on prescription. Only after experience proves them safe (antihistamines, for example) does FDA release new drugs for over-the-counter sale. To attribute such an attitude to FDA is reasonable. If deaths or serious illness result from an over-the-counter drug approved by the FDA, a large measure of public wrath will be directed toward the agency. The organization, in addition to its humanitarian instincts, does not wish to be the recipient of a barrage of public outrage nor does it wish to be the subject of a Congressional inquiry. Therefore, it seems reasonable to believe that the FDA would be extremely cautious and require a given drug to be sold only under prescription if there is any known danger involved.[27]

The argument that all drugs are potentially harmful is also weak; but not because the statement is false, for all drugs *are* potentially harmful. Almost everything has a potential for harm, and as many people are accidentally poisoned by nondrug substances as by nonprescription drugs. Poisonings of children are indeed tragic, but these deaths can be attributed to carelessness on the part of parents who do not place drugs, bleaches, insecticides, etc. beyond the reach of children. Even if proprietaries were limited to drugstore sale only, evidence suggests that proprietary drug purchasers are apt to be served by an untrained clerk.

It appears that FDA does its job well—too well to suit some in the drug industry. Therefore, considerable abuse and total disregard for the label are necessary before there is any hazard in the free distribution of nonprescription drugs. This view is supported by various outside parties whose objectivity seems to be real.

Therefore, there is no public health reason why nonprescription drugs should not be sold in any outlet. In this respect the proposal of The Proprietary Association, that advertised nonprescription drugs be sold in any outlet, does not go far enough. As far as public health is concerned, any drug (perhaps excepting exempt narcotics) cleared for over-the-counter sale by FDA is safe enough to be sold in all retail outlets.

[27] Recently there has been some publicity in connection with FDA's withdrawal from the market of cough drops and lozenges containing antibiotics. The action was premised on lack of efficacy, not on the danger involved in using the items.

CHAPTER SIX

Litigation and Legislation Concerning Sales Restrictions

As revealed by the preceding chapter, the advocates and opponents of restrictions on retail drug sales can marshal several arguments to support their positions. The extent to which these arguments are accepted by the courts and legislatures is more important that the philosophy espoused by the parties. This chapter will indicate the legislative and judicial reactions to the constraints imposed upon the sale of proprietary drugs. Recent court actions will be discussed in some detail to delineate the positions taken by the adversaries and to gain an understanding of current appellate court opinion.

Before delving into specific statutes and cases, it is necessary to understand the basis for state regulation of the sale of drugs. The source of the states' authority to control drug distribution derives from their obligation to protect the health and welfare of their citizens. To accomplish this task, the states are granted police powers to compel individuals to conduct themselves and their businesses in such a way that the health and welfare of citizens in general are not impaired. Thus, the states, in the name of public health and welfare, may demand from natural persons and corporations the performance of certain deeds and prohibit the exercise of other acts.[1]

Under the police power umbrella, every state has enacted laws to control drug distribution. The first pharmacy law, enacted in Rhode Island in 1870,[2] required all drugs to be sold in a drugstore but included

---

[1] The courts have long agreed that state regulation of drug sales is above reproach and is a legitimate exercise of police power, so long as the regulatory laws bear a reasonable relationship to and are designed to protect the public health. See *Louis K. Liggett Co.* v. *Baldridge*, 278 U.S. 105 (1928); *Pike* v. *Porter*, 126 Mont. 482, 253 P.2d 1055 (1953); *State* v. *Donaldson*, 41 Minn. 74, 42 N.W. 781 (1889); *State* v. *Wood*, 51 S.D. 485, 215 N.W. 487 (1927).

[2] *Rhode Island Session Laws of 1870* c. 856, s. 8.

a provision permitting general merchants to sell items classified as patents and proprietaries. This grant was not a special dispensation, for such medicines had been widely sold in the United States ever since they became popular in England. Rhode Island was merely allowing the continuation of an economic fact by taking notice of and approving the unrestricted sale of these common medications.

Some states followed the Rhode Island precedent. Others did not include the proprietary exemption in their statutes regulating drug distribution. Contests of these laws were based on the allegation that without the proprietary exemption the statutes violated the due process principle since they granted a special privilege to one group *without a corresponding benefit to the public health*. That is, the states were accused of abusing their police powers because limiting proprietary sales to drugstores bears no reasonable relationship to maintaining the public health. The various state supreme courts agreed with the contention and declared such state pharmacy laws to be unconstitutional.[3]

In Minnesota, the state Supreme Court, rather than holding the pharmacy law unconstitutional, interpreted the statute to include the proprietary exemption even though it was not mentioned in the law.[4] The courts of the other states followed the lead of the Minnesota Supreme Court.[5]

As the years passed, state pharmacy laws were amended and the judicially required proprietary exemption was incorporated in the law of forty-nine states and in the District of Columbia.[6] Kansas relies on the judicial interpretation[7] and until 1967 Nevada specified which products could be sold by general merchants.[8]

Despite the remarkable degree of uniformity that has evolved, the proprietary exemption clause has evoked numerous litigations and conflicting court decisions. The disputes arose over the meaning of the phrase "patent and proprietary medicines" and the words "harmless," "nonpoisonous," and "not deleterious" found in the laws.

Prior to 1952, the restrictionists' position (i.e., prohibiting general merchants from selling patent and proprietary medicines) was vindicated in Iowa, Minnesota, and Oregon.[9] The restrictionists feel that

[3] *State* v. *Childs*, 32 Ariz. 222, 257 Pac. 366 (1927); *Noel* v. *People*, 187 Ill. 587, 58 N.E. 616 (1900); *Wood, supra* note 1.
[4] *Donaldson, supra* note 1.
[5] William F. Weigel, "State Legislation Restricting the Sale of Drugs," *Food Drug Cosmetic Law Journal*, Vol. 13, No. 1 (Jan. 1958), p. 50.
[6] See Appendix I.
[7] *State* v. *Hanchette*, 88 Kan. 864, 129 Pac. 1184 (1913).
[8] The Nevada law was enacted too late to be included in Appendix I.
[9] *State ex rel Board of Pharmacy Examiners* v. *Jewett Mkt. Co.*, 209 Iowa 567, 228 N.W. 288 (1929); *State* v. *F. W. Woolworth Co.*, 184 Minn. 51, 237, N.W. 817 (1931); *State* v. *Combs*, 169 Ore. 566, 130 P.2d 947 (1942).

the technical definition of a proprietary medicine should determine its classification—only a preparation with a secret composition that is not included in the *United States Pharmacopoeia* (U.S.P.)[10] or other compendia[11] would have proprietary status. (If the sale of all pharmacopoelial items were to be limited to drugstores, only druggists would be allowed to sell honey sherry, soap, some spices, sugar, turpentine, and whiskey.)

Also prior to 1952, the proponents of the proprietary exemption clause (nonrestrictive) had won in California, Illinois, Kentucky, Montana, and Nebraska.[12] These states adopted the common-usage interpretation of the term "patent and proprietary medicines." According to this definition virtually all trademarked nonprescription drugs which are sold in their original packages are eligible for the proprietary exemption.

The patent and proprietary sale cases presented in detail date from the early 1950's. Peculiarly, peace descended upon the litigative front of the restrictive sales controversy in the 1940's. One possible explanation for the tranquil interlude is that the restrictionists tired of the battle after losing some cases. A more likely reason for this period of truce is that nondrug (mainly food stores) outlets did not constitute a competitive threat to drugstores during that decade.

There are several plausible explanations for the lack of food-drug outlet competition for proprietary sales in the decade of the 1940's:

1. The 1940's were a period of general shortage of most consumer goods. Drug manufacturers and wholesalers may have been able to be selective—selling mainly to drugstores.
2. Food chains may not have been greatly interested in nonfood lines at this time, preferring instead to complete their penetration of the retail food market before selecting new fields to conquer.
3. There may have been informal pressure by state pharmacy boards against food chains entering the field—accepted tempo-

[10] The U.S.P. sets forth (1) quality standards for drugs and medicines currently used and (2) testing procedures to assure that accepted standards are measured the same way each time a test is performed. The publisher of U.S.P., The United States Pharmacopoeial Convention, is composed of medical and pharmacy schools, federal agencies, and national medical and pharmaceutical associations. The U.S.P. is old and respected—it was originally developed at the request of George Washington.

[11] Other compendia include the *National Formulary* (published by the American Pharmaceutical Association), *New and Non-Official Remedies,* and *Homeopathic Pharmacopoeia of the United States.*

[12] *People* v. *Heron,* 34 Cal. App. Dec. Supp. 755, 90 P.2d 154 (Super. Ct. 1939); *State* v. *Ridgeway Drug Co.,* 324 Ill. App. 585, 59 N.E. 2d 351 (1945); *Kentucky Bd. of Pharmacy* v. *Cassidy,* 115 Ky. 690, 74 S.W. 730 (1903); *State* v. *Stephens,* 102 Mont. 414, 59 P.2d 54 (1936); *State* v. *Geest,* 118 Neb. 562, 225 N.W. 709 (1929).

rarily by the outlets until they could become entrenched in the retail food market.

4. Food chains may not have been aware of the profit potential of distributing proprietaries.

Whatever the reason, the sale of traditional nonprescription drugstore items did not begin to shift to food stores in significant proportions until the early 1950's. While drugstore proprietary sales volume remained almost stationary, food store sales of these items rapidly expanded. Druggists were not ignorant of this loss of business.[13]

The pharmacists' awareness of the changing distribution pattern, combined with their conviction that supermarkets had no right to invade drugstore sales territory, probably prompted many of the litigations to be discussed below.[14] These cases are presented for two reasons: (1) to elucidate the judicial view as to what the proprietary sales restriction issue means and (2) to indicate the prevailing views in the various states. In addition to court actions, legislative attempts to grapple with the problem will be mentioned. The goal is to bring to the surface the preponderant learned opinion concerning the validity of restricting the distribution of nonprescription drugs.

Sales Restrictions in New Jersey

New Jersey was one of the first states to become embroiled in the restrictive sales issue after the lull of the 1940's. Although neither of the opposing parties really instituted the first action, the case led to many other suits which one or the other of the original parties initiated.

DECLARATORY JUDGMENT ACTION OF 1952

In the fall of 1952, the Attorney General of New Jersey asked The Proprietary Association and the New Jersey Board of Pharmacy to join in a declaratory judgment action that asked court definition of statutory terms used in connection with the proprietary exemption clause in the New Jersey pharmacy law. Apparently this was an effort

[13] A magazine widely read by pharmacists stated that drugstore proprietary sales were virtually stagnant from 1952 to 1954, rising from $713 million to $740 million, a 2.39 percent increase, while sales in other retail outlets were rising from $272 million to $310 million, a 14.5 percent increase. This was particularly noticeable to druggists, especially since other outlets market only thirty or so of the several hundred proprietaries sold by drugstores ("What People Spent in 1954 for Products Sold in Drugstores," *Drug Topics*, June 27, 1956, p. 2).

[14] Sol A. Herzog, " 'Twixt Supermarket and Courts—Whither Pharmacy,' " *Journal of the American Pharmaceutical Association*, Vol. XIV, No. 12 (Dec. 1953), pp. 764–770.

to settle a long-smouldering dispute in which The Proprietary Association supported (and the Board rejected) a liberal interpretation of the exemption clause.

New Jersey Superior Court. Many issues and witnesses were brought before Judge Colie—all intended to support or invalidate the theory that proprietary drugs should be sold only in drugstores. The trial was exhaustive—the transcript of the proceedings ran to some 1,000 pages.[15]

Judge Colie waited seven months before handing down his decision. The opinion defined the legal terms as requested by the litigants,[16] and in doing so, followed the nonrestrictive interpretation advocated by The Proprietary Association. Judge Colie found that the words "patent" and "proprietary" mean

completely compounded packaged drugs, medicines and nonbulk chemicals which are held out for sale and sold by or under the authority of the proprietor thereof directly to the general public and the packages of which drugs, medicines and non-bulk chemicals bear, or are accompanied by, printed matter specifying affections, symptoms or purposes for which the remedies are recommended and the directions for their use, and with respect to which ownership is claimed or asserted by the proprietor thereof as to name, composition or process of manufacture, by secrecy, patent, trademark, copyright, or in any other manner which may be the basis for legal action by the proprietor with respect to said drugs, medicines and non-bulk chemicals in any of the courts of this state.[17]

A "nonpoisonous" medicine was held to be "a substance that, being in solution in the blood or acting chemically on the blood, neither destroys life nor impairs seriously the functions of one or more of the organs."[18]

In addition, the bench declared the Pharmacy Board definition of "drug" and "medicine" to be unreasonable because it bore no reasonable relation to the public health and welfare. The Board, by regulation, had described drugs and medicines as:

(1) articles recognized in the official United States Pharmacopoeia, official Homeopathic Pharmacopoeia of the United States, or official National Formulary, or any supplement to any of them; and (2) articles for use in the diagnosis, cure, mitigation, treatment or prevention of disease in man or other animals; and (3) articles (other than food) intended to

[15] "N.J. Board Won't Press to Collect Fines from Non-Rx Men," *American Druggist*, January 5, 1953, p. 18.

[16] The Proprietary Association withdrew its request for a definition of "domestic remedies" at the close of the trial.

[17] *Proprietary Assn'n v. Board of Pharmacy,* 27 N.J. Super. 204, 218, 99 A.2d 52, 59 (1953), *rev'd*, 16 N.J. 62, 106 A.2d 272.

[18] *Ibid.*

affect the structure or any function of the body of man or other animals, and (4) articles intended for use as a component of any article specified in clauses (1), (2) or (3); but does not include devices or their components, parts, or accessories.[19]

The definitive regulation was of such scope that it included virtually every medicinal agent known to man plus several nonmedicinal articles. This provision for all practical purposes eliminated drug items that could be sold in nondrug outlets.

The reasoning which led to the definitional conclusions was based on four points that Judge Colie considered important:

1. No other New Jersey court had ever ruled on definitions of this nature. Previous cases had dealt with deciding whether a specific product was a patent or proprietary medicine.[20] It was therefore necessary to rely on out-of-state authorities,[21] with which Judge Colie felt he abided.

2. The legislative history of the law (N.J.R.S. 45:14–29) indicated that the legislature did not intend to restrict the sale of medicines that were not legal patents or proprietaries, especially in view of the testimony of pharmaceutical history scholars that established that the words "patent" and "proprietary" have long since lost their meaning in drug trade circles.

3. Instances of injury or death caused by the consumption of proprietary medicines result from misuse or carelessness after purchase and where the purchase is made has no significance for that reason.

4. The Pharmacy Board's 1950 Annual Report had stated that "the owners of super-markets and other general store establishments are encroaching more and more upon the sale of drug items under an out-dated provision in the law enacted many years ago when New Jersey was more of a rural state, which permits the sale by any merchant of non-poisonous patent or proprietary medicines."[22]

---

[19] *Ibid.*

[20] *Board of Pharmacy* v. *Braunstein*, 2 N.J. Misc. 454 (Sup. Ct. 1924); *Board of Pharmacy* v. *Abramoff*, 6 N.J. Misc. 437 (Sup. Ct. 1928); *Kratky* v. *Board of Pharmacy*, 7 N.J. Misc. 970 (Sup. Ct. 1929); *Board of Pharmacy* v. *Hutchin*, 10 N.J. Misc. 641 (Sup. Ct. 1932); *Board of Pharmacy* v. *Quackenbush & Co.*, 22 Misc. 334 (C.P. Ct. 1940); *Crescent Bottling Works* v. *Board of Pharmacy*, 121 N.J. Eq. 237 (Ct. Err. & App. 1937).

[21] *Donaldson, supra* note 1; *Noel, supra* note 3; *Childs, supra* note 3; *Wood, supra* note 1; *Heron, supra* note 12; *Wrigley's Stores, Inc.* v. *Board of Pharmacy*, 336 Mich. 583, 59 N.W. 2d 8 (1953); *Culver* v. *Nelson*, 237 Minn. 65, 54 N.W. 2d 7 (1952); *Woolworth's Ltd.* v. *Wynne* (Ct. App. New Zealand 1951).

[22] *Proprietary Ass'n, supra* note 17.

Judge Colie's opinion on "non-poisonous" medicine seemed to confuse the adversaries. The Proprietary Association wanted the definition amended to include "when used in accordance with the specified directions."[23] The trade press also questioned the meaning of the definition, and the Board seemed to think that sales restrictions were still possible under the new ruling.[24]

At first Judge Colie refused to amend the "non-poisonous" definition,[25] but finally he relented and changed it to:

[A non-poisonous medicine is] a substance that, *when bearing or accompanied by proper printed directions for use thereof, and when used in accordance therewith, and* being in solution in the blood or acting chemically on the blood, neither destroys life nor impairs seriously the function of one or more of the organs.[26]

New Jersey Supreme Court. Upon appeal, Judge Colie's ruling was reversed and the action dismissed by a six to one vote. In delivering the majority opinion, Justice Jacobs reasoned that:[27]

1. It has been the practice in New Jersey to rule only upon specific items.
2. That practice has not been followed in this case.
3. The definition given by Judge Colie would nullify earlier New Jersey court decisions.
4. "The important underlying problems are legislative in nature and new enactments which clearly fix our State's current social policies and embody adequate definitions are urgently needed. In the meantime, however, our courts ought [to] confine themselves in this field to their customary function of deciding particular cases involving such undecided items as may, from time to time, properly be presented for adjudication."[28]

---

[23] "Judge Colie Refuses to Amend His 'Non-Poisonous' Definition," *American Druggist*, August 17, 1953, p. 6. According to "Court Redefines 'Non-Poison' Rule; Restrictions Fall," *Drug Topics*, October 5, 1953, p. 2., The Proprietary Association wanted the opening phrase of the definition to be "In circumstances of ordinary use . . ."

[24] Matthew L. Salonger, "The Jersey Proprietary Case," *The New York State Pharmacist*, Vol. 28, No. 8 (Aug. 1953), pp. 16–17; "Effect of Judge Colie's Decision Hinges on Sense of 'Non-Poisonous' Definition," *American Druggist*, August 3, 1953, pp. 5–7; " 'Don't Worry Over Non-Poison Ruling,' " *Drug Topics*, August 10, 1953, p. 94.

[25] "Judge Colie Refuses . . . ," *loc. cit.*

[26] As quoted in "Colie Amends 'Non-Poisonous' Definition," *American Druggist*, October 12, 1953, p. 7. Italicized words are those added. There were no other changes.

[27] 16 N.J. 62, 64–71, 106 A.2d 272, 273–277 (1954).

[28] *Id.* at 66, 106 A.2d at 274.

In his concluding remarks, the Justice (1) noted that no declaratory relief sought by either party should be granted because such a declaration probably would not terminate the controversy; (2) reemphasized the need for legislative action and the course to be followed by the courts in the interim:

Vital social issues are involved upon which the Legislature ought [to] have full opportunity to express itself in the form of modern legislation which fixes the current policy of the State and embodies suitable definitions and enumerations. Pending such legislation the courts will, as heretofore, be obliged to deal, in particular cases involving individual items . . . This may entail the danger that . . . judicial rather than legislative judgment as to the controlling social interests will dominate; but on this score the Legislature . . . has the counterbalancing and readily available remedy [of new legislation].[29]

Although the supreme court decision was hailed as a victory for the Board of Pharmacy,[30] neither party obtained its declaratory plan. The court refused to accept Judge Colie's definitions (following The Proprietary Association's recommendations), but the tribunal also declined to approve the definitions desired by the Board. In effect, the Supreme Court placed matters in the same position as before the declaratory judgment action was started.

LITIGATION ARISING FROM NEW JERSEY SUPREME COURT DECISION

It soon became clear that the Board and the New Jersey Pharmaceutical Association intended to press forward with restrictionism while the supreme court decision was still prominent in all minds. In the fall of 1954, a few months after the supreme court decision was handed down, the Board promulgated a regulation banning the self-service display of drugs in all outlets.[31] It is evident that if the "self-service rule" were enforced, food outlets would not be able to sell any drug item because in most food stores all merchandise generally is sold on a self-service basis.

New Jersey pharmacists warned The Proprietary Association what it could expect in the way of litigation if it continued its efforts to secure the generalized sale of proprietaries. Addressing the 1955 convention of the American Pharmaceutical Association (APhA), John

---

[29] *Id.* at 72, 106 A.2d at 278.

[30] "N.J. Rx Board's Right to Restrict Sales Is Restored by State Supreme Court," *American Druggist*, July 5, 1954, pp. 9–10.

[31] "2 Showdowns Near On Restricted Sales," *American Druggist*, June 6, 1955, p. 9.

Debus, Secretary of the New Jersey Pharmaceutical Association said that if The Proprietary Association carried its efforts too far, druggists might be "forced to conduct a 'chamber of horrors' to preserve restrictive sales laws."[32]

The threat was not an idle one. Several suits designed to block the sale of proprietaries by nondrug outlets had been filed before the declaratory judgment action had begun, but were held in abeyance pending the outcome of this action.[33] In the fall of 1954, supermarkets were warned to stop selling packaged medicines whose distribution the Board had restricted to drugstores only.[34] By the following summer, the Board had filed fifty complaints in various courts.[35]

The supreme court decision also provoked activity in the New Jersey legislature. Beginning in 1955 and continuing to the present, bills have been introduced nearly every year to change the pharmacy law.[36] Usually one proposal is introduced by antirestrictionists and another by advocates of the Board position. So far none of the proposed amendments has managed to secure approval of the legislators.

American Stores Corporation. The first case to be heard after the declaratory judgment action was a consolidated case involving six food stores owned by American Stores Corporation. The decision was handed down by Judge Martino of the Camden County District Court on October 19, 1955. The case involved the sale by the corporation of Bayer Aspirin Tablets and Phillips's Milk of Magnesia.[37]

The questions to be decided were:

1. "Is 'Bayer' Aspirin Tablets a non-poisonous patent or proprietary medicine within the meaning of N.J.S. 45:14–29?"
2. "Is 'Phillip's' Milk of Magnesia a non-poisonous patent or proprietary medicine within the meaning of N.J.S. 45:14–29?"

[32] As quoted in *Ibid.*

[33] "N.J. Board Won't Press to Collect Fines from Non-Rxmen," *American Druggist,* January 5, 1953, p. 18.

[34] "N.J. Supers Warned To Stop Selling Drugs," *American Druggist,* September 13, 1954, p. 21; "N.J. Board Warns Grocery Stores To Drop Drug Lines," *Drug Topics,* September 20, 1954, pp. 2, 77.

[35] "2 Showdowns Near . . . ," *loc. cit.*

[36] "N.J. Bill Seeks To Nullify Board's Court Victory On Restrictions," *American Druggist,* February 14, 1955, p. 25; "N.J. Gets Controversial Bill," *American Druggist,* February 27, 1956, p. 9; "N.J. Bill To Free Remedy Sales for Non-drug Outlets Is Killed," *American Druggist,* January 14, 1957, p. 16; "Full Package Criterion Pushed In N.J. As Basis For Restricting Sales," *American Druggist,* February 10, 1958, p. 8; "N.J. Lawmakers Recess Without Acting On Sales Hems Measures," *American Druggist,* June 15, 1959, p. 14; "N.J. Bill Lists '19 RxMan-Only' Drugs," *American Druggist,* April 1, 1963, p. 17; "N.J. Bill Limits 19 Types Of Drugs To Pharmacies," *Drug Topics,* April 6, 1964, p. 27.

[37] *Board of Pharmacy* v. *American Stores Corp.,* Consolidated Civils No. 31507 through No. 31512, Camden Co. Dist. Ct. N.J., October 19, 1955.

3. "Has plaintiff the right to restrict the sale of . . . [these products] to registered pharmacists and registered assistants of the State of New Jersey?"
4. "If plaintiff has the right to restrict said products under the statute, as aforesaid, does the statute violate the Constitution of the United States or the Constitution of the State of New Jersey?"[38]

Although the judge explored precedents, legislative intent, and several definitions contained in dictionaries and published by APhA, he based his decision on the testimony presented before the court:

An analysis of the testimony presented indicates that "Bayer" Aspirin and "Phillip's" Milk of Magnesia were the types of medicine which the legislature intended to fit the category of non-poisonous patent or proprietary medicines and, therefore, the defendants are not guilty of violating the provisions of N.J.S. 45:14–16.

The disposition of these main questions disposes of the other points [questions 3 and 4] raised by the defendant.[39]

Despite this adverse ruling, the Board continued with a number of other cases. The plan was to institute litigations at the rate of one per week during 1956 until the summer recess of the state district courts. By the end of February, the Board had won several uncontested cases: twelve in Camden County, four in Toms River, and one in Cape May, Jersey City, Mercer County, and Mt. Holly. The products whose sale was restricted as the result of the decisions were boric acid, citrate of magnesia, and tincture of iodine.[40] None of these nonprescription medicines are advertised proprietary medicines.

Honey Dew Food Markets. Later in 1956, the Board filed a suit in the Bergen County District Court against Honey Dew Food Markets for refusing to pay a $375 fine imposed by the Board on the company for selling Alka-Seltzer, Anacin, Aspergum, Bromo-Quinine, Bromo-Seltzer, Bufferin, Carter's Little Liver Pills, Ex-Lax, Fletcher's Castoria, Pepto-Bismol, Plough Children's Aspirin, Phillip's Milk of Magnesia, Sal Hepatica, and Vick's Va-Tra-Nol.[41]

In the spring of 1957, Judge John D. Lynn dismissed the case, vindicating the position of Honey Dew Food Markets. The opinion was rather lengthy, but was mainly a synopsis of testimony given

[38] *Ibid.*
[39] *Ibid.*
[40] "N.J. Board: We'll Fight A Case A Week," *American Druggist,* January 16, 1956, p. 7; "We'll Sue All Supers With Drug Depts,' " *American Druggist,* February 27, 1956, p. 9.
[41] "New Trial In New Jersey Tests 'Harmlessness' of 14 Drug Items," *American Druggist,* December 3, 1956, p. 10.

before the court. The testimony indicated no significant disagreement as to the proprietary status of the products. The major conflict was whether the products are poisonous. Evidence demonstrated that if the disputed items were consumed in sufficient quantity the products could be poisonous. The testimony also showed, however, that virtually all poisonings attributed to the preparations had occurred in adults with personality maladjustments and children who had ingested the products without the knowledge of their parents. Regarding the poisoning of children, the judge said:

Just as the forces of law and order must look to parental control to guard against juvenile delinquency, so we must look to the same quarter for watchful restraint over the use of domestic remedies with which every medicine cabinet abounds.

It appears quite conclusively that there is no causal relationship between the ingestion of excessive amounts, or the improper use, of the products under examination and the manner in which they are purchased or the place where the purchase is made. . . . It matters not whether a drug or medicine is purchased in a drugstore or in a corner grocery; the fact is that, when the purchaser walks out of the store, all control over the drug or medicine passes from the seller and from that time on the responsibility for proper usage lies entirely with the purchaser.[42]

The Attorney General's office finally decided not to prosecute the appeal that had been filed. In his letter informing the Board of his decision, Attorney General Grover C. Richman, Jr. said:

It would seem that the meaning of the statutory terms . . . expressed in the [1901 Pharmacy] Act has become so confusing and ambiguous that the courts cannot intelligently apply the statute to present-day regulatory problems.[43]

Anderson's Market. Some people apparently thought that the adverse ruling in the Bergen County case did not impair the Board's power to restrict the sale of the products in other counties. On this assumption, it appeared that the Board could compel adherence to its restrictive sales policy and force the payment of fines by violators or institute court actions elsewhere in the state.[44]

It was not until 1963 that this assumption was tested before the New Jersey Supreme Court. The case came from Cape May County,

[42] *Board of Pharmacy* v. *Adelman*, Bergen Co. Dist. Ct. N.J., Civil No. 63195, March 18, 1957. A fifteenth product, Sentrol, was declared by the judge to be poisonous.
[43] As quoted in "N.J. Restrictions Stay, Despite Loss Of Test By Court," *Drug Topics*, December 23, 1957, pp. 3. 40.
[44] *Ibid.*

where the presiding judge had ruled that citrate of magnesia was not a proprietary and that therefore the defendant, Anderson's Market, must pay a $50 fine levied by the Board for the illegal sale.[45]

The supreme court, in a very brief (one-page) decision unanimously reversed the lower court's ruling and found the defendant not guilty. The court recalled its 1954 decision that (1) it would not define the term "patent or proprietary" and (2) legislative action was needed because of the difficulty of discovering the legislative will from the statute. The court then said:

As yet the Legislature has not spoken.

We think we should go no further than to say we are not persuaded that the statute was intended to regulate the sale of the commodity here involved, and hence the judgment is reversed.[46]

In his concurring opinion, Justice Francis said:

I concur in the result decided upon, but in so doing I cannot escape a sense of unfinished business. . . .

The statute does not define "patent or proprietary" medicine. . . . But how can the command of the Legislature be . . . enforced if it is not . . . expressed in terms which are reasonably susceptible of definition? Obviously a state cannot issue commands to its citizens in language so vague . . . as to afford no fair warning to what conduct might transgress them. . . .

I do not believe vagueness of such extreme degree exists here. . . .

It is common knowledge that pre-packaged . . . preparations are sold to the public by reference to a trade or manufacturer's name. Such products are labeled with the name which is brought to public attention by advertising media, and the label or an . . . insert contains directions for their use and the conditions for which they are specifics. There is nothing about them which calls into use any skill or science of the person who sells them. Anyone who can read the label and make change is capable of complying with the request of the purchaser. No physician's prescription is needed. The druggist does not perform any professional function when he sells them. He is relieved of responsibity for the efficacy or safety of such products which are regulated and controlled by federal and state food and drug legislation. . . .

Under the circumstances, in my judgement, "patent or proprietary" medicine within the contemplation of the statute in question signifies:

Any non-prescription medicine or drug which is pre-packaged, fully prepared by the manufacturer or producer for the use of the consumer, and is accompanied by adequate directions for use.[47]

---

[45] Board of Pharmacy v. Anderson, 40 N.J. 40, 190 A.2d 664 (1963).
[46] Ibid.
[47] Id. at 42–43, 190 A.2d at 665–666.

STATUS OF NEW JERSEY SALES RESTRICTIONS

The twelve most recent years of litigation and legislative efforts have not produced a clear statement as to which medicines may be sold by nondrug retail outlets in New Jersey. The legislature, faced with pressure from two sides, has been unable to act. New Jersey courts have not demonstrated uniformity in their decisions since opposing county court rulings are valid in their jurisdictions until the supreme court renders a judgment and the high court has ruled on only one product—citrate of magnesia. It appears that the courts will continue to hear cases on a product basis, and if sufficient actions on various preparations reach the supreme court over the years, a nonrestricted and restricted drug list could eventually be developed.

One difficulty associated with this solution is the length of time involved: despite the number of cases that have been heard in the lower courts only one has so far reached the state supreme court. Such a process also presents a great danger of a miscarriage of justice, especially with respect to small grocers. The Board, if it chooses, can levy fines against these individuals. They must either pay the levies or face an expensive court action which costs the Board nothing since the Attorney General is the regulatory agency's counsel. Thus, small grocers can be intimidated into removing proprietary and other nonprescription drugs from their shelves when it is not at all clear that that is the intent of the law.

Sales Restrictions in New York

In New York, as in New Jersey, sales restrictions have been a subject of legislative contemplation. In 1953, New York pharmacists defeated the Donovan-Carlino Bill which would have allowed almost all nonprescription drugs to be sold in nondrug outlets.[48] In 1954, the food stores had a similar measure introduced and a bill to further restrict the sale of proprietary goods, which was supported by druggists, was also proposed. The general merchants had a third bill introduced as a compromise between the two extremes, but the New York State Pharmaceutical Association refused to accept the compromise, so no bill was passed.[49]

The following year a comprehensive restrictive sales bill was passed by the legislature. The enactment provided that manufacturers and

[48] "The Donovan-Carlino Bill," *The New York State Pharmacist*, August 1953, p. 15.
[49] "N.Y. Assn. Bars Drug Sales Compromise," *American Druggist*, March 15, 1954, p. 15.

wholesalers could sell restricted drugs, including veterinary products, only to outlets registered by the New York State Board of Pharmacy (drugstores and rural retailers). Although the druggists expected Governor Harriman to sign the bill into law,[50] the executive vetoed the measure because "while purporting to regulate more adequately the sale of drugs, this bill would impose restrictions that are unwarranted."[51]

The year 1956 again saw opposing bills introduced with no action taken, but a standing committee, the Joint Legislative Committee on Imitation Food Products and Problems (Drumm Committee), was authorized to study the control, distribution, and sale of proprietary drug remedies.[52]

THE DRUMM COMMITTEE REPORTS

The Committee held a hearing at Cooperstown, New York, on September 20, 1956, and heard the arguments of both sides of the restrictive sales issue. The report of the hearings and other information the Committee had gathered was published early in 1957.[53] Other hearings were held and additional statements were published (notably 1958 and 1960) but the contents and recommendations were primarily repetitions of the original report.

The Committee saw no harm in the unrestricted sale of nonprescription medicines and strongly favored the elimination of such sales constraints in New York:

It is the considered understanding of the Committee that these products, known as proprietary medicines, are fully packaged medicines, labeled in accordance with the provisions of the Federal Food, Drug and Cosmetic Act which do not require a prescription for their purchase. We have all used these products on countless occasions since our childhood, and we know of their efficacy and harmlessness from personal experience. These harmless home remedies are sold without restriction in 40 states today. . . . Even in New York State they may be sold with Pharmacy Board approval in rural areas if three miles distant from a drug store. . . . [These] stores have stocked and sold aspirin and milk of magnesia along with other drugs and medications with no ill effect on the health of our people. It therefore concomitantly follows, that if such sale in rural . . . stores

[50] "Harriman Is Expected To Sign Restricted-Sale Bill," *American Druggist,* April 25, 1955, p. 19.

[51] "Restricted Drug Sale Bill Vetoed In N.Y.," *American Druggist,* May 23, 1955, p. 23.

[52] "N.Y. Seeks Agreement on Proprietary Sales," *Drug Topics,* February 4, 1957, p. 12.

[53] New York, *Annual Report of the Joint Legislative Committee on Imitation Food Products and Problems,* Legislative Document No. 34, March 30, 1957.

is lawful and for the public interest and health, an extension of authorization to sell such drugs and products in urban outlets would not create any different result.[54]

The Committee also roundly criticized and recommended repeal of Section 6823, Subdivision 2 of the New York Education Law which permits the Board of Pharmacy to fine nonpharmacists up to $500 on any violation of the state pharmacy law. Under this provision, the Board acts as investigator, prosecutor, judge, and jury. Denied the accused are (1) the right to trial by jury, (2) the right of an impartial tribunal, (3) the right to have the case heard in accordance with established legal procedures and rules of evidence, and (4) the right to introduce facts not admitted by the Board if the defendant wishes to appeal to the courts.[55]

In its 1958 report, the Committee reemphasized this "kangaroo court" system and strongly supported the New York Bar Association and New York County Bar Association Legislative Committee demands that the provisions be repealed.[56] Other quarters have also criticized the arbitrary nature of the law.[57]

The result of the efforts by the Drumm Committee was the Drumm-Cooke Bill, introduced during the 1957 state legislative session. The New York State Pharmaceutical Association fought the bill vigorously[58] and as the result a revised version of the proposal was introduced.[59] The association was also opposed to the amended bill.[60] An example of its disapproval was the March appearance of 1,200 pharmacists in Albany to register their disapproval.[61] The bill did not pass.

Another battle between the restrictionists and nonrestrictionists erupted in 1958, but no action was taken.[62] After 1958 the Loblaw

[54] *Ibid.*, p. 63.

[55] *Ibid.*, p. 65.

[56] New York, *Annual Report of the Joint Legislative Committee on Imitation Food Products and Problems*, Legislative Document No. 56, March 31, 1958, pp. 66–69.

[57] Betty N. Collins, "Does New York State Have a Kangaroo Court?," *Albany Law Review*, Vol. 23 (May 1959), pp. 315–335.

[58] "N.Y. Men Mobilize Against Passage Of Drumm-Cooke Bill," *Drug Topics*, March 18, 1957, pp. 2, 102.

[59] "Amended Drumm Bill Limits Proprietaries To Outlets Selling Goods For 'Personal Use,' " *American Druggist*, April 8, 1957, p. 19.

[60] "N.Y. Assn. To Take Fight To The Public," *American Druggist*, September 23, 1957, p. 14.

[61] "Drumm Unit: Let Non-RxMen Sell Drugs," *American Druggist*, November 18, 1957, p. 15.

[62] "N.Y. Bill Bans Sales Of Drugs by Clerks," *American Druggist*, January 27, 1958, p. 13; "Restrict Sales of Dangerous Drugs, N.Y. Lawmakers Are Urged," *American Druggist*, March 10, 1958, p. 14; "N.Y. Men Battle Proposals To Weaken Drug Sales Curbs," *Drug Topics*, March 17, 1958, pp. 2, 76, 79.

case was in progress and little interest was displayed in legislative enactments, but restrictive bills were introduced every year from 1958 to 1966.

THE LOBLAW CASE

With its broad power exercisable in civil cases, it is not surprising that the New York Board of Pharmacy used that procedure to enforce its restrictive policies. Appeal of the agency's rulings to the courts was virtually stymied by the statutory provision that the Board's evidence had to be accepted without additions or deletions.

This chain of events was finally disrupted when Loblaw, Inc., a supermarket chain, instituted a suit against the Board that was not an appeal from an action of the agency. This was the first instance of a New York court hearing original evidence presented by both sides. This action was a plea for (1) a summary judgment declaring that the plaintiff Loblaw had the right to continue to sell Bayer Aspirin without a pharmacy license and without utilizing the services of registered pharmacists, and (2) a permanent injunction to prevent the Board of Pharmacy from interfering in any way with Loblaw's sale of Bayer Aspirin.

Supreme Court of Erie County.[63] The two major points of contention around which the litigation revolved were whether Bayer Aspirin is a proprietary medicine under the New York Education Law, Section 6816, Subdivision 2, Paragraph 6 and whether, if Bayer Aspirin is not a proprietary item, the statutory provisions used by the Board to deny the grocery store sale of Bayer are constitutional.

Loblaw pointed out that the courts have used "common-usage definition and a technical or restricted meaning for the term" proprietary medicine. Whichever interpretation the court selected, contended Loblaw, Bayer Aspirin was a proprietary. The plaintiff further alleged that even though Bayer Aspirin meets the minimum standards of the U.S.P., there are secret processes used which make Bayer far superior to any U.S.P. equivalent. The methods of manufacture and the binder used make Bayer disintegrate within thirty seconds after ingestion, far faster than other products. The U.S.P. itself says that the maximum aspirin dissolving time allowable is fifteen minutes. This difference, in addition to the proprietary right attaching to the Bayer name, makes Bayer a proprietary using even the narrow technical definition.

---

[63] *Loblaw, Inc.* v. *Board of Pharmacy*, 22 Misc. 2d 131, 202 N.Y.S. 2d 711 (Sup. Ct. 1960), *rev'd* 12 App Div. 2d 180, 210 N.Y.S. 2d 709 (1961), *rev'd*, 11 N.Y. 2d 102, 220 N.Y.S. 2d 681 (1962), *affirming*, 22 Misc. 2d 131, 202 N.Y.S. 2d 711 (Sup. Ct. 1960).

The defendants maintained that Aspirin—Bayer's or anyone else's—could not be a proprietary. The reasoning was: (1) aspirin is a synonym for acetylsalicylic acid; (2) acetylsalicylic acid is a drug intended to, and does, affect the human body; (3) aspirin is a medicine in general use; (4) the ingredients of aspirin are the common property of pharmacists and pharmaceutical manufacturers; (5) aspirin tablets can be prepared by any pharmacist or pharmaceutical manufacturer; (6) therefore, Bayer Aspirin is not a proprietary product, even though the binder used may hasten the solubility of Bayer as compared to other aspirin.

Judge Moule, the presiding justice, ruled in favor of Loblaw on the basis that even with the use of the technical definition, Bayer is a proprietary medication. In reaching the decision, the bench reasoned as follows:

1. The defendants contend that all aspirins capable of disintegration within fifteen minutes are the same, irrespective of secret ingredients and processes. This is not so. One does not arrive at the same end product if different processes are used, even though the base materials used are the same.
2. The defendants say that by virtue of aspirin's U.S.P. listing, it cannot be a proprietary, but the evidence shows that the U.S.P. does indeed list proprietaries.
3. Defendants claim that Bayer's processes and binder ingredient can be determined by other producers, but until that is done such processes and ingredient are in exclusive possession of the Bayer manufacturer.
4. The listing of such items as cotton, sugar, starch, lemon peel, orange peel, chalk, salad oil, salt, and yeast in the U.S.P. clearly refutes the defendants' claim that no drug or medicine appearing in the U.S.P. can be sold except in pharmacies.

In regard to the constitutionality question, the judge dismissed the charges of any conflict of the state pharmacy law with the federal constitution. The court declared that the state constitutionality depended upon whether the statute in question bears a close enough relationship to the public health and welfare to warrant the exercise of police power. Judge Moule found no such relationship for Bayer Aspirin:

1. Evidence shows that 10,000 tons of aspirin were consumed in the United States in 1959 and since the incidence of side effects of such ingestion was extremely low, aspirin is not a dangerous drug.

THE RETAIL DRUG INDUSTRY

2. A survey of one hundred drugstores revealed that none of their personnel offered any consumption advice when aspirin was purchased and that in fifty-three cases the sale was not even made by a pharmacist.
3. The defendants assume a strange position when they say professional advice is needed in aiding a customer to determine which aspirin to buy, when the Board has already stated that all aspirins are the same.
4. The State Commissioner of Education is apprehensive that the monetary inducement for prospective pharmacists will be insufficient if the sale of proprietary drugs is not restricted, but there is no reason for giving a distribution monopoly to druggists on economic grounds—especially when it is common knowledge "that most of the so-called drugstores are engaged in a wide field of merchandising having no connection with drugs."

Supreme Court—Appellate Division.[64] Upon appeal by defendants, the judges of the appellate tribunal overturned the lower court ruling by a four to zero vote. In the majority opinion given by Justice Williams, the reasons for declaring Bayer Aspirin not to be a proprietary medicine were:

1. A drug cannot be established as a proprietary medicine—when the drug's essential elements are known and used by the public—merely by claiming that secret manufacturing processes are used and that a well-known trademark is possessed.
2. If a drug is to be exempted from Board control, the right to exemption must be clear and in this case it is not.

As for the constitutionality issue:

1. Restricting the sale of Bayer Aspirin is a valid exercise of the state's police power even though (a) the item may be harmless and (b) some other states have ruled differently on the question.
2. The claim of the law's unconstitutionality on the theory that the public is no more protected when buying from a retailer than when buying from a druggist overlooks the basic fact that aspirin is a drug and as such may be regulated under police power.

Although Judge Goldman voted for the reversal of the lower court's findings, he wrote a vigorous opinion in which he agreed with everything that Judge Moule had said, except the ruling that aspirin is

[64] *Ibid.*

harmless. As a result, he voted for the reversal because the record did not present sufficient evidence to show that aspirin is harmless.

Court of Appeals of New York State.[65] Loblaw appealed the adverse decision to the highest tribunal in New York State. The opinion of the Court of Appeals, written by Justice Van Voorhis, declared that the main inquiry before the court was the question posed by Justice Goldman in his dissent at the intermediate court level: does the fact that the Bayer patent had expired from seventeen years ago make the sale of Bayer by nonpharmacists illegal when the practice had been sanctioned by law while the patent was in force?

The court held unanimously for Loblaw, saying that the Supreme Court-Appellate Division had not applied either the common usage or technical definition of a proprietary, but had established its own criterion that any U.S.P. item cannot be a proprietary. Since the active ingredients of all drugs are required by law to appear on the label of the drug's container, the Appellate ruling was equivalent to saying that there can be no proprietary medicines except those medicines that have outstanding patents. The Court of Appeals then stated that *all* previous cases of a similar nature had adopted either the technical or common-usage definition of proprietary medicine.

The court concluded:

> We believe the purpose of the Legislature in enacting this exception of proprietary medicines to have been to exempt pharmacists from the responsibility [liability] otherwise imposed upon them by the language of the article in case of pre-packaged nonprescription drugs (not poisonous, deleterious or habit forming) prepared under a federal or state law by responsible manufacturers and sold under their brand names without opportunity for inspection or analysis by the pharmacist.

This was a very important judgment. Although the Court said that it was not necessary to write an all inclusive definition of a proprietary in order to rule for Loblaw, its concluding paragraph essentially does just that. The implication of the paragraph is that any trademarked drug cleared by the Federal Food and Drug Administration for over-the-counter sale may be sold in any outlet.

It is interesting to note in this connection that the New York State Board of Pharmacy has been trying to convince the Attorney General's office that a suit should be instituted to test the status of Dristan.[66] In view of the Court of Appeals decision, the reluctance of the Attorney General's office is not surprising.

[65] *Ibid.*
[66] Interview with Kenneth S. Griswold, Secretary, New York State Board of Pharmacy, March 29, 1966.

Sales Restrictions in Minnesota

Although there have been several Minnesota Supreme Court decisions regarding the limitation on the distribution of proprietaries, the sales restriction issue is not yet settled there. In cases dating back several years, the court has upheld the pharmacy law and the theory that a very narrow view must be taken with regard to interpreting statutory provisions that apply to proprietary items. The Red Owl case and/or legislation arising therefrom would, it was hoped, put an end to the long struggle between grocers and pharmacists.[67] Those hopes proved to be futile, however, when the case was ruled upon by the state's highest court.

THE RED OWL CASE

The Minnesota State Board of Pharmacy originally brought separate suits against Groves-Kelco, Inc., a wholesaler, and Red Owl Stores, Inc., a supermarket chain, to enjoin the chain store from selling a specified list of drugs and to prevent the wholesaler from distributing the same drugs to Red Owl and other similar outlets. The medication in question included Alka-Seltzer, Anacin, Aspergum, Bromo-Quinine, Bromo Seltzer, Bufferin, castoria, Ex-Lax, Feen-A-Mint, 4-Way Cold Tablets, Lysol, Murine, Pepto-Bismol, Pinex, Sal Hepatica, Vick's Cough Syrup, and Vick's Va-Tra-Nol. The Board contended that these items could be sold only by those stores with a pharmacy permit and that since neither Red Owl nor Groves-Kelco possessed such licenses, they should not be permitted to merchandise the items.[68]

When the two cases came before the court,[69] defendants Red Owl and Groves-Kelco asked that they be tried by a criminal action rather than by an equity action asking injunctive relief as instituted by the Board. The defendants apparently thought that a decision in their favor was more likely if the proceedings were heard by a jury rather than by only a judge.[70]

The lower court judge granted the defendants' request, dismissed the suit, and instructed the Board to institute criminal actions if it

---

[67] *State* v. *Zotalis*, 172 Minn. 132, 214 N.W. 766 (1927); *F. W. Woolworth Co.*, supra note 9; *Culver*, supra note 21; *Donaldson*, supra note 1; *State* v. *Hovorka*, 100 Minn. 249, 110 N.W. 870 (1907); *Minnesota State Pharmaceutical Ass'n* v. *State Bd. of Pharmacy*, 103 Minn. 21, 114 N.W. 245 (1907).

[68] "Criminal Action Sought In Minn. Sales Hems Case," *American Druggist*, October 8, 1956, p. 16.

[69] The cases were combined and considered as a unit, a standard judicial practice when pending cases present essentially the same issues.

[70] "Criminal Action Sought. . . ," *loc cit.*

felt the pharmacy law was being violated. The Board had protested the defense plea, saying that such a procedure would necessitate the initiation of criminal cases in every county. The presiding judge, however, disagreed with this contention, asserting that an injunction proceeding would be binding only on the parties to the litigation just as would a criminal action.[71]

The Board appealed the decision to the Minnesota Supreme Court. The Supreme Court overruled the lower court's opinion of the correct judicial procedure, reversing the previous decision and instructing the lower court to proceed to hear the merits of the case in equity proceedings.[72]

District Court of Hennepin County.[73] The procedural questions having been settled, the District Court of Hennepin County began to hear the case on its merits. The tribunal adopted a lenient attitude toward the receiving of testimony and other evidence. As a result, the trial consumed fourteen weeks and produced about 7,000 pages of recorded testimony which included evidence given by forty-nine witnesses and a compilation of 204 exhibits. The judge found for the defendants, declaring that the facts of the cases did not warrant the issuance of the injunctions prayed for by the State of Minnesota.

Judge William C. Larson's findings of fact and memorandum opinion concerning the case were no less formidable than the court record. He listed thirty-four findings of fact and wrote a fifty-two page memorandum opinion in support of his decision not to issue the injunctions requested by the Board. An abstract of the significant findings of fact are:

1. The Minnesota State Board of Pharmacy has recognized that the sale by nonpharmacists of the products in dispute constitutes serious economic competition for the pharmacists. Concern over that increased competition is a motivating factor in this action. One of the manifest purposes of this litigation is the curtailment or restriction of free competition in the sale of medicines.

2. Each of these products is sold both in drug and nondrug outlets in extremely large volume throughout the United States since they first began to be manufactured. The amount of these products sold in nondrug outlets exceeds 50 per cent. It is common knowledge that products similar to these are sold freely without any attempt at supervision by pharmacists and often without any contact between a pharmacist and the purchaser.

[71] *State* v. *Red Owl Stores, Inc.,* 253 Minn. 236, 9 N.W. 2d 103 (1958).
[72] *Ibid.*
[73] *State* v. *Red Owl Stores, Inc.,* Fourth Judicial Dist. Ct. Minn. Civil No. 512684, March 9, 1960, *modified by,* 262 Minn. 31, 115 N.W. 2d 643 (1962).

3. The records of the Minnesota State Board of Pharmacy contain no proof that harm ever resulted to anyone from the sale by any of those products.

4. Rural "permit" stores are authorized by the Board to sell those products and such outlets consist of every conceivable type of retail outlet. This record does not show that any harm ever came to anyone from these rural sales.

5. Not a single instance has been shown where these products, when used as directed, have caused harm to anyone.

6. The record does not indicate any danger, past, present or future, to the public health from the sale of these products by defendants or by any other persons.

7. None of these products contain any narcotic or hypnotic substances; none will cause addiction; none has any tendency to give withdrawal symptoms upon discontinuance of use; none has a tendency to create tolerance through continued use; and none of the products is habit-forming.

8. There is no causal relationship between the ingestion of excessive amounts of these products and the manner in which they are purchased or the store where the purchase is made.

9. All control over the usage or dosage of the products covered ceases with the purchase. It makes no difference whether the medicine is purchased in a drugstore or in a corner grocery store. When the purchaser leaves the store all control over the medicine passes from the seller and from that time on the responsibility for proper usage lies entirely with the purchaser, regardless of where the item is purchased.

10. The retailer of these products, whether a pharmacist or grocer, is merely a conduit through which these products pass on their way from the manufacturer to the public. The public is adequately protected by the integrity of the manufacturer and by the supervision of the Federal Food and Drug Administration. The public is afforded no further protection whether the product is sold in a grocery or drugstore. The products have the same potential for danger, if any, no matter where they are purchased.

11. Each of the products is, according to popular usage and custom, a proprietary medicine.

12. The manufacturer of each product has an exclusive proprietary right to the trade name, secret formula, and active and inert ingredients. Each product is the exclusive property of the manufacturer concerned. *Each of the products concerned is a proprietary medicine within the strict and technical definition of a proprietary medicine.*

The memorandum opinion accompanying the findings of fact dealt with many issues, procedural and otherwise. Most of the material, however, concerned three central points: (1) the realization that the court was being asked to arbitrate between two economic interests and that economics was the basis of the case, regardless of other issues that, on the surface, were of paramount importance, (2) there was no public health issue involved in the sale of the enumerated items, and (3) the products are of proprietary status.

After stating that an equity court would not grant an injunction in economic matters, except when there is strong proof that injunctive relief is sought primarily in the interest of the public health and welfare, the judge proceeded to demonstrate that the pharmacists were concerned with the economics involved. The court illustrated this factor by excerpts from the Board's annual reports that indicated the agency's displeasure at the competition being caused drugstores by the grocery store sale of proprietaries. Excerpts from the same publications were also used to indicate that the maintenance of public health was not at issue. These documents were buttressed with testimony from pharmacy board officials and employees that no proof existed which indicated that consumers had been harmed by the sale of these products by outlets other than drugstores. The judge also noted the presence and presumed safety of a miscellany of rural stores that were allowed by the Board to sell the disputed items without a pharmacist participating in the sale.

As his authority for declaring the products to be proprietary medicines on the basis of either the technical or common-usage definition, the judge cited and discussed at length a number of cases, all of which, in the judge's opinion, supported his position. Concluding his argument on the proprietary status of these items, the judge quoted a *Yale Law Review* article which stated that restricting the distribution of such products to pharmacies serves no legitimate end.

In the course of ruling in favor of the defendants, Red Owl Stores, Inc., and Groves-Kelco, Inc. the judge stated his belief that the products fell within the exemption clause of the Minnesota pharmacy law. This finding was gratuitous in view of the State's failure to establish its right to injunctive relief. To be eligible for exclusion from the provisions of the law, the medicines had to be harmless, nonhabit forming proprietary medicines. The fact that the preparations were not dangerous, aside from the economic and health issues, was stressed throughout the opinion.

After the decision was handed down, the plaintiffs petitioned the judge for (1) a modification of his ruling or (2) a new trial. The plaintiffs contended that there were several errors of fact, law and judgment. This plea was dismissed summarily by the judge, who, by way of explanation, stated that no new evidence had been introduced to contest his previous conclusions.

Minnesota Supreme Court.[74] The Pharmacy Board appealed their second failure to the Supreme Court of Minnesota. This court also rendered a lengthy opinion at the conclusion of the proceedings. Of the lower court's two main findings, safety and proprietary status, the Supreme Court agreed with the several findings and opinions on safety. The proprietary status conferred by the lower court, however, was not allowed to stand.

All the out-of-state authorities cited by the lower court, the Supreme Court declared, were inapplicable because the Minnesota law differs slightly from that of other states. In ruling that the products are not proprietary in nature, the Supreme Court relied on expert testimony given in the lower court that indicated the products could easily be duplicated and in some cases had been so duplicated by the witnesses themselves. When the products can be analyzed and reproduced, they are not secret and are therefore not proprietaries, reasoned the court. This amounted to an adoption of a very narrow definition (technical) of the term proprietary. The court could not, it said, adopt the common-usage reasoning as other states had done since the Minnesota law was different from the statutes of the other jurisdictions.

The court, on the basis of the above line of thought, also declared that the statute relating to the sale of proprietary medicines was obsolete and largely meaningless. It then stated that a new law was needed to clarify the legislature's intent, since the conditions giving rise to the original law no longer exist. The tribunal concluded by affirming the lower court's denial of an injunction, but its decision that these items are not proprietary products, and were not covered by the exemption classes for proprietaries, apparently left open the possibility for criminal prosecution of the defendants.[75]

The Minnesota Supreme Court, instead of clarifying the rights of the grocers and the Board, only added to the confusion. Its denial of the Board's request for an injunction and agreement with the lower court's findings relating to public health matters implied that the grocery stores cannot be prevented (via injunction) from selling items approved by the FDA for over-the-counter sale. That is, the court would not grant an injunction because it had not been shown that

[74] *Ibid.*

[75] It is interesting to note that such prosecutions have not, so far as is known, been instituted. The Board perhaps realizes that a victory in a jury trial would be exceedingly difficult to achieve, since jurors would probably be sympathetic to the free distribution of the products that they frequently use.

the sale of the products constitutes an injury to the public health. This showing was necessary because the statute does not specify injunctive relief without showing some injury.[76] On the other hand, the court's decision that the items in question are not proprietaries means that the food stores are violating the law and are subject to prosecution. As a result, neither party can be sure that its previous actions are lawful.

LICENSE DENIALS TO WHOLESALERS

Under Minnesota law, drug wholesale firms must have licenses from the Board of Pharmacy in order to operate. While the Red Owl case was being heard by the courts, the Board revoked the licenses previously granted to two wholesalers, J. F. Wallerus & Sons and H. & S. Co., Inc. for selling proprietary medicines to supermarkets. The firms appealed to the courts. A restraining order was issued against the Board until there could be a trial. The presiding judge at the trial, Judge Jaroscak, said the Board had no basis for the license denials.[77]

Also, while Groves-Kelco was involved in court, the Board refused to issue it a renewal license. The regulatory agency claimed to have denied the license because Groves-Kelco was selling baby foods and toiletries as well as drug items. Judge Earl J. Lyons of the Hennepin County District Court ruled that the Board's decision had been arbitrary and without authority or jurisdiction.[78]

LEGISLATIVE ACTIVITY

The first meeting (1963) of the state legislature after the confusing Minnesota Supreme Court decision in the Red Owl case resulted in a flurry of proposals and counterproposals for new legislation to remedy the criticisms voiced by the Supreme Court. The two opposing parties, pharmacists (led by the Minnesota State Pharmaceutical Association) and grocers (led by the Minnesota Retail Grocers' Association) were strong enough to prevent the passage of a bill favoring either faction.

[76] Counsel for Red Owl feels that the Board's main endeavor was to have a provision judicially inserted into the law to allow injunctive relief (prohibit the grocery store sale of the product) without showing any injury to public health (Letter from Alf L. Bergerud, General Counsel, Red Owl Stores, Inc., August 11, 1966).

[77] "Minn. Board Loses Suit to Prohibit Sales to Grocers," *Drug Topics*, August 17, 1959, p. 2.

[78] "Court Decides Minnesota Board Must Issue Wholesaler Permit to Supermarket Supplier," *Drug Topics*, February 26, 1962, p. 8.

It was finally agreed to establish the Interim Commission on the Sale of Home Remedies to study the problem and to propose legislation.[79]

During the interval between the 1963 and 1965 sessions of the legislature, the Interim Commission held several hearings and was ready with a report of its activity and proposed legislation when the 1965 legislature opened. The main features of the proposed bill were (1) all prescriptions, habit-forming medications, ethical proprietaries, all drugs containing narcotics, and all injectible drugs to be sold only in pharmacies, (2) the responsibility for declaring any other (nonprescription) drug unsafe for self-medication to be shifted to the Department of Health, which would conduct hearings to determine the status of questionable drugs, and (3) trademarked nonprescription drugs advertised directly to the public by the manufacturer to be sold in any retail outlet.[80]

Notwithstanding the report and recommendations of the Iterim Commission, the proposed legislation soon bogged down in the 1965 legislature and several substitute proposals were offered, none of which was enacted. A second commission was created later in 1965 to conduct another study of the problem.[81]

Sales Restrictions in Other Jurisdictions

In addition to the three states already discussed, there have been important decisions rendered in other jurisdictions concerning the sales restriction controversy. In many instances, the courts of New Jersey, New York, and Minnesota relied on the reasoning exhibited in the cases below. This is particularly true of the *Wakeen* case in Wisconsin, the *Wrigley* case in Michigan, and the *Safeway* case in the District of Columbia. Other less important cases are discussed mainly to demon-

[79] "RxMen, Grocers Push Rival Bills for Control of O-T-C Products," *American Druggist*, March 4, 1963, p. 16; "Minneapolis MD Tells Legislature Supermarkets Ok for Proprietaries," *Drug News Weekly*, March 13, 1963, p. 8; "Minnesota Druggists Attack OTC Drug Sales at Hearing," *Drug News Weekly*, March 27, 1963, p. 7; "Grocers Offering New Minnesota Pill Bill," *Drug News Weekly*, April 17, 1963, p. 10; "Minnesota 'Pill Bill' Headed for Shelf as House Unit Votes 2-Year Study," *Drug News Weekly*, April 24, 1963, p. 7.

[80] Minnesota, *Report of the Interim Commission on Sale of Home Remedies*, March 1965, p. 9.

[81] "Showdown On Minnesota O.T.C. Drug Sales Measure Is Imminent," *American Druggist*, March 15, 1965, p. 28; "Minnesota Pill Bill Puts Home Remedies In All Stores; RxMen Gird For Fight," *Drug Topics*, March 22, 1965, p. 4; "Proprietary Bill Is Tightened By Solons," *Drug Topics*, April 19, 1965, p. 8; "RxMen's Sales Bill Gains In Minnesota," *American Druggist*, April 26, 1965, p. 23; "H.F. 1869 Defeated by State Senate as Legislature Adjourns," *Minnesota Pharmacist*, Vol. 19, No. 8 (May 1965), p. 11; "Minn. Drug Curbs May Again Be Delayed. . .by Another Legislative 'Study Committee,'" *American Druggist*, May 10, 1965, p. 15.

strate that the sales restriction problem has plagued a substantial number of states.

The status of sales restrictions in Wisconsin is unusual in several respects. First, there was a state Supreme Court decision early in the period of renewed warfare between restrictionists and anti-restrictionists that began in the early 1950's. In addition, the case did not involve any name-brand products in the proprietary field; rather, the items questioned were nonbranded nonprescription drug items. Further, there was a direct challenge to a statute's constitutionality early in the litigation. Finally, the early and adverse decision for anti-restrictionists allowed the Board of Pharmacy to promulgate a series of restrictive regulations that, as Chapters 10 and 11 will demonstrate, makes Wisconsin one of the most difficult places in which to perform as a businessman in a drugstore.

The case began when the defendant, Wakeen, a food outlet, was charged in LaCross County Court with the unlawful sale of drugs. The firm was adjudged guilty on March 19, 1951, and immediately appealed the decision to the Circuit Court for LaCross County. The defendant moved for dismissal of the case on the grounds that the medications in question (aspirin, milk of magnesia, and camphorated oil) are proprietaries and therefore exempt from the general rule that all drugs must be sold in drugstores. Wakeen also contended that the statute classifying all items listed in the U.S.P. as drugs is unconstitutional because (1) it is an unlawful delegation of a legislative power, (2) it is arbitrary and discriminatory, and (3) it is indefinite and meaningless.

The appellate court agreed with the lower court's ruling that the contested items were not exempt proprietaries but dismissed the complaint against Wakeen on the basis of the unconstitutionality of the statute in question—the provision unlawfully delegated a legislative power to the Board. The circuit court judge felt that the legislature could not delegate to an independent body the lawmakers' power to define terms.

Upon appeal to the Wisconsin Supreme Court, the circuit court was reversed. A large number of authorities were cited to show that the legislature's action was proper and that about the only nondelegatable power is that of enacting new laws. Thus, the original conviction was sustained and the case remanded to the lower court for continuation of the proceedings.

[82] *State* v. *Wakeen*, 263 Wis. 401, 57 N.W. 2d 364 (1953).

The effect of the *Wakeen* case is that grocery stores and other nondrugstore retail outlets may not sell unbranded nonprescription drugs. This is the result of the Supreme Court's upholding of (1) the U.S.P. as a proper identifier of drugs and (2) the provision in the state law that only druggists may sell drugs.

MICHIGAN: THE WRIGLEY'S STORES CASE[83]

The *Annotated Statutes of Michigan*, Section 14.740, lists thirty-nine drug products that grocers may sell and also permits the general sale of "any patents and proprietaries." Since the Michigan Pharmacy Act did not contain a definition of "drugs," the Michigan Board of Pharmacy adopted a definition by regulation in the early 1950's which it had copied from the Michigan Pure Food and Drug Act:

The term "drug" shall include all medicines and preparations recognized in the United States Pharmacopoeia or National Formulary for internal and external use, and any substance, or mixture of substances, intended to be used for the cure, mitigation, or prevention of disease of either man or other animals.

According to the Board, its regulation forbade food stores to sell any item listed in the U.S.P. or N.F., notwithstanding the exemptions contained in the body of the pharmacy act. When the Board threatened prosecution of grocery stores that sold U.S.P. or N.F. items, a group of food retailers appealed to the courts for a declaration of their rights to merchandise the disputed items.

The lower court held for the grocers:

1. Regardless of how suitable the definition of a drug (adopted by regulation to apply to pharmacy law) may be for purposes of the pure food and drug act, it is not a proper basis upon which to assert monopolistic selling rights by pharmacists.
2. There is no reason to limit the sale of the articles in dispute to pharmacists because (a) both grocers and pharmacists purchase these products from the same sources, (b) the goods are sold in the original containers of the various manufacturers under their trademarks, (c) the items are legally salable to the general public without restriction, (d) the potions fall within the common understanding of the words "patent and proprietary medicines," and (e) the disputed remedies are no more dangerous (and in most cases are less dangerous) than items explicitly named in the pharmacy act as salable by grocers.

[83] *Wrigley's Stores, Inc.* v. *Board of Pharmacy*, 336 Mich. 583, 59 N.W. 2d 8 (1953).

3. The preparations in question, the evidence shows, are commonly sold in drugstores by clerks, and frequently by self-service methods, so there is no difference between the way drugstores distribute the items and the way they are sold by grocery stores.

The defendant Board, upon appeal to the Michigan Supreme Court, marshalled a number of arguments in its defense. All were refused by the court, which affirmed the lower court's decision. The arguments of the Board and the comments of the Supreme Court are presented below in tabular form.

Defendant's Argument	*Supreme Court Reply*
1. The definition for a drug was properly adopted because the Pure Food and Drug Act is the same sort of promulgation as the pharmacy act.	1. The defendants have no power to adopt a definition which changes the scope, purpose and meaning of the pharmacy act as respects exemptions.
2. The pharmacy act, as amended in 1921, should be construed to negate the exemptions in the pharmacy act promulgated earlier.	2. The 1921 amendment did not negate the exemptions because a 1927 enactment specifically referred to and continued to allow the exemptions previously enacted in 1901.
3. Patents and proprietary medicines mentioned as exemptions apply only to preparations protected by patent or a secret manufacturing process.	3. The legislative intent, as exemplified by the original list of exemptions and its 1927 affirmation, is to permit the sale of ordinary or domestic household remedies, as well as the so-called patent and proprietary medicines. "We conclude that the permission given . . . to sell patent or proprietary medicines, was not intended to be limited to the rare class of patented medicines or secret formulas, but does include authorization to sell prepackaged, non-prescription, mass-produced remedies put up for sale to the general public . . . under the trade name of the manufacturer."

4. Only the legislature may determine which articles are to
be exempted.

4. Since the plaintiffs have been
"virtually threatened" with
prosecution, they are entitled
to the protection of the court
when they can prove that the
articles whose sale is contested
fall within the general terms
of the exemption.

DISTRICT OF COLUMBIA: THE SAFEWAY CASE[84]

On April 29, 1958, two police officers assigned to the Narcotics
Squad of the Metropolitan Police Department purchased a sealed 100-
tablet bottle of Bayer Aspirin from a nonpharmacist store checker
"at the Safeway store located at 21st and K Streets in Washington,
D.C." The store was then charged with violation of Section 2-601 of
the District Code. This section provides that only pharmacists may
sell drugs, with certain exceptions, one of which permits persons other
than registered pharmacists to "sell in original sealed containers, properly labeled, such compounds as are commonly known as 'patent' or
'proprietary' medicines . . ."

In his September 15, 1958 decision, Judge Harry L. Walker noted
that in view of the provision of the law allegedly violated by Safeway,
the only question to determine was whether Bayer Aspirin is a proprietary medicine. If so, the defendant was innocent; otherwise, the defendant was guilty.

Judge Walker found Safeway innocent by concluding that Bayer
Aspirin is a proprietary:

1. The Chairman of the District Commissioners had stated (in a
letter), to the Senate Committee considering the bill which became a law, that the proposed enactment specifically exempted
from its provision patent and proprietary articles not containing
poisonous ingredients.

2. At the time of passage of the law, Bayer was a patented product
and continued to be so until 1921. Mere expiration of a patent
does not change the product's innocuous nature. Therefore, it
is reasonable to presume that Congress intended all patents to
be included in the exemption regardless of the expiration date
of the patent.

3. Safeway is permitted to sell Bayer and other aspirin in the adjoining states of Maryland, Virginia and Pennsylvania.

[84] *District of Columbia* v. *Safeway Stores, Inc.*, Criminal No. DC9538-58, Munic.
Ct. D.C., Sept. 15, 1958.

4. In the District, the defendant is allowed to sell Anacin, Bufferin, Bromo-Seltzer and Alka-Seltzer, all of which contain aspirin. Hence, the public health is seemingly not served "by enforcement of the rule proscribing the sale of aspirin tablets other than under the supervision of a licensed pharmacist."

5. "It is a cardinal rule of statutory interpretation that in the absence of any definitions to the contrary the words in a statute should be given their commonly accepted connotation." Although Webster's Dictionary gives a technical definition of proprietaries (patented or using a secret process), a survey of 1,000 District of Columbia citizens revealed that 78 percent considered Bayer a proprietary, 7 percent had no opinion, and only 15 percent did not consider Bayer a proprietary.

6. It may be true, as the plaintiff contends, that aspirin tablets do not fall within the technical definitions of patent and proprietary items, but the Yale Law Journal has said that such a definition is unacceptable, arguing that if a product is found to be dangerous, it should be placed on prescription basis.

The court concluded by warning that its finding of innocence should not be construed as a precedent for products other than aspirin.

IOWA: THE MAC'S GROCERY CASE[85]

In Iowa, it had been decided that nondrug outlets could not sell aspirin because it is not a proprietary medicine.[86] In 1957, however, the Iowa legislature amended the pharmacy law by adding a definition of proprietary medicine that generally conforms to the common-usage meaning of the term.

On behalf of the Board of Pharmacy, the State brought suit against Walter McEwen, who had been selling Bayer Aspirin at his Mac's Grocery without a pharmacy license. The plea was for an injunction (to prevent the illegal sales) and a declaratory judgment (that the newly enacted definition did not apply to the entire pharmacy act). Judge Dring D. Needham denied the plaintiff's requests, noting that the legislature had recently revised the law to bring such items as aspirin within the proprietary medicines definition.

On appeal to the Iowa Supreme Court, the plaintiff's main argument was that when the legislature revised the law, the amending act itself was the only part of the statute to which the definition was applicable. This contention was based on the fact that the addition to the law

---

[85] *State ex rel Board of Pharmacy Examiners* v. *McEwen*, 250 Iowa 721, 96 N.W.2d 189 (1959).

[86] *State ex rel Board of Pharmacy Examiners* v. *Jewett Mkt. Co.*, 209 Iowa 567, 228 N.W. 288 (1929).

began "for the purpose of this Act, . . . proprietary medicine . . ."
The state (for the Board of Pharmacy) alleged that the word "act"
meant that the new definition was to apply only to the new enactment
and not the whole chapter. In that case the new definition would not
apply to the exemption for proprietaries clause in another part of the
chapter and hence the plaintiff's case would be sustained.

The Supreme Court rejected this line of reasoning and sustained
the lower court's decision. The state's highest tribunal explained that
one has to look beyond a word or a phrase and see the chapter as
an entity as far as legislative intent is concerned. The justices concluded
that the purpose of the new definition was to apply to the entire
chapter.

IDAHO: THE SLUSSER WHOLESALE CO. CASE[87]

An Idaho case involving a wholesaler acting as a rack jobber[88]
is important for purposes of this study because of the nature of the
products involved. The Idaho Board of Pharmacy brought suit against
Slusser Wholesale Company to enjoin it from placing certain items
in retail outlets not licensed as pharmacies. These products were all
antihistamines: Super Anahist Cough Syrup, Super Anahist APC Compound, Super Anahist Antibiotic Nasal Spray, Dristan Decongestant
Nasal Mist, and Dristan Decongestant Tablets.

The Board initiated the suit under its authority to regulate the
sale of "poisonous, habit forming or dangerous drugs." District Judge
Henry Martin ruled that the products were proprietaries and that
therefore they did not come under the Board's jurisdiction.

This appears to have been a rather important decision. In other
cases, the products where sale was being questioned were innocuous
unless consumed in massive doses. With antihistamines, however, an
individual may experience drowsiness if the medication is taken.[89]

Important Issues in Sales Restriction Litigation

In the many sales restriction cases that have come before the higher
state courts, two questions have been of paramount importance: Are
the contested products safe when sold in unsupervised outlets and are

[87] "Top Court May Get Antihistamine Case," *American Druggist*, December
11, 1961, p. 8.
[88] A rack jobber sets up displays of products in various outlets and keeps the
displays stocked. The rack jobber sells at slightly above wholesale prices to the
store owner, but by employing the services of the rack jobber, the store owner
does not have to order merchandise or stock shelves.
[89] To counteract the drowsiness tendency, FDA requires the inclusion of caffein
(or other stimulant) in nonprescription decongestant compounds containing
antihistamines.

the products proprietaries according to state law? When these questions have been answered affirmatively, sales restriction barriers applicable to proprietary items have fallen.

Every high court has concluded that the products involved in the particular litigation before it are safe enough to be sold and consumed without the supervision of a pharmacist, even taking into account that some danger is involved because of surreptitious overdosages by children and mentally deranged persons. Taken as a group, the court cases have included twenty-five nationally advertised nonprescription remedies.

The area in which the tribunals have disagreed is the proprietary status of the products under examination. Table 6-1 summarizes the courts' positions regarding the proprietary status of various products. There seems to be three different definitions of proprietary medicines that the courts have used. These interpretations have always been the crucial points in the cases because all state laws except Nevada allow the unrestricted sale of proprietary medicines.

The definition used in some of the early sales restriction cases and in two of the suits (Minnesota and Wisconsin—see Table 6-1) discussed in this chapter was the technical definition. According to this interpretation, a medicine can be a proprietary only if its ingredients are secret, if its manufacturing process is secret, or if the product is patented (not trademarked). Using this definition, courts have reached different conclusions regarding a particular product's proprietary status. In the cases mentioned in this chapter, of the two state high courts embracing the technical definition, only one held it unlawful to sell the items.

When the two other definitions were adopted, the courts have rather uniformly concluded that the particular products they were considering were proprietary medicines. These two definitions are similar but are not identical. The one most frequently used is that any trademarked product not requiring a prescription is a proprietary. Under this ruling, all of the nationally advertised products may be sold on an unrestricted basis. This definition, called the "common-usage" definition, appears to have been applied by the high courts of New Jersey, New York, Michigan, and Iowa and by courts in the District of Columbia and Idaho.

A third definition used is what might be termed the FDA definition. In this case, any product cleared by the FDA for over-the-counter (nonprescription) sale may be sold in any outlet. This differs from the "common-usage" definition in that a product need not be trademarked to be a proprietary—and therefore unrestricted sale—product. FDA itself does not determine the proprietary status. It merely decides

TABLE 6-1: Summary of Court Decisions on the Restrictive Sales Issue

State and Year	Court or Location	Products and Declaration as to Proprietary Status	Definition Used	Defendant
New Jersey (1955)	Camden County District Court	Bayer Aspirin and Phillip's Milk of Magnesia are proprietaries.	Common Usage	American Stores Corp.
New Jersey (1956)	Camden County, Toms River, Cape May, Jersey City, Mercer County, and Mt. Holly	Boric acid, citrate of magnesia, and tincture of iodine are not proprietaries.	Technical	—
New Jersey (1957)	Bergen County District Court	Anacin, Aspergum, Alka-Seltzer, Bromo-Quinine, Bromo-Seltzer, Bufferin, Carter's Little Liver Pills, Ex-Lax, Fletcher's Castoria, Pepto-Bismol, Phillip's Milk of Magnesia, Plough Children's Aspirin, Sal Hepatica, and Vick's Va-Tra-Nol are proprietaries.	Common Usage	Honey Dew Food Markets
New Jersey (1963)	Supreme Court	Citrate of magnesia is a proprietary.	Common Usage	Anderson's Market
New York (1962)	Court of Appeals	Bayer Aspirin is a proprietary.	Common Usage	Loblaw, Inc.
Minnesota (1962)	Supreme Court	Alka-Seltzer, Anacin, Aspergum, Bromo-Quinine, Bromo-Seltzer, Bufferin, castoria, Ex-Lax, Feen-A-Mint, 4-Way Cold Tablets, Lysol, Murine, Pepto-Bismol, Pinex, Sal Hepatica, Vick's Cough Syrup, and Vick's Va-Tra-Nol are not proprietaries. (The court, however, refused to issue an injunction to prevent the sale of the products by defendants.)	Technical	Red Owl Stores, Inc. and Groves-Kelco, Inc.

TABLE 6-1 (*Continued*)

State and Year	Court or Location	Products and Declaration as to Proprietary Status	Definition Used	Defendant
Wisconsin (1953)	Supreme Court	Aspirin, milk of magnesia, and camphorated oil are not proprietaries.	Technical	Wakeen
Michigan (1953)	Supreme Court	No specific product	Common Usage	Wrigley's Stores, Inc.
District of Columbia (1958)	Municipal Court	Bayer Aspirin is a proprietary.	Common Usage	Safeway Stores, Inc.
Iowa (1959)	Supreme Court	Bayer Aspirin is a proprietary	Clarified Amended Proprietary Exemption Clause	Mac's Grocery
Idaho (1961)	State District Court	Dristan Decongestant Nasal Mist, Dristan Decongestant Tablets, Super Anahist Antibiotic Nasal Spray, Super Anahist Cough Syrup, and Super Anahist APC Compound are proprietaries.	Common Usage	Slusser Wholesale Co.

prescription or nonprescription status. The reason for the use of this definition seems to be that the courts employing it have determined that the proprietary exemption clause is intended as a safety measure. That is, the legislatures intended to permit unlimited retail distribution of all medicines where it is safe to do so, and the only reason for restricting the sale of drugs to drugstores is to effect a safety device.

In addition to their judicial opinions, the courts have criticized legislatures for not modernizing this section of the state law. This criticism, however, has not provoked the promulgation of new laws in the states where they are most needed—Minnesota and New Jersey. Apparently the inaction is because of the strength possessed by the two opposing factions, grocers and druggists. Neither has the power to force through the state legislature its own bill, and neither will compromise enough to suit the other.

A fourth definition for proprietary drugs has, as discussed in Chapter 5, been advocated by The Proprietary Association. Under this definition, all trademarked and advertised nonprescription drugs would be proprietaries and therefore could be sold in any retail outlet. This proposal is primarily intended as a compromise between pharmacist groups who prefer the technical (restrictive) definition and general merchants who prefer the common usage or FDA definition. Pharmacists object to this definition because it leaves the initiative to the manufacturers, who, having already trademarked their products, only have to begin advertising to change the classification of the products.

It might be supposed that the various court actions have obviated the need for legislation in many jurisdictions. The contrary seems to be true. For those who have had decisions rendered against them in the various states, the rulings indicate a greater need for new legislation than existed previously. That the issue is not dead is indicated by the fact that restrictionist bills were proposed in Massachusetts and New York in 1966 and in South Dakota in 1967.

The problem before the state legislatures has been to select the appropriate definition for proprietary medicines. Eight states have selected that advocated by The Proprietary Association. Four additional states have appointed commissions to study the problem and to submit recommendations to the legislatures. The New York Commission supported the FDA definition, while the Minnesota Commission recommended adoption of The Proprietary Association definition. When the Minnesota Commission recommendation failed to produce a new law, the matter was studied by a special subcommittee of the Minnesota Senate Civil Administration Committee. The subcommittee's conclusion was "that the regulation of the sale of home remedies is not a proper matter for a state agency [Board of Pharmacy], given the current state and federal laws applicable and the questions of public interest involved."[90] Noting that there were several methods of clarifying the fact that the Board is not to have authority to regulate the distribution of proprietaries, the subcommittee recommended as the easiest, altering the wording of the proprietary exemption that essentially conforms to the wording of The Proprietary Association proposal.[91]

In Massachusetts, the commission's job was to study the three drug class proposal of the Massachusetts Board of Registration in Pharmacy. This proposal was similar to the legislation advocated by the American Pharmaceutical Association and the National Association of Retail Druggists. The commission's report stated that three classes of drugs are not needed in Massachusetts and noted that the present Massachusetts law allowed the sale of trademarked prescription drugs which are advertised directly to the general public.[92] The commission recommended that, rather than establish a third class, the Massachusetts law be amended to require a prescription only status for "harmful drugs." The Connecticut commission's primary conclusion was that no additional state legislation is needed, i.e., there is no need to establish a third class of drugs. Presumably there is no confusion concerning the meaning of proprietary exemption clause. The major recommendation was that FDA require the inclusion of quantities as well as ingredient names in the information on the label.[93]

The definition that seems most appropriate for proprietary drugs is a modification of the FDA definition. The so-called FDA definition, it will be remembered, classifies as proprietaries all drugs designated by FDA as nonprescription items. To further protect the public health, each state could authorize its health department to hold hearings and to confer prescription only status to those FDA-cleared drugs when necessary to preserve public health—the Massachusetts commission recommendation.

[90] Letter Report from H. Blair Klein to Henry M. Harren, Chairman, Minnesota Senate Civil Administration Committee, dated December 27, 1966, p. 2.

[91] *Ibid.*, p. 14.

[92] Massachusetts, *Report of the Special Commission Established to Make an Investigation and Study Relative to Establishing and Regulating a New Category of Over-the-Counter Proprietary Preparations Used for Self-Treatment to Be Known as "Potentially Harmful" Drugs*, House Document No. 3075, January 1966, pp. 4–10.

[93] Connecticut, *Report of the Commission to Study Potentially Harmful Drugs*, submitted to the January 1967 session of the Legislature, pp. 9–10.

PART THREE

Restrictive Pharmacy Laws and the Resulting Litigation

CHAPTER SEVEN

Pharmacy Ownership Restrictions

Simply stated, pharmacy ownership restrictions are intended to prohibit certain nonpharmacist classes from owning drugstores. The objective of the limitations evidently is to enhance the competitive position of the independent proprietor-pharmacist by obstructing entry into the retail drug market.

Not all ownership restrictions exist in the form of statutes. Some are imposed through the regulations promulgated by the various state boards of pharmacy. These regulations have the force of law until and unless it is shown through the adjudication process that the particular regulation in question is (1) beyond the power conferred upon the board by the state legislature, (2) unreasonable, (3) unrelated to public health, or (4) unconstitutional.

It is the purpose of this chapter to (1) examine some of the early litigation involving ownership legislation, (2) explain existing and proposed ownership requirements, (3) indicate recent legislative activity in the field, and (4) detail the rationale of the advocates of pharmacy ownership legislation. In addition, the groups excluded from drugstore proprietorship and the degree of exclusion (when it is not complete) are analyzed in the course of this chapter.

Historical Validity of Pharmacy Ownership Legislation

Pharmacy ownership legislation is rooted in the traditional opposition of independent retail druggists to chain store operations. This antagonism was inspired by the tremendous growth of chain stores (in all retail industries) between 1910 and 1930.[1] The drug chains moved aggressively to capture a share of the retail drug market and their rapid expansion (a twenty-fold increase in twenty years) instilled

[1] See Chapter 2.

in the independents the fear that they soon would be driven from the market.

One result of this anxiety was the enactment of several state laws that proscribed the corporate ownership of drugstores by nonpharmacists. The first restrictive law was passed in New York State and became effective April 24, 1923. Pennsylvania enacted a similar provision in 1927, as did Michigan. A few other states, including Delaware, added ownership laws to their statutes during the same period.[2]

As the following cases illustrate, pharmacy ownership laws have consistently been declared unconstitutional.

LIGGETT V. BALDRIDGE[3]

The 1928 *Liggett* case was one of the first legal contests involving pharmacy ownership legislation. The decision has become a landmark in that area.

The Liggett Company, a Massachusetts corporation, was operating a chain drugstore business in Pennsylvania when that state passed its ownership law. Liggett, contrary to the new law, opened two additional outlets and applied for pharmacy permits. The Pennsylvania Board of Pharmacy refused to issue the licenses. In addition, the State's Attorney General and the District Attorney of Philadelphia County reportedly "threatened and intend to and will prosecute [Liggett] . . . for its violations of the act, the penalties for which are severe and cumulative."

Liggett brought suit to prevent the officials from fulfilling their threats. The plea for relief was based on the assertion that the Pennsylvania ownership law denied equal protection under law, as guaranteed by amendment fourteen to the U.S. Constitution. The offending law stated:

Section 1. Every pharmacy or drug store shall be owned only by a licensed pharmacist, and no corporation, association, or copartnership shall own a pharmacy or drug store, unless all the partners or members thereof are licensed pharmacists; except that any corporation organized and existing under the laws of the Commonwealth or of any other state of the United States, and authorized to do business in the Commonwealth, and empowered by its charter to own and conduct pharmacies or drug stores, and any association or copartnership which, at the time of passage of this act, still owns and conducts a registered pharmacy or pharmacies or a drug store or drug stores in the Commonwealth, may continue to

---

[2] P. H. Costello, "Survey of Pharmacy Law," *Proceedings of the National Association of Boards of Pharmacy* (Chicago, 1951), p. 60.
[3] *Louis K. Liggett Co. v. Baldridge*, 278 U.S. 105 (1928).

own and conduct the same; but no other or additional pharmacies or drug stores shall be established, owned, or conducted by such corporation, association, or copartnership, unless all the members or partners thereof are registered pharmacists; but any such corporation, association, or copartnership, which shall not continue to own at least one of the pharmacies or drug stores theretofore owned by it, or ceases to be actively engaged in the conduct of a pharmacy, shall not thereafter be permitted to own a pharmacy or drug store . . .

Section 2. Any person, copartnership, or corporation, violating the provisions of this act, shall be guilty of a misdemeanor and, upon conviction thereof, shall be sentenced to pay a fine of not more than one hundred dollars. Each day any such pharmacy is owned contrary to the provisions of this act shall be considered a separate offense.[4]

Defendant Baldridge, the Pennsylvania Attorney General, asked that the law be sustained on the ground that its purpose was to promote the public health. The lower courts (the Court of Common Pleas for Philadelphia County and the U.S. District Court for Eastern Pennsylvania) ruled in favor of the defendant. In support of finding the law reasonably related to preserving the public health, the District Court said:

1. Medicines must be in a store before they can be dispensed.
2. The drugs that comprise the firm's inventory are dictated not by the judgement of the pharmacist but by those who have financial control of the outlet.
3. The Pennsylvania legislature may have thought that a corporate owner might give greater regard to price than quality in ordering drugs.
4. If that was the thought of the legislature the court will not undertake to say that the law was without a valid connection to the public health or so unreasonable to render the statute invalid.

The U.S. Supreme Court, to which the decision was appealed, also viewed the law's relation to the public health as the salient issue. But the Court held that there was no reasonable association between the law and the preservation of public health and declared the ownership law unconstitutional.

In speaking for the majority in the seven-two decision, Justice Sutherland reasoned as follows:

1. There is no doubt that the legislature can regulate pharmacy to protect the public health.

[4] *Pa. Stat.* s. 9377a-1 and 9377a-2 (Supp. 1928).

2. The Pennsylvania legislature has already done this by enacting a number of laws to assure drug quality, to prevent all except physicians from prescribing drugs, and to outlaw the filling of prescriptions by nonpharmacists.
3. It would seem that every point at which public health is likely to be injuriously affected by acts of the owner or a drug firm is adequately safeguarded.
4. The ownership law does not deal with safeguards, but with denial of a property right which the Constitution guarantees.

Justice Sutherland's concluding paragraph is long, but worthy of a direct and complete quote, especially since it summarizes the issue so forcefully:

In the light of the various requirements of the Pennsylvania statutes, it is made clear, if it were otherwise doubtful, that mere stock ownership in a corporation, owning and operating a drug store, can have no real or substantial relation to public health; and that the act in question creates an unreasonable and unnecessary restriction upon private business. No facts are presented by the record, and, so far as appears, none were presented to the legislature which enacted the statute, that properly could give rise to a different conclusion. It is a matter of public notoriety that chain drug stores in great numbers, owned and operated by corporations, are to be found throughout the United States. They have been in operation for many years. We take judicial notice of the fact that the stock in these corporations is bought and sold upon the various stock exchanges of the country, and, in the nature of things, must be held and owned to a large extent by persons who are not registered pharmacists. If detriment to the public health thereby has resulted or is threatened, some evidence of it ought to be forthcoming. None has been produced, and, so far as we are informed, either by the record or outside of it, none exists. The claim, that mere ownership of a drug store by one not a pharmacist bears a reasonable relation to the public health, finally rests upon conjecture, unsupported by anything of substance. This is not enough; and it becomes our duty to declare the act assailed to be unconstitutional as in contravention of the due process clause of the Fourteenth Amendment. Decree reversed.[5]

OTHER EARLY LITIGATION

A week after the *Liggett* decision, an almost identical case came before the Pennsylvania Supreme Court. The defendant in this second action noted that in the *Liggett* case the U.S. Supreme Court had remarked upon the failure of the state to demonstrate that the Pennsyl-

[5] *Liggett, supra* note 3, at 113–114.

vania legislature had considered the relationship between an ownership law and the public health. The defendant's argument thus attempted to illustrate that the legislature had enacted the law because: (1) a pharmacy owned by a licensed pharmacist is more likely to give proper service to the public in the compounding and sale of drugs than one owned by a nonpharmacist, and (2) the legislation would tend to lessen violations of the National Prohibition Act and laws restricting the sale of narcotics. The court did not see the relevance of the arguments. It cited *Liggett* and declared the Pennsylvania law unconstitutional.[6] The decision was not appealed.

Shortly after the second Pennsylvania case was decided, New York's ownership law came before that state's highest court. The same argument that was advanced in the second Pennsylvania case was used in trying to establish the constitutionality of the New York law. The court, by referring to the *Liggett* proceedings and the second Pennsylvania case, declared the New York law unconstitutional.[7] The decision was not appealed.

Three years later, in 1934, the Court of General Sessions of Delaware heard a case testing that state's ownership law. The bench ruled the law unconstitutional in a rather brief decision:

This case involves "ownership" alone.

The consideration of this case need not be unduly extended for the almost identical language of the Delaware act has been considered and statutes embodying it held unconstitutional by the Supreme Court of the United States and by the courts of last resort of Pennsylvania and New York.[8]

Types of Ownership Restrictions

The various ownership laws and regulations in force or under consideration are not uniform. The individual states have endeavored to draw their proposals in such a way as to fit their own needs. Still, a model ownership law designed to surmount the constitutional obstacles raised by *Liggett* is being circulated among advocates of the legislation.

PHYSICIAN OWNERSHIP

Perhaps the least restrictive of all the various types of ownership laws is that prohibiting physician ownership of pharmacies—because

---

[6] *Evans* v. *Baldridge,* 294 Pa. 142, 144 Atl. 97 (1928).
[7] *Prather* v. *Lascoff,* 261 N.Y. 509, 185 N.E. 716 (1933).
[8] *State* v. *People's Drug Stores, Inc.,* 36 Del. (6 W. W. Harr) 120, 172 Atl. 257 (Ct. Gen. Sess. 1934).

such laws allow anyone except physicians to own drugstores. Such a law was enacted by California in 1963. Known as the Holmes Act, the California statute stipulates that after June 1, 1967, physicians shall not have a proprietary interest in pharmacies. The law also does not permit owner relationships already in existence to continue—physicians had almost four years after passage of the bill to divest themselves of their pharmacy interests. The constitutionality of this legislation is now being tested in court.

A similar act has been promulgated in Maryland. Although the Maryland law does not specifically prevent doctors from owning pharmacies, the statute achieves that effect. Pharmacists are prevented from being employed in a physician-owned drugstore or from being a co-owner of a pharmacy with a physician.[9] These activities are categorized as part of a group of functions defined by the law as "grossly unprofessional conduct" for which the board of pharmacy is authorized to suspend or revoke a registered pharmacist's license. The law permits preexisting arrangements between pharmacists and physicians to continue. Nevertheless, the effect of the prohibition is to produce a gradual attrition of physician-owned drugstores as pharmacists associated with physicians terminate their employment, retire, or die. A Pennsylvania law and a Mississippi regulation resemble the Maryland statute.

Colorado has adopted still another way of protecting against physician ownership. Pharmacists are required not to "accept professional employment from any persons who, for compensation, prescribe drugs used in the compounding or dispensing of prescriptions." This clause is contained in the rules of professional conduct promulgated by the Board of Pharmacy as regulations.[10] Since pharmacists are subject to suspension or revocation of their licenses if they violate either pharmacy regulations or law, the ban is as effective as a statutory provision—unless a judiciary body construes such a regulation as assumption by a board of legislative authority. It is this possibility of court negation that has caused the Colorado Board of Pharmacy not to attempt to enforce its 1963 restrictive regulation until litigation currently in progress is settled.[11]

[9] As is true in California, this same relationship with dentists, veterinarians, and other medical practitioners is outlawed.

[10] Recently there has been a growing trend toward the compiling of rules or codes of professional conduct applicable to druggists. Sometimes the codes are enacted directly by the legislature, while in other states the legislature specifically authorizes the board of pharmacy to promulgate the rules. In a few cases, such as Colorado, a code is issued as part of a board's general rule-making authority. Most of the rules generally are innocuous, but in nearly every case one or two provisions that constitute free market restrictions can be found.

[11] The suit was initiated by a group of Denver clinics. "Board Defers Enforcement of Ban on Employment in Doctor-Stores," American Druggist, October 25, 1965, p. 32.

Utah also prohibits physician ownership of pharmacies by regulation, but it is a standard regulation, not part of a code of conduct. The rule states that the board of pharmacy will refuse to issue a pharmacy license to "any pharmacy which is owned by a physician, group of physicians, clinic or any other group of medical practitioners, which group of practitioners is authorized by law to prescribe drugs or medicines. . . ." So far as is known, no court test of the regulation is pending.

Altogether, then, six states have moved to exclude physicians from owning retail drug outlets. Three states (California, Maryland, and Pennsylvania) have enacted laws to that end, and three boards of pharmacy (Colorado, Mississippi, and Utah) have adopted regulations, designed to preclude the existence of physician-owned pharmacies. In this connection, it is interesting to note that an Alabama regulation specifically authorizes physician ownership of a pharmacy if the pharmacy fills only that physician's prescriptions.

PHARMACIST OWNERSHIP

Only four states, Michigan, North Dakota, South Dakota, and Montana,[12] now have laws or regulations that require pharmacies or a certain percentage thereof to be owned by pharmacists. The Michigan law is a relic of pre-*Liggett* days, having been enacted before the rendering of that famous decision. This regulation requires a minimum 25 percent pharmacist ownership of all drugstores.

Minnesota has a regulation of this type, but the state supreme court's decision in the *Red Owl* case would seem to have nullified the effectiveness of the rule. See Chapter 8. Wyoming had a regulation requiring 51 percent of the stock of an incorporated pharmacy to be owned by a pharmacist, which regulation was struck down by the state attorney general in 1957.

The only state to have enacted a comprehensive ownership law since the early 1930's is North Dakota. The state's Board of Pharmacy previously had promulgated a regulation similar to the present law, but the prior restriction was struck down by the North Dakota Supreme Court early in 1957. The present law was signed into effect on March 11, 1963.[13] The statute requires (1) drugstore proprietorships to be wholly owned by a North Dakota registered pharmacist, (2) drug enterprises operated as partnerships to be jointly owned by North Dakota registered pharmacists, and (3) drugstores organized as corpo-

[12] "Wyoming Atty-Genl Rules That Grocers May Accept Rxs To Be Filled Elsewhere," *American Druggist*, April 22, 1957, p. 5.

[13] "North Dakota Owner Law Passes; No Protest Heard," *Drug News Weekly*, April 10, 1963, pp. 1, 9.

rations to be majority owned by North Dakota registered pharmacists, with the majority stockholders being regularly and actively employed in the corporation-owned pharmacies. The South Dakota law is similar to the North Dakota statute, but a board regulation allows the South Dakota board to waive the law if the regulatory agency so chooses.

Montana, by Board of Pharmacy regulation, requires pharmacist ownership of pharmacies. It is not likely that the regulation would be sustained in court, since, on the basis of the 1957 North Dakota Supreme Court Decision, such a rule amounts to legislation, an activity reserved exclusively for the legislature.

NARD MODEL LAW[14]

For many years the National Association of Retail Druggists (NARD) has favored ownership legislation. At some time during nearly every NARD annual convention a resolution is passed reiterating the organization's dedication to the principle. The current model law advocated by NARD was drafted in response to a convention resolution of October 10, 1963. The euphemism now being used designates the proposed statute as a "pharmacy control law."

The basic provision of the model law is based on the fact that all the states require a permit (or certificate of registration) for operation of a pharmacy in addition to the employment of a licensed pharmacist.[15] The suggested language is as follows:

On and after the effective date of this Act, no person shall be granted a (permit or certificate of registration) to operate a pharmacy, as defined in this Act, or practice pharmacy except:

(1) A registered pharmacist in good standing in this state;
(2) A partnership, each active member of which is a registered pharmacist in good standing in this state; or
(3) A corporation, or association, a majority of the board of directors of which are registered pharmacists of good standing in this state and any one statutory officer of which is a registered pharmacist in good standing in this state and which officer is actively and regularly engaged in, and responsible for the management, supervision, and operation of each such pharmacy. If there are only two or less directors in such corporation or association, at least one (1) shall be a registered pharmacist in good standing in this state.

[14] Herman S. Waller and Sidney Waller, *Pharmacy Ownership Legislation*, A Report Prepared for the National Association of Retail Druggists (Chicago: National Association of Retail Druggists, *ca.* 1964).
[15] Until May of 1966, Kentucky was the lone state not requiring pharmacy licenses ("Kentucky Law Requires License For Hospital Pharmacies & Others," *Drug Topics*, May 2, 1966, p. 22).

The term "pharmacy control" is the phrase invested with significance in the proposed language—nowhere is ownership per se mentioned. Moreover, it is not clear whether a nonpharmacist could *own* a pharmacy and have it managed and controlled by a pharmacist. But it is definitely stated that only a pharmacist can apply for a permit for the pharmacy, except for corporations that have a pharmacist majority sitting on the board of directors.

Although ownership of property is not mentioned in the model law, such a statute would result in a pharmacist monopoly of retail drug outlets. Even if a merchant could own, but not supervise a pharmacy, it is almost a certainty that he would not invest capital in an enterprise that he could neither control nor manage.

ESCAPE CLAUSES

Most ownership laws, existing and proposed, have various escape clauses that permit the continuance of previously established marketing relationships. California is a notable exception. Its law specifically orders physicians to divest themselves of any retail drug interests by June 30, 1967.

Grandfather Clause. The provision that usually prevents interference with proprietorship arrangements that antedate ownership statutes is the grandfather clause. In the case of Maryland, a pharmacist employed by or in partnership with a physician before enactment of the law cannot be prosecuted as a violator. A similar provision is contained in the Michigan law. Corporate "grandfathers" can continue in business and even expand their operations.

The NARD model law would also grant grandfather status to existing corporations, but it appears that future expansion is prevented by giving this standing only to "existing . . . pharmacies owned by . . . [a] corporation" and by preventing the "sale, exchange, or other transfer of an existing pharmacy" except to pharmacist dominated corporations.[16]

Grandfather clauses exist because the U.S. Constitution proscribes *ex post facto* laws—statutes which make illegal and prosecutable actions which were within the law at the time the action was taken. Grandfather provisions, then, demolish one possible legal attack against ownership laws on a constitutionality ground.

Grandfather clauses are also included in proposed ownership statutes for tactical reasons. Legislation that would have an adverse effect on those currently engaging in some pursuit are vehemently opposed; a grandfather provision mutes this group's claim that injury would

---

[16] Waller and Waller, *op. cit.*, p. 5.

be inflicted upon them by the proposed law. Not being prescient, potential entrants into the commercial area affected can hardly be expected to be heard.

Inheritors' Clause. In almost every contemplated ownership legislation, there is a provision allowing the widow or child of a deceased drugstore proprietor to continue to operate the business. If the heir decides to sell the firm at some future date, the transfer must be to a registered pharmacist. The California physician-ownership act, however, does not allow nonpharmacist heirs who are physicians to continue in the retail drug business. Under the NARD model law, the widow or estate representative would have a period of five years in which the property could be operated before divestment becomes mandatory.[17]

The exclusion (or modified exclusion) of heirs is inserted into the law for the similar reasons that grandfathers are allowed. In addition to these constitutional and tactical reasons, there also is the danger of a drastic reduction in the value of the deceased's estate if his heirs are immediately required to liquidate the property to settle federal estate tax levies.[18]

Recent Legislative Activity

In the past few years, as may be inferred from the preceding comments, interest in ownership legislation has once again been aroused. Although efforts for gaining acceptance of the concept were once to be found only in state legislative halls, there now is some activity present at the federal level.

U.S. SENATE HEARINGS

In August 1964 the Subcommittee on Antitrust and Monopoly of the Senate Judiciary Committee conducted hearings concerning physician ownership of pharmacies and drug repackaging companies. The investigation evolved from earlier (Kefauver) hearings that culminated in the 1962 amendments to the Food and Drug Act.

Committee members participating in the Kefauver probe received complaints that some doctors were purchasing drugstores near their offices and that others were establishing clinic operations that included pharmacies. The Subcommittee convened in 1964 to investigate these

---

[17] *Ibid.*, p. 6.
[18] William J. Bowe, *Estate Planning and Taxation: Chartered Life Underwriter Edition* (2nd ed.; Buffalo, N.Y.: Dennis and Co., Inc., 1965), pp. 1–22.

charges and the allegation that drug packaging firms were being established by physicians, thus depriving other drug houses of competitive opportunities.[19]

Incidence of Physician-Owned Pharmacies. The investigation and testimony received during the 1964 hearings established that physician-owned pharmacies are growing in number in so many areas that a national trend toward this type of proprietorship has been created. According to Mr. Philip Jehle, then associate counsel of NARD:

Until 3 years ago . . . the *American Druggist* . . . made an annual . . . survey of M.D.-owned pharmacies. . . . At the end of 1961 . . . it counted about 1,200 such enterprises . . .

The last *American Druggist* survey . . . showed a 15-percent [sic] increase in the number of . . . [physician-owned pharmacies] over the previous year . . . And information which NARD has received from sources such as State pharmacy boards, pharmaceutical association officials, and individual druggists reveals that M.D.-owned pharmacies have substantially increased every year since 1961. We believe that M.D.-owned pharmacies now totals [sic] about 2,200.[20]

Referring to a midwestern state, Mr. Jehle said:

In some cities and towns in this State, every physician is associated with one or more clinic pharmacy. It is estimated the dollar volume of clinic pharmacies in this State will exceed $1 million. Ten percent of the pharmacies in the state are owned by physicians. Physicians involved in ownership of clinic pharmacies number from a low of 3 to a high of 30.[21]

Another witness, Joe H. Arnette, secretary of the Texas State Board of Pharmacy, testified that the number of physician-owned pharmacies was on the increase in Texas. According to Mr. Arnette, in 1960 there were 66 such firms, in 1962 there were 93, and by 1964 there were 117 drugstores controlled by doctors. The secretary further stated that these figures could be understated since the board has no way of determining whether a pharmacy is owned by a physician and registered in a relative's name.[22]

[19] U.S. Senate, Committee on the Judiciary, Subcommittee on Antitrust and Monopoly, *Report, Physician Ownership in Pharmacies and Drug Companies*, 89th Cong., 1st Sess., 1965 (Washington: U.S. Government Printing Office, 1965), p. 1 (hereinafter cited as *Report on Physician Ownership*).

[20] U.S. Senate, Committee on the Judiciary, Subcommittee on Antitrust and Monopoly, *Hearings, Physician Ownership in Pharmacies and Drug Companies*, 88th Cong., 2d Sess., 1964 (Washington: U.S. Government Printing Office, 1965), p. 147 (hereinafter cited as *Hearings on Physician Ownership*).

[21] *Ibid.*, pp. 148–149.

[22] *Ibid.*, p. 6.

A similar trend was noted in California by Benjamin J. Kingswell, president of the California Pharmaceutical Association:

Fifteen years ago we were able to document 39 physician-owned pharmacies in California. . . . In 1962, we documented the fact that 213 pharmacies were owned by physicians in California. . . . From February 1962 to February 1963, there were an additional 39 doctor-owned pharmacies licensed. . . . These figures are minimums because they include only those persons who identified themselves as doctors on the pharmacy application.[23]

Paul Pumpian, secretary of the Wisconsin State Board of Pharmacy, cited comparable statistics. He pointed out that although there are only twenty-four physician-owned pharmacies in Wisconsin, all but five have been established since 1960.[24]

In addition to these specific statements, the Subcommittee received a host of letters from pharmacists describing the prevalence of physician-owned drug firms in such widely separated locations as east Tennessee; Watertown, South Dakota; and Clovis, New Mexico.[25] Hawaii, too, apparently is experiencing the phenomenon:

A private report states that between 60 and 70 percent of all medicines in that State is dispensed by physicians or physician-owned pharmacies. In Honolulu, 12 to 15 clinic pharmacies, owned by doctors, reportedly handle 50 percent of all prescription business in the city.[26]

Despite the evident nationwide trend, physician ownership of pharmacies is concentrated in four states that, combined, contain about 60 percent of all the doctor-owned drugstores. The four (Texas—125, California—95, Illinois—45, and Louisiana—33 encompass 298 of 510 known physician-owned pharmacies. Although these figures are not too recent, they indicate that physician-ownership of pharmacies tends to be more prevalent in certain areas, a situation that is verified by the fact that thirty-eight other states have less than ten physician-owned pharmacies each.[27] Conversations with executive secretaries of boards of pharmacy indicate that physician-owned pharmacies constitute a problem in certain sections of Arkansas, Missouri, and Iowa.

Competition and Physician-Owned Pharmacies. The major objection pharmacists have to physician-owned drugstores is the contention that it is difficult to compete effectively with the doctors. This com-

[23] *Ibid.,* p. 163.
[24] *Ibid.,* p. 204.
[25] *Report on Physician Ownership, op. cit.,* pp. 22–29.
[26] *Ibid.,* p. 28.
[27] "Number of MD-Owned Clinic Pharmacies Resumes Rise; 510 Found in Survey," *American Druggist,* November 23, 1958, pp. 5–6. Statistics do not include Hawaii.

plaint would seem to be justified in view of the economic peculiarities associated with the sale of prescriptions.[28] Because of his intimate relationship with the patient, the physician can, if he wishes, easily influence the patient to purchase any needed medication from the doctor's pharmacy. Various methods such as coded prescriptions, imprinted prescription blanks, direct telephone connection with the drugstore, and suggestive statements ("Get this filled downstairs.") may be used to great advantage.[29]

Over and above these business (and hence profit) procuring tactics, physician-owned pharmacies have several cost-saving possibilities not available to other type drugstores:

1. Doctor-owned outlets can achieve a lower inventory level than other firms by the adoption of a sort of formulary system. That is, only one brand of a given drug is prescribed, and thus stocked. Other pharmacies must carry several varieties since more than one type may be prescribed and since it is illegal to substitute another brand for the one called for in a prescription.
2. Stocking only one brand permits bulk-rate purchases of that drug as opposed to the more expensive small lot buying of several varieties of a drug.
3. Samples distributed to doctors by the representatives of pharmaceutical manufacturing firms can be sent to the pharmacy and sold (usually not legal).
4. Generic drugs can be prescribed (in lieu of brand products) and sold at higher than ordinary prices.[30]

That physicians who own pharmacies are interested in profits is illustrated by the testimony given in connection with hearings held by the California Department of Professional and Vocational Standards in 1962. One witness, describing the hospital pharmacy owned by six physicians practicing in the hospital, was asked, "What is the purpose in filling a prescription with the generic name 'reserpine' rather than filling it with Serpasil?" The reply: "Possibly this will wrap that up pretty fast. On an inventory of less than $10,000 [and by prescribing generic drugs], this operation showed a profit of $90,000 last year."[31]

During the same investigation, the following exchange occurred between Dr. Donald C. Shelby (one of twelve doctor-owners of the

---

[28] See Chapter 12 for a discussion of the economic concepts involved.
[29] Hearings on Physician Ownership, op. cit., p. 189.
[30] Report on Physician Ownership, op. cit., pp. 28–32.
[31] California, Department of Professional and Vocational Standards, California Board of Pharmacy, Hearings, Re Changes in Rules and Regulations of Proposed Section 1769, Vol. II, p. 213. Hearing held in Los Angeles on Feb. 21, 1962.

Moore-White Medical Clinic Pharmacy in Los Angeles) and the questioner:

Q. Did you have anything in mind regarding the profit you may take out of the pharmacy?
A. I should think so. Anybody would.[32]

The conclusion to be drawn from the revelations of the various hearings is fairly obvious. Since doctors are in a better competitive position than pharmacists with respect to procuring retail drugstore trade and, as owners, physicians are interested in increasing profits (through increasing sales), the economic repercussions for other drugstore proprietors can be severe.

Competitive Effects of Physician-Owned Pharmacies. With economic power at their disposal, physicians can and do force pharmacist-owned enterprises out of business. A perhaps typical example was exposed during the California investigation. The incident involved Ross Ferrar, owner of the Beverly Hill Clinic pharmacy, which was located in a building owned by several doctors with offices in the building. In 1957, Ferrar's rental fee to the proprietors was 6 percent of the store's gross sales. Shortly thereafter, the charge was raised to 12 percent. In 1959 pressure was put upon Ferrar to sell his establishment, but he refused. Then, according to Ferrar:

And it got to the point where Dr. Smith said to me, "Well, you're going to sell, or else."
And I said, "Or else what?"
He said, "Well, we could put up another pharmacy in this building somewhere."
Well, the situation continued along those lines 6 or 7 months and I finally decided to sell.[33]

The 1964 Senate hearings revealed a further example of the economic power-wielding potential of physicians. Involved was a two-pharmacy county in Kansas, one of which was owned by a doctor. In the second quarter of 1964, of all the welfare drug claims originating from the two pharmacies, 94 percent were submitted by the physician-controlled store. In another Kansas county, one physician-owned drugstore filled 50 percent of the welfare prescriptions for the quarter.[34]

Further complaints that the Subcommittee received by letter voiced the competitive situation in various locations:[35]

[32] *Ibid.*, p. 113.
[33] *Ibid.*, p. 200. This testimony was substantiated by Edward Berger, manager of the pharmacy when it was owned by Ferrar.
[34] *Report on Physician Ownership, op. cit.*, p. 27.
[35] *Ibid.*, pp. 28–29.

North Dakota:

The doctor writes the prescription and if a woman succeeds in bringing it to her hometown pharmacist, the latter still has to bring this private formula medication from the clinic formula. Just lately they made the medication available through a wholesaler. This private formula is manufactured only for them . . . so that they make a profit on the prescription regardless of where it is filled.

Clovis, New Mexico:

Within the last 2 years, 2 pharmacies have been established there, with 11 of the 12 physicians in Clovis connected with one or the other of them. . . . with only one physician left without an interest in a pharmacy, the other eight [drug] stores there tell me they have suffered considerable financial loss.

North Dakota:

[Before the clinic pharmacy opened, there were two drugstores employing five pharmacists.] Within 9 months [of the opening of the clinic pharmacy] two pharmacists had to seek employment elsewhere. Prescriptions dropped from 60 to 70 daily to less than 10; refills were not honored but were advised or directed to call at the clinic for rechecks. The old vials and bottles were disregarded and new prescriptions issued and filled in their own pharmacy.

Watertown, South Dakota:

Out of the 21 doctors, only 3 practice the ethics of writing the prescription and letting the patient go to the drugstore of their choice. . . . One clinic which has nine doctors own their own pharmacy . . . Another clinic with seven doctors have [sic] a young pharmacist . . . [the doctors] get a large percentage of the gross profit . . . We now have five drugstores in town and I am sure that we don't fill as many [prescriptions] all together as one clinic.

Since the conclusion of the Senate hearings another doctor-ownership situation that resulted in a competitive advantage for the proprietor has been made public. The facts are documented by county welfare records. Dr. George E. Kister, the county physician of St. Charles County, Missouri, holds a one-third interest in Soellner's Prescription Shop, a pharmacy adjacent to and which can be entered from his office. Table 7-1 reveals that over half of the expenditures for welfare prescriptions in St. Charles County have been paid to the doctor's pharmacy. County records indicate that before Dr. Kister became the county physician, the adjoining pharmacy did not receive any income from filling welfare prescriptions. An investigation by the St. Charles Medical Society absolved Dr. Kister of any wrongdoing. Nevertheless, he was roundly criticized by an editorial in the St. Louis Post-Dispatch.[36]

[36] "County MD's Store Gets 63% Of Welfare Business," *Drug Topics*, February 7, 1966, p. 6.

TABLE 7-1: Welfare Prescriptions Filled by Soellner's
Prescription Shop, 1960–1965

Year	Dollar Amount of Welfare Prescriptions Filled in St. Charles County	Welfare Prescriptions Filled by Soellner's	
		Amount	Percent
1960	$ 3132	$ 2672	84.7
1961	5258	3846	73.1
1962	4999	3201	64.0
1963	5571	3682	66.3
1964	5161	2245	43.5
1965[a]	3190	1808	56.7
Total	$27,311	$17,454	63.9

Source: "County MD's Store Gets 63% of Welfare Business,"
Drug Topics, February 7, 1966, p. 6. Used by permission of the
publisher.
ᵃ Does not include all of December.

If only a few of the remarks quoted from the hearings are accurate,
that testimony is sufficient evidence to induce the belief that physicians
who own drugstores exploit the pharmaceutical competitive situation
through the professionally dominant position they occupy in relation
to pharmacists.[37] Such actions may result in an unnatural pattern
of commodity (i.e., drug) distribution that can result in higher prices.
As the Subcommittee concluded:

The possibility of [patient] exploitation would seem sufficient justification for banning doctor-ownership of pharmacies. The record testimony
that doctors have indeed used their prescription power to increase business
of their pharmacies—to the severe financial harm of independent competitors—increases the concern. In either case, it appears that unfair competition practices are involved.[38]

Possibility of Federal Legislation. At the conclusion of the hearings,
Senator Hart, who is chairman of the Antitrust and Monopoly Subcommittee, sent copies of the records of the proceedings and the Subcommittee's report to the Justice Department and the Federal Trade Commission. His purpose was to determine whether some existing federal law

[37] In the physician-pharmacist relationship, the pharmacist is inferior to the
physician even though pharmacists are generally conceded to possess a greater
knowledge of drugs than physicians. State laws enforce the relationship. Physicians
are authorized to prescribe and dispense medication whereas pharmacists are limited
to the dispensing function. Pharmacists, then, are dependent upon physicians' con-
senting to limit themselves to the diagnostic and prescriptive functions, thereby
providing work for pharmacists in the dispensing of drugs.
[38] *Report on Physician Ownership, op. cit.*, p. 33.

could be invoked to force the cessation of the practices disclosed by the investigation. Both agencies replied that there was no federal statute that could be applied to halt the described activities.[39]

The Senator then introduced a bill (1965) intended to remedy the abuses brought to light during his hearings. Appendix II is a copy of the proposal. The purpose was to strengthen antitrust laws by making it unlawful (and punishable by a fine of up to $5,000 and/or up to one year's imprisonment) for a medical practitioner to receive, directly or indirectly, any profit from referring patients to pharmacies or from the sale of prescribed drugs or devices.

Although a spot check of individual pharmacists disclosed that 87 percent favored the Hart Bill,[40] the state pharmaceutical associations took three different positions: (1) direct support, (2) support of the "principle" espoused by the bill, but no support for the bill, and (3) opposition to the bill. The two national associations, the American Pharmaceutical Association (APhA) and the National Association of Retail Druggists (NARD) took opposite positions. NARD favored the bill, while APhA opposed federal legislation on the issue.[41]

One reason for the lack of uniform advocacy is that many pharmacists still feel that the problem is one to be resolved by the professions involved. These druggists contend that a concerted effort to resolve the issue at the professional level would be successful. Another cause of the lack of support is the apprehension that pharmacists have about the American Medical Association (AMA) and the power of the physicians behind it. A careful reading of the proposed federal law seems to indicate that physicians could have eradicated pharmacist-owned drugstores by operating nonprofit drug outlets. The result is that druggists were cautious about endorsing an ownership philosophy that would antagonize those on whom their livelihood depends. Illustrative of pharmacists' reluctance to anger physicians is the resolution adopted by the Minnesota State Pharmaceutical Association in opposition to the Hart Bill. The resolution passed only after a bitter floor fight and after Henry M. Moen, Executive Secretary of the association, said:

> You'll never come out of this alive. When the day comes that they pass the Hart bill you're licked. You know what doctors are going to do. They're going to give the medicine away.[42]

[39] "Justice Dept. Sees Nothing Illegal In Physician-Owned Pharmacies," *American Druggist*, August 16, 1965, p. 14.

[40] "Bill to Curb MD-Owned Pharmacies Receives Strong Support Of RxMen," *Drug Topics*, July 11, 1966, p. 18.

[41] "NARD And APhA Take Opposite Views Of AMA Action On Doctor-Ownership," *American Druggist*, July 18, 1966, pp. 11–13.

[42] As quoted in "Minnesota Pharmacists Nix Hart Bill," *Drug News Weekly*, May 9, 1966, pp. 1, 15.

Finally, some druggists that do not endorse the Hart proposal contend that there has been some indication that the AMA may change its current position (physician-owned pharmacies are ethical if there is no patient exploitation) and return to its 1954 stand (doctor-ownership of pharmacies is strictly unethical). A reversal of the AMA attitude might solve the conflict if AMA can and will apply sanctions to insure that physicians abide by this code of conduct. But a change in AMA policy does not appear to be likely, for even after the June 24, 1966 issue of *Life* magazine, in a main article, criticized physician ownership of drugstores, AMA did not reverse its policy.[43]

Lacking full support from pharmacy organizations, the bill made no headway. Early in 1967, Senator Hart introduced a new bill with the same purpose, but with the features objectionable to pharmacists revised.[44] The new bill makes it unlawful for physicians to have any beneficial interest in pharmacy or to dispense medicines and appliances except that physicians could (1) own pharmacies and dispense in local areas where there are no drugstores, (2) dispense drugs in emergency situations or in unit dosages in their offices.

Support for the bill among pharmacists is more uniform than for the earlier one. About 91 percent of the rank-and-file pharmacists contracted in a survey favored the new bill,[45] as compared to 87 percent in favor of the original bill. APhA also supports the new bill. The reversal of position, according to Chester Bowles, Chairman of the APhA Board of Trustees, is the result of APhA's failure to solve the problem at an interprofessional level.[46]

It is important to note, however, that as the bill is now worded, its passage would not permit vindictive physicians to dispense drugs at cost in their offices as would have been possible under the original bill. Viewing the two bills in terms of the cost of drugs to patients, it may be that the original bill would be better if physicians woud seek revenge (as feared by pharmacists) by selling drugs at cost. The present bill arbitrates the interests of opposing economic groups and favors all drugstores not owned by physicians. In addition to the extra volume to be derived by closing physician-owned drugstores, the bill would also increase total drugs prescribed by virtually eliminating office dispensing by physicians—even if the drugs were free to the patients.

[43] "AMA Is Adamant On Its Stand That Medics Can Own Pharmacies," *Drug Topics*, July 11, 1966, p. 4.

[44] See Appendix III.

[45] "91% Endorse Hart Bill As Long Needed Legislation," *Drug Topics*, May 15, 1967, p. 15.

[46] "Both APhA, NARD Will Back New Hart Bill That Flatly Forbids M D Ownership," *American Druggist*, January 30, 1967, pp. 18–19.

The Economics of Physician Ownership of Drugstores. A large number of physician-owned drugstores have been initiated as a result of the changing methods of the practice of medicine. Two trends, not mutually exclusive, have been noticed: (1) a growth of clinic practice and (2) an increasing tendency of physicians to locate their offices near the hospitals with which they are associated. A clinic practice can be characterized as a one-stop medical service. A group of physicians of various specialties cooperate in the clinic establishment and share the cost of the building and the specialized equipment physicians use. The clinic allows centralized patient records, shared secretarial and nursing assistants, and quick referrals between the specialists. The joint venture is advantageous to the doctors and their patrons. The specialists lower their operating costs through high utilization of secretaries, bookkeepers, and general purpose diagnostic paraphanalia. Patients benefit because more equipment is available for use than in individual offices.

Recently, physicians have exhibited a proclivity toward establishing their offices near hospitals. Physician commuting is reduced to crossing the street. Moreover, close proximity to a hospital permits the doctor to draw upon the wide range of hospital diagnostic services not available elsewhere. Hence, patient commuting is also eliminated. Often, a "medical arts building" is provided to house the offices of physicians who prefer the hospital location.

The clustering of physicians, whether in clinic practice or not, seems to induce the desire to own the drugstore serving the group. This is especially so if the building is owned by the physicians. Naturally, there is a profit motive pure and simple; and pharmacy profits can be used to reduce the mortgage on the building. Rather than considering (1) the interprofessional problems that arise or (2) the competitive edge that the doctors enjoy (over independents and chains) due to their influence and the drugstore's location, it may be best to consider the situation from the consumer's viewpoint.

To the consumer, the most important point in connection with prescriptions is price. (He assumes that his physician will prescribe a good—in the quality and therapeutic senses—drug.) Some complaintants have charged that physicians' drugstores price generics higher than do conventional drugstores, but no prominence is given to the possibility that a high proportion of drugs dispensed are generics, as opposed to the usual 95-5 percent ratio in favor of the more expensive name brand drugs. Thus, it may well be that the overall annual drug bill is lower for the patients of the doctors owning drugstores. Before physician-owned pharmacies can legitimately be outlawed, some statistical evidence must be forthcoming to prove that patients are being exploited. Otherwise, this bizarre form of vertical integration may be taken to be as beneficial (to the consumer) as the typical ones.

ATTEMPTED STATE LEGISLATION

Many attempts have been made in the past few years to have state legislatures adopt comprehensive ownership laws. Failure has been universal, mainly because of vigorous opposition by the National Association of Chain Drug Stores (NACDS). In a few instances, ownership bills have passed a state legislature despite the efforts of NACDS, but in these cases the governors of the states have vetoed the bills.

Table 7-2 lists the pharmacy ownership bills introduced since 1955 and indicates the action taken on the bills. As the compilation indicates, repeated legislative rebuffs do not seem to deter the pharmacists—they keep reintroducing the proposals. Another interesting feature is the deceptive titles frequently given the bills, a practice which gives rise to the feeling that the sponsors do not want heralded what they are trying to achieve.

The positions of the parties at interest with respect to pharmacy ownership legislation are well known. NARD, APhA, state pharmaceutical associations, and most pharmacists favor the legislation. Labor unions, consumer groups, NACDS, chain drug corporations, and similar organizations, as well as chain store pharmacist-executives oppose the legislation.

Rather than noting the attitudes of these groups, however, it is more instructive to observe the division of presumably less interested parties in supporting the ownership laws. Two of these supposedly less biased groups advocate ownership legislation: deans of the various colleges of pharmacy and (usually) state medical societies.[47] On the other hand, other so-called disinterested factions oppose the bills. The opposition groups are represented by some spirited editorial and executive comments prompted by the ownership legislation proposed in New York in 1964. The editorial opinion stated:

A bill deserving quick rejection passed both Assembly and Senate by four-to-one margins. Is restricts ownership of pharmacies . . . to licensed pharmacists . . . The bill is largely an effort by pharmacists to restrict competition. . . .[48]

[47] Nicholas S. Gesoalde, "Executive Secretary's Page," *New York State Pharmacist*, Vol. 39, No. 4 (April 1964), p. 7. Some state medical societies apparently do not object to physicians not being able to own pharmacies, so long as everyone else except pharmacist-owners are also excluded from the field.

[48] *Times Union* (Albany, N.Y.), April 8, 1964.

TABLE 7-2: Introduction of State Pharmacy Ownership Bills Since 1955

Year	State	Action Taken
1955	Illinois	Did Not Pass Legislature[a]
1955	Washington	Did Not Pass Legislature[b]
1959	Colorado	Did Not Pass Legislature[c]
1963	New Jersey	Did Not Pass Legislature[d]
1963	North Dakota	Became Law (Governor Guy signing)[e]
1964	New York	Vetoed by Governor (Rockefeller)[f]
1965	Alabama	Did Not Pass Legislature[g]
1965	Alaska	Did Not Pass Legislature[g]
1965	Arizona	Did Not Pass Legislature[h]
1965	California	Did Not Pass Legislature[g]
1965	Colorado	Did Not Pass Legislature[g]
1965	Connecticut	Did Not Pass Legislature[g]
1965	Illinois	Did Not Pass Legislature[h]
1965	Maine	Did Not Pass Legislature[g]
1965	Maryland	Did Not Pass Legislature[g]
1965	Massachusetts	Did Not Pass Legislature[g]
1965	New York	Did Not Pass Legislature[g]
1965	Oklahoma	Vetoed by Governor (Bellmon)[g]
1966	Massachusetts	Vetoed by Governor (Volpe)[i]
1966	New York	Did Not Pass Legislature

Sources:

[a] "Illinois Law: RxMan Need Spend Only 'Major Time' in Store Daily," *American Druggist*, August 1, 1955, p. 20.

[b] "Harriman Is Expected to Sign Restricted-Sale Bill," *American Druggist*, April 25, 1955, p. 19.

[c] "Rx Business Must Be Owned by RxMan, Colorado Bill Provides," *American Druggist*, March 9, 1959, p. 20.

[d] "Bill Seeks Curb on 'Commercial' Control," *American Druggist*, February 4, 1963, p. 20.

[e] "North Dakota Adopts 'Ownership' Law," *American Druggist*, April 29, 1963, p. 15.

[f] "N.Y. Will Again Seek Ownership Law, This Time with MDs' Aid," *American Druggist*, December 7, 1964, p. 28.

[g] Letter from James H. Merritt, Executive Vice President, National Association of Chain Drug Stores, March 29, 1966.

[h] Charles Butterfield, Jr., *Legislation Affecting Pharmacy Introduced in State Legislatures During the Year 1965*, October 9, 1965, 17 pp. Mimeographed report submitted by the Legislative Committee of the National Council of State Pharmaceutical Association Executives to the Council.

[i] Jan Calkins, "Bay State Pharmacy Bill Killed," *Drug News Weekly*, September 12, 1966, pp. 1, 9.

According to the governor of New York in his veto message:

Stripped of its unsupported connection to the public health, this bill stands as an unmistakable effort to restrict competition, restrict free entry into a business, restrict the free employment of plant and capital—all to the benefit of a few and at the expense of the consumer who would ultimately have to pay the price.[49]

Other noteworthy comments of nonsupporters were made in New Jersey in 1963, and in New York in 1965. In New Jersey:

It is distressing at times to see legislation from special interest groups come to me veiled and cloaked with only their own narrow and special goals in mind.

. . . .

[I want the pharmaceutical association to ask itself:] Are your proposals fair to everyone? Are they in the public interest?[50]

And for New York:

The obvious purpose of the [1965 New York pharmacy ownership] bill is limitation of the number of pharmacies and protection from competition which its proponents present to the Legislature under the guise of protecting the public health and safety.[51]

Here we seem to have another example of regulators too eager to guard special interests rather than the public. . . .

. . .

. . . Indeed evidence reported by Howard S. Knowles of our Boston Bureau strongly suggests that the Legislature ought to take a hard look at the board itself. The regulatory agency apparently is using its present powers to limit competition in he drugstore business.[52]

Most of the recent legislatures have refused to assent to pharmacy ownership bills and even when the lawmakers of a state are willing, the governor generally is not. Exceptions to this generalization are Maryland and California, whose laws eliminate physician-ownership of pharmacies, and North Dakota, which specifies that a certain percentage of a drugstore must be owned by a pharmacist. Michigan's

[49] Nelson Rockefeller, Memorandum filed with Senate Bill, Introductory Number 2208, Print Number 2300, entitled: An Act to amend the education law in relation to the ownership of a pharmacy. As quoted in "The Veto Message," *New York State Pharmacist*, Vol. 39, No. 4 (April 1964), p. 13.

[50] Arthur J. Sills, Attorney General of New Jersey, quoted by Peter Albertson, "Ask Laws Only in Public Interest NJPHA Is Admonished," *Drug News Weekly*, February 6, 1963, p. 8.

[51] New York State AFL-CIO, "Memorandum in Opposition to New York Ownership Bills Introduced in 1965 in N.Y. Legislature" (Mimeographed memorandum to legislators).

[52] *Worcester Telegram* (Worcester, Mass.), April 13, 1965.

law cannot be included in this category since it was enacted thirty-nine years ago. In addition to being spurned by state legislatures, nearly all other interested parties, except pharmacists' associations and allied health groups, reject the ownership notion.

Rationale Underlying Pharmacy Ownership Legislation

Having mentioned the opinions of various opponents of pharmacy ownership laws, it is worthwhile to note briefly the reasons behind the introduction of the bills.

The stated (i.e., publicized) motivation that has led to agitation for enactment of the laws is that they are necessary to protect the public health. During the field work phase of this study, many of the individuals interviewed emphasized this point. Instances of unprofessional conduct forced upon pharmacists by nonpharmacist owners, chain stores, and discounters were frequently cited. Nevertheless, when pressed, the persons citing the situations were unwilling (perhaps unable) to identify the firms involved. Court opinion of this type of evidence has been made abundantly clear—no concrete facts, no favorable ruling.

A second argument advanced in favor of ownership legislation is that independent retail druggists need to be protected from the competitive threat of chains and discounters. The disappearance of "mom and pop" grocery stores is cited as evidence of what will happen to independent drugstores. According to this line of reasoning, the existing distribution pattern of retail drugs should be perpetually maintained. This is a plausible argument. As Chapter 12 explains, it is proper to ask the legislature to make such a political decision (i.e., preservation of "small business"), and it is proper for an affirmative decision to be rendered, if the lawmakers feel that the economic consequences of the action are not intolerable.

But ownership advocates do not say, "Please protect us. Small business viability is more important than economic consequences." Rather, the advocates endow their proposals with an emotional appeal: "Do your duty and enact these laws to protect the health of the American public." Nor are the ownership law proposals framed to promote generally small business in the retail field. The suggested bills would protect small business in the retail drug field and then for only a specified group of these entrepreneurs—registered pharmacists.

What appears to be the primary cause for the recent spate of ownership bills is the belief (or hope) that the philosophy of the U.S. Supreme Court has changed since the *Liggett* decision was rendered and that ownership laws now would be upheld if appealed to that highest tribunal. This opinion has been voiced several times in the trade press,[53] and is given emphasis by NARD's brochure promoting its model owner- ship law.[54]

It is useless to speculate how a particular court will rule on a question at any given time, regardless of legal precedents and the direc- tion of prevailing political winds. Nevertheless, it would seem that ownership advocates are overly optimistic as to the outcome of the hypothetical future U.S. Supreme Court decision. The Court has dis- played strong interest in the protection of the rights of individuals. Since ownership laws deprive a large segment of the population (all nonpharmacists) of a basic property right, it is difficult to conclude that the Court would sustain a law that achieved that result. The judiciary decisions in the two following chapters support this view.

[53] See especially " 'Court Would Okay Ownership Law Now,' " *American Drug- gist*, June 24, 1963, p. 17 and Nathan I. Gruz, "Professional Licensing Legislation," *The Maryland Pharmacist*, Vol. 39, No. 12 (September 1964), pp. 746, 748, 750, 752–753.

[54] Waller and Waller, *op. cit.*, pp. 7–13.

CHAPTER EIGHT

Recent Pharmacy Ownership Litigation

Entrepreneurs generally will acquiesce, as a matter of expediency, in some state-imposed restrictions on their business operations. These same individuals will vigorously protest any administrative or statutory steps that might restrict the right to enter and remain in a particular commercial enterprise. One consequence of this attitude is several court actions that were initiated to contest the pharmacy ownership laws and regulations that exist in a small number of states.

Five of these cases are analyzed in this and the following chapter. Only two of the five suits to be discussed have been completed and no constitutional issues have been settled. Nevertheless, all of the litigations merit examination since they explicitly illustrate the actions and tactics of the various state boards of pharmacy in their attempts to reserve the retail drug industry solely for pharmacists.

This chapter is concerned primarily with the Red Owl case (Minnesota) and a North Dakota case. For the sake of completeness, two pending actions—in California and Colorado—are mentioned. The final suit (Superx Drugs, Inc.) is discussed in the following chapter.

The Red Owl Case

Snyder's Drug Stores, Inc., a Minnesota corporation, was originally organized as a partnership in 1931. In 1939 it assumed its corporate form. Snyder's expanded until by 1961 it included twenty-one drug stores—all within its home state of Minnesota. At that time there were thirty-one individual stockholders, none of whom were pharmacists.[1]

---

[1] *Petition for Writ of Certiorari*, pp. 1–3, *Snyder's Drug Stores, Inc.* v. *Minnesota State Bd. of Pharmacy*, Fourth Judicial Dist. Ct. of Minn., Filed August 17, 1962 (hereinafter cited as *Petition for Writ*).

In November of 1961 negotiation was begun for the purchase of Snyder's (via a stock exchange) by Red Owl Stores, Inc., a Delaware food corporation headquartered in Hopkins, Minnesota. When it learned of Red Owl's interest in the drug chain, the Minnesota Board of Pharmacy sent the following telegram to Snyder's:

IN VIEW OF THE APPARENT NEGOTIATIONS BETWEEN RED OWL AND SNYDER'S DRUGS INC YOUR ATTENTION IS DIRECTED TO THE REGULATIONS OF THE BOARD OF PHARMACY STATE OF MINNESOTA AND PARTICULARLY REGULATIONS 14, 15 AND 18.

Despite this communication, the conferences between the two corporations continued. As a result the Minnesota Board of Pharmacy held a meeting in Minneapolis and again telegraphed Snyder's:

THE PROPOSED STOCK EXCHANGE AND PROPOSED METHOD OF OPERATION OUT-LINED BY YOUR OFFICERS MR LLOYD D BERKUS MR WILLIAM SMITH AND DIRECTOR SIDNEY LORDER WOULD IN THE OPINION OF THE BOARD OF PHARMACY CONSTITUTE A VIOLATION OF REGULATION FOURTEEN[3]

Regulation fourteen states that the Board will refuse to grant licenses for the operation of pharmacies to individuals or corporations unless: (1) for individuals, the applicant is a pharmacist registered by the state of Minnesota, or (2) for corporations, the corporation is owned and controlled by pharmacists registered by the state of Minnesota. The Board may, however, exempt a firm from the rule if it is deemed necessary for the protection of public health and welfare.[4]

The stance taken by the Board is peculiar since regulation fourteen also states:

Provided, however, that this regulation shall not affect pharmacies or drug stores for which licenses have already been issued and which are in actual operation at the time this regulation is adopted.[5]

Since the regulation was adopted in 1941 and Snyder's had been formed prior to that date and had been conducting business activities for many years, it would seem that the drug company was exempt from the restrictive provisions by virtue of its "grandfather" status.

At any rate, the Board's warnings had little effect on the corporations' discussions. On April 4, 1962, Snyder's informed the Board that the stock exchange had been consummated. The Board was also re-

[2] *Id.* at 10.
[3] *Ibid.*
[4] *Id.* at 3.
[5] *Ibid.*

quested to forward stock transfer forms so that the facts of the transaction could be revealed as demanded by Board regulations.[6]

BOARD HEARINGS OF MAY 1962

On April 19, 1962, Snyder's filed with the Board an application for new operating permits for its branches, a procedure that is required by state law when there is a change in the ownership of a drug establishment. On May 7, 1962 the Board met and denied the licenses. During the hearing, the point was brought out that even if regulation fourteen was legally enforceable, it was not applicable because of Snyder's grandfather status. It was also noted that Red Owl, Snyder's new owner, sold items that, according to the Board's interpretation of the state pharmacy law, could only be marketed in pharmacies. These "restricted sale" items included Alka-Seltzer, Anacin, Aspergum, Bromo-Quinine, Bromo Seltzer, Bufferin, castoria, Ex-Lax, Feen-a-Mint, 4-Way Cold Tablets, Lysol, Murine, Pepto-Bismol, Pinex, Sal Hepatica, Vick's Cough Syrup, and Vick's Va-Tro-Nol. It was primarily because of Red Owl's alleged violations that Snyder's application for new licenses was rejected.[7]

Snyder's did not seek court relief from the ruling since the new licenses would have expired on June 30, 1962, and the question would have become moot before it could be appraised by a court. Hence, Snyder's deferred any action until June 12, 1962, and then filed for new licenses for the period from July 1, 1962, to June 30, 1963.[8]

BOARD HEARING OF JULY 1962

The Board held hearings on July 20, 1962, to receive and consider evidence concerning Snyder's second application for licenses for its twenty-one drug stores.

Testimony of Lloyd Berkus. The first person to be called during the proceedings was Mr. Lloyd Berkus, President and General Manager of Snyder's Drug Stores, Inc. His testimony established the following:

1. The technical relationship between Red Owl and Snyder's is that Red Owl is the sole stockholder of Snyder's. This was accomplished by Red Owl's exchanging some of its previously unissued stock for the Snyder's shares held by the thirty-one individuals mentioned previously.

[6] *Id.* at 4.
[7] See Chapter 6 for the facts of the Red Owl case involving the sale of these items.
[8] *Petition for Writ,* p. 4.

2. Red Owl has in no way interfered with the operation of Snyder's. Managerial personnel are the same as before the stock exchange. Further, Red Owl conditioned the stock exchange upon Mr. Berkus continuing as chief executive officer of Snyder's.[9]

Following these statements, Ivan E. Peterson, President of the Board, attempted to establish that noninterference by Red Owl could change at any time. Charles S. Bellows, attorney for Snyder's, demolished that position by remarking that the prospectus filed with the Securities and Exchange Commission in connection with the Snyder-Red Owl stock exchange "specifically states that there will be no material change in the operation of Snyder [sic] Drug Stores and that none is contemplated."[10]

Robert Mattson, attorney for the Board, questioned whether the prospectus would be binding on Red Owl, to which Mr. Bellows replied:

It is binding in the same sense that all statements made to the Securities and Exchange Commission . . . are binding on the corporation. I can only state that any stock which is traded on the New York Stock Exchange, as the Red Owl stock is—any such company when they make representations to the Securities and Exchange Commission is bound by it [sic].[11]

Mr. Mattson then pointed out that, despite the prospectus, a change of circumstances in the future could mean an alteration by Red Owl of Snyder's management and operations. Mr. Bellows instantly agreed, saying, however, that the hearing was concerned with the present and the next one-year interval. Should an act by Snyder's be disapproved, the Board could revoke the licenses immediately or refuse to reissue permits for the following year.[12]

Testimony of Earl Schlekau.[13] The only other witness was Earl Schlekau, an inspector for the Minnesota Board of Pharmacy. His testimony disclosed that Red Owl was still illegally selling items (Alka-Seltzer, etc.) as it had been doing at the time of the May hearing. The witness did agree that other supermarkets were currently vending the same items.

Snyder's attorney objected to the entire line of questioning of the inspector on the basis that the manner in which Red Owl operated its grocery stores was irrelevant to the proceedings. He asserted that

---

[9] Minnesota State Board of Pharmacy, *In the Matter of: Application for Licenses to Operate Pharmacies or Drug Stores, Snyder Drug Stores, Inc.*, pp. 3–14, 28. Transcript of hearing held on July 20, 1962, at the Board office.

[10] *Id.* at 19.

[11] *Id.* at 22–23.

[12] *Id.* at 23.

[13] *Id.* at 30–35, 37, 41.

THE RETAIL DRUG INDUSTRY

Snyder's operations were what should be considered. In addition, he contended that if the Board had a quarrel with Red Owl concerning its sales, it should consult a city or county attorney and initiate prosecution. The attorney further noted that the disputed items had been sold since 1949 and that there had been no attempt to indict Red Owl or other food chains that followed the same practice.

In Mr. Bellows' concluding remarks to the Board he said:

> It appears to Snyders [sic] that if you should deny these applications . . . solely because Red Owl Stores own [sic] the stock of Snyder's, and because Red Owl . . ., [along with] other grocery stores in Minnesota, is continuing to sell Alka Seltzer, and the like, . . . what you are trying to do is to, in effect, pressure Red Owl to stop selling these items and therefore, penalize Snyders [sic] . . . You are making, in effect . . . a condition that the stockholder of Snyders [sic] stop selling these items even though all other grocery stores are doing this. It seems very clear to us that what you are doing is employing, in effect, economic sanctions against the stockholder of Snyders [sic] even though there is no complaint against Snyders [sic].[14]

The foregoing is the substance of the proceedings at the July hearing. The major questions involved were control of Snyder's by Red Owl, the possibility of future changes in management and operations of Snyder's, and Red Owl's sale of certain nonprescription medicines. At no time was there an allegation that Snyder's past and present operations constituted violations of the pharmacy laws of Minnesota. In fact, at one point Ivan Peterson, President of the Board, explicitly stated that there was no complaint to be made about Snyder's activities and that Snyder's had always been operated "in accordance with the law of the State of Minnesota and . . . [had] been very reputable operators in the past."[15]

FINDINGS AND DECISION OF THE BOARD[16]

At the conclusion of the July hearings the Board continued its meeting in executive session. By unanimous vote the members denied the request for the licenses. The Board found that:

1. All of the outstanding capital stock of Snyder's Drug Stores, Inc., consists of 5,000 shares of common stock and all 5,000 shares are issued to and held by Red Owl Stores, Inc.

[14] Id. at 42–43.
[15] Id. at 32.
[16] Minnesota State Board of Pharmacy, "Minutes of the 379th Meeting," July 20, 1962 (in the files of the Board).

2. Snyder's Drug Stores, Inc., is a wholly owned and controlled subsidiary of Red Owl Stores, Inc.

3. The applications for pharmacy licenses are in fact those of Red Owl Stores, Inc., acting by and through its wholly owned subsidiary, Snyder's Drug Stores, Inc.

4. Red Owl Stores, Inc., through its retail grocery outlets has been for some time, and even as of the date of the hearing, selling drug items in violation of the state law.[17]

5. No evidence or testimony was presented at the hearing to indicate that Red Owl Stores, Inc., intends to discontinue the illegal drug sales.

6. Red Owl Stores, Inc., has, within recent months, been charged with and convicted of violation of the Federal Food and Drug Act.[18]

The license denial was based upon five conclusions. The first four were restatements of the Board's findings. The fifth conclusion was:

5. Mr. Lloyd D. Berkus and Attorney Charles S. Bellows, appearing for the applicants, admitted that they did not represent nor could they speak for Red Owl Stores, Inc., and therefore any statements which they made regarding the Snyder's Drug Stores, Inc., were meaningless and without effect since Snyder's Drug Stores, Inc., is wholly owned and controlled by Red Owl Stores, Inc.

STATE DISTRICT COURT

On August 17, 1962, about two weeks after notification of denial,[19] Snyder's petitioned the Hennepin County District Court for a writ of certiorari to review the Board's decision. The plea outlined the history of the problem and took exception to the Board's findings. The petition further declared that the final determination by the Board justified a writ of certiorari because:

[The] determination by . . . [the Board] is unsupported by evidence, is arbitrary and capricious, constitutes an attempt to exercise legislative powers reserved to the legislature, bears no reasonable relationship to the public health, is contrary to the laws and Constitution of the State of Minnesota and of the United States, has as its manifest purpose the restraint of trade . . . and . . . the Board and the individual members thereof have exceeded the authority in it and them vested by the Minnesota Pharmacy Act, to the substantial prejudice of . . . [Snyder's].[20]

[17] This refers to the sale of products such as Alka-Seltzer.

[18] This matter was not mentioned during the hearings.

[19] Although the Board reached a decision on the day of the hearings (July 20), Snyder's was not informed of the ruling until July 31. Snyder's did not receive the Board's "Reasons for Denial and Order" until August 6.

[20] *Petition for Writ*, p. 8.

Specifically, the plaintiff asked for (1) an order to compel the Board to appear in court to answer the allegations in the plea, and (2) an order prohibiting any action based on the hearings (i.e., an attempt to close Snyder's pharmacies) until the court had reviewed the case.[21]

Judge Lewis M. Hall ordered the issuance of the writ of certiorari on the same day that the petition was filed,[22] and the mandate was simultaneously issued.[23]

DISTRICT COURT DECISION[24]

A change of venue was requested by the Board and was not contested by Snyder's. Hence, the December 17, 1962, decision was handed down from the Ramsey County District Court rather than from that of Hennepin County. The presiding justice, Judge Parks, reversed the Board's decision and ordered the Board to issue the twenty-one licenses to Snyder's.[25]

In commenting on the decision, the bench first complained of evidence introduced to support the Board's sixth finding. This new evidence was improper in the court's opinion since it was not introduced during the course of the hearings. Moreover, said the judge, the Federal Food and Drug Act convictions against Red Owl could have been nuisance settlements of violations either not done or done by mistake, but less expensive to discharge by a guilty plea than by a trial. In any event, he said, the "crimes" were not felonies.

[21] *Id.* at 8–9.

[22] *Order for Writ of Certiorari, Snyder's Drug Stores, Inc.* v. *Minnesota State Bd. of Pharmacy*, No. 579593, Fourth Judicial Dist. Ct. Minn., August 17, 1962.

[23] *Writ of Certiorari, Snyder's Drug Stores, Inc.* v. *Minnesota State* Bd. of Pharmacy, No. 579593, Fourth Judicial Dist. Ct. Minn., August 17, 1962.

[24] While this case was pending, the Superx case in Michigan (see Chapter 9) came to light. Snyder's attorneys felt that even if Snyder's current court action was favorably adjudicated, more problems might be generated than solved. Superx was accused of violating the law that written prescriptions are required for all legend drugs. Apparently the fear was that Snyder's would be subjected to continual inspection until an infraction "justifying" license revocation was found.
Snyder's attorneys said there had been an indication that if Red Owl would voluntarily withdraw objectionable items (Alka-Seltzer, etc.) from its grocery shelves, the Board would grant Snyder's licenses. (There is no available explanation of the source of the "indication.") The lawyers recommended this course of action since they felt it would absolve the existing difficulties and avoid court expenses and possible harassment. Letter from Charles Bellows to Alf L. Bergerud, General Counsel, Red Owl Stores, Inc., dated October 11, 1962.
Apparently Red Owl did not share the apprehensions of the attorneys since the case was continued. Also, so far as is known, the fear of harassment has proved unwarranted.

[25] *Snyder's Drug Stores, Inc.* v. *Minnesota State Bd. of Pharmacy*, No. 324715, Second Judicial Dist. Ct. Minn., December 17, 1962 (hereinafter cited as *Order of the District Court*), aff'd, 268 Minn. 8, 127 N.W.2d 682 (1964).

Further, the court noted that the Attorney General, in defense of introducing the evidence during the trial, alleged that Snyder's had not been entitled to a hearing; hence, the Board could rightfully consider extraneous evidence. Remarked the judge:

The court considers this specious reasoning and construes the . . . [law] as allowing a hearing when a petition by a drug store already licensed has been denied.

. . . Whether this interpretation is correct or not, the respondents assumed that the petitioner had such a right . . . for the respondents served notice on the petitioner of such a hearing, granted such a hearing and held such a hearing. Hence it is not for the respondents at this time to claim that the petitioner was not entitled . . . to a hearing . . .[26]

Having demolished the argument of the Attorney General and the sixth finding of the Board, the judge proceeded with an orderly explanation of his opinion:

1. The law requires the Board to license everyone who is eligible, unless there has been a violation of the law.
2. Snyder's past licensure indicates it is eligible to continue to receive such permits and there is no evidence that Snyder's has violated a law.
3. Hence, unless Snyder's is to be held accountable for the merchandising actions of Red Owl, the "all-important point to decide here" is whether the Board can refuse to register Snyder's merely because the stock of Snyder's is held by Red Owl.
   a. The undisputed testimony is that Snyder's is and will be operated by the same people following the same policies as before the stock exchange.
   b. The *Liggett* case settled the question of whether Red Owl had the right to buy all of the Snyder's stock.
   c. What Red Owl might do in the future, as regards policy, is of no consequence since the Board can suspend or revoke pharmacy licenses at any time.
   d. "It is not for the Board to say that one corporation cannot hold stock in another corporation, even if the other corporation is a drug store . . ."[27]

Having spoken about the case specifically before it, the court shifted its attack to pharmacy ownership matters implicit in the case:

1. Regulation fourteen . . . "pays tribute to vested interests and casts reflection on the claim that the paramount issue is the health and welfare of our people."

[26] *Order of the District Court*, at 4–5.
[27] *Id.* at 6–8.

2. The grandfather clause in regulation fourteen protects Snyder's from being denied a license because of the other provisions of Regulation fourteen.

3. "It is obvious from . . . [the Board's] findings and from a perusal of the evidence taken at the hearing that the Board is attempting by rules to govern the proprietorship of drug stores in such a manner as to prevent anyone from owning a drug store except pharmacists. This has never been the law, is not the law today, and the court doubts very much if it will ever become the law because it is not in the province of a Board of Pharmacy to make a regulation amounting to law establishing who can and who cannot own or participate in the ownership of a drug store . . ."

4. "In conclusion: the court is of the opinion that the Board did not proceed upon a proper theory of law and that its action in denying the licenses was arbitrary, oppressive, unreasonable and capricious, and the evidence upon which the [Board's] decision was predicated does not afford a reasonable and substantial basis for the determination [made by the Board]."[28]

MINNESOTA SUPREME COURT[29]

The Board appealed the adverse decision to the State Supreme Court and a decision was not rendered for over a year. Finally, on April 10, 1964, the Court affirmed the lower court's decision that Snyder's should be granted its licenses.

The opinion, given by Justice Thomas Gallagher, perceived the central question to be as the lower court had stated: Does the stock ownership of Snyder's by Red Owl give the Board the right to deny Snyder's licenses?

While the court answered negatively, it said that it was entirely proper for the Board to inquire into the affairs of the corporate parent. Since no evidence of wrongdoing was in the record, the court held that the licenses could not be denied, for such action would be arbitrary.

SUMMARY

The Pharmacy Board erred in trying to deny Snyder's licenses merely because it is a corporate child of Red Owl. There was also an attempt to establish guilt by association, and had there been credible evidence against Red Owl, the Supreme Court may have reversed the lower court ruling since the higher court approved of the idea of investi-

[28] *Id.* at 9, 13, 15.
[29] 268 Minn. 8, 127 N.W.2d 682.

gating the activities of the corporate parent. But since guilt is not established by allegations, the Board's legal legs were rather weak.

Neither court took upon itself the burden of declaring regulation fourteen unconstitutional, probably because there was no request for such a determination. Also, the courts may have felt that such a ruling should be based on an action specifically testing the constitutionality of the regulation. This is suggested by the district court judge's remarks that two cases contesting the constitutionality of regulation fourteen had federal jurisdiction originally and were held pending by the U.S. Court of Appeals until the litigants exhausted all remedies in the state courts.[30]

Although the constitutionality question was bypassed, it is possible to infer that the courts involved in the Snyder case were dubious of regulation fourteen's validity. The Minnesota Supreme Court quoted freely from the lower court's decision, and as has already been shown, the lower court made a venomous, if circuitous, attack upon the regulation. The Board, however, must not have drawn a similar conclusion— regulation fourteen still appears in the Board's listing of its rules and regulations.

North Dakota Case[31]

Medical Properties, Inc. is a firm organized in connection with the Dakota Clinic in Fargo, North Dakota. Stockholders of the corporation are the physicians who practice in the clinic and the manager of the clinic.

The owners of Medical Properties, Inc., applied to the North Dakota Board of Pharmacy for a pharmacy license to be issued to the corporation. The stated purpose of the pharmacy was to serve those patients of the clinic—especially the handicapped—who preferred to have their prescriptions filled in the building where the doctors are located. The pharmacy itself was to be operated by a registered pharmacist and presumably in accordance with the state pharmacy law and the rules and regulations of the Board of Pharmacy.

The application for a license was denied upon two grounds. One reason for denial was that the applicant did not comply with regulation (k) of the Board which states:

The Board of Pharmacy of the State of North Dakota shall hereafter refuse to grant a permit or license for the operation of pharmacies or

[30] *Snyder's Drug Stores, Inc.* v. *Taylor*, 227 F. 2d 162 (8th Cir. 1955); *Walgreen Co.* v. *Donovan*, 227 F.2d 162 (8th Cir. 1955).
[31] *Medical Properties, Inc.* v. *North Dakota Bd. of Pharmacy*, 80 N.W. 2d 87 (Sup. Ct. 1956).

drugstores in the State of North Dakota to individuals who are not owners thereof and who are not registered pharmacists in the State of North Dakota or to corporations which are not owned and controlled by pharmacists registered in the State of North Dakota, unless the issuance of permits to individuals or corporations is a necessity from the standpoint of public health and welfare.[32]

BURLEIGH COUNTY DISTRICT COURT

Medical Properties, Inc. appealed the license denial to the state district court. Judge George Thom, Jr. ruled that nowhere did the statutes of North Dakota authorize the promulgation of regulation (k) and that therefore it was invalid and void. He reversed the Board's ruling and ordered a pharmacy permit to be issued to the corporation.

NORTH DAKOTA SUPREME COURT

The North Dakota Board of Pharmacy appealed the adverse decision to North Dakota's highest court, contending that the lower court had erred in its findings and conclusions. Myron Bright, attorney for Medical Properties, Inc., charged that the Board's ruling was in violation of the due process and equal protection clauses of amendment fourteen to the U.S. Constitution. His appellate brief charged:

[The Board's regulations] are arbitrary and unreasonable and are for the purpose of giving registered pharmacists a monopoly on ownership of drug stores and pharmacies in North Dakota.[33]

The North Dakota Supreme Court's ruling, given by Judge Grimson, agreed with the reasoning of the lower court. The following points were made:

1. The state pharmacy law gives the Board authority to promulgate rules and regulations.
2. The Board may not make a regulation that includes any substantive matter not included in the statute under which it is acting, because such a regulation would constitute legislation.
3. Legislative authority is vested exclusively in the legislature and such authority may not be delegated to some other body.

[32] *Id.* at 89. Apparently this is not an exact quote, but a precise enough presentment for the State Supreme Court's purposes. The other reason for denial was noncompliance with certain physical requirements. See Chapter 10 for a discussion of this facet of the case.

[33] As quoted in "N.D. Court Oks Permit for MD-Owned Store," *Drug Topics,* June 25, 1956, p. 10.

4. The pharmacy law under which the Board operates does not mention conditions of ownership. Moreover, it specifically allows corporations to obtain licenses if they meet the law's requirements in other respects.
5. The Board's regulation seeks to prescribe the kind of corporation eligible for licenses and hence is a new feature affecting property rights and ownership and amounts to new legislation.

The court then concluded that regulation (k) was void. It is interesting to note that the court's analysis did not broach the subject of the constitutionality of the regulation. The entire chain of reasoning leads to a ruling based on the court's belief that the Board has exceeded its authority by adopting a regulation which amounted to new legislation. The promulgation of laws by an administrative body is an improper action since, according to the court, it is a settled question that the legislature—and no other group—can enact new laws.

It should not be assumed that the question of constitutionality did not occur to the judges. The court simply said that since there was no *statute* limiting pharmacy ownership there was nothing to rule upon and that it would be improper to issue a decision on a nonexistent statute. This is in keeping with judicial practice of not ruling even on an existing statute until that law is challenged and the court is asked to render an opinion.

Pending Cases

At present two similar cases are in litigation, one in Colorado and one in California. That is, the cases are alike in that ownership of pharmacies by physicians is involved. In Colorado, the Board regulation that prohibits a pharmacist from being employed by a physician or other medical practitioner is being contested.[34] It is difficult to apply the decision in the North Dakota case to this suit since employment rather than ownership is the issue. Colorado courts may feel (unlike North Dakota courts) that the regulation is within the Board's authority. If so, an opinion may be given on the regulation's constitutionality. Otherwise, the regulation will be nullified (as in North Dakota) by the judicial opinion that the regulation amounts to legislation.

The California action is based on a law rather than a regulation. The question to be resolved is whether the Holmes Act, which outlaws physician-ownership of pharmacies, excludes a physician-owned pharmacy in a clinic owned by doctors. Three clinics owned by physicians

[34] See Chapter 7 for a discussion of this regulation.

have brought suit against the California State Board of Medical Examiners asking that the law be declared unconstitutional.

Los Angeles Superior Court Judge Edward Olstyn has held that the Holmes Act violates neither the state nor the federal constitution. The bench also ruled that the law exempts corporately owned clinics that have a pharmacy.[35]

This means that two of the three clinics will be in violation of the law when it becomes effective (June 1, 1967) since they are partnerships. The decision was unsatisfactory to both plaintiffs and defendents, and it is likely that both will appeal the decision.

[35] "Calif. Doctor-Ownership Law Is Upheld," *American Druggist*, May 9, 1966, p. 29.

CHAPTER NINE

Recent Pharmacy Ownership Litigation: The Superx Case

This chapter is a chronology of The Kroger Company's efforts to obtain a Michigan pharmacy license for its drug subsidiary, Superx Drugs Corporation. The primary aim in devoting an entire chapter to one company's problems with a board of pharmacy is to provide a case study of (1) conscious and arbitrary license denials, (2) irregular procedures on the part of a pharmacy board, (3) discriminatory application of standards, (4) delaying tactics, (5) questionable actions by board officials, and (6) falsification of testimony—or poor memory. All of these events, and others, have occurred during Superx's four-year confrontation with the Michigan Board of Pharmacy.

Superx and Its Parent

The Kroger Company is a giant in the field of retail grocery sales. It ranks only behind The Great Atlantic and Pacific Tea Company, Inc. (A&P) and Safeway Stores, Inc. in terms of sales and number of outlets. In 1965, Kroger had 1,458 stores in operation and sales of $2,555,109,466,[1] while Safeway had 2,128 outlets and $2,939,004 in sales.[2] The leader, A&P, had 4,625 stores in 1965, which generated a $5,118,977,800 sales volume.[3]

Just as these figures emphasize the fact that Kroger is a very large company other figures indicate that its drug operation is rapidly be-

[1] *Kroger Annual Report, 1965* (Cincinnati, Ohio: The Kroger Co., 1965), pp. 1–2.

[2] *Safeway Stores, Incorporated Annual Report, 1965* (Oakland, Calif.: Safeway Stores, Inc., 1966), p. 2.

[3] *The Great Atlantic and Pacific Tea Company Annual Report for Fiscal Year Ended February 26, 1966* (New York: The Great Atlantic and Pacific Tea Co., 1966), p. 2.

coming one of the more substantial in the retail drug industry. At the end of 1965, Kroger operated approximately 180 stores and supposedly ranks as the sixth largest in the retail drug field.[4] Most of these drugstores art Superx stores, but there is also the Sav-On Drug Chain—operating in New Jersey and on Long Island—and the Gasen chain operating in St. Louis, Missouri.[5]

The expansion plans of most firms are carefully designed and are not made as off-hand decisions. This is true also for Kroger. The company reviewed retail drug distribution and concluded that entry into that industry would prove to be a profitable venture. Once this assessment had been made, and sensing that the drug and grocery areas are quite different, Kroger wisely sought and employed executives who were experienced in the drug field.[6] After gathering together a managerial nucleus and organizing Superx Drug Corporation, Kroger began to open its pharmacies in 1961. Kroger purchased the Sav-On chain and appointed its president and founder, James P. Herring, to head up the Kroger drug business. Herring, in turn, recruited additional drug executives.[7]

The vast majority of the Superx outlets are "freestanding" (i.e., separate) buildings adjacent to Kroger supermarkets. The Kroger and Superx stores compete with one another in selling health and beauty aids.

Superx Attempts to Penetrate the Michigan Market

It was not long before Superx's entrepreneurial eye fell upon Michigan. Such an expansion is a natural since there is a magnetic attraction between retailers and large population centers and since the Michigan marketing area is near the Superx headquarters (Cincinnati, Ohio). Even more important, Kroger has a large concentration of food stores in Michigan and prefers to install Superx stores adjacent to Kroger stores. By this time (early in 1962) Superx was operating in several jurisdictions and had learned that the various states have some pecu-

---

[4] The five largest firms, and the number of their stores, are: The Walgreen Company (470), Cunningham Drug Stores, Inc. (214), Peoples Drug Stores, Inc. (211), Marrud, Inc. (210), and Thrifty Drug Stores Company (200). Following Superx in size are Gray Drug Stores, Inc. (135) and Liggett Drug Company (115). David Mahler, "What the 1963 Census Shows . . . and What It Fails to Show," *Chain Store Age—Drug Executives Edition*, February 1966.

[5] Letter from Arthur L. Ferguson, Law Department, The Kroger Co., dated August 3, 1966.

[6] The writer was assured by many drug and grocery executives, sometimes with chagrin, that their experiences indicated that administrative skills in these related fields are not interchangeable.

[7] Letter from Arthur L. Ferguson, dated August 3, 1966.

liarities in their pharmacy laws. The Superx attorneys were aware of the Michigan pharmacy ownership law and realized that some method of circumventing the law was necessary if Superx was to enter the Michigan market. Kroger's knowledge of the law resulted from a letter from the Michigan Board of Pharmacy advising Kroger of the ownership requirement. The letter was received before Kroger had reached a decision on entering the Michigan drug retailing market.[8]

DECISION TO COMPLY WITH GRANDFATHER CLAUSE

There is no evidence that extensive deliberations transpired before Superx reached the "comply with grandfather clause" decision. Once the ownership law was made known, however, Superx had several alternatives: (1) focus expansion activities on other states and ignore the Michigan market, (2) build or buy a drugstore and defy the Michigan Board of Pharmacy by attacking the constitutionality of the statute, or (3) become a Michigan grandfather.[9]

The first alternative is unsatisfactory because of reasons previously mentioned: (1) Michigan is an extremely large merchandising area in terms of population and is conveniently located in relation to Superx's Cincinnati, Ohio Headquarters and (2) Kroger has a large food business in Michigan.

The second possibility is also undesirable. The Board may have acquiesced in the demand for a pharmacy license, but such amenability was unlikely in view of the hostility encountered in a few other states and the Board's apparent intention (the letter from the Michigan Board to Kroger) to apply the statute very strictly. Superx would have to be prepared to fight any decision by the Board to deny the company an operating permit. A court action, however, could prove to be poor strategy: (1) the law might be declared constitutional, (2) litigation is very expensive, (3) a law suit probably would earn the undying enmity of the Board, and (4) Superx might experience adverse publicity.

The third conceivable action—to become a grandfather—wins by default. Presumably Kroger conducted a preliminary investigation of

---

[8] *Ibid.*
[9] It would also have been possible to subvert the Michigan law by organizing a corporation that would be one-fourth owned by Michigan pharmacists, but with a contract executed between the pharmacists and Superx requiring the druggists to surrender any stockholder dividends to Superx. This device has been used by other companies. Superx could also have leased the prescription department in each store to a separate corporation, 25 percent pharmacist owned, under an arrangement whereby the rents paid by the lessee would be equal to prescription department profits. Superx apparently chose against such subterfuges.

the feasibility of grandfathering before the decision was made. Grandfathering had several advantages on the surface: (1) an expensive, time-consuming, and possibly unsuccessful legal action was avoided, (2) the possibility of developing harmonious relations with the Michigan Board of Pharmacy was retained, and (3) there would be no adverse publicity.[10]

The Search for Grandfathers[11]

Once it had been decided to pursue the grandfather route, a search was instituted to locate the appropriate company. The strategy was to buy a grandfather, change its name to Superx, and expand through the acquired store's grandfather status. Kroger obtained a list of drugstore corporations from the Michigan Revenue Department and then, from the records of the Michigan Corporation Commission, determined which of these had grandfather status (incorporation prior to 1927). Following this the size and strength of these firms were estimated by various investigations.

It was now possible to strike from the roster several firms that were so large as to require an outlay beyond the amount Superx wished to invest. This refinement reduced the possible candidates to four.

Superx officials approached the four prospects to determine whether they would be favorably inclined toward a purchase proposal. Two indicated interest and negotiations with those two were carried forward. One firm, Owl Drug Company, seemed to meet all requirements and was reasonably priced. Superx accordingly entered into a purchase agreement with that company and on May 25, 1962, acquired all outstanding shares of Owl Drug Company.

[10] A fourth advantage, the importance of which should not be underestimated, is that by grandfathering only Superx would be in a favorable competitive position compared to other chains that might later attempt to enter the Michigan market. The Michigan pharmacy law is old (1927). The result is that there are not many drug firms in that area with grandfather status. Of these existing grandfathers, possibly only a few would be willing to sell their establishments. Many of those probably would demand an exhorbitant price. Hence, Superx, being the first to acquire a grandfather firm, would have the entire group from which to choose. Other chains that later endeavored to enter the market by becoming grandfathers might be blocked by the same circumstances that limited Superx's selection. As a result, the new chains might be forced to challenge the Michigan ownership law in order to operate in the state. In the meantime, Superx would be expanding and, by the time the litigation was settled, the firm would have an enviable competitive situation while its potential opponent (assuming the suit was decided in its favor) would just be getting established. Kroger officials strongly deny that the fourth advantage was considered. The denial is given credence by the food chains', and particularly Kroger's, traditional opposition to restrictive legislation of all types.

[11] Interview with Arthur L. Ferguson, December 30, 1965.

Owl had been incorporated in 1909 and had at one time operated several stores in Battle Creek. By 1962, Owl's holdings had declined to a single store operated by Herbert Herman, a pharmacist, president and principal shareholder of Owl.

Events Preceding the Board Hearing of September 1962

On June 5, 1962, Owl applied for a license renewal for its Battle Creek store, under the name of Superx Drugs. Previously, the drugstore license had been issued under the name of Herman Pharmacy. Applications were also filed for licenses for three new stores in Mount Clemens, Plymouth, and Ypsilanti.[12]

At a regular meeting of the Michigan Board of Pharmacy held in Lansing in June 1962, Superx was told that the only obstacle to the issuance of licenses was an inspection of the stores and that the inspections would be made before the Board's July meeting. Despite this assurance, no inspections were conducted prior to the meeting and no licenses were issued at the July meeting.[13]

Representatives of Superx attended the next Board meeting, held in Munising, Michigan, on August 28, 1962, to ascertain why no action had been taken on the license applications.[14] The Board explained that it was illegal for Superx, then still named Owl Drug Company, to operate under the assumed name of Superx Drugs or under any other assumed name. Superx was instructed to submit an amended license application in the legal name of the corporation. The drug chain was informed that once this was done, there would be no other impediments to issuance of the permit.[15] Prior to this meeting Superx investigated several current businesses and found that some drug corporations were operating in Michigan under assumed names. Superx officials pointed out this fact at the meeting. One Board member was employed by Cunningham Drug Stores, which then and now operates under assumed names in Michigan.[16]

Following this August meeting, events seemed to progress smoothly. On September 7, 1962, Superx amended its articles of incorporation to change its Michigan affiliate's name to Superx Drugs Corporation,

---

[12] *Appendix to Brief for Plaintiff*, Vol. I, p. 4a, *Superx Drugs Corp.* v. *State Bd. of Pharmacy*, State Supreme Court File No. 50087 (hereinafter cited as *Plaintiff's Appendix*).

[13] *Ibid.*

[14] Munising is the county seat of Alger County and is located in the western portion of Michigan's sparsely populated Upper Peninsula.

[15] *Plaintiff's Appendix*, Vol. I, p. 5a.

[16] Letter from Arthur L. Ferguson, dated August 3, 1966.

filed amended license renewal applications, and the stores were duly inspected. There was no intimation by the Board or its inspector that any violations of laws or regulations had been uncovered during the examinations.[17]

In addition to these events, David M. Moss, Director of Drugs and Drug Stores for the Board, declared: "As far as we are concerned, the Kroger Company has purchased a corporation and is entitled under the law to that corporation's license."[18] Apparently Moss' position was based on a ruling of the Michigan Attorney General[19] that Owl Drug Company had grandfather status and that Superx acquired the same standing when it purchased the corporation. The Board of Pharmacy had requested the Attorney General to give an opinion as to the authenticity of Owl Drug's grandfather status. The ruling had been rendered some time before it was publicly announced. Superx had no knowledge of the opinion until the statement appeared in the newspaper. The ruling was given in an August 7, 1962 letter from the Attorney General to the Board. The Attorney General, Frank J. Kelley, also said that Superx could secure as many licenses as it desired for individual drugstores owned and operated by Owl Drug Company.[20]

From what had transpired, then, Superx's right to a license seemed to be well established on grandfather grounds, especially since there had been no other allusions by the Board to possible reasons for denial.

But the newspaper article in which Moss' statement appeared carried bad omens. The title and context of the article indicated that the Michigan independent retail druggists intended to oppose the granting of the Superx application. The independents retained a Plymouth, Michigan, Attorney, Edward F. Draugelis, to review the Superx licensing situation. The lawyer's resulting comments portended problems. He stated that Kroger's use of the grandfather clause was "sheer subterfuge." Further:

The neighborhood drugstore would be confronted with the same fate that befell the independent grocers when the chain supermarkets started.

. . .

If Kroger can succeed in entering the pharmacy field there is nothing that will stop the A.&P. grocery chain or other supermarkets from going into the drug business.[21]

---

[17] *Plaintiff's Appendix*, Vol. I, p. 5a.
[18] *Lansing State Journal*, September 19, 1962.
[19] *Plaintiff's Appendix*, Vol. I, p. 860.
[20] *Lansing State Journal*, September, 22, 1962.
[21] Lansing State Journal, September 19, 1962. Apparently the attorney was retained by Plymouth pharmacists who could visualize a Kroger-size drug chain. As if to feed this fear, Superx announced that outlets were under construction in Mt. Clemens, Plymouth, Saginaw, and Ypsilanti.

Board Hearing of September 1962

Superx was not notified of the September 26 hearing to be conducted by the Board until September 24. Notice was relayed by telegram.[22] Michigan law specifies that:

All necessary parties shall be notified of hearings by registered mail, which shall be posted at least 15 days prior to the date of hearing and shall state the date, time, place, issues involved and reasons involved for holding said hearing . . .[23]

The hearing was an uproarious affair. So many pharmacists were present that it was necessary to hold the meeting in a "small" auditorium of Lansing's Civic Center. Some 600 pharmacists were present[24] in addition to the members of the Board, Superx officials, and the attorneys for each of the three interests represented. The Board heard Superx's arguments and considered a multitude of written objections, affidavits, and petitions by assorted parties.[25] This procedure was followed despite the state law's requirement that written briefs or arguments be presented to the Board "and *all other parties directly interested* at least five days prior to the date set for the hearing,"[26] and the fact that Superx, a "directly interested party" involved, was not served with the documents that the Board reviewed during the hearing.

The meeting was tumultuous and the arguments, statements, petitions, and oral complaints consisted of several subjects and alleged infractions, but dwelt upon the various aspects of the grandfather clause. Following the public hearing, the Board retired into executive session. That same afternoon it announced that the license application had been denied because the firm's pharmacist had violated the pharmacy law. The infraction was the filling of barbiturate and amphetamine prescriptions telephoned in by physicians. Nothing had been said of this violation at the hearing.[27] What had been a grandfather issue suddenly became an issue of violations of the Michigan pharmacy act.

Appeal to Michigan Supreme Court[28]

Superx immediately appealed directly to the Michigan Supreme Court, asking it to issue a writ of mandamus ordering the Board to

[22] *Plaintiff's Appendix*, Vol. I, p. 7a.
[23] *Mich. Admin. Code* R338.485.15(b) (Supp. 37). Emphasis supplied.
[24] *Lansing State Journal*, September 26, 1962. Others placed the number of pharmacists present at 900 to 1200.
[25] *Plaintiff's Appendix*, Vol. I, p. 7a.
[26] *Mich. Admin. Code* R338.485.15(d) (Supp. 37). Emphasis supplied.
[27] *Plaintiff's Appendix*, Vol. I, pp. 8a-9a.
[28] *Id.* at 1a-13a, 48a-55a, 68a, 85a.

grant the license. In its petition, Superx traced the history of its problems with the Board and particularly pointed out (1) the procedural irregularities at the hearing, (2) the high ratings given in inspection reports on the store, (3) the fact that the firm was given no chance to reply to the Board's allegation of violations, (4) that the files of the drugstore had contained similar "violations" for many years and a license had never been denied on that (or any other) basis, (5) the Superx belief that the law is unconstitutional because it has no reasonable relation to safeguarding public health and welfare.

On October 2, 1962, the court ordered the Board to reply to the Superx petition. The Board was to explain why "an order [for the Board to appear and] to show cause should not be issued." In its answer the Board denied several Superx allegations and asked the court not to issue an "appear and show cause" decree. The court refused the request and on October 16, 1962, ordered the Board to appear and show cause why the writ of mandamus should not be granted. Also ordered was that the Board not interfere with the operation of the pharmacy (which was still open) until the case was settled.

Meanwhile, the Board initiated criminal charges against Mr. Herman based on the allegation that he had filled barbiturate and amphetamine prescriptions on oral orders from physicians. These charges are *still* pending. Also, after Superx filed suit the Board called a second meeting in which additional reasons were put into the minutes for denial of the Superx pharmacy licenses. Included in the supplemental reasons was ineligibility under the grandfather clause of the pharmacy ownership law.

The supreme court eventually declared that it could not make a judgment on the writ of mandamus because the facts of the case were in dispute. The court therefore decreed that the proceeding be remanded to a lower court for determination of the facts and that those facts be submitted to the supreme court in the form of a report. The supreme court then would render a judgment based on the facts and not on allegations.

Circuit Court of Calhoun County

THE PRE-TRIAL ORDER

Pursuant to the directions of the Michigan Supreme Court, Judge Creighton R. Coleman, circuit judge of Calhoun County, on November 16, 1962, ordered that the testimony presented be limited to evidence directly related to facts to be established. The only issues to be settled, according to the judge, were:

1. Did Superx (by virtue of its grandfather status) operate a drug store in September 1927 (the date of enactment of the ownership law) and has it continued to operate one from that date through October 1, 1962?
2. Did Superx (not actually owned by Superx at that time) cease to be actively engaged in the practice of pharmacy in the fall of 1958?
3. Has the Board been guilty of an abuse of discretion in handling Superx's application for a license renewal at its Battle Creek store?
4. What was the reason for the September 26, 1962, denial of Superx's license application?
5. Does the Michigan 25 percent ownership law bear a reasonable relationship to the public health?
6. What has been the common practice of pharmacists with respect to dispensing barbiturates and amphetamines on oral prescription?
7. What evidence of alleged violations of the Hypnotic Drug Act and the Pharmacy Act was before the Board when it denied Superx's renewal license?[29]

The parties stipulated that these were the only facts in dispute.

REVEALING TESTIMONY CONCERNING ISSUE FOUR[30]

According to the Board, the answer to question four was simple: the only reason for denying the license application was that Superx's pharmacist had violated that provision of the Michigan law which required written prescriptions for the dispensing of barbiturates and amphetamines. Mr. Herman, the previous owner and now pharmacist-manager of the store, had allegedly filled such prescriptions by oral order from physicians—a fact which was verified by two inspection reports of the store's files. The two audits that provided this data were conducted on August 30, 1962, and on September 20, 1962.

Inspection of August 30, 1962. Kenneth French, inspector for the Michigan Board of Pharmacy, stated that he had observed violations (i.e., unsigned prescriptions received over the phone) in the company's barbiturate and amphetamine file on August 30, 1962. The following exchange occurred when Mr. French testified. Mr. Warren is attorney

---

[29] *Id.* at 85a-86a.
[30] The evidence submitted in connection with the fourth issue is analyzed in more detail than that pertinent to the other questions since the fourth area of inquiry reveals some unexplained inconsistencies in the testimony of a board employee.

for Superx and Mr. Bilitzke is the Assistant Attorney General representing the Board.

MR. WARREN: On August 30, 1962, you didn't look at the prescription files on barbiturates and amphetamines . . . did you?
MR. FRENCH: I did sir, I always do.
MR. WARREN: Did you find anything wrong with them?
MR. FRENCH: Yes sir, I did.
MR. WARREN: On August 30 you did?
MR. FRENCH: Yes sir.[31]

. . .

MR. BILITZKE. Did you, at this time, go through the prescription file . . . ?
MR. WARREN: What time?
MR. BILITZKE: August 30, 1962?
MR. FRENCH: Yes sir, I did.
MR. BILITZKE: Did you find any violation?
MR. FRENCH: Yes, I did. Violations in both the amphetamine and barbituric acid prescriptions files.[32]

This testimony did not go unchallenged. Cogent opposing evidence was submitted. The following comments are by Mr. Chambers, the part-time pharmacist on duty at the time of the August 30, 1962, inspection; Mr. Warren, the Superx attorney; and Mr. Moule, a Board attorney:

MR. WARREN: Were you working . . . at the Owl [Drug Company] store on August 30th of this year [1962]?
MR. CHAMBERS: Yes I was, I remember distinctly.
MR. WARREN: All day?
MR. CHAMBERS: No, I worked the afternoon shift . . . I think I came to work at twelve o'clock and worked until six.
MR. WARREN: Did you see Mr. Kenneth French then?
MR. CHAMBERS: Yes.[33]

. . .

MR. WARREN: I will ask you two questions, the answer [sic] to which I would like you to consider very carefully, Mr. Chambers, because I know you know the penalty for perjury.
MR. CHAMBERS: Oh yes.
MR. WARREN: Did, at any time that day, Mr. French look in the perscription files in the store . . .
MR. CHAMBERS: He did not.
MR. MOULE: This was on August 30, Mr. Chambers, of this year?
MR. CHAMBERS: That was August 30th of this year, Thursday afternoon.

[31] *Plaintiff's Appendix*, Vol. II, p. 311a.
[32] *Id.* at 331a–332a.
[33] *Id.* at 541.

MR. MOULE: Did Mr. French ask you about the prescription files for barbiturates and amphetamines on that day?

MR. CHAMBERS: He said nothing about prescriptions at all, never asked me anything about them on that day.

. . .

THE COURT: I have been puzzled constantly since the beginning of this hearing as to whether I should comment on my attitude to the various witnesses. The Supreme Court occasionally in its opinion, will state they do not see the witness, of course, they do not observe them, and they don't quite say it but almost say it, but I feel the situations which the Supreme Court indicated often goes to the truth and veracity of the witness. I have not been a judge for a very long time, but I am now completely aware of why the Supreme Court makes those comments from time to time. I therefore wish to state, at this time, that I have known Mr. Chambers for many, many years. I have observed his demeanor on the witness stand, and I know personally he couldn't, under any possible situation, make a false statement. It would be impossible for him to do so; now he could make a mistake, but not a false statement. I want that to show on the record in regard to this witness. Thank you.[34]

By his statement, Judge Coleman apparently placed more faith in Mr. Chamber's testimony than in Mr. French's statements. The judge's feeling was probably also based on the fact that Mr. French's recollections had proved defective on two other occasions in connection with the events and actions arising from the August 30, 1962, inspection and the resulting report.

First Area of Questionable Testimony—One of the occasions that caused confusion to arise during the proceedings concerned the time at which the reference to prescription file violations had been typed on Mr. French's report of his August 30, 1962, inspection. Establishing this fact was important because the Board could not very well have refused to grant a license on the basis of the alleged violations if knowledge of the infractions had not been placed before the Board on September 26, 1962. Furthermore, if the disputed lines in the report had been added to it at a date much later than, say September 5, it would suggest that the entire record might be of questionable validity. Attempts to clarify this situation resulted in the following exchange:

MR. WARREN: Mr. French, is it your testimony that this typewritten portion on proposed Exhibit Y [the inspection report] was filled in by you on August 30, 1962?

MR. FRENCH: No.

[34] *Id.* at 542a–543a, 545a–546a.

MR. WARREN: When was it filled in?

. . .

THE COURT: The 30th was a Thursday.

MR. FRENCH: That would be Saturday or Sunday then that I typed it.

. . .

MR. WARREN: And then what did you do with this exhibit?

MR. FRENCH: I turned it into the office with my other reports.

MR. WARREN: It [sic] it please the Court, very sincerely I resist the offer of this exhibit because I think it shows on its face this typewritten part, which is of some importance here, was printed over the stamp of the State Board of Pharmacy, marked "Received, September 4, 1962."

THE COURT: . . . Mr. Warren, your argument is that if this witness is incorrect as to when he put this on that, that invalidates the entire exhibit.

MR. WARREN: Yes, sir . . . To go to the heart of my objection, I don't think the notation was contemporaneously made. . . . I very strongly submit . . . [that] what has obviously occurred on that exhibit . . . [places] its credibility greatly in doubt.

. . .

THE COURT: . . . Mr. French, in regard to Exhibit Y, the argument has been made that it appears that the stamp "Received September 4, 1962—David M. Moss, Director, Michigan Board of Pharmacy" was placed on this exhibit prior to your typewriting beginning on August 30, 1962 and I don't know when, I call your attention to the fact that the first two lines of this typing are not parallel with the last four lines of typing. Is it possible that the first two lines of typing which recite as follows: "Narcotic, barbiturate and regular prescriptions are filled here. Violations in the A and B prescriptions filled" was [sic] placed on this exhibit at a different time than the last four lines.

MR. FRENCH: The part of the irregular typing, it is very possible is [sic] was typed at different times, yes; that is all I can think of.

THE COURT: Do you have any recollection that the words I read were placed on there at a different time than the last four lines?

MR. FRENCH: I can't answer that sir.

THE COURT: Do you have any recollection that after this was filed with the Board, evidently on the 4th, that for some reason you took the exhibit from the file and typed that on?

MR. FRENCH: Well, it's a possibility, but I don't remember it.

. . .

MR. WARREN: Do you recall typing in the first two lines after August 30, 1962, at the office of the State Board of Pharmacy?

MR. FRENCH: No sir.

MR. WARREN: Is it your testimony that all of those lines were put on there at the same time?

MR. FRENCH: As far as I know, yes.

MR. WARREN: You are the only one that filled that out, aren't you?

MR. FRENCH: Yes.

MR. WARREN: So you should be the only one that knows.
MR. FRENCH: That's right.

The court decided to submit the questioned document to an expert for examination. By the time the trial resumed the next day (November 28, 1962), the expert had completed his analysis:

THE COURT: Mr. French, I want to swear you in myself. Do you solemnly swear to tell the truth and nothing but the truth, so help you God.
MR. FRENCH: Yes sir.
THE COURT: You may be seated, sir. I think, gentlemen, I am going to make a statement here on the record. . . . One of our officers took it [Exhibit Y] to the State Police laboratory this morning, stayed with it, and brought it back to me in a sealed envelope. With the return of the exhibit there was a statement . . . as follows: "It is my [the expert's] opinion that the typing is over the rubber stamped impression, (the typing was made after the stamp was affixed to the paper)."
    Now, in light of this development, . . . Mr. French, we wish to question you about how this happened. . . .
MR. BILITZKE: Have you, since . . . [yesterday] thought about this matter?
MR. FRENCH: Yes sir, very seriously.
MR. BILITZKE: Do you have any further recollection at this time?
MR. FRENCH: Yes sir, I remembered that I saw the directive in the office and picked it up and felt it wasn't a neat, I might say, looking record; I had intentions of going to a typewriter and setting [sic] down and making out a special report form which I probably should have done in the first place.
MR. BILITZKE: When did you see this in the office?
MR. FRENCH: I can't answer that.
MR. BILITZKE: Was it before or after September 24th—pardon, September 4th?
MR. FRENCH: After September 4th.
MR. BILITZKE: That you saw it in the office?
MR. FRENCH: Yes sir.
MR. BILITZKE: Did you do anything with the report?
MR. FRENCH: Yes, I took it home with me, and it is very possible—I am quite sure—I did type additional information onto the report.

. . .

MR. BILITZKE: Then did you return this report to the office?

. . .

MR. FRENCH: Yes.

. . .

MR. BILITZKE: Do you know when you returned it to the office?
MR. FRENCH: No, I don't.
MR. BILITZKE: Was it before September 26, 1962? [This was the date of the meeting at which Superx was denied its licenses.]
MR. FRENCH: I can't be positive about that.

. . .

MR. WARREN: Mr. French, are you aware of the penalties of perjury?

MR. FRENCH: No sir, I am not.

MR. WARREN: Are you aware of the penalties for falsifying a public record?

MR. FRENCH: No, I am not, sir.

MR. BILITZKE: Your honor, I would like to know the purpose of this line of questioning.

MR. WARREN: I want to make sure the witness understands the context of incrimination . . .

THE COURT: I think I am going to interrupt at this point. I want this witness excused from the courtroom. Mr. Burns (Court Baliff) will you take him from here into my office, please, and shut the door?[35]

Mr. French's testimony thus revealed that he could not remember when he had typed the incriminating lines on his August 30, 1962, report. In light of all the publicity the case had been receiving in Michigan at that time, this is most unusual. The significant thing, however, is that the report, so far as the record shows, could have been altered after the hearing at which the Superx license was denied.

Second Area of Questionable Testimony—Mr. French suffered another lapse of memory on the same day that he partially improved his recall in respect to his original testimony. The next day, the court questioned French concerning his erroneous answers to the court:

THE COURT: Mr. French, yesterday, when you were on the stand I asked you the following questions and I want to ask you if you remember these: Have you talked to anyone about this particular exhibit between the time you testified yesterday and the time you were called on the stand today? And you answered: "No, sir." Do you remember that testimony?

MR. FRENCH: Yes, sir, I do.

THE COURT: The Court then said this: Not a single soul? And you said "No, sir." Do you remember that question and answer?

MR. FRENCH: Yes, sir, I do.

THE COURT: Then I asked you, "Not even your wife?" do you remember that question?

MR. FRENCH: Yes sir.

THE COURT: Now I want to ask you again, Mr. French, whether you talked to anyone between the time that you testified the day before yesterday and the time you were called to the stand yesterday.

MR. FRENCH: I'm sorry. I did talk to Mr. Bilitzke in the other room

[35] *Id.* at 334a–343a.

there. I hadn't thought about it in that sense. I was telling him what I had remembered and I think Mr. Moss was present at the table.

THE COURT: Is there anyone else that you talked to between your testimony the day before yesterday and the time you took the stand yesterday? You forgot, for instance, Mr. Bilitzke and Mr. Moss. Who else have you forgotten?

MR. FRENCH: I can't think of a soul, sir. Unless there was somebody else present at that table that I didn't—

THE COURT: Can you only remember things after they have been brought to your attention?

MR. FRENCH: No, sir, I am trying very hard to remember the actual fact.

THE COURT: This is the second time you had to correct your testimony, is it not?[36]

Seriousness of Violations.[37] As indicated previously, the Superx license was not renewed, according to the Board, because of the seriousness of the offense of filling (and/or refilling) prescriptions for barbiturates and amphetamines on the basis of a telephone call from a physician. The general procedure in filling oral prescriptions is to write the name of the prescribed drug on a blank form as it is dictated by the physician and then fill the prescription and file the unsigned order.

According to David M. Moss, Michigan Director of Drugs and Drug Stores, such actions had a deleterious effect on public health and fully justified a license denial. Despite these assertions, Mr. Moss' testimony cast doubt on the seriousness of the violations. It was established that Mr. French had told Mr. Moss about the unsigned prescriptions on September 4 or 5 (1962). It would appear that if the alleged violations were so dangerous, Mr. Moss would have instructed Mr. French to immediately revoke the license of the pharmacy and close it. Instead, Mr. French was directed only to re-inspect the operation as soon as it was convenient and the re-examination of the Superx Michigan store was not made until September 20.

The supposed seriousness of Superx's purported indiscretion was further de-emphasized by Mr. Moss' admission that he had supported a legislative measure (which was enacted) that would authorize the very practice in which Superx had reportedly been engaged, that is, the practice of accepting oral prescriptions for amphetamines and barbiturates became legal. Mr. Moss never satisfactorily explained why he supported a change in the law to permit the filling of oral prescriptions, assuming they were as detrimental as he contended.

[36] *Id.* at 357a–358a.
[37] *Id.* at 432a–472a.

FINDINGS OF FACT

After listening to the testimony and other evidence presented to identify the facts of the issues listed in the pre-trial order, Judge Coleman assembled his conclusions for the Michigan Supreme Court. The opinion followed precisely the pre-trial order and presented a finding for each issue to be resolved.

Questions One and Two.[38] According to the pre-trial order, the first two questions to answer were:

1. Did plaintiff [Superx] operate a drug store in September, 1927, and has it continued to operate one from that date through October 1, 1962.
2. Did plaintiff cease to be entirely engaged in the practice of pharmacy in the fall of 1958?

These questions were proposed to determine Superx's grandfather status. The fact to be established was whether the drug company had been operating continuously since 1927. If it had, it was a grandfather regardless of changes in corporate name, company officers, and/or owners. (The Attorney General had stipulated that Superx had continuously operated a drugstore except for a period in the fall of 1958.)

Specifically, the period of time under scrutiny between 1927 and 1962 was the three months from August 30, 1958, to November 24, 1958. Immediately prior to August 30, 1958, ownership of the old Owl Drug Company passed to Mr. Herman, the pharmacist who later sold the drugstore to Superx. Since the three months between August 30, 1958, and November 24, 1958, were the first months of Mr. Herman's ownership, he closed the store during that interval and sorted stock, discarded out-of-date drugs, negotiated for and purchased new fixtures, and generally did all the things required to refurnish a rundown shop.

The crucial point involved was whether the store was "out of business" or merely "closed for business" for those three months. If the pharmacy was simply "closed for business," it did not cease being a going concern and was thus a bona fide grandfather. If the firm was "out of business," the continuum had been broken and its venerable status was lost.

Judge Coleman found that Mr. Herman had indeed been closed for business, but that this was not the same as being "out of business." The opinion emphasized the difference between the two situations and cited a mass of evidence—receipts, invoices, etc.—to show that Mr. Herman was steadily occupied during the entire three months in ques-

---

[38] *Plaintiff's Appendix,* Vol. I, pp. 115a–117a.

tion readying the store for reopening. The pharmacist had not disconnected his phone and did, in fact, receive a number of calls at the pharmacy during the three-month period. Had Mr. Herman been out of business, the bench reasoned, he hardly would have been spending his time at the store. Hence, the Superx grandfather claim was substantiated.

Questions Four and Seven. The court also considered questions 4 and 7 together:

> 4. What was the reason for the denial of plaintiff's license application, which took place on September 26, 1962?
> 7. What evidence of alleged violations of the Hypnotic Drug Act and the Pharmacy Act was before the Pharmacy Board when it denied plaintiff's renewal license?

The only *evidence* before the Board on September 26, 1962, was a report stating that a September 20, 1962, inspection revealed that Mr. Herman had dispensed barbiturates and amphetamines on oral orders from physicians. There were allegations of other violations and conjectures as to the grandfather status of Superx, but none of these charges constituted evidence. Thus, the only reason for denial of the license was the September 20, 1962, inspection.[39] As for the August 30, 1962, inspection, Mr. French's testimony that he had looked at the prescription files (and had found violations) was, in Judge Coleman's words, "flatly denied by pharmacist Howard Chambers (T 578), whom this Court believes. This Court finds that French did *not* look at the prescription files on August 30, 1962."[40]

Question Five.[41] Another issue was:

> 5. Does an Act requiring that registered pharmacists hold twenty-five (25%) percent of the stock of a corporation owning a drug store bear a reasonable relation to the health, safety, and morals of the people of the State of Michigan?

The court found it difficult to rule upon the relevance of some of the questions asked in connection with the ownership law. Hence, the judge took a lenient position, feeling that the entire testimony pertinent to issue five should be made a part of the record so that the supreme court could decide for itself which part of the evidence was relevant.

Among those who testified in connection with the fifth question was George F. Archambault, an employee of the United States Public

[39] *Id.* at 117a–124a.
[40] *Id.* at 120a.
[41] *Id.* at 124a–127a.

Health Service and then President of the American Pharmaceutical Association. Archambault (1) said that a 25 percent ownership element could not select a member of a company's board of directors, (2) said that drugstores are in competition with supermarkets, (3) would not say that in every case a drugstore operated by a nonpharmacist would be less ethical than one supervised by a pharmacist, (4) said, as to commercial motive, that he knew of gifts from owner-pharmacists to physicians at Christmas, (5) said his ethics were not damaged by his early association with the Liggett Company—a chain operation, and (6) could not say that chain members of APhA are less ethical than independent members.

Dr. Thomas D. Rowe, Dean of the University of Michigan School of Pharmacy, also testified during the proceedings concerning issue five. He stated that it was his feeling that a nonpharmacist-owned store would tend to buy drugs of an inferior quality, but he admitted that the pharmacists employed by chains are just as competent as those not associated with chains. Dr. Rowe also revealed, upon further questioning, that he did not know who owns the corporate stock of Quarry Drug, the pharmacy where he purchases his drug needs.

Maurice Seevers, M.D., Chairman of the Department of Pharmacology of the University of Michigan, disagreed with his colleague, Dr. Rowe. Dr. Seevers contended that the 25 percent ownership requirement does not have a reasonable relationship to the objective of protecting the public health, welfare, and morals. It is his opinion that the pharmacist is the most important individual or factor in achieving the statutory goals of public safety. Dr. Seevers indicated that he buys his drugs from a pharmacy and does not know whether it is incorporated.

Another witness, Dr. Stephen Wilson, Dean of the College of Pharmacy of Wayne State University, stated that the 25 percent ownership rule is reasonably related to the protection of public health, welfare, and morals because pharmacists might be subjected to improper pressure from nonpharmacist managers. He admitted, however, that (1) chain store pharmacists are just as ethical as others in that profession, (2) improper pressure could exist in independent pharmacies, and (3) a 25 percent ownership law does not mean that the pharmacist-owner will take an active interest in the business.

Two practicing physicians also testified before the court with respect to the fifth issue. Dr. Robert H. Trimby stated that the 25 percent ownership law was necessary and should be even more stringent. Dr. Paul J. Diamante took the polar position. He said the public was protected through the individual pharmacist filling the prescription, not by a business arrangement. He also indicated that a pharmacist-owner is just as interested in making money as a nonpharmacist-owner; further, there is no difference between a drugstore owned by a corporation and one owned by a pharmacist.

Another witness, Philip E. Cowan, Chairman of the Michigan Board of Pharmacy, stated (1) he has never bothered to find out how the corporate stock is divided in the firm by which he is employed, (2) he does not believe the 25 percent ownership requirement has any bearing on public health, and (3) he does not feel that filling amphetamine and barbiturate prescriptions on oral orders from physicians endangers public health.

Based on the testimony given, Judge Coleman ruled that the 25 percent ownership law is not reasonably related to the objective of preserving public health. He agreed with those who maintained that the pharmacist dispensing medicines is the controlling factor in fulfilling the statutory goal. In addition, he noted that a 25 percent interest does not give control of the firm.

Question Six.[42] This question was:

6. What has been the common practice of pharmacists with respect to dispensing barbiturates and amphetamines on oral prescription?

Of the evidence collected during the trial, an overwhelming amount demonstrated that it was common practice for pharmacists to dispense these items on oral orders from a physician. Moreover, a law had been enacted in Michigan in 1962 that would make the practice legal beginning in March 1963. All of the interests affected by the new law knew and approved of it. Moreover, prior to the passage of the act, many similar dispensing violations had been observed by Board officials and none utilizing the practice had been prosecuted. The bench reached the conclusion supported by the bulk of the evidence and declared that it was common practice among pharmacists to dispense barbiturates and amphetamines on oral prescription.

Question Three. The findings with respect to the third question were reserved by the court as the last area to be analyzed because those findings depended, in part, on the disposition of the other questions before the court.

The question was as follows:

3. Have the defendants been guilty of an abuse of discretion in treating plaintiff's application for renewal license at its Battle Creek store?

[42] *Id* at 128a–132a.

Judge Coleman first stated that he could not make a definite ruling because the issue was one that could be properly decided only by the Michigan Supreme Court based on (1) the standards of conduct demanded of administrative boards by that court, (2) an interpretation of the statutes and cases in this area, and (3) an interpretation of the statutes relating to the creation and operation of the Michigan Board of Pharmacy. The bench then proceeded to point out a number of facts that would indicate that the Board had abused its discretionary powers, but did not explicitly state that there had been such abuse.

In a parenthetical paragraph appended to the findings of fact, Judge Coleman said:

(If the Supreme Court desires this Court to make a determination as to fact issue number three, . . . this Court hereby determines on the basis of the findings set forth above, that defendant [Board of Pharmacy] did abuse its discretion when it denied plaintiff's [Superx] said application. Defendants, in denying plaintiff's application, clearly held plaintiff to "standards" not practiced by members of defendant Board, to "standards" not believed in by members of defendant Board, discriminated against plaintiff via a vis [sic] other drugstores, did not grant plaintiff a fair hearing, was not justified [in denying the license] on the basis of current practice or statement of legislative standards to be adhered to in the future. . . .)[44]

Decision of the Michigan Supreme Court[45]

On December 5, 1963, a full year after testimony was taken in the Circuit Court, the Supreme Court of Michigan granted the 1962 writ of mandamus requested by Superx and directed the Board to issue the requested license. In the five to three decision, Chief Justice Carr and Justice Smith wrote separate opinions for the majority and Justices Black, Kavanagh, and Souris wrote for the dissenters.

The Justices were split into two camps, primarily because of two reasons. One complaint by the minority was that the case had become embroiled in politics. Judge Coleman's findings had somehow been relayed to Governor Romney and banner headlines[46] announced Romney's demand for Director Moss' resignation. The judges were

[43] *Id.* at 131a–133a.
[44] *Id.* at 134a–135a.
[45] *Superx Drugs Corp.* v. *State Bd. of Pharmacy*, 372 Mich. 22, 125 N.W. 2d 13 (1963), 375 Mich. 314, 134 N.W. 2d 678 (1964), 233 F. Supp. 705 (W.D. Mich. 1964), 375 Mich. 314, 134 N.W. 2d 678 (1965), Michigan Supreme Court, June 6, 1966, filed Nov. 11, 1966.
[46] See *The Detroit Free Press*, March 2, 1963.

astounded—the Governor had seen the findings before they were available to the court.

The main objection of the dissenters, however, was that proper legal procedure had not been followed since the inception of the case. The justices maintained that Superx should not have appealed directly to the Michigan Supreme Court when the Board refused the license. Rather, the litigation should have come to the court only after proceeding through the lower courts. The majority, on the other hand, held that the case had been properly brought and that since the case had originally been accepted jurisdictionally by the court, it should not at this late date be sent back to the lower courts for adjudication.

There was substantial agreement that the Board had acted arbitrarily in denying the Superx licenses. Judge Black, one of the dissenting judges, said:

The Board proceeded not only to summary denial; it provided plaintiff no fair or due process and assumed to render its decision solely on *ex parte* proof tainted much by pure hearsay and the recorded hoorahs of a not too well controlled public gathering; referring to the presently described assembly of plaintiff's pharmaceutical competitors. This was an offense to state and national guaranties of due process. . .

Elsewhere in his opinion, Justice Black said:

The obvious reason for such controversy. . .is that the druggists foresaw from plaintiff's application statewide chain store pharmacy by a formidable competitor. . .

Subsequent Events

The Board did not grant the Superx license and instead asked for a rehearing before the court. By the time the request was acted on (February 3, 1964), the complexion of the court had changed. Chief Justice Carr had retired on December 31, 1963 and Paul Adams, who had previously been elected, was sworn in as Associate Justice to succeed him.

In considering the rehearing request Justice Adams adopted what had been the minority view. The result was a four-four vote which was a denial of the rehearing requested by the Board. The result, however, was a deadlock: four justices favored approving the original petition for a writ of mandamus ordering the Board to issue the license and ordered the clerk to issue the writ; the new Chief Justice and three other justices preferred granting the rehearing and ordered the clerk not to issue the writ. The clerk did not issue the writ.[47]

[47] 375 Mich. 314, 134 N.W. 2d 678.

In response to this bewildering situation, Superx filed damage suits[48] against the Board, individually, and sought from a Federal district court a writ of mandamus ordering the issuance of a license. Superx's plea was based on the Michigan law governing court procedure. In instances of a tie on the state supreme court, the lower court decision is to serve as the breaking vote. In the Superx case, however, there was no lower court decision, so Superx contended that the first supreme court decision should serve as the tie breaker. Since the supreme court did not follow that procedure, matters were deadlocked and therefore it was, Superx contended, being unconstitutionally denied due process of law and therefore the federal district court should act. To place the issue before the supreme court again was not satisfactory for two reasons, according to Superx: (1) a proliferation of litigation would result and (2) the law does not require plaintiff to seek a remedy where none will be given.

Judge Fox denied the Superx plea. In response to Superx's reasons why the case should not be brought before the supreme court again, Judge Fox said (1) Superx created the proliferation of litigation in the first place by choosing to appeal directly to the supreme court at the outset, and (2) the Michigan Supreme Court may still give a remedy. Although the Judge based the denial of the Superx plea on several points, they all related to the fact that there seemed to be a conflict in the state law regarding the judicial procedure followed by the supreme court and that the supreme court itself, not a federal district court, should clarify the correct procedure to be followed in this "unusual case." Judge Fox did, however, retain jurisdiction pending further action by the supreme court.[49]

Early in 1965, the Michigan Supreme Court agreed to another review.[50] This time there was a decision. On May 10, 1965, the Michigan Supreme Court voted five to three to send the case back to the Board to consider whether or not a license should be granted.[51] The Board was directed to proceed "as expeditiously as possible," but Allen G. Weatherwax, who had become Board secretary in the interim, replied that "there are so many factors involved it [the new analysis] could run to September [1965]."[52]

---

[48] "Kroger Sues Board In $1.3 Million Permit Case," *Drug Topics*, May 18, 1964, p. 2. Superx eventually dropped these suits.

[49] 233 F. Supp. 705.

[50] 375 Mich. 314, 134 N.W. 2d 678.

[51] *Ibid.*

[52] As quoted in "Superx Case Sent Back to Mich. Board," *Drug News Weekly*, May 17, 1965, p. 20. Mr. Weatherwax proved so prescient, one wonders if this statement was intended to evoke a reaction as to whether the Supreme Court would tolerate such a delay. Apparently the court took no notice of the remark.

SECOND HEARING BEFORE MICHIGAN BOARD OF PHARMACY

The review, ordered by the supreme court was begun by the Board on September 29, 1965. Various evidence was received during this second hearing, the bulk of it concerning Superx's current operational procedures.

Testimony of Lorenzo Ippolito.[53] Lorenzo Ippolito, an inspector for the Board of Pharmacy, stated that he had conducted inspections of the Superx store on July 7 and July 22 of 1965. During the July 7 inspection, it was revealed, the pharmacy section of the firm was closed and blocked off to prevent entrance. The fact that the Rx department was not open was proclaimed by large signs. Mr. Herman, the pharmacist, was in the hospital and prior to his confinement had instructed an employee who was temporarily in charge of the store to sell only cigarettes, newspapers, candy, and similar items. The inspector saw no drugs being dispensed and did not observe anyone in or near the prescription department. Despite this, Mr. Ippolito closed the store because there was no pharmacist on duty.

The July 22 inspection disclosed that Mr. Herman was filling prescriptions without a pharmacy permit or state narcotic license. The pharmacist-manager explained to the inspector that the permits were being delayed by the Board. Mr. Ippolito also found two bottles of outdated drugs in the store's inventory, but upon further questioning by Superx's attorney, it was shown that outdated drugs are often present in drug stocks. The inspector further stated that had he given the store a performance rating, it would have been 89 percent, a mark above average. The Board voiced some objection to Mr. Ippolito's quoting the evaluation since he had not actually rated the store in accordance with the procedure used in connection with a pending license.

Testimony of Allen G. Weatherwax.[54] Allan Weatherwax assumed the duties of Executive Secretary of the Michigan Board of Pharmacy on February 10, 1965, succeeding David Moss.

While being questioned by Superx's counsel about the results of the July 7, 1965, inspection, the new secretary indicated that he could not remember an instance in which a short absence of a pharmacist from the pharmacy had resulted in license forfeiture proceedings by the Board. He further said that a brief absence caused by a lunch break or a trip to a bank might be acceptable in a one-man drugstore operation. He would not say that the Superx pharmacy, closed by

[53] Michigan Board of Pharmacy, *In the Matter of the Application of Superx Drugs for: Pharmacy License*, pp. 7–12, 15–23 (hereinafter cited as *September 1965 Hearings*). Proceedings held at the Board office, September 29, 1965. Chapter 11 discusses the requirement that a pharmacist must be on duty at all times when a drugstore is open.

[54] *Id.* at 29–38.

the inspector at 10:00 a.m. on July 7 had been open without the presence of a druggist for only a short time. Moreover, Mr. Weatherwax pronounced a hospital confinement to be dissimilar to the situation where a pharmacist leaves the premises for lunch.

With reference to the July 22, 1965, inspection and the issue of outdated drugs, the Executive Secretary never definitely stated that a pharmacy license revocation had or had not been made in situations where outdated drugs had been found in the stock of other drugstores. He did note, however, that several stores with outdated drugs in their stocks had closed voluntarily and ceased to be in business. Further questioning by Superx's lawyers revealed that these firms were marginal stores, on the verge of economic collapse.

It was also developed during the cross-examination that the presence of outdated drugs on a shelf in the drug department is not as serious an occurrence as it might appear since all pharmacists are trained to read the label of a bottle very carefully before filling a prescription from it. Since the expiration date is on the label, there is little chance that an outdated drug will be dispensed.

Testimony of Fred G. Valdivia.[55] Fred Valdivia is employed by Mangini and Associates (Chicago, Illinois), an inventory specialist firm operating primarily in the drug field. The company specializes in taking physical counts of the inventory in drugstores and pharmacies.

Mr. Valdivia testified that he knew of 397 drugs whose labels include expiration dates. Further, in taking drugstore inventories around the country, he said that virtually every store with which he was familiar had outdated drugs in stock, provided a conscientious crew similar to his had not inventoried the store in the preceding few months. The statement by Mr. Valdivia was of special significance since Mangini and Associates performs its services for various firms in Michigan.

Other Testimony.[56] The Board members displayed an interest in the managerial status of the pharmacists in Superx stores. Accordingly, several Kroger and Superx officials were called as witnesses to explain the general operation of Superx. The chain store representatives reported that in most instances their store managers were pharmacists and that in all cases the pharmacists managed the prescription department.

SECOND LICENSE DENIAL[57]

The outcome of the second hearing before the Board was again a denial of the Superx request for a pharmacy license. In its December

[55] *Id.* at 40–51.
[56] *Id.* at 52–105.
[57] Michigan Board of Pharmacy, *In Re: Application of Superx Drugs Corp.,* December 16, 1965, p. 4.

16, 1965, decision, the Board found that the Superx store had been violating the law at the time of the July 7 and July 22 (1965) inspections and that the "violations could present sound grounds for denial of application. However, it is the decision of this board that a denial forever [sic] based on these grounds would not be well founded."

The rejection was therefore based on the Board's opinion that Superx did not qualify for a license renewal because it is not a grandfather. This conclusion was based on the ownership status of the old Owl Drug Company during the January 2, 1958–November 6, 1958, time period. In the first part of that period, the stock of the drugstore was pledged to an insurance company;[58] during the latter portion of the interval (September through November), the store was closed while Mr. Herman was remodeling preparatory to reopening the store.[59] Also, according to the Board, the name Herman Pharmacy that appeared on the window of the store after its reopening in November 1958 proved that Mr. Herman and not Owl Drug Company (i.e., Superx) was operating the establishment.[60] These facts, according to the Board, destroyed the concept of the corporation's continuity of existence and thus its grandfather status and Superx's right to a pharmacy license.

Despite the license denial, the Board said:

If, upon appeal, the Supreme Court should determine that the decision of the Board was incorrect, and that the Owl Drug Co. and the applicant have continued to be actively engaged in the practice of pharmacy so

---

[58] The owner of Owl Drug Company before Mr. Herman acquired control was a man named Briggs, who encountered financial difficulties while operating the firm. Briggs was able to get Wolverine Insurance Company, owner of the building where Owl Drug was located, to assume the Owl Drug Company debts for which Briggs pledged the Owl Drug Company stock as collateral. Briggs still owned the stock, but was paid $100 a week by Wolverine for his pharmaceutical services. A Wolverine executive testified before Judge Coleman that it entered into the escrow agreement merely to keep a drugstore tenant in the building and that the insurer had never owned the stock or contemplated entering the drug business. *September 1965 Hearings*, pp. 127–128.

[59] Judge Coleman had disposed of the grandfather issue:

"It appears clear from the record that plaintiff corporation operated a drugstore from before September, 1927 and has continued to operate a drugstore from that date to the fall (August 30) of 1958. While the stockowners may have changed, the name may have been changed, the officers may have been changed, the stock may have been pledged, the corporation continued to be empowered to and in fact operated a drugstore from that fall to November 16, 1962." *Plaintiff's Appendix*, Vol. I., p. 115a.

[60] *In Re: Application of Superx Drugs Corporation, supra* at 4–6. There was no testimony regarding ownership or grandfather status at the September 1965 Hearing, but counsel for Superx did point out to the Board that the Attorney General had stipulated during the proceedings before Judge Coleman that Superx had operated a drugstore during the January to September period.

as to come within the provisions of . . . [the grandfather clause of the ownership law], then there is nothing further of this record to deny applicant a license.[61]

Final Appeal to the Michigan Supreme Court[62]

The Supreme Court order remanding the case of Board gave Superx twenty days in which to appeal the Board's decision—such appeal to be made directly to the Supreme Court. Superx duly instituted the action and the Court's decision was rendered on November 11, 1966. The justices' opinions provided an appropriate terminal point for the case—their varied views paralleled the tortuous legal path that characterized the entire litigation.

Superx argued that it had bona fide grandfather status and was therefore entitled to licenses. If that was not the Court's finding, Superx asked that the ownership statute be declared unconstitutional as violation of "equal protection of the law" guaranteed by the Fourteenth Amendment to the U.S. Constitution and as specifically enunciated by the U.S. Supreme Court in the *Liggett* case which also dealt with a drugstore ownership law.

The Board was allowed the unusual privilege of raising a new issue in this, the final stage of litigation. The new issue was that Superx had never had grandfather status because the legislature's intent when the law was passed (1927) was to allow no exemptions to those drugstore corporations then complying with the 25 percent requirement.

Justice Dethmers' opinion sustained the Board position on the grandfather status of Superx and further declared the ownership statute to be constitutional. His constitutional ruling was based on his beliefs that (1) the U.S. Supreme Court no longer substitutes its economic beliefs for acts of legislation (citing cases), (2) the connection between drugstore ownership and public health and safety had been established in the Superx case, whereas it had not in the *Liggett* case, and (3) the second point had been the deciding factor in the *Liggett* decision.

Justice O'Hara disagreed with Justice Dethmers, saying that the only reasonable interpretation of the grandfather clause was to exempt those corporations operating when the law was passed. He further held that Superx had not lost its grandfather status at any time after 1927 and was therefore entitled to a license. As a result of this conclusion Justice O'Hara saw ample reason to vote for a writ of mandamus

---

[61] *Id.* at 7.
[62] Michigan Supreme Court, June 6, 1966, filed Nov. 11, 1966.

and saw no reason to go into the constitutionality question since the real issue was whether Superx was entitled to a license. Justices Kelley and Smith concurred.

A lengthy opinion by Justice Adams, Justice Souris concurring, dwelt upon the constitutionality of the statute and after citing a number of cases declared the statute unconstitutional for a number of reasons and voted for an order to the Board to issue the licenses.

Justice Black, with Justice Kavanaugh concurring, voted not to issue the writ of mandamus. His reasoning was that under such an order the Board would have no latitude to resurrect issues not associated with the ownership law's constitutionality. (This referred to the Board's original contention that the Superx pharmacist had filled barbiturate and amphetamine prescriptions upon oral prescription from a physician rather than by written prescription as required by the law. This would seem to have been a moot question since the law had been changed in the meantime to legalize oral prescription of those drugs.)

Justice Black did, however, repudiate constitutionality of the ownership law, saying that *Liggett* was binding on the Michigan Supreme Court and that even if it were not he agreed with the reasoning of the U.S. Supreme Court in the *Liggett* case.

In summary, five justices voted for issuance of a writ of mandamus to compel the Board to issue a license to Superx; three were opposed to the writ. Of the five voting for the writ, two further held that the ownership law is unconstitutional. Two of those voting against the writ did so for procedural reasons—even though they declared the law to be unconstitutional they preferred to return the case to the Board with that ruling so that the Board could then take appropriate action, i.e. issue licenses or renew some of the original charges and/or raise new questions.

Justice Dethmers was conspicuous by his being the only member of the Court to hold (1) that Superx was not a grandfather, or (2) that the ownership law was constitutional.

The Board had twenty days in which to file for a rehearing or to appeal to the U.S. Supreme Court. No action was taken. Though constitutionality is now highly questionable in view of the opinions given, the ownership law is still operative and the Board will presumably enforce it until there is another court challenge.

After expiration of the time limit for filing an appeal, the Board issued pharmacy licenses to the grandfather store and the additional Superx stores in Mount Clemens, Plymouth, and Ypsilenti. Mr. Herman also received his personal pharmacist's license and state narcotic license.

Summary and Conclusions

An analysis of the records of the various proceedings indicates that there are three central questions involved in the controversy: (1) are the Superx drug law violations serious enough to warrant a license denial, (2) does Superx have grandfather status, (3) is correct judicial procedure being followed, and (4) is the Michigan ownership law constitutional? The constitutional question had not received much attention prior to the final Michigan Supreme Court decision because it had not previously been necessary for the courts to reach issue (3). Only if the courts had decided that Superx did not have grandfather status would they have had to consider the constitutionality of the ownership law.

The decisions by the courts on the drug law violation issue verify that the drug law violations (filling amphetamine and/or barbiturate prescriptions on a telephone order from a physician) are of little consequence. The Board officials themselves testified that that was true in the proceedings before Judge Coleman. Judge Coleman and the Supreme Court (in its first 5–3 decision) duly noted the testimony and the issue did not have much weight thereafter. (It will be remembered that in its first decision the Board did not even mention the grandfather question—the license was denied *solely* on the grounds of drug law violations. It was only later that the Board focused attention on the grandfather clause.) By its December 1965 decision, the Board itself has now resolved that the original drug law violations and those found in 1965 are not sufficient grounds for license denial "forever."

The issue of the grandfather status of Superx appeared to have been settled in the Supreme Court's first 5–3 decision granting the writ of mandamus sought by Superx. The majority commented favorably upon Judge Coleman's finding that Superx had grandfather status. Nevertheless, the three dissenters addressed themselves only to the procedural questions and the retirement of one of the majority could have resulted in a reversal when the case made its final appearance before the Supreme Court.

The subsequent Board decision that Superx did not have grandfather status (reason for license denial) in effect overruled Judge Coleman and the Michigan Supreme Court. Upon appeal, the Board attorneys (perhaps feeling that the Supreme Court would not sustain the Board decision) sought to repudiate the Superx grandfather claim by trying to prove that the legislature had never intended to grant grandfather status to corporations meeting the 25 percent ownership requirement at the time of enactment but which later came to be less than 25 percent owned by pharmacists.

Despite the previous court decisions, it appears that the grandfather issue was the one that determined the final outcome. Three judges said that the position adopted by the Board's attorneys could not be sustained because the Board had not questioned original grandfather status and since the Board was incorrect in its determination that grandfather status had later been lost, licenses should be issued. Two additional judges concurred. Of the other three judges, one said the Board attorneys were correct (no original grandfather status) and the other two said that the Board's determination had been correct.

The correct judicial procedure was a concern of all of the Supreme Court justices in all of the appearances of Superx and the Board before the tribunal. These issues, while important, need not be discussed in detail. The important point is that disagreement as to correct procedure was a major factor in prolonging the litigation.

The issue of the constitutionality of the Michigan ownership law is still not settled, as has been indicated previously. The constitutionality question did not really become an issue until the September 1965 hearing by the Board. It had, however, been mentioned in Judge Coleman's findings and the first Michigan Supreme Court decision arising therefrom.

After Superx attorneys had raised the constitutionality question at the September 1965 Board hearings, it became incumbent upon the Supreme Court to consider the constitutionality issue *if* it decided that Superx was not a grandfather. Six of the justices followed the grandfather-constitutional sequence. The other two went directly to the constitutional question.

Of the six following the standard sequence, three found Superx to be a grandfather and did not therefore need to consider the constitutionality of the ownership law. The other three found Superx not to be a grandfather and continuing on to constitutionality, one found the law constitutional, while two did not. The two who went directly to the constitutionality question found the law to be unconstitutional.

The tally, then, on constitutionality of the Michigan ownership law as expressed by the Michigan Supreme Court is: no—4, yes—1, no opinion—3. In the absence of a majority for either position, the Michigan Supreme Court cannot be said to have ruled either way on the law's constitutionality.

As for the Board's original license denial, it appears that it was a partly concealed attempt to prevent Superx from entering the Michigan market. Filling telephone prescriptions from physicians for amphetamines and barbiturates was an established practice among Michigan pharmacists and became legal a few months after the license denial. Another indication of the Board's intent is delays encountered by Superx between the application date and the first hearing. A third suspect act was the short (two day) notice given to Superx of the first hearing. Finally, Superx was not aware that it would be charged with drug law violations and hence had no chance to prepare rebuttal evidence. Several other incidents, such as Inspector French's notoriously poor recall and erroneous testimony, lead to the conclusion that the Board and its employees were unfair, biased, and careless in the Superx license denial.

CHAPTER TEN

Operating Constraints: General Prohibitions, Physical Requirements, and Advertising Restrictions

In addition to pharmacy ownership laws and regulations, the state pharmacy acts and board of pharmacy regulations contain a number of other restrictive features. The intent in this and the following chapter, is (1) to determine the pervasiveness, (2) to analyze the nature and enforceability, and (3) to explain the purpose (stated and implicit) of these other restrictive laws and regulations. This will be accomplished by (1) explaining what a particular rule means in terms of operating practice, (2) analyzing cases contesting some of the regulations, and (3) noting some recent legislative and regulatory developments. In addition, a summarizing section is included in the next chapter to draw together the thoughts in this and the following chapter.

Appendix I contains an itemization of the restrictive practices as they are embodied in the various laws and regulations. These laws and regulations may be divided into five categories: (1) general prohibitions, (2) physical requirements, (3) advertising restrictions, (4) restrictions relating to employees, and (5) limitations on nondrugstore drug sales. This chapter discusses the first three categories and the next chapter analyzes the remaining two and some miscellaneous license denials.

General Prohibitions

General prohibitions are those pharmacy board rules that specifically deny a license to discount drugstores, general merchandise discount operations, and supermarkets. Also, a general prohibition can be imposed by refusing to license firms that do not observe the fair trade law.

Only two states, Maine and Minnesota, now publish regulations that prohibit licensure as a pharmacy because of the type of business in which the drugstore operation is to be located. The Maine regulation states that a pharmacy shall not be an adjunct to a general merchandise store. In Minnesota, pharmacy licenses are denied to "super stores . . . , super markets, self-service stores, and other similar establishments." Although there is no regulation in Wisconsin, "it is the policy of the Board to discourage establishment of a drug department as an adjunct of larger, unrelated business enterprises." Other states, notably Maryland and Pennsylvania, have had similar rules, but they have fallen into disuse—probably because the economic motivation behind the regulations is so obvious.

There have not been any court actions involving these general bans and, since they now exist in only two states, they are not very important as restraints. The general restrictions on pharmacy departments in general merchandise stores are very important, however, as an insight to the attitudes of boards of pharmacy—an explanation of license denials discussed under other headings may be more accurately categorized if placed in this section.

Although there have been no litigations with respect to the licensing ban on general merchandisers per se, court actions have resulted from such stores being denied operating permits because of their nonadherence to state fair trade laws. Strangely enough, no litigation has developed in Mississippi, the only state with a regulation allowing license revocation for violation of the state fair trade law.

An Arizona license denial was based on the existence of a fair trade law. The Arizona State Board of Pharmacy refused to grant a pharmacy license to Fed Mart, a discounter. The Board reasoned that since a provision of the pharmacy law required an applicant to observe all other laws of the state to be eligible for a pharmacy license, Fed Mart was not qualified because it did not comply with the Arizona Fair Trade Law. The discounter took the issue to court. The Maricopa County Superior Court disagreed with the denial of the permit and ordered the Board to issue the license, which it did. An appeal to the Arizona Supreme Court apparently was rejected.[1]

It is noteworthy that (1) at this time Alfred J. Duncan was executive secretary of both the Arizona Pharmaceutical Association and the Arizona State Board of Pharmacy and (2) shortly after the Maricopa

---

[1] "Flout Fair Trade in Ariz. and You Lose Your License," *Drug Topics*, December 22, 1958, pp. 3, 30; "Arizona Court Rules Board Cannot Enforce Fair Trade," *Drug Topics*, June 22, 1959, p. 3.

County Superior Court decision the U.S. Justice Department filed suit against the Arizona Pharmaceutical Association for conspiring to fix the retail price of prescription drugs.

A case similar to the Arizona one later developed in Delaware. On December 1, 1961, the Wilmington Vitamin & Cosmetic Corp. filed an application with the Delaware State Board of Pharmacy for a pharmacy permit. The premises of the proposed pharmacy were inspected on December 15, 1961, but no action was taken on the license application. On February 7, 1962, the company instituted an action seeking a preemptory writ of mandamus directing the Board to issue the permit or to state its reasons for not doing so.[2]

Following a hearing on the petition and the Board's answer, the writ was issued (March 7, 1962). It directed the Board to take action on the application and to give notice of the action by March 31, 1962. The Board met on March 25, 1962 and denied the license on the grounds that (1) one Edward Pastor, allegedly employed by the company, had a record in the Narcotic Division of the U.S. Treasury Department and had had his license as pharmacist suspended in Pennsylvania from July 13, 1960 to September 17, 1961, and (2) the company had violated the Delaware fair trade law.[3]

On March 29, 1962, the company appealed the license denial to the Superior Court of Delaware at New Castle. The court said it was disregarding all references to Pastor because (1) the president of the company had signed an affidavit stating that Pastor, or a person with a similar name, had never been an employee, officer, or director of the corporation, (2) Pastor had violated no Delaware law, and (3) Pastor was presently in good standing in Pennsylvania.[4]

Regarding alleged fair trade violations, the judge concluded that where the pharmacy act said the board was to enforce "the law," it meant provisions relating to public health and safety, not economic questions like fair trade. The judge also quoted several portions of a letter from the Delaware Attorney General to the Board (at the time the Board was considering the application) which gave the opinion that there were not sufficient grounds for a license denial. The court criticized the Board for ignoring the Attorney General's advice and said:

> If the permit was to be denied, then the reasons must have been other than the ones asserted by the Board and appearing in the record. I find and hold that the reasons stated in the record did not justify the Board to deny the application.[5]

[2] *Wilmington Vitamin and Cosmetic Corp.* v. *Tigue*, 183 A. 2d 731 (1962).
[3] *Ibid.*
[4] *Ibid.*
[5] *Ibid.*

Thus the judge ordered the case remanded to the Board with instructions to issue the license.

Another general prohibition, the like of which exists in no other state, has recently been promulgated in Arkansas. The regulation states:

In determining whether to issue a registered pharmacy permit for a new pharmacy or for a new location of an existing pharmacy, the board will determine whether public need and convenience will be served by the granting of the permit at the particular location sought. The board will not grant a permit where the granting of the permit will not serve the public need or convenience.[6]

The Arkansas Board of Pharmacy has, in effect, vested in itself the authority to limit competition. If the Board determines that a neighborhood is *adequately* served by the existing pharmacies, no license for an additional pharmacy will be issued. The Board ignores (1) the possibility that a new pharmacy might do a better job of serving the public and (2) the standard practices of allowing patronage by the public to determine the number and types of establishments that shall exist.

The chairman of the Arkansas Board, Joseph B. Harris, Jr. of Fort Smith, Arkansas, gave three reasons for the need for the regulation:

1. The Board has seen instances where price competition became so intense that pharmacists "may be tempted to cut professional corners."
2. There is a shortage of pharmacists and it is therefore necessary to limit the number of drugstores that those presently licensed will have a sufficient number of pharmacists.
3. Only one out of five Arkansas hospitals has a pharmacist. This, combined with the expected demand for pharmaceutical service for nursing homes because of Medicare provisions, means more service off drugstore premises will be required of those pharmacists practicing the profession in drugstores. The limitation of drugstores will allow more pharmaceutical service for these hospitals and nursing homes.[7]

Soon after the regulation was passed, it came under attack. In January, Superx Drugs Corporation had applied for a pharmacy license for a prescription department to be located in a discount store (Fort

---

[6] "Arkansas Pharmacy Board Will Curb New Stores on Basis of Public Need," *American Druggist*, August 29, 1966, p. 11.
[7] *Ibid.*, pp. 11, 12.

Smith, Arkansas) owned by Superx. When no action was taken, Superx officials approached the Arkansas Board to ascertain the reason. Superx was told that no formal hearing was necessary since things seemed to be in order. Superx was informed that a separate outside entrance would be required. After complying, it was learned that a formal hearing would be necessary after all.

Between the application date and the hearing date of June 15, the Board had promulgated its "demonstrated public need" rule. At the hearing, Superx was told that a license could not be granted unless the public need could be shown. A Superx attorney then introduced statistics indicating that Fort Smith has fewer pharmacies per capita than the rest of the state. Also, a real estate agent testified that there were no pharmacies in the immediate area surrounding the discount store. The Board, however, denied the license on the basis of letters from a number of pharmacists asserting that there was a sufficient number of drugstores in Fort Smith.

Superx then filed suit to force issuance of the license. Within three weeks the court heard the case and ordered issuance of the license. The regulation itself did not come under attack. The judge ordered the license to be issued because Superx had applied for a license before the regulation had been passed and therefore could not be bound by the requirements of the regulation.[8]

Other individuals have filed suit to contest the merits of the regulation. These are R. Lewis Riegler, doing business as Gibson's Pharmacy of Fayetteville, Arkansas and his pharmacist, G. T. Brown.[9] Although it is inconceivable that the regulation can survive court scrutiny, the Massachusetts Board must feel that the Arkansas idea has a chance of viability as a law as evidenced by the Massachusetts Board's support of a similarly worded bill in Massachusetts. Part of the Massachusetts Board argument is that when there is one drugstore for every 2500 residents, there is no public need for additional drugstores. Although the Massachusetts Medical Society has severely criticized the Board position editorially in the *Massachusetts Physician*,[10] according to a *Drug Topics* national survey, 51 percent of the pharmacists support the Arkansas and Massachusetts Board position. But some pharmacists vehemently oppose this attemp to limit the number of drugstores.[11]

[8] Telephone conversation with Arthur Ferguson, Law Department, The Kroger Co., December 1966.
[9] "Courts Asked to Blow Whistle on Arkansas Pharmacy Restriction," *Drug Topics*, November 28, 1966, pp. 3, 33.
[10] "Mass. MDs Oppose Curbs on Pharmacy Numbers," *American Druggist*, May 8, 1967, p. 31.
[11] See "Voice of the Druggist" in *Drug Topics*, especially the January 23, 1967 issue.

The Arkansas Board must be regarded as innovative in another way. The Board has decided to rate pharmacies: Grade A, Grade B, and Grade C. Each pharmacy must have at least a "C" rating and may have its license revoked if it cannot obtain a higher rating than "C" for two consecutive years. Also, only a Grade A pharmacy may train pharmacy interns.

The rating each pharmacy receives is based on the points earned (100 possible) by meeting certain standards set forth on the rating form. Several of the standards are required by law: generally good condition of the prescription department (24 points), prescription department equipment (16 points), pharmacy reference books (6 points), and a general orderly appearance in the rest of the drugstore (5 points). A total of 66 points, then, can be earned by complying with the law and by having an orderly store. An additional 15 points is available to those who offer "full pharmaceutical service," i.e., pharmacist on duty at all times the drugstore is open, pharmacist subject to emergency calls when prescription department is closed, waiting area with seating for prescription patrons, full delivery service, and prescription compounding and credit service.

Even if all the requirements above are met in full, a pharmacy only qualifies for a "B" rating (70–84 points). To be a Grade A pharmacy, the pharmacist must have, within the year, attended a state pharmaceutical association meeting (5 points) or a district (3 points) and a national pharmaceutical (2 points) association meeting. But if the pharmacist (9 points) or the pharmacy (9 points) is a member of the Arkansas Pharmaceutical Association, or if the pharmacist is a member of the American Pharmaceutical Association (6 points), deficiencies in several areas required by law will not prevent an "A" rating.[12]

Physical Requirements

Pharmacies must comply with several physical requirements to which most people would not object. Drugstores must be neat and clean and must maintain certain technical equipment, reference books, narcotic records, and other drug records. Some pharmacists and drugstore executives do, however, complain that much of the reference data and compounding equipment is superfluous (and expensive, by the way) since the filling of 95 to 97 percent of all prescriptions requires only the counting of pills or the placing of a liquid or ointment into a smaller container.

[12] "Ark. Board Grades Stores on Basis of 'Extra' Pharmaceutical Service," *American Druggist*, January 30, 1967, pp. 22–23.

Although many of the requirements appear to be helpful in protecting the public health, there are many others that seem to serve no distinguishable public health interest. Rather, the restrictive physical requirements appear to have been promulgated (1) to prevent supermarkets and discounters from entering the retail drug industry and (2) to limit the size of conventional drugstores.

The specific restrictions to be discussed below deal with (1) physical separation of the drug department from the other sections of a drugstore or a general merchandise store, (2) entrances into the drug department, (3) size of a drug department, (4) self-service limitations, and (5) inventory requirements. The court actions arising from these rules are also discussed.

PHYSICAL SEPARATION

In twelve states, according to one law[13] and twelve pharmacy board regulations,[14] any drug department in a nondrugstore must be completely separated from the rest of the store. These requirements are frequently quite detailed, specifying the type of material to be used (transparent or opaque) in constructing the walls of the pharamacy and the height (usually eight feet) of the structures. The walls, say the promulgators, are needed as a security device, so that the department may be locked by the pharmacist when he leaves, thus preventing unauthorized persons from entering the drug area.[15]

If such a degree of security is necessary, it is no less essential for standard drugstores. Yet physical separation of the prescription department is usually not required in conventional drugstores. The real goal of the physical separation idea seems to be to make drug departments less attractive to supermarkets and discount stores. By requiring the isolation, the traffic pattern of the stores can be disrupted since the patron must go through a door to receive service from the prescription department. This procedure causes a decline in the volume that the prescription department would ordinarily obtain.

[13] The Delaware law applies to drugstores, but an exemption is granted to stores that always have a pharmacist on duty when the stores are open.

[14] Arkansas, Connecticut, Delaware, Indiana, Kansas, Michigan, Minnesota, Montana, New York, Pennsylvania, South Dakota, and Virginia.

[15] The South Dakota regulation is not applicable to a pharmacist-owned general merchandise store, if a pharmacist is always on duty when the store is open. An exemption is definitely not available for a general merchandise store in Delaware even if prescription department hours correspond to the hours during which the rest of the store is open. The other states do not mention exemptions.

The Canadian province of Quebec, through the Quebec College of Pharmacy (equivalent to a board of pharmacy in the United States) has also adopted a physical separation rule. "Quebec Board Rules: All New Pharmacies Must Be 'Separated'," *American Druggist*, June 5, 1967, p. 31.

The separated arrangement also is more expensive than the usual high counter arrangement common to drugstores. Erecting the partitions and providing vacant floor space for a waiting area entails additional expenditures in building and operating the pharmacy. As a result, prescription prices will be slightly higher to offset the added expense.[16]

ENTRANCES TO PRESCRIPTION DEPARTMENT

On the surface, requirements concerning the entrances into a pharmacy are a trivial regulatory matter. Similarly, the connection between doors and public health is difficult to visualize. Nevertheless, the regulation of entrances has been the subject of seven board of pharmacy regulations officially[17] and several others unofficially.

Separate Entrances. One such restrictive regulatory device states that if a drug department is contained in a general merchandise store (department store, discount outlet, supermarket), that pharmacy must be provided with a separate street entrance opening directly into the prescription department.

There does not seem to be any good reason for such a rule and it has been the subject of court action. Giant Food, Inc., of Washington, D.C. applied to the Maryland Board of Pharmacy for an operating permit for one of its Peco, Inc. supermarkets in Tacoma Park, Maryland. The license was denied because there was no separate outside entrance into the drug area and because there was inadequate identification on the exterior of the supermarket that there was a pharmacy within the store.[18] Giant Food, Inc. appealed to the Montgomery County Circuit Court, but the action was dismissed for procedural reasons: the firm had not filed a supplementary petition with the clerk of the court explaining the action from which it appealed, the alleged error made by the Board, and the relief sought.

Believing that it eventually would be upheld in a court action, Giant Food, Inc. immediately filed an application for a new pharmacy license with the Board.[19] This second application (July 19, 1962) was denied by the Board on November 7, 1962. The refusal was based

[16] Physical separation of drug departments is somewhat analogous to such items as separate Negro and white employee wash rooms formerly required by those states practicing racial segregation. An employer may be reluctant to hire Negroes if it increases his cost of doing business.

[17] Kansas, Maine, Minnesota, Montana, Pennsylvania, Virginia, and Utah.

[18] "Board's Denial of Rx Permit to Super Upheld," *American Druggist,* July 23, 1962, p. 11.

[19] "Peco Supermarkets Apply for Pharmacy Permits in Maryland," *American Druggist,* August 20, 1962, p. 19.

on four grounds: (1) the location and appointments of the pharmacy were such that it could not be operated without endangering the public health and safety, (2) there was no separate entrance into the pharmacy, (3) the drug area was inadequately identified on the outside of the supermarket building, and (4) the pharmacy would be closed on Sundays, denying to the public the health, safety, and convenience of filling prescriptions on Sunday.[20]

Giant Food, Inc. attorneys claimed that the license permit was denied because the pharmacy was to be located in a supermarket.[21] They said, correctly, that there was an unpublished regulation to the effect that food stores would not be granted pharmacy licenses. The text of the anti-supermarket regulation (adopted May 1947) was:

> Because of its firm belief that it would be detrimental to the public health and welfare, the Maryland Board of Pharmacy will refuse to permit to operate a drug store or pharmacy in any establishment operating a food store, grocery store, food market, food fair, self-service store, or any such establishment.[22]

In explaining why the regulation had not been printed, Frank Balassone, Secretary of the Maryland Board of Pharmacy, stated that he had thought the regulation was a resolution, but that in reviewing the minutes, he found that it was a regulation and that "it was an oversight on the part of the Board, not having it available in printed form."[23]

Balassone reportedly agreed with Giant Food, Inc. attorneys that the license denial was based on the fact that the applicant was a supermarket:

> Mr. Balassone admitted that the permit was denied because Giant is primarily a grocery store. He said the board would have issued a permit if the firm's name were different. "Giant Pharmacy" or "Super Drugs" would have solved the problem, he said.[24]

After the November 1962 license denial, Giant Food, Inc. filed—for the third time—for an operational permit in January 1963. In April

[20] Betty Morris, "Expect Court Decision on Rx in Discounters," *Drug News Weekly*, June 6, 1962, p. 11.

[21] The Board granted pharmacy licenses to two discount operations owned by Giant Food, Inc. after they had complied with physical requirements—no inside entrance, physical separation, and outside entrance. "Giant Food Gets Rx License for Discount Center," *American Druggist*, November 12, 1962, p. 15.

[22] As quoted in "Maryland Board Will Fight Court Decision That Hits Curb on Supermart Pharmacies," *Drug Topics*, November 4, 1963, p. 6.

[23] "Expect Court Decision . . . ," *loc. cit.*

[24] *Ibid.*

of 1963 the Board again rejected the license application. The decision was appealed and the presiding judge ordered the Board to conduct a hearing concerning the matter. The hearing was held in August 1963. In September, the license request was denied for the fourth time.[25]

Following this, Giant Food, Inc. initiated its third appeal to the courts. Montgomery County Circuit Judge James H. Pugh reversed the Board's denial of the license. The judgment was based on the opinion that the Board had gone beyond its statutory authority in adopting the regulation detailing the physical requirements of a drugstore. The judge held that the Maryland Board "has power to make rules only for the administration of duties assigned it by the statute."[26] Since the establishment of physical requirements was not specifically a duty assigned to the Board and since the regulation had "no connection with the public health, safety and morals . . . [it was] therefore unreasonable."[27]

The case was taken to Maryland's highest court, the Court of Appeals, by the Board. This appeal was dismissed on March 12, 1964, without a hearing because of procedural reasons. According to the Court of Appeals, when a lower tribunal's power to review a case depends upon a statute, the statute specifies who may appeal from the lower level review. In this particular case, said the court, only "an aggrieved party" may appeal. The court held that the Board, in acting upon an application, performed a quasi-judicial function, not an adversative one, and hence was merely a "party" and not entitled to an appeal.[28]

Entrances to Adjoining Stores. A second rule relating to entrance facilities states that a pharmacy may not have entrances between it and adjoining stores. This rule is found only in the Maine regulations, but it is frequently combined unofficially in other states with the physical separation and separate entrance requirement. The effect of the regulation, although not stated in so many words, is the outlawing of the establishment of prescription drug departments as an integral part of nondrugstores.

This rule was used by the Connecticut State Pharmacy Commission to rescind a pharmacy license previously granted to the Insurance City Pharmacy located in a Topp's Discount Store in Wilson, Connecticut. Prior to this, the same regulation was used to revoke a license held by a Topp's store in Berlin, Connecticut. The pharmacy in Berlin

---

[25] "Maryland Board Will Fight . . . ," *loc. cit.*
[26] As quoted in *Ibid.*
[27] As quoted in *Ibid.*
[28] *Maryland Bd. of Pharmacy* v. *Peco, Inc.,* 234 Md. 200 (1964).

had appealed the voidance to the Superior Court and the Wilson store threatened to do the same.[29]

The Pharmacy Commission admitted that the regulation was designed to prevent the establishment of pharmacies in discount operations on the grounds that such drug outlets are detrimental to professional ethics and engender supervision problems.[30] Apparently the Commission decided that the rule would be unenforceable. The regulation was accordingly suspended—evidently to avoid the embarrassment of a court reversal. Later, at a second hearing, the Berlin license was reinstated and no punitive action was taken against the Wilson pharmacy.[31]

FLOOR SPACE RULE

Another method used to prevent the inclusion of prescription drug departments in nondrugstores is the requirement that the prescription area in all new retail drug outlets encompass 10 or 15 percent of the floor space available in the entire store.

If enforced, the "percent rule," as it is known, prevents supermarkets and discount operators from entering the prescription drug business. A store with 50,000 square feet would be required to have a pharmacy of 5,000 square feet, twice the size of many neighborhood pharmacies! Sometimes boards will permit the enclosure of the pharmacy department and consider it to be a separate building for applying the rule, thus reducing the floor space requirement.

As an adjunct to the percent rule, an absolute large square footage may be compulsory. Any obligatory area that exceeds about 220 square feet may be regarded as unreasonable, even for a very active prescription department filling several hundred prescriptions per day.[32] Using this as a rule of thumb, four states specify (by regulation) an excessive square footage[33] in addition to the nine states having unreasonable

---

[29] "Conn. Board Outlaws Drug Dept. In Super," *Drug Topics*, October 23, 1961. p. 3.

[30] *Ibid.*

[31] "License Granted For Pharmacy In Conn. Cut-Rate," *Drug Topics*, January 15, 1962, p. 10.

[32] Very, very few retail drug outlets fill "several hundred prescriptions" daily. Of all interviewees, only one indicated that his company had a store that consistently fills between 400 and 500 prescriptions daily, on the average. The interviewee said that the prescription department in the store, the largest in any of the company's outlets, was slightly larger than 200 square feet and that it is adequate for the high prescription volume. This is the basis for declaring a square footage requirement in excess of 220 to be unreasonable.

[33] California, 240 square feet; Minnesota, 400 square feet; Montana, 400 square feet; New Mexico, 250 square feet.

floor space rules (Delaware and Mississippi by law, the others by regulation) based on percent of total floor space.[34]

Generally, conventional chain drugstores were happy to have the rule—it reduced competition for them as well as for independents. As the chains have grown, however, their individual stores have also grown larger so that they too have run afoul of the floor space requirement. To accommodate the larger stores, some states have bent the rules to include such items as the shelving in front of the prescription counter and stock rooms for drugs to allow larger drugstores to meet the rules.

The excessive (as previously defined) floor space rule has been contested only once in court, but that single precedent seems to have implications for similar rules in other states. The subject of the litigation was the typical three-pronged rule adopted by the North Dakota Board of Pharmacy. It provides:

No pharmacy shall be licensed hereafter unless (1) the space which it occupies has an entrance which affords the public direct access from the street, (2) the space which it occupies is separated from the remainder of the building in which it is located by walls extended from the floor to the ceiling, which walls may contain doors to the interior of the building which may be closed and locked when the pharmacy is not in charge of a registered pharmacist, and (3) the space which it occupies contains no less than 400 square feet.[35]

A license application for a pharmacy in a North Dakota clinic was refused by the Board, citing this rule as one of the grounds for denial. The clinic corporation appealed to a state district court,[36] which held the rule unreasonable and therefore invalid and void. The Board appealed to the North Dakota Supreme Court and that court sustained (5-0) the lower court:

The . . . regulation [is] . . . clearly arbitrary and unreasonable. . . . Under the regulation one drugstore with sufficient overall space may operate as a general merchandise emporium and devote a small cubbyhole of much less than 400 square feet . . . [to the prescription department] while a true pharmacy [such as the one involved here] which deals in prescriptions exclusively must have 400 square feet of space in which

[34] Delaware—7.5 percent; Louisiana, Mississippi, New Jersey, and Rhode Island—10 percent; Oklahoma, Pennsylvania, and Wisconsin—15 percent; Massachusetts—20 percent.

[35] As quoted in *Medical Properties, Inc.* v. *North Dakota Bd. of Pharmacy*, 80 N.W. 2d 87 (Sup. Ct. 1956). The regulation differs from those of other states because it is stated in terms of the *pharmacy* rather than the *prescription department*.

[36] There was also a pharmacy ownership regulation involved. See Chapter 8 for this aspect of the case.

to store drugs and compound prescriptions. Such a regulation is discriminatory and has no reasonable relationship to public health and safety. The regulation that the public must be afforded direct access to the pharmacy from the street is on its face unreasonable. Certainly if the pharmacy is in other respects a proper place for dispensing drugs, the fact that its entrance is from an arcade, a hotel lobby or a corridor in a railroad station does not in any respect affect its character as a proper place to sell drugs or prescriptions. . . .[37]

The court held that a regulation must be within the Board's power, consistent with the law, and reasonable. Of these three requisites, the court disputed only the reasonableness of the regulation. From this decision it appears that the only necessary fault in a regulation to cause it to be declared null and void is to demonstrate that the regulation is unreasonable.

SELF-SERVICE RESTRICTIONS

A few years ago, the regulations of several state pharmacy boards included the prohibition of the self-service sale of proprietary drugs. These regulations were never observed to any appreciable extent. One of the defenses in many of the sales restriction cases concerning this rule was evidence that proprietaries could be selected and purchased by the customer without conversing with the pharmacist.

Wisconsin has not been part of this general legislative pattern. The favorable *Wakeen* decision allowed anti-self-service regulations[38] to endure in that state.[39] In Wisconsin, the "restricted drugs" (i.e., certain nonprescription drugs) sold in drugstores are confined to an area that must be constructed so that the only exit is at the cash register near the prescription department. In this way, the pharmacist is always involved in the sale—he takes the customer's money for the purchase.

To assure that new drugstores include a proper restricted drug area, Wisconsin has about six approved layouts that it will explain to those contemplating the construction of a drugstore. A railing surrounding the restricted drug area, one-way doors or gates as entrances

---

[37] *Medical Properties, Inc., supra* note 30.

[38] Minnesota and South Dakota also ban self-service sales by regulation and specify a restricted drug area for proprietaries. The Red Owl case demoralized enforcement in Minnesota. How stringently South Dakota enforces its rules is not known.

[39] *Wakeen* did not specifically endorse self-service restrictions, but it did permit the continuance of allowing only drugstores to sell aspirin, camphorated oil, and milk of magnesia. By extension, this decision includes a number of nonprescription drugs. Interview with Paul Pumpian, Secretary, Wisconsin Board of Pharmacy, January 12, 1966.

and exits, and a separate cash register for drug sales are mandatory. As a further control, blueprints must be submitted and approved before the store will be considered for a license.[40] Many of these practices are not specifically itemized in the Board's rules and regulations.

With its requirements of approved layouts of the prescription and restricted drug areas, blueprint approval, and percentage space requisites (15 percent of the outlet's total floor space must be the prescription department and the restricted drug area), Wisconsin exerts a great deal of control over what the final drugstore layout will be and can effectively prohibit the creation of self-service establishments.

Other states, especially those with floor space requirements, have adopted the approach of requiring a copy of the blueprints of a new store (whether or not self-service) before a license is issued to it. Drugstore chains have not objected to this procedure. They much prefer real or imagined design deficiencies to be identified during the planning stage. In addition, blueprint approval partially obligates approval of the physical layout once it has been constructed—the chance of license denial or delay for some trivial matter is reduced.

INVENTORY LAW

The demand that a retail drug outlet maintain a certain percent of its inventory in prescription drugs is, like self-service restrictions, not widely used. Probably this is because of (1) the ease with which the rule can be circumvented and (2) the difficulty of enforcing the requirement. Indiana attempts to enforce its 10 percent inventory law by making it a part of the pre-opening store inspection. In Mississippi, the only other state with an inventory requirement, the mandatory 10 percent inventory in prescription drugs is also a law.

It is not difficult to over-order an amount of drugs initially and, once the license is granted, return some drugs to the supplier or to allow inventory to decline until it reaches its proper level. Theoretically, an inspection and an inventory count could occur at any time, but a physical count for special occasions such as this would be extremely time-consuming for the state inspectors. If these examinations were made, they would have to be conducted by an inspector and his assistants to assure accuracy, and that procedure would result in no other auditing work being accomplished for several days. Since the official examining force is usually understaffed, such inspections are not feasible. Using the figures of year-end inventory for an outlet is also unsatisfactory—it would result in the same situation that evolves from a pre-opening inspection.

[40] *Ibid.*

CLOSED DOOR OPERATIONS

In the drug trade, a "closed door operation" refers to a discount store that requires a purchaser to have a membership card. Before a person may enter the store, he must present his membership card. There is usually some sort of electrical control on the door that keeps it locked until a guard pushes a button which unlocks the door for the member.

The members of these stores are theoretically restricted to some class of consumers, usually government employees.[41] The government category is pervasive enough for almost anyone to become a member of the stores. For example, members of reserve armed forces components, employees of companies with government contracts, and employees of state-supported educational institutions are eligible for membership in addition to all persons directly employed by a federal, state, or local governmental unit. For a small membership fee, transferable to other such stores and good for life, nearly everyone may shop at these stores.

Many of the closed door operations contain a prescription department where allowed by the state pharmacy board. In six states, two by law (Maryland and Mississippi) and four by regulation (Florida, Massachusetts, Pennsylvania, and South Carolina[42]) this is not allowed because the boards of pharmacy have decided that a drugstore must be open to the public at large if it is to benefit the public health. Hence, licenses are denied closed door pharmacies on the contention that they are contrary to the public health. Some closed door discounters provide a separate entrance for the prescription department— open to all—to surmount the obstacle.

It is by no means certain, however, that a closed door operation must serve the general public to be qualified for a pharmacy license. One state supreme court, that of Indiana, has ruled that a closed door status is no hindrance so far as pharmacy license eligibility is concerned. The Indiana case arose when that state's Board of Pharmacy denied an operating permit to Hook Drugs, Inc. for a prescription department to be located in a Gov-Co closed door store in Indianapolis. Hook Drugs, Inc. appealed the license refusal to the Marion County Superior Court.[43] The court upheld Hook Drugs, Inc. and the Board appealed to the Indiana Supreme Court.

[41] Two of the better known closed door operations are GEM (Government Employees Mart) International and GEX (Government Employees Exchange).

[42] South Carolina issues pharmacy permits for closed door operations if a separate entrance for the general public is provided for the prescription department.

[43] *Indiana Bd. of Pharmacy* v. *Hook Drugs, Inc.*, 242 Ind. 287, 288, 177 N.E. 2d 654–655 (1961).

The Board based its argument on paragraph 3 of Section 63-1214 of the Indiana law which states:

A registered pharmacist shall be in personal attendance and on duty in the drug department of the drug store at all times when the drug department is open to the public and be responsible for the lawful conduct of such pharmacy.

The Board asserted that the phrase "open to the public" makes it mandatory that a drugstore be open to the general public if it is to be granted a license. Hook Drugs, Inc. argued that the phrase meant only that a pharmacist had to be on duty when the drug department is open for business, and that therefore a license should be granted for a pharmacy included in the closed door operation.[44]

The four justices hearing the case agreed with Hook Drugs, Inc.:

Section 63-1214 . . . provides six minimum qualifications . . . [for] a permit to operate a drugstore. . . . [in] in our judgment, not one of such qualifications requires a drug store to be open to common or general use by the public.

Paragraph 3 of . . . [Section 63-1214] requires that a registered pharmacist shall be "in personal attendance and on duty." When? At all times when the drug department is open for business, so that some qualified person will be responsible for the lawful conduct and operation of the drug department.

Paragraph 3 of . . . [Section 63-1214] does not require that the drug department be *open to the public* but does require that when such department is open for business it shall be operated by a registered pharmacist who shall be responsible for its operation.

Consistent with the foregoing construction of the phrase "open to the public," . . . the evidence was not sufficient to support the finding of the Board, and the judgment of the trial court reversing the [Board's] order . . . must be affirmed.[45]

Judge M. Walter Bell then set aside the Board's denial and ordered issuance of the permit.

On November 1, 1961, the Board filed for a rehearing before the Indiana Supreme Court. The rehearing was denied on December 14, 1961.[46]

PENNSYLVANIA LICENSE DENIALS ARISING FROM PHYSICAL REQUIREMENTS

Several pharmacy license rejections in Pennsylvania have been attributed to noncompliance of the proposed drugstore with physical

[44] *Id.* at 288–289, 177 N.E. 2d at 654–655.
[45] *Id.* at 289–290, 177 N.E. 2d at 655.
[46] *Id.* at 287, 177 N.E. 2d at 654.

requirements. In these instances, the applicants supposedly committed infractions of several provisions of the state's physical requirements. But there generally were other factors influencing the Board, as most of the following situations will indicate.

Best Markets, Inc. In 1951 Benjamin Glassman and Philmore Solotoff filed an application for licensing a pharmacy that was to be located in Best Markets, a food market in the Philadelphia suburb of Cheltenham. The Board of Pharmacy scheduled a hearing on the application, but the Department of Public Instruction, to which the Board of Pharmacy is subordinate, ordered the issuance of the license.[47] Although at that time Pennsylvania had a regulation prohibiting pharmacies in supermarkets, the state attorney general expressed the opinion that the regulation was not valid. For this reason the state director of permits instructed the issuance of the licenses.[48]

Despite the action of the Department of Public Instruction, the Pharmacy Board questioned the right of Best Markets to receive a pharmacy permit. After two years of litigation the Dauphin County Court upheld the Board's contention that the pharmacy was not eligible for a license. Glassman and Solotoff did not appeal the decision so the Board was able to refuse the issuance of a permit in 1953.[49]

The Board's denial was commended by Chauncey E. Rickard, executive secretary of the Pennsylvania Pharmaceutical Association:

> The laws pertaining to the operation of a pharmacy are in the best interests of public health. . . . We do not feel that prescriptions should be filled in the same area in which meats and foods are being offered for sale.[50]

Bargain City. A few years later, in 1959 and 1960, the Pennsylvania Pharmacy Board rejected license applications made by Bargain City, U.S.A., a discount chain store. Again, noncompliance with the physical requirements of a drugstore was cited as a reason.[51] A contributing factor may have been the vigorous opposition by the Bucks County Pharmaceutical Association, The Delaware County Pharmaceutical Association, The Pennsylvania Pharmaceutical Association, and the Pennsylvania Association of Retail Druggists. The Bucks County group first warned:

[47] "Penna. Wins Fight To End Rx Depts. In Supers," *Drug Topics*, September 21, 1953, p. 3.
[48] "Penna. Board Revokes Super's Rx Permit," *American Druggist*, September 28, 1953, p. 19.
[49] *Ibid.*
[50] As quoted in "Penna. Wins Fight. . . .," *loc. cit.*
[51] " 'Bargain City' Centers Denied Rx Licenses," *American Druggist*, February 23, 1959, p. 21.

If this type of store is granted a pharmacy license, every large food store, supermarket, roadside auction stand, [and other nondrug outlets of all sorts will attempt to invade the discount prescription business.][52]

On another occasion, Jack Estes, president of the Bucks County Pharmaceutical Association, said:

Bucks County Pharmaceutical Association is unalterably opposed to the licensing of pharmacies in supermarkets, since such action . . . would lead to the degradation of the profession.

Pharmacy is an honorable profession, dedicated to the protection of public health and should not be practiced in an atmosphere as unprofessional as an auction market, supermarket, or discount house.[53]

Bazaar Pharmacy Inc. On October 25, 1961, the Pennsylvania Board of Pharmacy voted to grant a license to Bazaar Pharmacy, Inc., the prescription department concession to be located in the Bazaar of All Nations, a discount house located near Philadelphia. The Philadelphia Association of Retail Druggists (PARD) immediately filed suit in Dauphin County Court for an injunction to prevent the Board's issuance of the license.[54]

The license had not been mailed when the PARD initiated litigation. On November 14, 1961, the Pharmacy Board held an "emergency meeting" to further consider the matter. The outcome was a reversal of the previous affirmative action and a denial of a permit for Bazaar Pharmacy, Inc. The refusal was made after the Board (at a hearing concerning the license) heard complaints from the Philadelphia Association of Retail Druggists, The Pennsylvania Pharmaceutical Association, and the American College of Apothecaries.[55]

The Board attorneys stated that the reversal was made because Bazaar Pharmacy, Inc. had (1) sold dangerous drugs without prescriptions, (2) used the title "pharmacy" without permission, (3) called itself a pharmacy in the county telephone book, and (4) failed to meet physical and space requirements included in Board regulations.[56]

[52] As quoted in "Pennsylvania Groups Protest Issuance of Pharmacy Licenses to Discount Stores," *American Druggist*, January 12, 1959, p. 9.

[53] As quoted in "Pa. Assn. Battles Pharmacy Sections In Supermarkets," *Drug Topics*, January 18, 1960, p. 3.

[54] "Senator Urges Probe of Pharmacy Board," *Drug Topics*, December 4, 1961, pp. 3, 14. The suit also asked for injunctive relief to prevent the issuance of a pharmacy license to the International Ladies Garment Workers Union Clinic in Harrisburg on the ground that Board regulations outlawed mail order pharmacies. After defense attorneys pointed out that mail order prescriptions are permitted if they are written by Pennsylvania-registered physicians and filled by Pennsylvania-licensed pharmacies, the objection was withdrawn.

[55] *Ibid.*, p. 3.

[56] *Ibid.*

State Senator Donovan, counsel for Bazaar Pharmacy, Inc., then filed a cross petition in Dauphin County Court seeking an order to compel the issuance of the pharmacy license. He also wrote a letter to Governor Lawrence asking for an investigation of the Board:

I feel . . . that the operations of this board, not only in this case but in other cases should be thoroughly investigated. There are other matters which have happened in the past which I will be happy to present to any investigating committee.

There has been a strong feeling that the hidden reason for the opposition for the granting of the permit to Bazaar Pharmacy, Inc., is the fact that if such a permit is granted, the public will be able to purchase drugs at fair and reasonable prices and that this is the main reason why there is such great opposition from certain druggist associations to the granting of the permit.[57]

The resulting investigation[58] and court actions, however, did not decide the issue. As is explained below, the legal battles did not come to a decision point before various state agencies became involved in and finally settled the matter.

After the November 14, 1961, license denial and Bazaar Pharmacy, Inc.'s filing of the cross petition, the Board gave no further public consideration to the issue until a hearing held on January 16, 1962. At that meeting not much was accomplished. Most of the time was expended in heated exchanges between State Senator Donovan, attorney for Bazaar Pharmacy, Inc., and the Board members.[59] Additional hearings were held on February 8, but the licensing decision was postponed until the March 13–14 meeting because the Board members wanted to review the transcripts of the January 16 and February 8 hearings.[60]

At the March meeting the Board voted two to one to deny the license. Two members were absent. The decision was withdrawn, however, when the Assistant Attorney General Philip Wein and Deputy Attorney General Morris Dean warned the Board that it had no right to reject the Bazaar Pharmacy, Inc. application since all state investigations and inspections indicated that the firm was qualified to receive a permit. Still, no positive action was taken by the Board.[61]

---

[57] As quoted in *Ibid.*, p. 14.

[58] The "investigation" consisted of Governor Lawrence's request for, and receipt of, advice from officials from Pennsylvania's four schools of pharmacy. "Pharmacy Colleges Asked for Advice in Pa. Board Row," *Drug Topics*, January, 1, 1962, p. 2.

[59] Chester A. Moore, "Pa. Board Continues Hearing On Bazaar License to Jan. 29," *Drug News Weekly*, January 24, 1962, p. 13.

[60] "Penna. Board Postpones Ruling on Bazaar License," *Drug News Weekly*, February 28, 1962, p. 13.

[61] "Penna. Board Again Rejects Permit, Then Warning Causes Postponement," *Drug Topics*, April 9, 1962, p. 16.

In June, the Board again denied the Bazaar Pharmacy, Inc. license in a unanimous vote, despite further criticism from the state attorneys that had cautioned the Board previously about rejecting the permit. Following this refusal Senator Donovan readied a suit for the U.S. District Court in Philadelphia charging "some board members and at least one pharmaceutical association" with restraint of trade.[62]

Finally, in September 1962, the Pennsylvania Justice Department ordered the Board to issue the license,[63] and on November 15, Deputy Attorney General Dean personally mailed the permit. The license, however, had expired long before it was mailed, since the permit that had been in dispute was for the July 1, 1916–June 30, 1962, period.[64]

Upon receipt of the expired license, Bazaar Pharmacy, Inc. filed for a renewal. When the Board took no action on the renewal application, the drugstore instituted a mandamus action in the Commonwealth Court in Harrisburg to compel the Board to issue a renewal license. It was rumored that the Board feared it could not justify withholding the permit and would issue it, not wishing to have to justify its actions in court. The rumor proved to be correct—at least to the extent that the license would be granted. The Board, in a three to one vote, granted the operational permit on February 14, 1963, thus ending nearly two years of litigation, hearings, and maneuverings.[65]

Other Denials. While the Bazaar Pharmacy, Inc. episode was being played, E. J. Korvette, Inc. made several attempts to acquire pharmacy licenses for its two Philadelphia area general merchandise discount stores. All of Korvette's efforts failed—letters, visits, and personal appeals to the Pharmacy Board by Korvette officials notwithstanding. The Board, after a cursory inspection of Korvette's King of Prussia store, stated that a pharmacy permit for the outlet would not be in the best interests of public health because of failure to meet certain (unspecified) physical requirements. Korvette did not initiate court action to compel the Board to alter its position. There were at least four Korvette license denials made by the Board.[66]

[62] "'No Dice' On License For Penna. Unit," *Drug Topics*, June 18, 1862, p. 4.

[63] "Pennsylvania Board Ordered To Send Bazaar Permit," *Drug News Weekly*, October 3, 1962, p. 9.

[64] "Discount Permit Seen Near for Bazaar Pharmacy, Pa.," *Drug News Weekly*, February 13, 1963, p. 18.

[65] "Bazaar Pharmacy Issued Pa. Permit," *Drug News Weekly*, February 20, 1963, pp. 1, 18.

[66] "Pharmacy Permit for Discounter is Opposed by Philadelphians," *Drug Topics*, October 26, 1959, p. 3; "E. J. Korvette To Ask Permit for Pa. Store," *Drug News Weekly*, May 2, 1962, p. 12; "Korvette Stores to See Pa. Board about Rx Permits," *Drug Topics*, May 7, 1962, p. 8; "Penna. Board Mulls Permit for Korvette," *Drug Topics*, October 8, 1962, p. 3; "Pa. Board Keeps Ban On Supers," *Drug Topics*, January 28, 1963, p. 3; "Penna. Pharmacy Board Refuses To License Two Discount Stores," *American Druggist*, May 27, 1963, p. 17.

Considered in tandem with one of Korvette's license applications was Thrifty Drug Company's request for a pharmacy permit for a GEM closed door discount store located in Harrisburg. The Board denials were reversed when the emissary of the ex-officio Board member, the Superintendent of Public Instruction, attended a meeting consisting of two regular Board members and voted, along with one of the Board members, to grant the license. Such an appearance by the ex-officio member or his representative was a rare occurrence.[67]

S. Klein experienced the same difficulties as did Korvette, suffering several delays and four separate license denials. But Klein persevered. Meeting at the request of the License Commissioner and behind closed doors in the Attorney General's office, the Board finally voted 4–0 to issue a permit to S. Klein's northeast Philadelphia store.[68]

Advertising Restrictions

This third major category of restrictive operating practices involves controls over the way in which a company promotes its stores and the class of merchandise that is its *raison d'etre*—prescription drugs. The three major activities that are supervised are (1) advertisement of discounted prices, (2) communication of prescription drug prices, and (3) utilization of outdoor pharmacy signs. This section will describe the various restrictions in the three areas, analyze important pertinent court cases, and assess some recent legislative developments applicable to the activities.

OUTDOOR SIGNS

A vivid imagination is needed to find that public health is detrimentally affected by the signs used in advertising the type of business conducted in a pharmacy. Let it be conceded that such fanciful minds dwell in Michigan and New Jersey, for these states apparently possess the power to regulate the content of the exterior identification signs of pharmacies.

[67] "Ex-Officio Board Member OK Of Discount License Rapped," *Drug Topics*, June 3, 1963, p. 3. In protesting the vote, the Pharmacy Board secretary noted the peculiarity of the ex-officio Board member's approval of the Thrift Drug application while at the same time refusing to affirm a license application made by E. J. Korvette, Inc.

[68] "Two Discounters, For Fourth Time, Denied Licenses," *Drug Topics*, July 1, 1963, p. 3; "Pa. Board Defers S. Klein Plea," *Drug News Weekly*, December 18, 1963, p. 8; "Penna. Board Holds Up Dept. Store Rx Permit," *Drug Topics*, January 13, 1964, p. 3; "Cut-Rate Wins Permit For Pharmacy Section," *Drug Topics*, March 23, 1964, p. 4.

Requirements of the Laws. In Michigan, a corporate-owned pharmacy may not use such words as "drugstore," "drugs," or "pharmacy," to identify itself. Thus, the Arnold chain drugstores are known as "Arnold's Health Centers," a name somewhat confusing to out-of-state customers, and, it is suspected, to many of the local residents. These outlets, of course, perform the same services as the drugstores and pharmacies of other states.

Another idiosyncrasy of the Michigan law is the prohibition of exterior identification for pharmacies located in general merchandise stores. This is in contrast to the Maryland rule (mentioned earlier in this chapter) that contributed to a license denial because of inadequate notice that a drugstore was contained in a larger store.

The New Jersey authority for control over exterior signs derives from a law that became effective in 1965. Although the legislation was intended to prevent advertising of discount prescription prices, several drugstore corporations will be affected through their outdoor signs, since many of the companies' names imply that they grant discounts of some sort on sales. This law is now being contested by the Supermarkets Operating Company.

Supermarkets Operating Company Case. In June 1965 Governor Hughes of New Jersey signed P.L. 1965, Ch. 120 into law. The act was to become operative in September 1965. The statute provides that the New Jersey Board of Pharmacy may revoke or suspend the licenses of registered pharmacists who are, to the satisfaction of the Board, guilty of grossly unprofessional conduct. The law also allows the Board to refuse to issue an operating permit to a drugstore if it appears that the outlet will offer professional services under terms and conditions that tend to interfere with the full and complete exercise of professional skill.

Some of the actions constituting grossly unprofessional conduct are:

c. The promotion, direct or indirect, by any means, in any form and through any media of the prices for prescription drugs and narcotics or fees or for services relating thereto or any reference to the price of said drugs or prescriptions whether specifically or as a percentile of prevailing prices or by the use of terms "cut rate," "discount," "bargain," or terms of a similar connotation; but this shall not include . . . the advertising or issuance of trading stamps . . .

. . .

e. Fostering the interests of one group of patients at the expense of another, which compromises the quality or extent of professional services or facilities made available.

f. The distribution of premiums or rebates of any kind whatever in connection with the sale of drugs and medications, provided, however, that trading stamps and similar devices shall not be considered to be rebates . . ."[69]

Before this act became operative, Supermarkets General Corporation filed suit to determine the statute's constitutionality and to prevent it from becoming operative until its constitutionality is settled. The plaintiff is a New Jersey corporation and is located in Cranford, New Jersey. Supermarkets General controls several Shop-Rite supermarkets in New Jersey, New York, and Pennsylvania. Eight of the New Jersey Shop-Rite supermarket outlets contain prescription drug departments licensed by the Board of Pharmacy.[70]

The company has historically engaged in activities which are now unlawful under the new act. It violates provision (c) by use of the slogan "Why pay more?" which appears on its supermarket signs and on other items such as prescription delivery bags. Clause (e) is infringed by Shop-Rite's participation in such devices as union and senior citizen plans that give special price reductions to members of those groups. Provision (f) is violated by Shop-Rite's practice of distributing to patrons, from time to time, coupons worth fifty cents on the next prescription purchase.[71]

The company's first move, that of obtaining a temporary injunction to prevent the statute from being enforced, was accomplished on September 21, 1965.[72] Ordinarily, a temporary injunction is effective from three to five days, its main purpose being to allow a complainant—who is in imminent danger of being irreparably injured by an impending event—time to prepare a case that demonstrates an act would be harmful. This permits a plaintiff to obtain a preliminary injunction that remains in force while the merits of the case are heard in court. In this situation, however, the defendant Board of Pharmacy did not force the issue for some reason and the temporary injunction was in effect for over six weeks.

The firm's next step was a plea for a temporary injunction that would prevent the statute from becoming effective until the merits of the case (the law's constitutionality) were settled. Judge Herbert, the presiding justice, denied the plea on December 7, 1965, and stated that since the constitutionality of the statute had to be determined by the Appelate Division of the court, that tribunal should also decide whether or not a temporary injunction should be granted.[73]

[69] N.J. Stat. Ann. tit. 45, subtit. 1, c. 14, s.45:14–12.

[70] Brief for Plaintiff, pp. 1–2, Supermarkets Gen. Corp. v. Sills, Super. Ct. N.J.

[71] Id. at 3–6.

[72] Trial Brief for Plaintiff, pp. 6–7, Supermarkets Gen. Corp. 6 v. Sills, Super. Ct. N.J. (hereinafter cited at Trial Brief for Supermarkets Gen.).

[73] Id. at 7.

Supermarkets Operating Company appealed to the Appellate Division and, although the temporary injunction was refused, the denial was conditioned upon a stipulation by the Board of Pharmacy that no action would be taken against the company for use of its sign and slogan until the constitutionality litigation had worked its way through the courts.[74] Hence, the company's goal—temporary immunity—was attained without the injunction, and the Board is free to apply the law to others, although it does not intend to do so until the law's constitutionality is established.

Supermarkets General has attacked the constitutionality of the statute on several grounds:

1. The law deprives plaintiff and others of liberty and property without due process.
   a. The law bears no relation to the public health, safety, morals or general welfare.
   b. The statute deprives plaintiff and others of valuable property rights.
   c. The provisions are so confusing, vague and ambiguous that attempted enforcement would deprive plaintiff and others of their liberty and property without due process of law.
2. The statute provides unconstitutional restraints upon freedom of speech and press.
3. The statute is discriminatory class legislation violative of the requirements of equal protection of the laws.
4. The statute violates the New Jersey constitutional requirement that every law shall embrace but one subject, which shall be expressed in the title.
5. The law violates the commerce clause of the U.S. Constitution.
6. The statute imposes unconstitutionally excessive fines and cruel penalties.[75]

The final decision may rest with the U.S. Supreme Court since the suit raises federal questions.

The first decision,[76] given by Judge Mintz on December 8, 1966, held the act to be constitutional. In essence, the ruling sustained the Board defense that enactment of the law was a valid exercise of the police power of the state of New Jersey.

[74] *Ibid.*
[75] *Id.* at 8–55.
[76] *Supermarkets Gen. Corp.* v. *Sills,* Civil No. C-262-65, Super. Ct. N.J., Dec. 8, 1966.

The judge first pointed out that any legislative act regulating business must not be arbitrary or discriminatory and must be related to the health and general welfare of the public. Nevertheless, observed the bench, there is a strong presumption of constitutionality and factual support in every legislative action. This places a strong burden upon the plaintiff in a constitutionality suit to clearly show that a law is arbitrary or discriminatory or unrelated to the general health and welfare of the public.

The judge, citing several cases, then declared that pharmacy is clearly related to the general health and welfare of the public and that the legislature is entitled to regulate the field, including advertising, as evidenced by court rulings dealing with advertising and other matters relating to various other professions. Judge Mintz's view was that plaintiffs presented no affirmative proof of this matter and that "defendants offered testimony from which it might be thought that" the law was drawn to correct an existing evil:

(1) If a person uses one pharmacy for all his prescription needs, the pharmacist is able to check the records to determine whether a new prescription is contra-indicated by the patient's prescription history. If advertising is allowed, a person may purchase prescriptions from several pharmacies, thereby nullifying the pharmacist's surveillance function. Even if the monitoring is the rare rather than the usual case, the few cases where it does occur justifies the law.

(2) If discount price advertising is allowed, small retailers may be encouraged to buy large quantities of drugs to capitalize on quantity discounts. These drugs may be on the shelf for a long time and may therefore lose their potency. (The judge was apparently influenced by expert testimony to the effect that not much is known about drug deterioration over time.) If the law discourages mass buying and thereby low inventory turnover, the public interest is served. This is true, according to the judge, even though the training of pharmacists and laws relating to drug dispensing set rigid standards that should prevent outdated drugs from being used to fill a prescription.

(3) Contrarily, courts have generally not sustained laws regulating the commercial aspects of professions. Instead, the courts have confined themselves to fostering "a personal relationship predicated upon a confidence in the one rendering the service rather than a relationship based upon price." Although "that rationale seems inapplicable to pharmacy, . . . defendant's evidence to which I have alluded [items (1) and (2)] . . . together with the strong presumption of constitutionality [of every legislative enactment] requires this court to adjudicate . . . [the law] as constitutional."

The judge quoted but did not comment upon the contrary opinion of the court in the Florida case discussed later in this chapter. In commenting upon the Oregon case, the judge said that that case was not applicable because the advertising prohibition had been declared invalid by the Oregon Supreme Court because regulation of advertising was beyond the Oregon Board's rule-making authority. Moreover, it was significant to Judge Mintz that the Oregon Supreme Court opinion had stated that the *legislature* could presumably enact statutes dealing with the advertising of prescription drugs.

Having used thirteen pages to answer yes to the question of whether the law constitutes a proper exercise of police power by the legislature, the judge disposed of the other (the first seven are constitutional) questions (raised by Supermarkets General) in just six pages:

1. *The law is not an unconstitutional interference with interstate commerce.* If a statute is the proper exercise of police power and only indirectly affects interstate commerce, the statute stands. This law affects interstate commerce only indirectly, if at all. It is designed as a public health measure.
2. The Federal Trade Commission Act is not a preemption of state regulation of advertising in the sphere of food and drugs. FTC is concerned with false or deceptive advertising. This is a health measure—an entirely different sphere of interest.
3. *Prohibition of price advertising does not violate constitutional guarantees of free speech and press.* Many cases indicate that the guarantees do not proscribe governmental regulation of commercial advertising.
4. *The state constitutional requirement that every law embrace but one topic has not been violated.* The title does not have to be a resume of the act; this act *does* concern the practice of pharmacy.
5. *The law does not impose cruel and unusual punishment.* License suspension or revocation is in order if a pharmacist does not conform to the code of conduct required by this law.
6. *The law is not arbitrary (violative of equal protection of the law) merely because it allows the use of trading stamps but not rebates.* Courts must uphold legislative classification unless they are clearly arbitrary. In addition, courts have previously recognized the distinction between trading stamps (not a cash rebate) and rebates.
7. *The law is not void by virtue of vagueness.* It reasonably specifies what will be considered grossly unprofessional conduct and it would be impossible to define the term to anticipate every form of grossly unprofessional conduct.

8. *It is not necessary to decide whether the words "shoprite" and "Why pay more" violate the law.* The complaint and pretrial order present the sole issue of constitutionality of the law.

Judge Mintz appears to have perceived the main issue to be whether the enactment of the law was a legitimate exercise of the legislature's police power. To rule in favor of plaintiffs, it was incumbent upon plaintiffs to convince the judge that because the law was (1) arbitrary, (2) discriminatory, or (3) unrelated to public health and welfare, it was not a proper exercise of the legislative police power. Cogent evidence on any one point would have been adequate, but in Judge Mintz's view none was given.

The court, therefore, refused to void the law because, seemingly, the unanimous judicial view has always been that a duly enacted law is constitutional until proved otherwise. This is analogous to the tradition in criminal proceedings that the person accused of a crime is innocent unless there is sufficient evidence presented to prove, beyond a reasonable doubt, that the accused is guilty.

In a criminal proceeding, the accused's defender need only induce doubt that the accused did not commit the crime. *Proof is not necessary,* Perry Mason's exploits notwithstanding. Constitutionality tests of laws proceed from the analogous assumption—those defending the constitutionality need only create doubt in the judge's mind. (Of course, doubt must be evoked in jury members in criminal cases.)

That such doubt was not induced in this case is self-evident. Moreover, even though it was not necessary, the judge found positive evidence that the law is related to the public health and welfare in that (1) the law indirectly exerts a positive influence on the monitoring function (which reduces the possibility of a patient taking contra-indicating medication) by reducing the patient's incentive to shop around (due to advertising) for prescriptions and (2) the law eliminates the possibility of dispensing outdated drugs because the incentive of drugstore owners or need to meet competition?) to purchase large quantities of drugs to take advantage of quantity discounts is muted.

It is pertinent to note that in two previous cases involving a professional board, the New Jersey Supreme Court has ruled that truthful advertising is permissible even though it might not be deemed good professional practice.[77] Paradoxically, the Superior Court brief of the intervenor-defendant New Jersey State Pharmaceutical Association relied heavily on these cases, but it did not point out the decision regarding legality of truthful advertising.

[77] *Abelson, Inc.* v. *New Jersey State Bd. of Optometrists,* 5 N.J. 412, 75 A. 2d 867 (1950); *Abelson, Inc.* v. *New Jersey State Bd. of Optometrists,* 19 N.J. Super. 408, 88 A.2d 632(1952).

ADVERTISING DISCOUNTED PRICES

Three states have laws[78] and seven states have regulations[79] that prevent a pharmacy from advertising discounted prices. The laws and regulations provide that such terms as "discount," "cut rate," or words with a similar connotation may not be used to promote the sale of prescription drugs. This rule is distinct from those that prohibit the naming of specific prices of particular prescription drugs, although the two rules usually are combined as one or are both contained in the laws or regulations of the states.

Complaints about violations of the rules ordinarily arise from newspaper advertisements. Pharmacists upon seeing an unsatisfactory ad send it to the Board, or Board members may see the ad and notify the secretary of the Board. Enforcement of the ban is accomplished by warning pharmacists and pharmacies that their licenses may be revoked for violation of the restrictions. Usually the admonitions are sufficient to induce a change in the words used in their drug advertisements. After several attempts the offending promoter usually composes an advertisement that satisfies the Board and which, it is hoped, still proclaims that savings may be obtained on prescription purchases made in that outlet.

There has been no litigation on this specific issue. Probably this is because of the beliefs by companies that (1) current permissible statements convey the cost saving message to consumers and (2) the issue is too minor to contest. Drugstores that do not explicitly advertise prices are not convinced that such promotion is a good business policy and hence will consent to abide by Board requirements that limit what can be said about prescription departments generally. Moreover, according to interviewees, drugstore executives feel that by advertising discounted prices of toiletries and related items, and including the phrase "visit our prescription department" on the same page, the public receives the impression that prescription prices are also discounted.

PRESCRIPTION DRUG PRICE ADVERTISING

Eight[80] states have laws and twenty-one[81] have regulations that prohibit the advertising of prescription drugs by name and/or price. Although the requirement is straightforward in most states, Washing-

---

[78] California, Maryland, and New Jersey.

[79] Colorado, Louisiana, Maine, Massachusetts, Mississippi, New York, and Pennsylvania.

[80] Florida, Maryland, Michigan, New Jersey, New York, Oklahoma, Pennsylvania, and Texas.

[81] Arkansas, Colorado, Connecticut, Georgia, Hawaii, Illinois, Indiana, Iowa, Kansas, Louisiana, Maine, Massachusetts, Minnesota, Nevada, Oregon, Rhode Island, South Dakota, Virginia, Washington, West Virginia, and Wisconsin.

ton demands that if a prescription drug is named, its generic name, chemical formula, possible side effects, and benefits all be given prominent display. This is a devious way of making a drug price advertisement impractical.[82]

A regulation to prohibit the advertising of prescription durgs was proposed by the Missouri Board of Pharmacy, but was declared invalid by the Missouri Attorney General, who noted that "it is difficult to understand how the public welfare can be prejudiced by the dissemination of truthful information concerning the name, nature, and price of drugs which can be purchased only upon proper prescriptions."

The Attorney General also refused the Board's reasons for adopting the regulation:

> The reasons given for the proposed regulation are:
>
> 1. The "demoralizing" of prescription prices.
> 2. The possibility of public confusion and misconception concerning the availability of such drugs.
> 3. The danger of self-medication.
> 4. "Intimidation of the prescribing prerogatives of physicians."

> If . . . "demoralizing" of prescription prices . . . mean[s] the "lowering" of prescription prices, let us say only that this type of control is not within the scope of the Board's duties or powers. The argument that such advertising will confuse the public and foster misconceptions as to the availability of the drugs not only is a contingency inherent in any advertising, but seems to contradict the other reasons given on behalf of the proposed regulation. If the advertised drugs are not available, no damage can be done and there is no danger to be avoided.

> Another contradiction is presented by the third argument in favor of the regulation. By the terms of the regulation, it is addressed to drugs available only by prescription. Inasmuch as 'self medication' imports purchase and use without prescription, this reason fails to provide any basis for action by the Board.

> The contention that physicians will be intimidated by the advertising, or by patients who have seen the advertising, is likewise rejected. Aside from the fact that the professional skill and integrity of Missouri physicians is more than enough protection against the feared mesmerization of those who behold the advertising, it is not the function of the Board to control the sources of information of physicians or the general public.

> Without further analyzing the arguments propounded on behalf of the regulation, let it be said that there is no threat to the health or safety

---

[82] Wisconsin does not permit the advertising of non-name brand nonprescription drugs, which it calls "dangerous drugs."

of the community which would warrant a regulation of the type proposed. On the contrary, the suggested regulation would encroach upon the valuable right of merchants to proclaim their wares in a truthful manner and that of the public to be informed. Curtailment of these rights by the State is justified only by substantial and compelling reasons. None exists here.[83]

The usual justification for prohibiting the advertisement of prescription drug prices is that the procedure is not in the best interests of public health. Supposedly, patients who see Drug A advertised at a lower price than Drug B (which they are taking) will attempt to have their physician prescribe the lower-priced drug whether or not it is in the patients' best interests. It is suggested that physicians would be amenable to such pleas. Hence, the laws protect the public by shielding the allegedly weak-willed physician.

The concern of pharmacists for their fellow health professionals is admirable, but suspicious. All retail outlets have dealt a blow to the nonprescription drug sales of independent drugstores in recent years and it is probable that the main objective of these laws is to protect this last bastion of nonprice-competitive products through the spurious public health issue. Litigations in five states, four of which will be discussed, have contested advertising bans based on the preservation of public health.

Litigation in Louisiana. In 1956 the Louisiana legislature passed a law granting the state Board of Pharmacy the authority to promulgate a code of ethics by regulation. The resulting code, which went into effect January 31, 1957,[84] outlawed the advertising of prices of prescription drugs. On two different occasions John Schwegmann, Jr., supermarket and pharmacy owner and despoiler of Louisiana's fair trade law, attacked that provision of the promulgation proscribing price advertising of prescription drugs and refused to abolish the practice. Schwegmann charged that the Board, through its code of ethics, was merely trying to find a device to replace the fair trade act he had defeated in the courts.[85]

Over five years later, the Board of Pharmacy sent a letter to Schwegmann's five pharmacists ordering them to appear before the Board and stating that their licenses were being considered for revoca-

---

[83] *Trial Brief for Supermarkets Gen., supra* note 68, at 25–26.
[84] "Rx Price Ads Are Banned in Louisiana," *American Druggist*, January 28, 1957, p. 21.
[85] "Schwegmann Wars On New Louisiana Rx Code of Ethics," *Drug Topics*, February 18, 1957, pp. 3, 70, 84; "New Orleans Businessmen Hear Both Sides Discuss New Rx Code," *Drug Topics*, March 4, 1957, p. 10.

tion. Schwegmann, a state representative, tried to have a bill enacted to suspend the code of ethics, but was unsuccessful. He was able to obtain, however, a temporary court injunction preventing the Board from taking disciplinary action against his pharmacists.[86]

Later, the temporary injunction was removed when Schwegmann's plea for a permanent injunction was refused. Although this decision was hailed as a victory for the Board, it does not actually seem to be one. The Board apparently had not attempted to revoke any of the pharmacists' licenses and accordingly was able to successfully argue that Schwegmann had no cause for action since he had not been injured by any Board action.[87] Presumably, the court felt that Schwegmann would not have an actionable complaint until a license was revoked.

Although it was reported that the Board intended "to enforce the law," there seems to have been no such activities directed toward either Schwegmann[88] or other druggists. It appears that the Board has its rule and Schwegmann has his advertising.

Litigation in Florida. A short time after the Louisiana code of ethics promulgation, the Florida Board of Pharmacy decided to ban prescription price advertising. The Florida Board, however, did not have a specific legislative power authorizing the creation of the restrictive regulation.[89] Early in 1961 Shell's City, Inc., a discount drugstore, instituted a suit to have declared unconstitutional (1) the prohibitive regulation and (2) that provision of the Florida pharmacy law which limits the time available for appeal to the courts after a board promulgation. This litigation step was taken after the Board threatened to enforce the restrictive advertising regulation against Shell's City, Inc.[90]

In its petition to intervene in behalf of the defendant, the Florida State Pharmaceutical Association stated several reasons why the contested regulation did protect the public health and welfare:

1. To permit the advertising of dangerous prescription-legend drugs results in their becoming mere items of price competition.
2. Such advertising inevitably results in discount operations which suggest to a patient with a prescription for a specific quantity of a drug that the drug can be obtained for less in larger quantities.

[86] "Schwegmann Gets Injunction Against Board's Ad Curb," *Drug Topics*, June 18, 1962, pp. 2, 40.
[87] "Louisiana Board Hits Schwegmann on Rx Advertising," *Drug Topics*, May 6, 1963, pp. 3, 77.
[88] *Ibid.*
[89] "Advertising of Rx Items Banned in Fla.," *American Druggist*, October 6, 1958, p. 15.
[90] *Shell's City, Inc.* v. *Board of Pharmacy,* 18 Fla. Supp. 138 (Cir. Ct. 1961), aff'd 140 So.2d 871 (Fla. 1962).

3. The advertising of dangerous or prescription-legend drugs to the public tends to encourage the obtaining of such drugs, sometimes lethal, in larger quantities than dictated by good medical or pharmaceutical practices.

4. The danger of such advertisement has been recognized by the United States Bureau of Narcotics and has resulted in the nonadvertising policy of the Bureau concerning any narcotic drug or preparation.

5. Insofar as public health and general welfare are concerned, the prohibition of advertisement of prescription drugs applies with equal force and vigor to pharmacists as does the prohibition of advertisements by the medical and legal professions.

6. Unrestricted advertising of prescription-legend drugs leads directly to an increased addiction to habit-forming drugs by the public.

7. The regulation is not directed at the advertising or promotion of simple household remedies but is directed exclusively against prescription-legend drugs which may only be dispensed pursuant to a prescription and which require professional supervision to insure sane, sensible and proper distribution and use of such drugs by the general public.

8. The advertising condemned by the regulation tends to disparage the profession of pharmacy and to destroy the public's confidence in this profession and to the special damage of all members of that profession in Florida including the members of the Association and to, thereby, channel the public to other non-professional sources to obtain dangerous, habit-forming and prescription-legend drugs.

9. The direct relationship between the regulation and the public health and general welfare has been recognized in the states of Connecticut, Maryland, Louisiana, New York, Texas, Virginia, and Wisconsin by the enactment in these states of similar statutes and regulations prohibiting the advertising of prescription drugs.

10. The advertising of prescription drugs has had a direct harmful and deleterious effect upon the medical profession in that doctors experience increasing difficulty in properly treating and prescribing medication for patients who have been erroneously influenced by false and misleading advertising of prescription drugs.[91]

In a very short opinion, Circuit Court Judge Pat Cannon granted Shell's City, Inc.'s pleas, declaring both the regulation and the appeal time limit unconstitutional.

The Board appealed to the Florida Supreme Court, requesting a reversal of the decree. This court upheld the lower court's decision in both respects. In reaching its decision on the regulation, the court first declared the matter to be a question of whether the regulation had a reasonable relationship to the public health and welfare. The

[91] *Id.* at 140–141.

court then pointed out the fallaciousness of the Board's public health argument. The bench said that while the Board purported to consider the welfare of physicians it actually cast aspersions upon their competency and suggested the probability of unethical conduct by physicians by implying that there would be irresistible pressures to prescribe on the basis of patient demand. Further:

> The rule has more resemblance to an economic regulation prohibiting price competition in the drug business than it does to a regulation guarding the public health. . . . There is simply no reasonable justification for such an administrative intrusion on private rights when the regulation is so completely lacking in public benefit.[92]

This decision was the first state supreme court ruling concerning prescription price advertising. The judgment appears to be acceptable to other states since lower court rulings in several other states have upheld the same principle.[93]

Litigation in Illinois.[94] Section 7 of the Illinois Pharmacy Practice Act permits the revocation or suspension of the licenses of pharmacists who are guilty of "gross immorality." The Illinois Board of Pharmacy adopted a regulation declaring the advertising of prescription drug prices to be "gross immorality."

Pullman Prescription Pharmacy brought suit in the Cook County Circuit Court seeking an injunction to prevent enforcement of the regulation since the firm engaged in the price advertising of prescription drugs. The presiding judge held the restrictive regulation to be "illegal, invalid and void" and issued the injunction.

Litigation in Oregon. In promulgating the Oregon regulation prohibiting the advertising of prescription drug prices, the Board of Pharmacy cited four reasons why such publications are contrary to the public interest:

1. This practice will destroy confidence and caution necessary in the use of legend drugs by placing them in the same category as proprietary remedies.
2. This practice will also tend to induce the request for the sale of such drugs or medications without proper authorization.
3. The average citizen is unable and unqualified to read and interpret such orders or to determine the name of needed medication.

---

[92] 140 So.2d at 875.

[93] "Ban Against Rx Drug Price Ads Attacked In Three States," *American Druggist,* September 3, 1962, p. 18; "Rx Prices In Ads Stirs Illinois Row," *Drug News Weekly,* November 29, 1965, p. 4.

[94] *Pullman Prescription Pharmacy, Inc.* v. *White,* Cir. Ct. Ill., 1964.

4. This practice may tend to cause or lend support to substitution of drugs and medications and, as a result, the Public Health, Welfare, and Safety of the citizens is [sic] in jeopardy.[95]

The Oregon litigation resulting from this state's no-advertising policy is unusual because the suit was instituted by four Oregon newspapers and the Oregon Newspaper Publishers Association. The plaintiff publishers alleged that (1) they had been damaged by a loss of advertising revenue,[96] (2) the regulation bears no reasonable relation to public health and welfare, and (3) the regulation is an unconstitutional abridgement of free speech.[97]

The defendant Board of Pharmacy contended that the advertising of prescription drugs is dangerous because it (1) encourages patients to engage in self-diagnosis and to exchange medicines with one another and (2) exerts pressure on physicians to prescribe the lower-priced drugs.

Marion County Judge Val D. Sloper ruled for the plaintiff publishers. He declared the regulation void on the theory that the regulation has no reasonable relationship to the public health. He did not rule on the free speech issue.[98] The judge also held that the Board exceeded its statutory authority in promulgating the regulation.[99]

Upon appeal to the Oregon Supreme Court, the Board presented the same defenses it used in the lower court proceedings: (1) the plaintiffs have no standing to sue, (2) the controversy is not ripe for decision, (3) there is no judicable controversy, (4) the action is barred by sovereign immunity, (5) the question is moot because of the recent Congressional enactment of 76 Stat. 791 (1962) and 21 USC 3529n (1964), and, finally, on the merits of the case (6) promulgation of the regulation was a valid exercise of powers granted under ORS 689.620.

The court considered the first five issues and brushed them aside by showing that they were not satisfactory defenses. Having found for plaintiffs on the first five defenses presented by the defendant board, the court reached the merits of the case; namely, whether the authority to promulgate regulations is sufficiently broad to include the regulation of advertising. The court decided that the legislature did not include

[95] As quoted in *Trial Brief for Supermarkets Gen., supra* note 68 at 24.
[96] The Pay Less drug chain had advertised prescription drugs before the regulation went into effect. " 'Rx Ads To Public Are A Health Menace,' " *American Druggist*, June 22, 1964, p. 20.
[97] "Oregon Judge Rejects Ban On Rx Ads," *American Druggist*, November 23, 1964, p. 17.
[98] *Ibid.*
[99] "Judge Likens RxMan To Shoe Salesman," *American Druggist*, February 28, 1966, p. 19.

regulation of advertising in the rule-making power, because it was not mentioned and was specifically provided for in other sections of the law, e.g., laws relating to dentistry. If the legislature had wanted to include regulation of advertising for the Board of Pharmacy, it would have done so. Therefore, the court struck down the regulation on the ground that the regulation was beyond the scope of authority vested in the Board. Since the regulation was struck down at this point, the court did not find it necessary to consider the merits of other (constitutionality) grounds asserted by plaintiffs.[100]

To dispel the notion that the advertising problem has been limited to the states previously mentioned, it should be noted that drugstores in other jurisdictions have encountered similar difficulties. Among these are California,[101] Pennsylvania,[102] New York,[103] and Canada.[104]

The courts that have ruled on the advertising of prescription drugs seem to agree that a board of pharmacy may not promulgate and enforce a regulation that proscribes advertising in that (1) such a regulation exceeds the grant of authority given to boards of pharmacy by the legislature and/or (2) such a regulation amounts to legislation—a function limited to the legislature.

The courts do not agree that regulation of prescription drug advertising is or is not related to public health and safety. If the relationship does exist (to the satisfaction of the courts), *laws* regulating prescription drug advertising are within the police power of the state and therefore constitutionally acceptable. Otherwise, the opposite line of reasoning (leading to a declaration of unconstitutionality) follows.

The Florida Supreme Court and the Missouri Attorney General have said the health relationship does not exist and the Oregon Supreme Court (seemingly) and the New Jersey Superior Court have said that the relationship does exist.

To get a reasonable understanding of the relationship (if any) of prescription drug advertising to public health, it must first be ascertained to what extent the pharmacists are responsible for public

---

[100] *Oregon Newspaper Publishers Ass'n.* v. *Oregon State Bd. of Pharmacy*, Sup. Ct. Ore., June 3, 1966.

[101] "Calif Board Orders Drug King Chain To Cease Its Rx Price Ads," *American Druggist*, November 13, 1961, p. 12; "Reduced-Price Ads Draw License Suspensions," *Drug Topics*, August 24, 1964, p. 10.

[102] "Hits Membership Discount Rx Plan," *American Druggist*, July 9, 1962, p. 18; "Penna. Board Asks Justice Dept. To Okay Citations For Unfair Ads," *Drug Topics*, January 27, 1964, p. 10.

[103] "Court to Study New York's Ban On Rx Price Ads," *Drug Topics*, November 4, 1963, p. 4.

[104] "Canadian Rx Ad Curb Hits Judicial Snag," *American Druggist*, November 22, 1965, p. 19; "Canadian Supreme Court Nixes Review Of Recent Ruling Allowing Rx Price Ads," *American Druggist*, January 17, 1966, p. 21.

health. Ordinarily, it is considered to be the fault of the prescribing physician and/or manufacturer if contra-indications or injuries result from a prescribed medication. If the injury was caused by improper manufacture or by the manufacturer not making the dangers and contra-indications associated with the drug known to physicians, it is likely that the manufacturer will be held liable. If, on the other hand, the injury results from ignorance on the part of the physician due to the physician's own shortcomings, (inadequate diagnosis, unawareness of the patient's history of contra-indications with specific drugs, etc.) the pharmacist is still not liable provided he filled the prescription correctly.

Other than the all-important function of filling prescriptions accurately, the pharmacist is responsible for keeping his drug stock from becoming contaminated or adulterated. Avoiding the dispensing of drugs that are not effective or are dangerous because of natural deterioration after manufacture (shelf life) is shared by the manufacturer and the pharmacist. The manufacturer must indicate on the package the expiration date and the pharmacist must not dispense from that package beyond that date.

It would then appear that the advertising-health relationship does not exist, unless it can be shown that a law prohibiting advertising would protect the public health by removing the incentive to break the law that requires the discarding of outdated drugs—the law-breaking proclivity having been generated by price competition which generates the need to buy large quantities of dated drugs to take advantage of quantity discounts which induces law breaking when these drugs do not sell fast enough. Such reasoning is tantamount to a belief that pharmacists are not trustworthy, especially if they are drugstore owners. If that is so, public health should further be protected by (1) requiring that only prescribing physicians dispense drugs or (2) preventing pharmacists from owning drugstores so they would not be tempted by the profit motive.

PROMOTIONAL TECHNIQUES

Drugstore operators employ a variety of promotional techniques to entice customers. One that is growing in prevalence is the offering of special discounts on prescriptions sold to union members and to older citizens, the latter popularly called senior citizens' plans. The reasoning behind such schemes is sound. By charging lower prices to older customers, the image of a druggist willing to sacrifice profit to help people with limited incomes is created. Relatives of older people generally will tend to patronize these drugstores because of their price reducing policy. Moreover, older people frequent drugstores more often than others (they use more medication than other age groups), and it is hoped that they will be grateful enough, or that for convenience they will purchase other items at the participating stores. The combination, judging from the prevalence of the plans, induces a sufficient volume to overcome the 10 or 20 percent price reduction on prescriptions given to the oldsters.

The plans involving unions are established for similar reasons. There is, however, an additional purpose. Unions have, in several states, organized pharmacies to service their members and druggists believe that it is better to retain this business at a reduced profit rate than to forfeit the sales completely. In the football vernacular, union plans are defensive as well as offensive formations.

Some states do not allow these plans to operate on the theory that a pharmacist's duty is to serve the public without discriminating in any manner between patients or groups of patients. As is true for all the restrictive practices, it is difficult to determine which states prohibit the senior citizen and union plans, but it appears that only six states outlaw such plans, one (New Jersey) by law, four (Colorado, Michigan, Pennsylvania, Virginia) by regulation, and one (Utah) by a ruling of the attorney general. There has been no litigation in this area and it is surprising that rules prohibiting these practices have not been more widely adopted. The dearth of such regulations is probably attributable to the pharmacy boards' not being aware of the economic arguments against price discrimination.

The American Pharmaceutical Association has, however, informed all state boards of pharmacy that the offering of special prices or discounts to groups can be attacked from several directions if the boards wish to do so:

1. Where there is a law or regulation prohibiting the advertising of prescription drugs by name or price, the offender can be charged with violating the provision.
2. A suit can be brought alleging unfair competition for charging an unreasonably low fee for service, if the state has an appropriate statute.
3. A suit may be initiated to enforce the fair trade law, if the state has one.
4. The offender may be charged with violating the state's antitrust law.
5. Opposing advertisements may be placed pointing out that if one group is receiving a special discount, the other customers are indirectly subsidizing the discount.

6. Proceedings may be instituted on the basis of fraud if it can be shown that the promised discounts are not actually given.[105]

RECENT LEGISLATIVE DEVELOPMENTS

In a few states, the advertising problem has shifted to the legislative halls, perhaps because of adverse court decisions on regulations and perhaps for other reasons. That a court reversal resulted in a recent Florida drug advertising law is probable since the statute declares that it is in the public interest to prescribe advertising on certain drugs because their use causes abnormal physical reactions "that may interfere with the user's physical reflexes and judgments, may create hazardous circumstances which may cause accidents to the user and to others." This, it appears, is to serve notice to the courts that the law is a public health and safety measure.

Maryland has enacted a law that specifically empowers the Maryland Board of Pharmacy to promulgate regulations concerning advertising and promotion to the extent that such regulations are "necessary to protect public health, safety and welfare." Sponsored by the Maryland Pharmaceutical Association, the bill as originally worded would have given the Board the authority to issue the regulations to proscribe advertising actions tending to lower professional standards of conduct. In the face of charges that the clause would give too much power to the Board, it was struck from the bill.[106]

When this writer interviewed the Executive Secretary of the Maryland Board of Pharmacy early in 1966, he expressed the intention to seek broader rule-making power for the Board. As described by the Executive Secretary, the impression received by this writer was that advertising is inappropriate for a professional pursuit such as pharmacy and that it would be desirable to limit advertisements to the name of the establishment, its proprietor and/or pharmacists, its hours, and its location.

[105] "Map Rx 'Club' Attack," *Drug News Weekly*, April 3, 1967, p. 4.
[106] "Law Requires RxMan To Transmit Data," *American Druggest*, May 8, 1967, p. 38.

CHAPTER ELEVEN

Operating Constraints: Employees and Nondrugstore Sales

This chapter analyzes pharmacy laws and regulations that restrict managerial practices in connection with the employment of pharmacists and drug sales in nondrugstore outlets. Also, various litigations pertaining to this area as well as some miscellaneous license denials will be examined. Finally, a summarizing section will be presented to crystallize the controversies which are the subject of this and the preceding chapter.

Restrictions Relating to Employees

The employee prohibitions included in the various state pharmacy laws and regulations adopted by state boards of pharmacy bear a dubious relationship to professionalism and/or the protection of public health. The restrictions are concerned with pharmacist-manager requirements, dispensing limitations and regulation of hours of pharmacists.

PHARMACIST-MANAGER REQUIREMENT

Sixteen states, fourteen by law[1] and two by regulation (Colorado and Wisconsin) require that each drugstore be managed by a registered pharmacist. The reasoning underlying the enactments is that a nonpharmacist manager of a drug outlet might order a pharmacist-employee to commit illegal and/or unethical acts. If the manager is a pharmacist this possibility is removed. There is no evidence to support the idea that pharmacists have been induced by their superiors to act

[1] Alaska, Connecticut, Maryland, Massachusetts, New Jersey, New York, Ohio, Oklahoma, Oregon, Pennsylvania, Tennessee, Vermont, Virginia, and West Virginia.

contrary to law. Despite this, the rule has been used as a basis of several license denials in Massachusetts, the theory being that even a pharmacist-manager of a corporate-owned store is an employee and not a manager (cannot control policy) since there are others to whom he must report. Three of the more important Massachusetts license rejections are discussed below.

Adams Drug Company. Early in 1965, at the close of a tempestuous hearing attended by many drug association leaders (The Greater Lowell Pharmaceutical Association and The Massachusetts State Pharmaceutical Association), the Massachusetts State Board of Registration in Pharmacy refused to issue an operating permit for an Adams Drug Company drugstore to be located in Newton Center, Massachusetts. One ground for the denial was that the management of the outlet would not be in the hands of pharmacists, even though a pharmacist named Irving Beck was scheduled to direct the activities of the store. The other reason for the license rejection was that the Lowell, Massachusetts, area in which the outlet was to be situated was overpopulated with drugstores. The national average of population per drugstore is 3,000; Lowell has a 91,000 population and 41 drugstores—about one drugstore for every 2,200 inhabitants.[2]

Newspaper reaction was sharply critical of the Board's decision. A cartoon appearing in *The Lowell Sun* depicted a barrel labeled "free enterprise" being tightly held shut by a rather obese pharmacist sitting on the barrel lid. An accompanying editorial stated that the Board's reasoning gave "rise to the thought that it is, indeed, fair business competition that the druggists fear most."[3]

Brooklyn, New York, pharmacists, on the other hand, agreed with the action of the Massachusetts Board:

There is little doubt that in many sections of our country there is an overabundance of pharmacies. There is also little reason to doubt that an overabundance of pharmacies causes excessive competition and a possible lowering of professional standards—when price-cutting enters the scene. . . .

The corner-cutting [which results from the entrance of a discount drugstore into an area where there are already enough drugstores] may take the form of curtailed services which sick people sorely need, such as deliveries and charge accounts. Or they may take the form of stocking lower-quality, unknown-brand drugs. Or it may even force some weak-willed, hard-pressed pharmacists to take chances on unauthorized refills, just to

[2] "The Massachusetts Board Denies License: Too Many," *Drug News Weekly*, January 25, 1965, p. 12; "Board Denies License: 'Too Many Shops,'" *American Druggist*, February 15, 1965, p. 17; "Mass. Board Refuses To Issue Store Permit; Cites Population, Non-Pharmacist Control," *Drug Topics*, March 8, 1965, p. 14.
[3] *The Lowell Sun*, January 28, 1965.

make a living. Any or all of these practices are bad for the public health. And all of these practices are spawned when too many pharmacies are permitted to congest a neighborhood or a city.[4]

Osco Drug Company of New England, Inc. Osco Drug of New England, Inc. is owned by Osco Drug, Inc., which in turn is a subsidiary of Jewel Companies, Inc., whose major business is the operation of a large midwestern supermarket chain, Jewel Tea, Inc. Jewel Companies, Inc. entered the retail drug industry about five years ago by pooling interests with Osco Drug, Inc., a chain of drugstores concentrated in the Chicago area and operating in six other midwestern states.

Interviews with Osco and Jewel officials indicate that Jewel and Osco strive to cooperate with the boards of pharmacy in the states in which Osco stores are located. Also, Jewel attempts to promote a certain quality image to the public in its drugstores.[5] The firm's cooperation with regulatory officials may be a reflection of image maintenance efforts, but whatever the reason, Jewel Tea and Osco have gone to great lengths to avoid conflicts with boards of pharmacy. For example, significant compromises were effected in Wisconsin (including floor to ceiling partitions and separate entrances) to avoid litigation with the Wisconsin Board of Pharmacy.[6]

In keeping with its policy, when Osco began to consider entry into the Massachusetts market, its officers approached Massachusetts pharmacy officials to explain Osco's proposed expansion.[7] When no overt objection was voiced by the Board, Osco proceeded to carry out its plans. If objections had been raised at this point, Osco may well have withdrawn, especially since Parkview Drug's troubles in Massachusetts were well publicized. In any event, Osco was given no indication that its plans would not be acceptable.[8]

Osco formed Osco Drug of New England, Inc., and applied to the Massachusetts Board for a pharmacy license in November 1964.[9] The application for a store to be located at 97 River Street in Boston was received by the Board on December 17, 1964, and was returned because it was incomplete. The application was refiled on January 6, 1965.

[4] "Too Many Pharmacies," *The Brooklyn Pharmacist*, March 1965, p. 11.

[5] Interview with George E. DeWolf, Attorney and Insurance Manager, Osco Drug, Inc.; Jack Skyles, Vice President in charge of Chicago-Osco stores; Craig T. Allen, Jr., Secretary and Treasurer, Osco Drug, Inc.; and Grant C. Gentry, General Counsel, Osco Drug, Inc., January 13, 1966. Interview with John P. Street, Director of Professional Services, Osco Drug, Inc., February 16, 1966.

[6] Interview with Grant C. Gentry.

[7] A major reason for wanting to enter the Massachusetts market was that the drugstore operation would fit in with the firm's supermarket, discount, and restaurant subsidiaries located in that area.

[8] Interview with Grant C. Gentry.

[9] *Ibid.*

A hearing was scheduled for March 2, 1965, but was postponed at the request of an Osco attorney. The hearing was rescheduled for June 8, but was again postponed, this time at the request of the Massachusetts State Pharmaceutical Association.[10]

The hearing was eventually held on July 13, but further proceedings were delayed once more because of the resignation of the pharmacist Osco had employed to manage the proposed drugstore.[11] A new license application (that named the new pharmacist-employee) was filed with the Board and the next hearing was set for September 7. This meeting was cancelled due to the illness of an attorney representing defendant-intervenor (Massachusetts State Pharmaceutical Association) in the case. The next hearing was held on October 19 and the final session convened on November 9. Full transcripts of the procedures were not available to the Board until February 11, 1966.[12] The Board revealed its negative decision about March 1, 1966, so the total elapsed time between the original license application and the Board's rejection was about sixteen months, during which time the completed Osco store remained closed.

The Board stated three reasons why Osco's license request was denied. (1) The Board did not believe that the managements of the store would be under the direction of a registered pharmacist as required by G.L. c.112, s.39 of the Massachusetts law. (2) The Board felt that registration of the pharmacy would be inconsistent with and opposed to the best interests of the public health, welfare, and safety. (3) The Board did not believe that the store would be independent of all businesses other than retail drugstores.[13]

According to the regulatory agency, its finding that management of the proposed outlet would not be in the control of a pharmacist was supported by several facts:

1. The registered pharmacist who was supposedly to be in charge of the store had no written contract with Osco that outlined the employee's duties or tenure.
2. Conrad Faber, a pharmacist and President of Osco Drug of New England, Inc., attempted to employ pharmacists after he had hired a manager. If the supposed manager really was in control

[10] Massachusetts Board of Registration in Pharmacy, *Application of Osco Drug of New England Inc. for Registration of a Store for the Transaction of Retail Drug Business at 97 River Street, Dorchester*, p. 1, March 1, 1966 (hereinafter be referred to as *Ruling on Osco Application*).

[11] It was revealed at the July hearing that the pharmacist had declared bankruptcy in behalf of drugstores in another state while owning a major stock interest in those drugstore corporations.

[12] *Ruling on Osco Applications, supra note* 10, at 1–2.

[13] *Id.* at 3, 6, 8.

of the drugstore's operations, he would have done the hiring rather than Faber.

3. John P. Street, an Osco executive, placed orders for drugs for the store rather than the store manager performing that function.

4. Faber's insistence that the man hired as manager would really be a manager was of doubtful veracity in the absence of (a) a contract between the manager and the company, (b) ownership of Osco stock by the manager, and (c) Osco bylaws that the store would be supervised by a pharmacist.[14]

The objections are of very little merit. The Massachusetts pharmacy law does not outline specific managerial functions that a pharmacist should perform, and it is doubtful that a strict enumeration of any manager's duties could be compiled.[15] The Board may have an opinion concerning the drugstore manager's area of responsibility, but there is no firm legal ground to justify the opinion. And the lack of a formal contract between employee and employer or stock ownership in the parent corporation by the pharmacist-manager are patently ridiculous charges. There are thousands of managers without either, but they are managers nonetheless.

To support the ruling that registration of the pharmacy would be inconsistent with the best interests of the public health, the Board cited the following:

1. Osco demonstrated a reckless disregard for laws regulating the use of harmful drugs by (a) stocking the store when the law prohibits harmful drugs from being kept on unlicensed premises and (b) keeping those drugs in unlocked cabinets even though unregistered personnel had access to the as yet unopened store.

2. Osco performed an inadequate job of selecting its professional personnel.[16]

3. Osco did not adhere to accepted standards of professional conduct when it solicited pharmacists at their places of employment during their working hours.

4. The words "Drug Store" were crayoned above the Osco store front. The law (G. L. c.112, 5.38) says that such words must not be used before an outlet is registered as a pharmacy.[17]

[14] *Id.* at 4–5.

[15] Colorado may soon define a pharmacist's managerial duties. The Colorado Pharmaceutical Association is drafting such legislation now. The bill will be introduced after it has been approved by the Association's Executive Committee and the Board of Governors and by the Colorado State Board of Pharmacy. "PhA Drafting New Code for Colorado," *Drug News Weekly*, May 9, 1966, p. 14.

[16] This refers to the pharmacist who had experienced bankruptcy.

[17] *Ruling on Osco Application, supra* note 10, 6–7.

Here again the Board's charges appear fallacious under close scrutiny. It is true that John Street ordered the drugs, but the Massachusetts pharmacy law also provides that a drugstore must be fully stocked and inspected before it can be considered for a license. The only person who had access to the drugs were Osco employees who were preparing the store for business operations and it would seem that one's employees have to enjoy a little trust or that the person supervising the employees would make them trustworthy.

The alleged inventory violation resulted from a February 2, 1965, inspection of the store by Edmund Fitzpatrick, an examiner for the Massachusetts Board of Registration in Pharmacy. He had been instructed by the Board to check a rumor that drugs were on the premises. Fitzpatrick did not find the drugs himself, but they were shown to him by Camille LeFrancois (the store manager at that time) and Conrad Faber (President of Osco Drug of New England, Inc.). Faber and LeFrancois, both registered pharmacists (Faber is not registered in Massachusetts), were the only persons with access to the drugs. The drugs were stored in two locked cabinets in a warehouse on the second floor of the store.[18]

As a result of Fitzpatrick's inspection, the Board registered a complaint with the Massachusetts Department of Public Health. William P. Kearney, an inspector of the Drug Control Section of the Department, was ordered to investigate the complaint, and was shown the drugs stored in the locked cabinets on the second floor warehouse. Kearney reported to his superiors that there was no violation of the law.[19]

The Board's complaint that Osco did not competently select its employee-pharmacists is not logical. If pharmacists registered by Massachusetts are unsuitable, the fault lies with the Board, not Osco. Also, the Board's disapproval of Osco's pharmacist recruitment technique is without merit. Whether or not the Board condones the practice, there is no law against it and, of course, the pharmacists interviewed do not have to become Osco employees.

As for the crayoned words "drug store" above the store front, it appears that the sign was lying on a counter inside the store, and could be seen by peering through a window where a corner of paper covering the window had come untaped. The sign would not have been visible to a casual passerby.

[18] Massachusetts Board of Registration in Pharmacy, *In the Matter of: Camille J. LeFrancois—Osco Drug of New England, Inc.* Hearing held on July 13, 1965, at 14 Beacon St., Boston, Mass.

[19] Massachusetts Board of Registration in Pharmacy, *In the Matter of: Osco Drug of New England, Inc.* Hearing held on October 19, 1965, at 14 Beacon Street, Boston, Mass.

The third reason stated for denial of the license, that the outlet would not be independent of any other type of business, is based upon the facts that (1) Osco's parent corporation owns supermarkets, bakeries, and ice cream parlors operating in Massachusetts, and (2) Osco's headquarters were apparently to be located at the local subsidiary supermarket headquarters.[20] This charge may be true. The law that drugstores must be independent of other business operations may, if the Board's interpretation is correct, be unconstitutional. The question arises as to how the public health is harmed by the fact that a company owns supermarket and drug chain subsidiaries.

Osco has retained Harold Rosenwald, a well-known appellate attorney who successfully argued the Parkview case. This is a strong indication that Osco intends to continue its efforts to enter the retail drug industry in Massachusetts. In addition, a spokesman at the 1966 annual meeting of Jewel Companies, Inc. stated that the license denial would be taken to Massachusetts' highest court if necessary. Meanwhile, the "drugstore" in question and another (in Rockland) were opened without a prescription department and another, in Attleboro is under construction.[21]

Parkview Drugs, Inc. Parkview Drugs, Inc. owns a chain of drugstores in the Kansas City, Missouri area and operates the prescription drug departments in GEM International discount stores and in other discount stores in nearly every section of the United States. It was standard procedure for Parkview to arrange for the opening of the pharmacy in the GEM store located in Hingham, Massachusetts.

Parkview located a manager, Martin Cohen, for the pharmacy (to be known as Hingham Pharmacy) and on February 28, 1962, Cohen applied for a permit for a pharmacy in the GEM store. The Massachusetts Board held a hearing on May 23, 1962, to consider the application, and on July 13, 1962, denied the license because, purportedly, the management of the store would not be in the hands of a registered pharmacist.

Parkview immediately appealed the refusal to the courts, but procedural and jurisdictional matters were to delay a final decision on the case for almost four years. Parkview apparently committed a procedural error in connection with filing its appeal for court review of the Board's decision. The petition for review was filed with the Superior Court well within the thirty-day period required by G.L. c.30A s.14(1). But intervenors in the Board proceedings (The Massa-

[20] *Id.* at 8.
[21] "Denied Permit, Osco Launches 2 OTC Stores," *Drug Topics*, June 27, 1966, p. 3; Jan Calkins, "Osco Vows to Fight Bay State Defeat," *Drug News Weekly*, June 20, 1966, pp. 1, 12.

chusetts State Pharmaceutical Association and fourteen Boston drugstores) were not given notice of the appeal until August 14, 1962, eleven days after the filing of the petition with the court. According to G.L. c.30A, s.14(2), an intervenor must be given notice within ten days after the petition is filed.

Apparently the error was noticed by both the plaintiff and the intervenors. Parkview, on February 14, 1963, filed a motion for permission to file a substitute petition for review. The intervenors, however, on March 14, 1963, moved to dismiss the original complaint on the ground that the Superior Court was without jurisdiction in the proceeding because of the plaintiff's failure to serve notice to intervenors within the required ten days. The Superior Court agreed with the intervenors, allowed their motion, and denied Parkview's motion for a substitute petition.[22]

First Supreme Judicial Court Decision—The plaintiffs appealed the dismissal of the case to the Supreme Judicial Court of Massachusetts. The high court reversed the lower tribunal and remanded the case to the lower court to be heard on its merits. The appellate court held that G.L. c.30A, s.14(2) does not state a jurisdictional requirement. Rather, said the court, it only deals with threshold matters. The bench held that the petitioners met the jurisdictional requirement of the law by filing a petition with the Superior Court within thirty days. Had there been an unreasonable delay in serving the intervenors, there would have been grounds for dismissal. But in this case, the appellate body held, no delay or prejudice resulted from having served intervenors one day late.[23]

When a new petition was filed with Superior Court on the basis of the Supreme Judicial Court decision, the Pharmacy Board filed a petition for a writ of prohibition to keep the Superior Court from hearing the Parkview petition. It was the Board's position that a license denial may not be appealed to the courts. The petition for the writ of prohibition took the form of a suit by the Board against the Superior Court. A single justice of the Supreme Judicial Court heard the prohibition case and allowed Parkview to become an intervenor in the case. The judge reserved decision and brought it to the entire Supreme Judicial Court for consideration.[24]

Second Supreme Judicial Court Decision—The Supreme Judicial Court combined the prohibition case with another case resulting from

[22] *Cohen* v. *Board of Registration in Pharmacy*, 347 Mass. 96–98, 196 N.E. 2d 838–839 (1964).
[23] *Id.* at 98–99, 196 N.E. 2d at 839–840.
[24] *Milligan* v. *Board of Registration in Pharmacy*, 348 Mass. 491, 492, 494, 204 N.E. 2d 504, 506, 508 (1965).
[25] *Id.* at 492–502, 204 N.E. 2d at 506–513.

a license denial by the Board of Registration in Pharmacy. In the second case, Milligan and Baker, Inc. (John J. Milligan and Chester A. Baker) had on May 9, 1963, applied for a permit to operate a drugstore at 520 Commonwealth Avenue in Boston. It was not until a petition for a writ of mandamus was filed that the Board assigned the matter for a hearing on December 3, 1963. On February 27, 1964, the Board denied the license. On March 27, 1964, Milligan and Baker filed a petition for court review of the Board's decision.

On July 3, 1964, the Board filed a petition for dismissal of the *Milligan* case, presumably on the theory that a license denial does not entitle the aggrieved party to court review. The plea was overruled and the case was heard. A final decree was entered in favor of Milligan: "The Board's decision 'unreasonably delayed the issuance of the permit . . . in violation of . . . [Milligan's] constitutional rights . . . [The License denial] was unsupported by substantial evidence, . . . [Was] based on error of law and . . . [was] otherwise arbitrary and an abuse of discretion.' "

The judges were of the opinion that the salient issue in both the Milligan and Parkview prohibition cases was whether a court review could be had from an agency's adjudicatory hearing. Since the Board is specifically authorized to conduct adjudicatory proceedings (G.L. c.112, s.40 and 42A), there was no question of the Board's status as an agency. In addition, G.L. c.30A, s.14 provides for judicial review of any "final decision of any agency in an adjudicatory proceeding." Thus, the only question to be resolved was whether the proceedings before the Board were adjudicatory proceedings.

The court next pointed out that if a hearing is constitutionally necessary under the fifth and fourteenth amendments to the U.S. Constitution and Articles 1, 10, and 12 of the Declaration of Rights of the Massachusetts Constitution, the proceedings were adjudicatory. The court decided that the hearings were constitutionally required and cited a number of precedent decisions involving several different professional licensing boards. The tenor of the decisions was that to be lawfully denied the right to engage in a permissible occupation (i.e., all except burglary, prostitution, etc.), the applicant must be given a hearing so as to learn of the evidence against him and to refute such evidence if possible.

Regarding the two cases under consideration, the court said:

The effect of the board's denial of the registration permits in the two cases before us is clearly to preclude the applicants, although the individuals are qualified pharmacists, from the pursuit of a vocation at places where they deem it advantageous for them to work. Whether there is any constitutionally valid and adequate reason for denying the permits involves the determination by the board of the facts concerning the applicant and the place in which he wishes to carry on business. In such circumstances a hearing is necessary . . . The proceeding . . . is adjudicatory . . . [and therefore license applicants are entitled to court review of Board decisions] because opportunity for a hearing was constitutionally required.[26]

Since in the *Milligan* case the lower court had already ruled that the applicant was entitled to a license the high court merely affirmed the lower court decision. In the *Parkview* prohibition case (*Board of Registration of Pharmacy* v. *Superior Court*) a dismissal was ordered, in line with the judge's decision that court review *was* appropriate. This meant that the trial on the merits of the Parkview (Cohen) license denial could continue.

Superior Court Decision—All the preceding legal maneuvers by Cohen (Parkview) seemed to be lost when Judge Eugene A. Hudson of the Superior Court decided that the Board's denial of the license had been proper, even though there was a possible conflict of interest since the Board members were also members of the Massachusetts State Pharmaceutical Association. According to the judge, the transcript, exhibits, and evidence heard in court supported his decision.[27]

When Judge Hudson handed down his final decree, however, less than three weeks after enunciating this position, he completely reversed his original opinion. The justice declared that the Board had failed to prove that, because of the pharmacy's connection with GEM and Parkview, the firm's management would not be under the control of a pharmacist. Also, the judge continued, the Board failed to prove that (1) a pharmacy location in a shopping center is detrimental to the reasonable conduct of the drugstore's business, (2) the physical location of the Hingham outlet inside the GEM store is indicative of control of the pharmacy by someone other than Higham Pharmacy, and (3) the "closed-door membership" feature of GEM would materially affect the pharmacy.[28] The reason for Judge Hudson's sudden change in his position was probably due to the second Supreme Judicial Court decision as it related to the *Milligan* case. This decision was handed down in the interval between Judge Hudson's original declaration and his final decree.[29]

During the Superior Court trial, some interesting facts were brought

[26] *Id.* at 499–500, 204 N.E. 2d at 511–512.

[27] "Court Okays Board Denial of License," *Drug Topics*, March 8, 1965, p. 14.

[28] "Mass. Board Loses Leased Dept. Fight," *American Druggist*, March 29, 1965, p. 26.

[29] "Mass. Supreme Court Asked to Deny Permit for Pharmacy in GEM Store," *Drug Topics*, April 5, 1965, p. 8.

to light (by Harold Rosenwald, Parkview's attorney) concerning the relationships between the Massachusetts State Pharmaceutical Association and the Massachusetts Board of Registration in Pharmacy. All the members of the Board had been directors of the Association, but resigned from their directorships in a body on February 20, 1962, eight days before Parkview's pharmacy application was filed.[30] It was also shown that there was a connection between the Association and the Massachusetts Fair Trade Commission:

> Q (By Mr. Rosenwald):   And that [Fair Trade Commission] was affiliated with the Massachusetts State Pharmaceutical Association?
>
> A (By Mr. Cusick):   Well, basically it was partly affiliated in one way, shape or form because it pertained to pharmacy.[31]

Mr. John E. F. Cusick, at one time, simultaneously held these positions: member of the Massachusetts Board of Registration in Pharmacy, member of the Massachusetts Fair Trade Commission, and director of the Massachusetts State Pharmaceutical Association.[32]

Third Supreme Judicial Court Decision—The Board's appeal to the state high court failed to produce a reversal. The court held that the majority stock ownership of Hingham Pharmacy by Parkview did not mean that Cohen, with a small minority stock interest, could not exercise full managerial powers over the outlet.[33] Although Cohen's meager stock holdings were relevant to the Board's deliberations, as were Cohen's year to year employment contract and the corporation's bylaws, they were not adequate to deny a license. If they were, said the court, the Board could refuse to license any incorporated pharmacy, the managing pharmacist of which is not a substantial shareholder, a corporate officer, or at least the possessor of a long-term contract.[34]

The court concluded by declaring that the lower court judge had been correct in ordering the Board to issue the license:

> After finding that the board's decision was unsupported by substantial evidence, the [lower court] judge property . . . [ordered] Hingman's registration and the issuance of a permit to Cohen. [The law] . . . provides

[30] *Transcript of Superior Court Proceedings*, Vol. II, pp. 69–79, *Cohen* v. *Board of Registration in Pharmacy*, Superior Court No. 79683 in Equity, January 4–5, 1965.

[31] *Id.* at 73.

[32] *Id.* at 69–79.

[33] "Mass. Top Court OKs Permit Despite Tie to 2d Rx Firm," *Drug News Weekly*, February 14, 1966, p. 2.

[34] *Cohen* v. *Board of Registration in Pharmacy*, 214 N.E. 2d 63 (Sup. Jud. Ct. 1966).

that where prejudicial error has been found, "the court may . . . compel any action unlawfully withheld or unreasonably delayed." The record reveals that nearly four years have elapsed since Hingham's application was submitted to the board. . . . This dispute has been before us on two prior occasions involving procedural issues. While caution should be exercised by a court in ordering the issuance of occupational licenses, we think that the judge below did not err in deeming this case an appropriate one for such relief. *Final decree affirmed.*[35]

The Board did not issue a license to Hingham Pharmacy as the court ordered. Instead, the agency filed for a rehearing before the high court, requesting that the case be remanded to the Board for further proceedings. The arguments advanced by the Pharmacy Board were (1) the court cannot substitute its judgment for that of the Board as to whether the drugstore's operation would be controlled by a registered pharmacist, (2) there had been no unnecessary delay in the licensing proceedings, and (3) the Board did not take the position that a pharmacist employed by a corporation cannot be in charge of a store. The court denied the plea and issued a final decree ordering a permit to be issued to Hingham Pharmacy.[36]

The Massachusetts Board evidently does not intend to be guided by the decisions handed down in the Parkview case. This conclusion is confirmed by the regulatory agency's actions after considering the Osco license application. The charges against Osco are, as has been indicated, minimal and not grounds for license denial. Yet, the license request was refused. Perhaps the Board anticipates that the huge litigation expense that Parkview incurred,[37] coupled with the Board's Osco decision, will deter similar prospective applicants from attempting to enter the Massachusetts market.

It is also interesting to note that here was no direct attack on the constitutionality of the pharmacist-manager requirement in the Massachusetts law—especially since there has been such a case in Florida.

Florida Case.[38] The State of Florida initiated litigation against one Salvatore Leone under section 465.18 of the Florida law which stated that anyone who:

(1) owns, operates, maintains, opens, establishes, conducts, or has charge of . . . a retail drug establishment that is not, while open for

[35] *Ibid.*

[36] "Parkview Chain Wins Long Battle For Mass. Permit," *Drug Topics,* April 18, 1966, p. 12.

[37] According to Philip Small, Parkview spent over $100,000 to obtain its license, including legal fees, costs of leases, and employees' salaries. Other persons say Mr. Small is definitely not overestimating the amount of the expenditure.

[38] *State* v. *Leone,* 118 So. 2d 781 (Fla. 1960).

business or while engaged in . . . compounding, dispensing, or selling drugs or medicinal supplies, under the constant and immediate supervision of a person licensed as a pharmacist in this state . . .

. . .

(5) . . . shall, upon conviction, be fined a sum not to exceed one thousand dollars, or be imprisoned for a period not to exceed six months, or shall be so fined and imprisoned for each violation.

The defendant contended that the statute was unconstitutional in that (1) enforcement of the law would be an abridgement of certain privileges of certain Florida and United States citizens and (2) the law discriminated against a certain class of citizens. The lower court agreed with the defendant's assertions and dismissed the case. The state then appealed the decision to the Florida Supreme Court.

The Supreme Court concurred with the lower court's ruling and held the statute to be invalid. The justices stated that the pharmacy supervision requirement, although right and proper as it related to the prescription department of a pharmacy, could not be extended to include unrelated drugstore operations. This ruling was based on the reasoning that the state's police power, founded on the sound principle that individual rights must give way before the public welfare, was not at issue. The Supreme Court opinion held that there was no public health or safety problem that would justify pharmacist supervision over the entire store. Many other stores, the justices asserted, sell the same items a drugstore merchandises (except for prescriptions) without pharmacist supervision.

The court also rejected the state's contention that enforcement of the law compelling a pharmacist to supervise the filling of a prescription would be impossible without the broader managerial requirement. The court conceded that enforcement of the prescription provision might be made a little more inconvenient if nonpharmacists managed drugstores, but would not be impossible. Had the court accepted the state's argument that administration of the basic provision necessitated the broader limitation, the tribunal would have permitted the statute to stand since the established doctrine is that some unnecessary statutory restriction can be tolerated if it is needed to enforce a law that is essential for the protection of the public health and safety.

The Florida Supreme Court decision evidently means that (1) drugstores need not be operated by a pharmacist-manager and (2) a pharmacist need not always be on duty when the store is open. The pharmacist must be on duty only when prescriptions are being accepted and filled.

HOURS OF WORK FOR PHARMACISTS

The Florida case has implications for those states that regulate the working hours of pharmacists, particularly those that specify a minimum number of hours that a pharmacist must be on duty in a given drugstore. The states use three different provisions to control the dispensing hours of a drug outlet. These are (1) requiring a pharmacist to always be on duty when the store is open, (2) delineating minimum operating hours for a drugstore, (3) establishing maximum and minimum working hours for pharmacists, and (4) specifying the number of pharmacists to be employed by a store.

Pharmacist on Duty Whenever Store is Open. Fifteen states demand (eight by law,[39] seven by regulation[40]) that a pharmacist be present when the store is open for business. In view of the Florida Supreme Court decision, it does not seem likely that these laws and/or regulations would survive court actions testing their constitutionality.

Considering just the regulations, they probably transcend the authority vested in the boards of pharmacy by their respective state legislatures. The Missouri Board at one time promulgated a regulation stating that a pharmacist had to be on duty when a drugstore is open for business. The Missouri Attorney General, however, ruled the provision invalid on the ground that the Board exceeded its authority since the state *law* merely requires that a drugstore must have a pharmacist in its employ. The Attorney General concluded that a store can keep its other departments open even if there is not a pharmacist on duty to service the prescription department.[41]

The laws requiring a pharmacist to be present when the drugstore is open for business (lunch breaks and the like excepted) also appear to be of doubtful validity in light of a 1967 Virginia court decision. While the pharmacist owner of a Virginia Beach drugstore was absent from his drugstore, his nonpharmacist wife sold prescription drugs— and without prescriptions, at that. The wife was fined $60 for her acts, and her pharmacist husband was fined $350 by a municipal court for violating the law requiring every pharmacy to be "under the personal supervision of a pharmacist."

A Virginia circuit court overturned the municipal court ruling as it pertained to the pharmacist. The circuit court judge reasoned that

[39] Alaska, Michigan, New York, Oregon, Pennsylvania, Rhode Island, Tennessee, and Virginia.

[40] Arizona, Connecticut, Massachusetts, Minnesota, Montana, New Hampshire, and Wisconsin. Virginia also has a regulation in addition to its law.

[41] "Atty. Gen. Says Other Depts. Can Sell When Rx Man Is Away," *Drug Topics*, February 12, 1962.

the phrase quoted above does not mean that a pharmacist must always be present when a drugstore is open for business. Had that been the legislature's intent, the judge contended, the law would have been worded "no pharmacy may be open for business unless a pharmacist is present in the store."[42]

In contrast to the Florida case discussed in the preceding section, the constitutionality question is absent from this Virginia case. Possibly the Virginia justice followed the common judicial practice of interpreting a law, when possible, in such a way that constitutionality of the statute is preserved. That option was not available in the Florida case because the pharmacy law clearly stated that a pharmacist had to be in constant and immediate attendance whenever a drugstore is open.

The Florida and Virginia court decisions seem to express similar views: a pharmacist must fill and dispense prescription drugs, but a pharmacist need not be present merely because the drugstore is open.

Minimum Drugstore Operating Hours. Analogous to the "pharmacist always on duty when the store is open" requirement, is the interest in compelling all pharmacies to provide "full service." The idea seems to be a method of assuring that all drug departments in general merchandise stores have equivalent hours to standard drugstores. This would prevent the shifting of a pharmacist from store to store to fill prescriptions left by customers while he was at another store.[43]

In keeping with the full service theory the Massachusetts Board has promulgated a rule requiring drugstores to be open eighty hours each week. The board included a clause which allows the store to remain open for fewer hours "for good cause shown." The board, if it so chooses, can use the rule to force unprofitable store hours on some while, at the same time, allowing competitors to close early. Past actions of the Massachusetts Board should make chains extremely

[42] As quoted in " 'RxMan Can Supervise While Absent,' " *American Druggist*, May 8, 1967, p. 31; "Court OK's Filling Rx in Absence of Pharmacist," *Drug News Weekly*, May 8, 1967, p. 7.

[43] "Illinois Law: Rx Man Need Spend Only 'Major' Time in Store Daily," *American Druggist*, August 1, 1955, p. 20; "Utah Edict Hits 'Roving' RxMan Setups," *American Druggist*, April 6, 1959, p. 23; "Utah Warns Re Breaches Of Ban On Part-time Pharmacies," *American Druggist*, November 16, 1959, p. 16; "New Colorado Code Requires RxMen to Give 'Full Service," *American Druggist*, December 24, 1962, p. 8; "Iowa Board Is Urged To Require Full Service Of All Pharmacies," *American Druggist*, April 1, 1963, p. 20; "Georgia Pharmacists Urge Board To Pass 'Complete Service' Rule," *American Druggist*, May 27, 1963, p. 22; " 'Hours Minimum for RxMen Should Omit Nursing Homes,' " *Drug Topics*, May 17, 1965, p. 8. The last article deals with a proposed eight-hour-minimum-day law for pharmacies in Florida. The Board has either forgotten its Supreme Court decision or thinks the law will stand if no pharmacist-manager requirement is included.

wary of this rule. Typically, the *American Druggist* sees the rule as stronger discipline over *pharmacists,* not *businesses.*[44]

Maximum and Minimum Hours.[45] Six states have established limits on the number of hours a pharmacist may work. New York law, for example, prohibits an employee pharmacist from working over fifty-four hours per week. Regulations in Colorado, Minnesota, and Montana correspond approximately to the New York law. A Louisiana regulation requires a pharmacist to be on duty a minimum of forty hours a week. Arkansas, also by regulation, has a forty hour minimum, but does not allow the use of several part-time pharmacists to meet the forty hour requisite. No part-time pharmacist may be employed unless a full-time pharmacist is also employed.

There is, perhaps, a public health interest behind the maximum pharmacist hours if it is presumed that too many hours on the job are fatiguing and might result in dispensing errors. But since self-employed pharmacists are not included in those to whom the hours requirement applies, the public health either is being jeopardized in their case or else there is another reason for the maximum hour provisions.

There are two possible reasons—other than public health considerations—for the New York maximum employee-pharmacist hours law. The number of pharmacies has declined rather sharply in New York City in recent years, creating the very unusual situation of a local surplus of pharmacists. The excess persists because the store closings forced into the labor market former owner-pharmacists who are usually old and who have been in New York City many years and refuse to seek work elsewhere. The surplus is further aggravated by the presence of four pharmacy schools in New York City, many of whose new graduates have the same affection for the city as do the oldsters.[46]

A second conceivable reason for the maximum hours of work law lies in the fact that many New York City drugstores are unionized. It may be that the union supported the law to reduce the disparity between union and nonunion hours so that unionized stores could compete on a more equal basis with nonunionized outlets.

[44] "Trend Toward Stricter Discipline Over RxMen Seen Growing Among Boards," *American Druggist*, October 24, 1966, pp. 13–14.

[45] Although not directly related to employment hours, it is of interest to note that the Connecticut Board of Pharmacy planned to deny license applications on the ground that there was a shortage of pharmacists in Connecticut. The Attorney General, in response to a query from the Chairman of the Pharmacy Board, said that denials had to be based on provisions of the law and that the law said nothing about denying licenses because of a shortage of pharmacists. "Limits Grounds For Store Permit Denial," *American Druggist*, July 5, 1954, p. 20.

[46] Interview with Kenneth S. Griswold, Secretary, New York, State Board of Pharmacy, March 29, 1966. Mr. Griswold supplied the facts, not the theory.

Number of Pharmacists to Be Employed. Although it is not formally stated in the rules and regulations, there apparently is a rule in the Pennsylvania pharmacy law that new corporate-owned drugstores must employ a minimum of two full-time pharmacists. This provision is another way of assuring that a drugstore will be open for long hours— eighty hours per week at a minimum unless two pharmacists are on duty at the same time. Alabama and New Hampshire have a similar rule, but the Alabama regulation does not exempt independent retail pharmacists from compliance with the requirement whereas the New Hampshire regulation does.

The requirement does not constitute an economic hardship in larger cities where there generally is a large prescription volume, especially since the store manager must be a pharmacist and would be engaged in activities other than filling prescriptions, except during peak hours. In smaller towns, having two pharmacists on duty in an outlet is not necessary and generally results in the store having longer business hours than are economically justifiable.

DISPENSING RESTRICTIONS

Some drugstores have developed such a high prescription volume that it is profitable to take advantage of the division of labor principle. When a customer presents a prescription to be filled, the following tasks are performed: (1) the prescription is taken from the customer; (2) the written order is read and interpreted; (3) the correct medication (pills, for example) is selected from the drugs on hand; (4) the number of pills designated in the prescription are counted out and placed in a container; (5) the label is typed and attached to the receptacle; (6) the filled prescription is given to the customer and the sale is rung up. In most drugstores all these functions are performed by one pharmacist without utilization of the division of labor concept since the prescription volume generally is not sufficient to justify full-time quasi-professional assistance for the pharmacist.

In a few drugstores and in many hospital pharmacies the prescription volume makes it desirable to have clerks who receive the written order, type the consumption instructions on the label, and ring up the sale on the cash register. Despite the obvious advantages of this technique, eight states, by regulation, declare the use of clerks in prescription filling to be illegal.[47] The prohibition is supported by the argument that it is not safe for anyone except a pharmacist to have any connection with the dispensing of drugs.

[47] California, Colorado, Illinois, Indiana, Iowa, Kansas, Louisiana, and Virginia.

In the summer of 1964, the Ohio Board of Pharmacy adopted a regulation saying that no one except a pharmacist could type a prescription label. The rule was contested in the Franklin County Common Pleas Court by the Toledo Health and Retiree Center which had all its prescription labels typed by clerks. The Center claimed that the rule worked a hardship on its pharmacies. The presiding judge concurred with the plaintiff.

In rejecting the dispensing restriction, the court cautioned that the decision did not negate the pharmacist's responsibility to interpret the physician's instruction for the clerks. Moreover, the pharamacist, not the clerk, would be held accountable for any typing errors found in the label. There was no appeal from this decision.[48] If this case is accepted as a precedent, boards of pharmacy cannot refuse to permit the practice of the division of labor principle in the filling of prescriptions.

Restrictions on Nondrugstore Drug Sales

In addition to the many statutory and regulatory restrictions that apply to the operation of drugstores, there are three important limiting provisions that do not pertain specifically to pharmacies. These are the outlawing of prescription agents, prohibitions on mail order drugs, and anti-vending machine laws.

PRESCRIPTION AGENTS

A prescription agent could theoretically be anyone acting on behalf of a person whose physician has prescribed a medication for him. In practice, a prescription agent is ordinarily a nondrug outlet that takes its patron's prescription to a pharmacy, has it filled, and then delivers the medication to the patron while he is still on the agent's premises.

This system first came to public attention in 1957 when the Wyoming Board of Pharmacy attempted to prevent Casper Commissary, a supermarket located in Aspen, from pursuing the activity. When the Wyoming Attorney General was asked by the Board to clarify its right to prohibit the functioning of the prescription agency, the Attorney General stated that there is nothing illegal about having an agent perform an act for a person rather than the person executing the step himself. This opinion voided a Board rule approved by the Attorney General in office at the time of promulgation.[49]

---

[48] "Ohio Board Won't Fight Type Rule," *Drug Topics*, November 1, 1965, pp. 3, 36.

[49] "Wyoming Atty-Genl Rules That Grocers May Accept Rxs To Be Filled Elsewhere," *American Druggist*, April 22, 1957, p. 5.

Following the revelations concerning the Wyoming case, it was reported that three Food Town supermarkets in New Orleans were acting as prescription agents. The Louisiana Board of Pharmacy soon extracted an agreement from the supermarkets that they would cease the operation. At that time only Louisiana and Massachusetts had a provision which could be construed as outlawing the existence of prescription agents. Moreover, queries to ten attorneys in the drug field produced a nine to one opinion that it would be legal for a supermarket to act as a prescription representative.[50]

The lawyers indicated several reasons why the use of prescription agents is in conformity with the law:

1. There is no legal objection to a nondrugstore acting as an agent for a customer, whether it is a gratuitous service or whether a fee is involved. It is comparable to the employment of a Western Union messenger to present the prescription and obtain the drugs, except that the nondrugstore would advance the cash for the purpose. Such a loan would not make the transaction illegal.

2. In merely acting as the authorized agent of its customers, the nondrugstore is not engaged in the practice of pharmacy. It is, therefore, not committing any unlawful act, unless such agency services are expressly, or by clear implication, prohibited by law.

3. There are certain nonprofessional activities which can be delegated to an agent. For example, a doctor can have his receptionist or assistant clean a skin area preparatory to an injection and a lawyer can send an office boy to file a petition with a court clerk.

4. Prescription agents would not be prohibited under the general law of agency unless there is deception as to the fact that the prescription will be filled elsewhere.

5. It would seem unlikely that such a transaction would be construed as a sale of drugs at retail under New York law. The drugs are not offered or displayed to the general public. The nondrugstore buys the drugs from a pharmacist on behalf of the customer, and not on its own behalf for the purpose of resale.

[50] "Need Seen to Close State Laws Against Rx Handling by Non-Druggist 'Agents,' " *American Druggist*, October 7, 1957, pp. 5–6, 8. The attorneys consulted were Walter Beachboard of Philadelphia, general attorney for Smith, Kline and French Labs; Murray Cleveland of New Orleans, counsel to the Louisiana Pharmaceutical Association; Ray O. Clutter of Indianapolis, manager of the legal department of Eli Lilly; Frank T. Dierson of New York City, associate counsel to the American Pharmaceutical Manufacturers Association; Lawrence Ehrhardt of New York City, secretary of McKesson & Robbins; Harold Harper of New York City, counsel to the National Wholesale Druggists Association; Thomas Kiernan of New York City, White & Case; Samuel Shkolnik of Chicago, counsel to the Illinois Pharmaceutical Association; Samuel Silverman of Boston, counsel to and secretary of Massachusetts State Pharmaceutical Association; and Joseph Stamler of Newark, counsel to the New Jersey Pharmaceutical Association.

6. It could be argued that the practice is legal because the prescription is being filled by a registered pharmacist, as required by law.[51]

Despite these legal opinions, Allan Reese, Dean of students at the University of Kansas School of Pharmacy, declared that state boards have the authority to issue a regulation banning agency prescription arrangements.[52] Apparently, the states have concluded that Dean Reese is correct. Sixteen states ban prescription agencies, Oklahoma by law and fifteen others by regulation.[53] A court action dealing with both mail order drugs and agency prescriptions will be discussed in the following section on mail order drugs.

MAIL ORDER PRESCRIPTIONS

A person may become aware of and participate in a mail order prescription purchase plan in several ways. A mail order company from which he buys merchandise (e.g., Spiegel) may announce such a plan in its catalog or in a letter to prospective drug customers. In addition, an association such as a senior citizens' club may initiate a mail order program for its members. Labor unions also have utilized the plan, sometimes in conjunction with a prescription agency system.

To effectively prevent the operation of mail order drug plans at the state level requires a viable law proscribing the existence of such devices in every state and the District of Columbia. Universality is needed because the regulatory powers of the boards of pharmacy are limited, even assuming that the restrictions (four laws,[54] thirteen regulations[55]) that now exist can survive a court test. Pharmacy Boards can prevent their registered pharmacists from engaging in mail order drug plans. The regulatory agencies, however, cannot take action against a citizen of the respective states who sends his prescription to a jurisdiction where mail order drug houses are permitted. The problem was, and still is, the District of Columbia.

The American Pharmaceutical Association (APhA) first became aware of the situation when it learned that two mail order drug plans, with a combined 10,000 per week prescription volume, were operating practically next door to the APhA's national offices. The programs,

---

[51] "Is 'Rx-Via-Agent' Legal?" *American Druggist*, October 7, 1957, p. 7.
[52] " 'Boards Have Right to Bar Rx Agents;' " *American Druggist*, July 14, 1958, p. 23. Kansas had just promulgated such a regulation.
[53] Alabama, Arkansas, California, Colorado, Florida, Georgia, Kansas, Louisiana, Maine, Massachusetts, Mississippi, Ohio, Pennsylvania, Rhode Island, and Washington.
[54] Michigan, Oklahoma, Pennsylvania, and Tennessee.
[55] Arizona, California, Georgia, Illinois, Massachusetts, Minnesota, Mississippi, Nevada, New Mexico, Ohio, Oregon, South Dakota, and Washington.

launched by the American Association of Retired Persons and the National Retired Teachers Association, were operating out of Washington, D.C. where APhA is headquartered. A meeting was called by Dr. William S. Apple, Executive Director of APhA to discuss "the mushrooming of mail order prescription services throughout the United States [which] presents a menace to pharmacy as practiced in the traditional way. . . ." The Federal Food and Drug Administration (FDA) was called upon by the participants at the meeting to stop this activity,[56] but the FDA has never attempted to do so.

Although, as previously indicated, eighteen states eventually enacted laws or regulations to prevent the sale of mail order drugs, the citadel of the practice, Washington, D.C., remains a free market. A 1960 attempt to amend the District of Columbia pharmacy law to prohibit the licensing of mail order pharmacies failed when the U.S. Justice Department assailed the bill as a proposal to restrain interstate commerce.[57]

Many of the state mail order prohibitions were legislated as a direct result of a nonprofit mail order prescription drug plan initiated in the summer of 1961 by Spiegel, Inc. of Chicago, the third largest mail order house in the United States. The company organized a non-profit foundation called Spiegel Non-Profit Prescription Drug Foundation in which its charge account customers automatically became members. The plan was featured on the back cover and a four page insert in the 1961 Spiegel catalog. The company stated plainly that it was not in the charity business and that the Foundation was intended to increase sales of its other items.[58] Spiegel ceased this operation when the Illinois Department of Registration and Education ruled that resident pharmacists could not receive and dispense prescriptions by mail.[59] There was no definite authority for the action and legislation granting specific power to ban mail order drugs was vetoed by Governor Kerner in 1963 and 1965.[60]

Also in 1961, Pennsylvania druggists tried to prevent a pharmacy license from being issued to a Harrisburg clinic operated by the Inter-

---

[56] Stephens Rippey, "Mail Order Rx Operations Called Menace To Pharmacy At Special APhA Meeting," *Drug Topics*, January 18, 1960, p. 3; "FDA Is Urged To Bar Mail-Order Rxs," *American Druggist*, January 25, 1960, p. 17.

[57] Stephens Rippey, "Justice Dept. Raps Proposed D.C. Ban on Mail Order Rxs," *Drug Topics*, May 23, 1960, pp. 3, 40.

[58] "Spiegel Sure Courts Will Back Mail Rxs," *American Druggist*, July 24, 1961, p. 8.

[59] "Ill. Forces Spiegel To Shut Down Its Rx Mail-Order Plan," *APhA Newsletter*, Vol. 1, No. 3, February 10, 1962, p. 1.

[60] "Illinois Okays Board Plan But Kills Rx Mail Order Ban," *Drug Topics*, September 9, 1963, p. 3; "Governor Kills Illinois Ban On Mail-Order Rx," *Drug Topics*, August 23, 1965, p. 3.

national Ladies Garment Workers Union which was to include a mail order prescription service for its Pennsylvania members. The license was granted "after the board was subjected to pressure from the governor's office."[61] The plan was set up and apparently is operating successfully.[62]

By the spring of 1962 *American Druggist* was able to report that mail order drug plans were of no consequence. The dozen or so schemes that had emulated the first plan established in the District of Columbia were all defunct except for the original plan for retirees and (1) Katz Prescription Co. of Kansas City, Missouri; (2) Peoples Prescriptions, Inc. of Kansas City, Missouri; (3) Save-More Drugs of Washington, D.C., and (4) National Epilepsy League, which fills prescriptions only for members and limits those prescriptions to epilepsy medication.[63]

Recently, however, there has been renewed activity in the mail order drug field. In 1965, the National Farmers Union, Greenbelt Consumer Services, and National Council of Senior Citizens unveiled a cooperative venture designed to supply their members with prescription drugs by mail. Potential customers are about 2.25 million. The group issued a chart to indicate the extent of savings possible under the plan.[64] Table 11-1 reproduced the chart.

In addition to this proposal, the Toledo Health and Retiree Center, a nonprofit union-sponsored organization, announced that it would introduce a prescription by mail service for Ohio residents, both union and nonunion. This operation will presumably avoid the legal obstacles imposed by the states when an organization attempts to operate on an interstate basis.[65]

The Health Insurance Plan of Greater New York (HIP), the second largest group health service organization in the United States, instituted a mail order prescription program in January, 1967. The plan is an optional feature that HIP's group health insurance contracts will include if an employer requests it. To date, the coverage has been extended to 20,000 federal government employees and 14,000 New York City employees. By the end of 1967, HIP plans to have enrolled the remainder of New York City employees. Such a large enrollment will have a noticeable effect on drugstores in the New York City area since

[61] "Penna. Men Battle Labor Union's Plan For Rxs By Mail," *Drug Topics*, November 20, 1961, p. 3.

[62] "Union Mail Rx Program In Penna. Held 'Reasonable Success'; Phila. Excluded," *Drug Topics*, January 1, 1962, p. 14.

[63] "Only Two Big Nationwide Operations Are Left In The Mail-Order Rx Field," *American Druggist*, March 5, 1962, pp. 5–6.

[64] "Mail Order Service for Elderly to Bow Wednesday—Result of 2 Years' Planning," *Drug News Weekly*, March 15, 1965, pp. 1, 20.

[65] "Union Store To Sell Rxs by Mail Throughout Ohio," *American Druggist*, October 25, 1965, p. 21.

a large proportion of the total 750,000 employees covered by HIP plans are New York City employees.

The purpose of the mail order arrangement is to facilitate the payment of prescription drug expenses by employers with HIP acting as a servicing agent. If an employer prefers to have his prescriptions filled by his local pharmacy, the employee must pay for the first $25 of prescription costs and 20 percent thereafter. Under the mail order scheme, the employee pays nothing—not even postage.

A retail pharmacy fills the prescriptions for HIP, but the organization is trying to obtain a pharmacy license in its own right. Permission to do so must be received from the New York State Insurance Department before an application can be submitted to the New York State Board of Pharmacy.[66]

When the prepaid drug plan was announced in the summer of 1966, the intent was to establish HIP-owned pharmacies throughout the city in a pattern similar to the HIP health centers. The mail order plan was secondary to the proposed HIP pharmacies. Pharmacists quickly organized the Emergency Committee for Pharmacy and Public Health to fight the prepaid plan and the establishment of HIP pharmacies.[67] The Committee's appeal to Mayor Lindsay failed. Another appeal to the New York State Insurance Department did not halt the prepaid plan, but the need for Insurance Department permission for HIP to open pharmacies was revealed. Since approval of HIP-owned pharmacies was being deliberated upon at length, the mail order idea assumed primary importance.[68]

Although mail order prescriptions do not comprise at present a large percentage of the total prescription volume, two recent court decisions in this area are of interest since they reveal the courts' attitudes toward mail order drugs. In Iowa, a state district court has held that the Board of Pharmacy, in the absence of a law to that effect, does not have the authority to prevent the operation of a mail order drug business. The Iowa Board had not promulgated even a regulation concerning the mailing of prescription drugs, but it revoked the license of Federal Prescription Service of Madrid for advertising a mail order plan. Judge Harvey Uhlenhopp agreed with the drug firm that revoca-

[66] "HIP Expands NYC Rx-By-Mail Service," *American Druggist*, June 19, 1967, p. 31.

[67] The Committee included officials of the National Independent Pharmacists, Consolidated Brooklyn Retail Pharmacists, Nassau-Suffolk Pharmaceutical Society, Empire City Pharmaceutical Association, New York Pharmacists Association, Queens County Pharmaceutical Society, and Staten Island Pharmaceutical Association. A similar committee was formed six years ago to prevent unions from establishing drugstores in Manhatten.

[68] Elsa Klensch, "NY Pharmacists Fight 'Ruinous' Prepaid Plan," *Drug News Weekly*, August 1, 1966, pp. 1, 10.

TABLE 11-1: Prices Announced by Cooperative Mail Order Drug Service of National Farmers Union, Greenbelt Consumer Services, and National Council of Senior Citizens

Established (generic) Name	Brand Name	Price When Doctor Prescribes by Brand Name		Direct Drug Service Price When Doctor Prescribes by Established (Generic) Name
		You are Probably Paying	Direct Drug Service Plan	
1. Dextro Amphetamine Sulfate (5 mg.) 100's	Dexedrin	$7.95	$6.90	$1.20
2. Prednisone (5 mg.) 100's	Meticorten	26.70	21.95	2.40
3. Digitoxin (1 mg.) 200's	Crystodigin	2.70	2.20	1.20
4. Meprobamate (400 mg.) 100's	Miltown Equanil	9.90	7.50	5.90
5. Reserpine (.25 mg) 100's	Serpasil	6.75	5.15	.75
6. Pantaerythritol Tetranitrate (10 mg.) 100's	Peritrate	7.50	6.50	1.40
7. Secobarbital (1.5 gr.) 100's	Seconal	3.25	2.80	1.70

Source: "Mail Order Service for Elderly to Bow Wednesday— Result of 2 Years' Planning," *Drug News Weekly*, March 15, 1965, pp. 1, 20.

tion of its license was not warranted. The justice declared that "the cardinal fact is that the board's objection of prohibiting dispensing of drugs by mail is a matter of policy determination for the legislature, not a question of application or enforcement by the courts or administrative bodies.[69]

In Virginia, a union was charged with operating a pharmacy without a license (a criminal offense) because it acted as an agent for its members in collecting their prescriptions once a week, sending them to a union pharmacy in New York City, distributing the filled prescriptions, collecting the money for the cost of the drugs and then sending it to New York City. Warren County District Court found the union, Local 371 of the Textile Workers Union of America, and its secretary,

[69] "Iowa Court Says Rx Board Has No Right To Bar Mail-Order Rxs," *American Druggist*, December 6, 1965, p. 16.

David Ramsey, guilty of the charges. Upon appeal to the Circuit Court, the jury reversed the lower court's decision and found the parties innocent.[70] The Virginia Board of Pharmacy has now filed a civil suit in the Richmond County Court seeking an injunction to enjoin the union from continuing its practice of mail order and agent prescription drug service.[71]

Although the restriction prohibiting the operation of mail order pharmacies appears to be of doubtful legal validity, the issue may be definitely settled by APhA and the Veterans Administration (VA). The VA operates a mail order drug service for veterans who are eligible to receive free prescriptions and the agency recently began dispensing narcotic preparations through the mail. APhA has asked the U.S. Post Office Department to rescind a regulatory change that allows narcotic medications to be distributed by mail. The reply was not favorable and now APhA is contemplating litigation to halt the practice. Pharmacists have sought to curtail the VA's mail prescription program for a number of years, and, theoretically, the veterans need not rely on the mail service, but can have prescriptions filled at a local pharmacy of their choice. The VA, however, strongly encourages participants to secure their maintenance drugs through the agency's mail order prescription service.[72]

The pharmaceutical association arguments against mail order drug sales have emphasized that (1) the patient cannot ask a pharmacist questions about medicines sent through the mail, (2) the pharmacist is not able to consult the physician if there is some question concerning the medication, (3) mail order prescription plans make it easier for persons habituated to narcotics, amphetamines, and barbiturates to acquire such drugs by using forged prescriptions, and (4) if the mail order practice becomes widespread, the number of drugstores in the country would decline sharply and that would not be in the interests of public health.

APhA's arguments are weakened when one considers that:

1. Most pharmacists consider it unethical to discuss with the patient his illness and medication.
2. Various sources of communication, such as long distance telephone service, are available if the druggist must consult the patient's doctor.

[70] "Virginia Jury Sees Nothing Illegal About Mail-Order Rx Depot Operated by Union," *American Druggist*, December 6, 1965, p. 16.
[71] "Virginia Sues To Bar Union Over Mail Order Pharmacy," *Drug News Weekly*, April 18, 1966, p. 2.
[72] "May Sue P.O. On Its New Reg. Allowing VA To Mail Narcotic Rxs," *American Druggist*, January 17, 1966, p. 23.

3. Mail prescription services could exclude the dispensing of narcotic and other habituating drugs, except perhaps for the VA which maintains records and can detect forged prescriptions.
4. There is no evidence that the number of drugstores would decline, or that a decline would endanger public health.

VENDING MACHINE DRUG SALES

Five states have laws[73] and eighteen have regulations[74] that prohibit the sale of drugs by vending machines.[75] These rules keep even the simplest proprietary, aspirin, from being sold in vending machines. The theory is that young children might purchase and consume the medicine as candy. Although there is some merit to the argument, the places in which the vending machines generally would be located (railroad stations, air terminals, and taverns) ordinarily are facilities where young children, if present, are escorted.

The only known court case involving the distribution of drugs through vending machines occurred in Maryland in 1956. National Enterprises, a Baltimore vending machine manufacturer, applied to the Mayland Board of Pharmacy for a pharmacy permit, stating that it planned to sell aspirin and vitamins through vending machines. The Board declined to issue the license and warned the company that it would risk criminal action if it installed the machines without the pharmacy permit.[76]

National Enterprises brought suit in the Baltimore state circuit court to compel the issuance of the license. The Board contended that:

The indiscriminate placing of vending machines containing aspirin in public places where they would be available for use any time of the day or night without supervision of any sort would constitute a serious threat to the public health.[77]

Judge Reuben Oppenheimer, the presiding justice, agreed with the Board. The court said that the Maryland statute that lets general mer-

[73] Georgia, Indiana, Maryland, North Dakota, and Oregon. Indiana allows the use of the Brewer system, but others do not mention it.

[74] Arizona, Arkansas, California, Colorado, Connecticut, Idaho, Iowa, Louisiana, Minnesota, Montana, New Hampshire, New Mexico, Ohio, Utah, Virginia, Washington, West Virginia, and Wisconsin. California specifically exempts the Brewer system from the general ban. Louisiana and New Hampshire specifically include the Brewer system in the ban. The other fourteen states do not mention the Brewer system.

[75] Three additional states, Kansas, South Carolina, and Texas, do not have rules to prevent vending machine drug sales, but they do have regulations authorizing the use of the Brewer system.

[76] "Firm Asks To Sell Aspirin & Vitamins Through Machines," *Drug Topics*, April 30, 1956, pp. 2, 66.

[77] "Vend Machine Co. Sues For Right To Put Aspirin Device In Taverns," *American Druggist*, May 7, 1956, p. 8.

chants sell proprietary drugs implies personal supervision over those sales by the merchant. The opinion concluded that since this supervision would not be present if the drugs were sold in an unattended vending machine, the use of the mechanism was not permissible.[78]

Miscellaneous License Denials

In the many litigations mentioned in previous chapters, refusals to grant pharmacy licenses were always based on a restrictive provision of the state pharmacy law or regulation promulgated by the board of pharmacy. This section deals with cases of a more general nature. The license denials discussed below were based on statutes not considered to be restrictive, but interpreted in a restrictionist manner. The five cases presented involve four states.

RHODE ISLAND[79]

The Ann & Hope Store of Cumberland was the first discount operation to secure a pharmacy license in Rhode Island. The firm's first application for a permit was refused by the Pharmacy Board on the basis that:

1. There is no public need for a pharmacy since there are already a sufficient number of pharmacies in the area.
2. The pharmacy cannot adequately serve the public since the discount store is closed on Sundays.

The Governor then asked the Rhode Island Attorney General to rule on the validity of the denial. The state attorney ruled that the license had to be granted if the store met all statutory requirements. Since the grounds on which the permit had been denied were not rooted in the law, the license was granted.

MISSOURI[80]

In the summer of 1964, Lester Steinhoff, a registered pharmacist employed by a Columbia drugstore, applied for a license to open a pharmacy in a building then under construction. The structure was

[78] "Maryland Board Wins Round Against Vending Machine Drugs," *American Druggist*, July 30, 1956, p. 8.

[79] "R.I. Forces Board To Grant License," *American Druggist*, July 23, 1962, p. 10.

[80] "Board May Restudy Controversial Permit," *Drug Topics*, October 5, 1964, p. 8.

to consist primarily of physicians' office space. In the area where the building was being erected, there is a municipal zoning ordinance restricting the hours that drugstores may operate and the items that they may sell. Reports were that the Missouri Board of Pharmacy intended to refuse Steinhoff's application because of the ordinance.

On August 21, 1964, the Missouri Attorney General informed the Missouri Board of Pharmacy that its function was not to enforce or implement a city ordinance. Nevertheless, the Board, on August 26, 1964, declined to issue the license and advised Steinhoff to get the ordinance amended to that the store could be operated without any limitations.

After the Board's rejection, the Attorney General was asked to give a formal opinion on the propriety of the action. He stated:

Restrictions imposed by city ordinance provide no basis for the Missouri Board of Pharmacy to refuse to license a pharmacy which is otherwise qualified.

. . .

If there be a conflict between the ordinance and the statutes of the state, which regulate operation of a pharmacy, then the ordinance, at least to the extent of the conflict, is invalid.[81]

The statement given by the Attorney General caused the Board to consider its position and issue the license.[82]

PENNSYLVANIA

Of more recent vintage is the experience of White Cross Stores, Inc., a discount drugstore chain. When the Board denied the firm's request for a pharmacy permit in Pittsburgh, the company simultaneously filed an antitrust suit (charging restraint of trade) in a U.S. District Court and a suit in the Dauphin County Court to force the Board to grant a pharmacy license.

In the federal case, White Cross charged the Allegheny County Pharmaceutical Association and its three principal officers with conspiring to prohibit the chain store from obtaining a pharmacy license. The main allegations were that the association had solicited funds from its members to finance its illegal activities and had tried to obtain promises from pharmaceutical wholesalers in the Pittsburgh area that they would refuse to sell merchandise to White Cross. This forced the company to buy its inventory through Virginia wholesalers.[83]

[83] "Discounter Sues Association For Conspiracy On Permit," *Drug Topics*, February 10, 1964, pp. 3, 66.

[81] *Ibid.*

[82] Interview with Lloyd W. Tracy, Secretary, Missouri Board of Pharmacy, January 7, 1966.

The Dauphin County Court suit alleged that the Board of Pharmacy cannot deny a pharmacy license on the assumption that the establishment might be operated on a discount basis. The White Cross attorney contended that (4) the Board deliberately delayed considerations of the license, (2) other applicants were not required to undergo similar treatment, and (3) complaints submitted to the Board by an unnamed third party had no basis in fact.[84]

The Dauphin County Court sustained the plea that the Board be ordered to issue the pharmacy license. The Board's contention that the applicant did not comply with the standard of professional character as required by the Pharmacy Act was rejected. The evidence offered by the Board of prescription irregularities contrary to Virginia and federal law had not been prosecuted by either Virginia or the U.S. government, the court noted. Besides, said Judge Homer J. Dreider:

> The State Board of Pharmacy will be able to exercise adequate supervision. The store will be under the board's supervision with respect to the applicant's pharmacy and with power to suspend or revoke its permit for just cause.[85]

The federal suit was dismissed at the request of White Cross.[86]

The Pennsylvania Board of Pharmacy also refused to grant a pharmacy license to the Health and Welfare Committee of the Harrisburg Central Labor Council. The first denial was based on the Board's belief that the drugstore would not be open to the public. Upon reapplication, the Board asked for the Health and Welfare Committee's minutes, bylaws, constitution and charter. While the Committee was considering the Board request, the Board denied the license.[87]

The Labor Council took the matter to court, and it is still being adjudicated. At one point, however, the judge did criticize the Board for raising the matters of authority and status of the Welfare Committee during the latter stage of the Board hearing that preceded the court action. The bench contended that if those items were of importance and the Board was confused, as it said, it should have sought to delve into the matters at the beginning of the hearings.[88]

[84] "Cut-Rate Sues Penna. Board To Obtain Pharmacy Permit," *Drug Topics*, May 4, 1964, p. 17.

[85] *State Board of Pharmacy* v. *White Cross Stores, Inc.*, 83 Dauph. 179, 186 (C. P. Dauph. Co. Pa. 1964).

[86] "White Cross Drops Suit Against ACPA," *Allegheny County Pharmacist*, November 1964, p. 7.

[87] "Penna. Board Again Denies Permit For Union Store," *Drug Topics*, April 3, 1967, p. 30.

[88] "Board Fights Competition, Union Tells Penna. Court," *Drug Topics*, June 26, 1967, p. 4.

IOWA[89]

For thirty years Woodbury County had operated a clinic containing a pharmacy that was jointly administered under a contract by the county medical and dental associations. In 1967, the two associations discontinued the relationship, apparently because federal and state welfare programs had reduced or eliminated the need for the prescription service.

The county then hired a pharmacist to continue the drugstore's operation and applied to the Board of Pharmacy for a license. The Board denied the license on the grounds that the county clinic is not a person as defined by pharmacy laws (i.e., the clinic was not an individual, partnership or corporation). The County Attorney asked for a ruling from the Attorney General's office, and the Board's position was sustained.

It appears that a license had not been needed before because the pharmacy was under the supervision of dentists and physicians practicing in the county. Now, according to the Executive Secretary of the Iowa Board of Pharmacy, the pharmacy would not have maintained the high standards required of drugstores and the pharmacy's patrons would have suffered as a result.

Summary of Operating Constraints

This and the preceding chapter have identified twenty-one separate operating constraints imposed by state pharmacy boards, either through existing statutes or promulgations of the regulatory agencies. Many courts in several states have ruled against the restrictions. Only one limitation, the prohibition of the sale of home remedies in vending machines, has been upheld. The overwhelming number of court rejections should convince state pharmaceutical associations, the American Pharmaceutical Association, legislators, and the public that no evidence exists to justify the existing restrictions on a public health basis.

Despite the multitude of negative court decisions, the constraints still remain as part of the state law and board of pharmacy regulations in states where the courts have not ruled on the restrictions. Table 11-2 shows the prevalence of the various restrictions. (Refer to Appendix I for each state's provisions.) In some instances the restriction declared invalid is still retained as part of the state law or board regulation. As one official explained in connection with an advertising rule,

[89] "County Pharmacy Is Ruled Illegal By Iowa Official," *Drug Topics*, May 29, 1967, p. 10; "Iowa Rx Board Rules: County Clinic Is Not A Person; So Doesn't Rate Pharmacy License," *American Druggist*, June 5, 1967, p. 33.

TABLE 11-2. Operating Restrictions in State Laws and Regulations

Restriction	No. States with Restriction Law	Regulation	State(s) where Declared Invalid	Authority Making Invalidity Declaration
I. General Prohibitions				
1. No Permit for General Merchandise Store	0	2	None[a]	
2. No Permit for Fair Trade Violator	0	1	Arizona, Delaware	Lower courts (Arizona Supreme Court refused to hear that case)
3. Limitation on Number of Outlets	0	1	None[a]	
II. Physical Requirements				
4. Physical Separation Required of Rx Dept. in General Merchandise Store	1	12	None[a]	
5. Separate Entrance Mandatory (Rx Dept. in General Merchandise Store)	0	6	Maryland	State Supreme Court
6. Entrance to Adjoining Store Prohibited	0	1	None[a]	
7. Floor Space Rule (% or over 220 sq. ft.)	2	11	North Dakota	State Supreme Court
8. Self-Service Prohibited	0	3	None[a]	
9. Inventory Rule	2	0	None[a]	
10. Ban on Closed Door Operations	2	4	Indiana	State Supreme Court
III. Advertising Restrictions				
11. Outdoor Sign Control	2	0	None[b]	
12. Implying Discounted Rx Prices in Advertisements	3	7	None[a]	
13. Advertising of Prescription Prices	8	21	California, Florida, Illinois, Missouri, Oregon[c]	Florida Supreme Court, Oregon Supreme Court, lower courts, and Missouri Attorney General
14. Promotional Schemes	1	4	None[a]	
IV. Restrictions Relating to Employees				
15. Pharmacist-Manager Requirement	2	14	Florida	State Supreme Court
16. Pharmacist on Duty Whenever Store is Open	8	7	Florida	State Supreme Court

TABLE 11-2—(*Continued*)

Restriction	No. States With Restriction Law Regu- lation		State(s) Where Declared Invalid	Authority Making Invalidity Declaration
17. Number of Pharma- cists to Be Employed	1	5	None[a]	
18. Dispensing Restrictions	0	7	Ohio	Lower Court
V. *Restrictions on Nondrug- store Sales*				
19. No Prescription Agents Allowed	1	15	Virginia	Lower Court
20. Mail Order Drug Sales Prohibited	4	13	Iowa, Virginia	Lower Court
21. Ban on Sale of Pro- prietary Drugs in Vending Machines	5	18	None[d]	

Source: Appendix I.

[a] No known litigation concerning this regulation.

[b] In litigation in New Jersey.

[c] In litigation in New Jersey.

[d] Upheld by a lower court in Maryland.

the provision is handy to show to people in an attempt to obtain volun- tary compliance with the rule and to mention the consequences of flouting the provision; once a "violator" calls attention to the rule's invalidity, harassment of the individual ceases. It was pointed out, however, it was possible to obtain "a lot of mileage" with the rule because most people are not aware that it has been declared invalid.

If the restrictions previously discussed are not designed to protect the public health, it is intriguing to ponder their true purpose, notwith- standing the complaints by pharmacy officials that the courts do not understand the issues. Great intelligence is not necessary to deduce that the restrictions are intended to limit competition. All of the limita- tions are designed to exclude discount stores, chain drugstores, and supermarkets from the retail drug industry business and/or inhibit advantages enjoyed by these large merchandisers. If one surveys the restrictions enumerated in Table 11-2 and asks what type firm's activi- ties are hurt by each restriction, the answer is monotonously the same. Not one injures the independent neighborhood pharmacy. All except the last three adversely affect the large drugstore operators.

Most large enterprises are resigned to the restrictions and abide by them even though they are an annoyance and are costly. The prob-

TABLE 11-3: Ranking of States by Number of Restrictions[a]

State, Rank, and No. of Restrictions	State, Rank, and No. of Restrictions
1. Pennsylvania (12)	23–28. South Dakota (4)
2. Minnesota (11)	23–28. Washington (4)
3–4. Colorado (9)	29–35. Alabama (3)
3–4. Virginia (9)	29–35. Arizona (3)
5–6. Massachusetts (8)	29–35. Florida (3)
5–6. Mississippi (8)	29–35. Illinois (3)
7–9. Louisiana (7)	29–35. New Hampshire (3)
7–9. Michigan (7)	29–35. Utah (3)
7–9. Montana (7)	29–35. West Virginia (3)
10–13. Arkansas (6)	36–40. Alaska (2)
10–13. Maryland (6)	36–40. Delaware (2)
10–13. New York (6)	36–40. Nevada (2)
10–13. Wisconsin (6)	36–40. North Dakota (2)
14–22. California (5)	36–40. Tennessee (2)
14–22. Connecticut (5)	41–45. Hawaii (1)
14–22. Indiana (5)	41–45. Idaho (1)
14–22. Kansas (5)	41–45. South Carolina (1)
14–22. Maine (5)	41–45. Texas (1)
14–22. New Jersey (5)	41–45. Vermont (1)
14–22. Ohio (5)	46–51. District of Columbia (0)
14–22. Oklahoma (5)	46–51. Kentucky (0)
14–22. Oregon (5)	46–51. Missouri (0)
23–28. Georgia (4)	46–51. Nebraska (0)
23–28. Iowa (4)	46–51. North Carolina (0)
23–28. New Mexico (4)	46–51. Wyoming (0)
23–28. Rhode Island (4)	

[a] Includes restrictions relating to pharmacy ownership.

lems created by the restrictions become much more severe and are much more prone to litigation when licenses are denied as a result of the rules. The larger corporations will abide by the rules of the game, but will raise quite a disturbance if they are not allowed to play. Even so, the restrictions make it possible for pharmacy boards to engage in delaying tactics through infrequent board meetings, postponement of action on license applications, and prolonged court actions.

Some assessment of the unfriendliness of the various states' pharmacy boards toward the large drugstore operators can be made by comparing the number of restrictions in each state. Table 11-3 draws such a comparison. This should serve as a guide to entrepreneurs in the drug field—be very careful in states ranked near the top and be prepared to initiate or to respond to court action or otherwise stay out.

PART FOUR

Results and Implications of Restrictionism

CHAPTER TWELVE

Economic Consequences of Free Market Restrictions

Introduction

It is not the function of economists to establish national economic policies just as it is not the function of aeronautical engineers to determine the number of airplanes that should be in the Air Force. Economic goals and defense budgets are political decisions to be made by the executive and legislative branches of the government.

The role of economic technicians in the political decision-making process is to explain how various alternative courses of action will affect the economy. Once the preferred course of action has been selected by the legislative and/or executive branches, the economist is available to assist by showing how to reach the economic goals.[1]

This generalized reasoning applies to regulation of the retail drug industry. Supervision of the drug area requires two basic decisions. First, it should be questioned whether the public health will be harmed (in a measurable way) by the proposal under consideration. If the conclusion is yes, the decision not to adopt the proposal should be a relatively easy one. The same argument is applicable if the question is reversed. Will the public health be enhanced (in a measurable way) by the proposal under consideration? In this case, if the answer is yes, there should be no problem in securing the adoption of the suggested law (or administrative regulation).

---

[1] This is not to suggest that economists are apolitical—quite the contrary is true—nor is it to suggest that there is unanimity among economists. No consensus could be established among economists that anti-inflationary measures are or are not needed at this time, but a sizable majority could be polled. Likewise, there would be substantial agreement as to what could be done to halt inflationary tendencies, even though a variety of possibilities would appeal to a diverse number of economists.

Only when public health is not the point at issue is there a need for a political decision. Consider, for example, physician-owned pharmacies. Assuming that such factors as drug prices, number of drug outlets, and quality and quantity of medication prescribed are satisfactory, the physician ownership problem becomes one of the desirability of assuring the viability of the druggist segment of small business. Hence, legislative action in this area should be premised on whether small business should be preserved.

Needless to say, the factors that affect public health are not as simple to isolate as the foregoing has intimated. In a given situation, each proponent is able to present formidable statements that seemingly validate his position. However, public health matters and political questions must be separated and investigated independent of one another if rational regulation of the practice of pharmacy is to prevail. The purpose of this chapter is to examine those factors that should be considered in the political arena. No attempt is made to conclude what course of action should be taken. Rather, in keeping with the opening paragraphs, the goal is to suggest the results of following certain regulatory practices.

Pertinent Economic Concepts

To analyze properly how free market restrictions relate to consumers and the economy, one first must make a subjective judgment as to what is most significant for these two elements. It appears that for consumers the most important consideration is how the restraints affect prices. Since political survival depends on keeping constituents satisfied, legislators are also extremely interested in how a given law will affect prices. In view of the current emphasis on the national growth rate it seems that, for the general economy, the most important effect of free market limitations is their influence on economic growth. Bearing these two thoughts in mind, some basic economic concepts are useful as a vehicle for discussing pricing, while the general economic effect of restrictions can be characterized in terms of resource allocation and innovation.

DEMAND SCHEDULE AND DEMAND CURVE

A demand schedule is a chart that indicates the quantity of a particular item that will be purchased at varying prices. In Table 12-1, the hypothetical example of men's suits demonstrates that as the price of suits changes, so does the number of garments purchased. The schedule is derived by asking at each price level, "If men's suits cost $X, how many will be bought?" The schedule does not purport to encom-

TABLE 12-1: Demand Schedule for Men's Suits

Quantity of Men's Suits Purchased	Price of Men's Suits in Dollars
50,000,000	20
10,000,000	50
6,000,000	75
1,000,000	100
500,000	150
400,000	200
250,000	250

pass more than one time period; i.e., it does not explain (for example) how many suits will be purchased at $200 if 250,000 of the garments had been sold at $250 and then the price fell to $200. The question answered by the schedule is: If at one point in time the prevailing price of suits is a given amount, what is the corresponding number of suits that will be sold?

The demand schedule, when plotted on graph paper with the horizontal axis being quantity purchased and the vertical axis being price, is known as a demand curve. Thus, the demand curve is nothing more than a graphical representation of the demand schedule.

The demand curve in Figure 12-1 is what is known as a conventional demand curve. This means that for most products, a demand curve empirically derived would have the characteristic shape illustrated by Figure 1—sloping downward and to the right. Stated another way, the conventional demand curve shows that if an item has a high price, few of that item will be purchased; conversely, at each lower price, more of the good will be purchased.

As might be expected, there are other types of demand curves that do not adhere to the conventional shape, but for the purposes of this chapter, these various other shapes need not be introduced in the discussion.[2]

To further simplify the complex real world, it is instructive to think of a conventional demand curve in linear terms; that is, a demand schedule which, when graphically presented, is a straight line. Typical linear demand curves are shown in Figure 12-2.

Demand curves shaped as the ones in Figure 12-2 indicate that there is a constant relationship between the various prices of an item and the quantity of the item purchased at each price. This relationship

[2] For a comprehensive analysis of such perverse demand curves, see Sidney Weintraub, *Intermediate Price Theory* (Philadelphia: Chilton Books, 1964), pp. 146–152.

is such that for every dollar decrease in price some constant additional amount of the item will be purchased.

It should be emphasized that the curves in Figure 12-2 refer to *market demand* rather than to each firm's demand for its product. The summation of the demand curve for each firm is the market demand, but there may be wide disparities in the individual firm demands. This is of especial importance in the pharmaceutical manufacturing industry where a revolutionary drug is protected by patent. The demand for drugs to cure ailment A will, in such cases, be dominated by one firm—the one producing the new drug.

The new drug will be so intensively promoted by brand name that physicians form the habit of prescribing by the brand name. Therefore, even when the protecting patent has expired, habit and continued promotion keeps demand concentrated on the one firm's (and

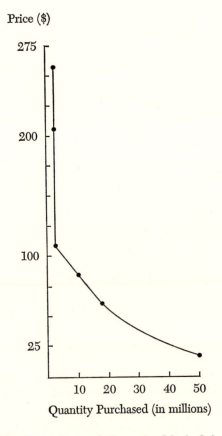

Price ($)

Quantity Purchased (in millions)

Fig. 12-1.—Demand Curve for Men's Suits

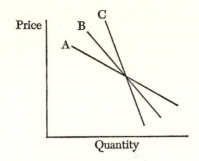

Fig. 12-2.—Linear Demand Curves

its licensees) branded product long after generically equivalent drugs appear on the market.

PRICE ELASTICITY OF DEMAND

The General Concept. Having determined that price and quantity are related to one another in a certain numerical way, it becomes necessary to define the relationship more precisely. What must be established is the strength of the price-quantity relationship. Specifically, it should be resolved whether a small price change will result in a small or large change in the quantity of the item consumed. If, for example, in one time period the price of a good drops from $2 to $1, the question arises as to what extent the quantity purchased will increase in the ensuing time period.

A method that utilizes an index number has been derived to cope with the problem. This index number, called the price elasticity of demand, is the ratio of the percentage change in the quantity purchased to the percentage change in the price of the commodity. Expressed mathematically: $e_d = -\%$ change in Q/% change in P. When numbers are inserted in place of words, a numerical value for e_d can be calculated. The value of e_d will always be equal to one, less than one or more than one. The values of e_d at particular points on a demand curve vary and these changing values are of extreme importance. Assume that e_d is less than one along a considerable portion of a demand curve. This means that the demand for the commodity for which the demand curve is drawn is insensitive to price changes. That is, there is very little change in the quantity purchased, even though the price of the good is changed considerably (curve C in Figure 12-2). As a result, prices of this commodity tend to be elevated.[3] On the other

---

[3] Firms attempt to maximize total revenue. If at P = $2, Q = 10 (TR = $20), a firm would be foolish to reduce P to $1 unless Q would surge to more than 20.

hand, where e_d is more than one along a significant portion of a demand curve, prices will tend to be depressed.

Price Elasticity and Drug Prices. The concept of price elasticity, or e_d, is of most importance with respect to various types of drugs. For most drugs the value of e_d probably is less than one most of the time, which means that prices are apt to be rather high. This conclusion is reached by visualizing the typical prescription drug sale.

A person becomes ill and consults his physician. The doctor performs an examination and diagnosis and then prescribes one or more medications in addition to an injection given to the patient by the nurse in the physician's office. Having been assured that the combination of the injection and the prescribed drug will remedy his ailment, the patient goes to a pharmacy to have his prescription filled.

The average person does not haggle with the pharmacist over the price of the drug, nor, in most cases, will he ask the price before having the prescription filled. Generally, the cost of the prescription is of secondary importance. The patient is convinced that he needs the medication and, as a consequence, price is not of major significance to him. He is more concerned with restoring his health. Hence, his demand for the medicine ordinarily is insensitive to the price he must pay, that is, the e_d is less than one.[4]

The individual probably is not completely ignorant of the price situation. It is possible that through his physician, or family or friends who have had similar maladies, the patient knows the price range of a particular drug. If one pharmacist attempts to charge a sum above the going market price in other pharmacies, the patient may seek another pharmacist.

In addition, people do not as a rule consider whether a prescribed medicine should be bought. The purchase is an automatic action and one that is in contrast to the usual economic view of man. The conceptual base of man as an economic animal revolves around the premise that a person has a given income and allocates it among his needs and wants so as to achieve optimum satisfaction. This view is not fully applicable to the purchase of a prescription drug, for, although an individual may decide to buy a power boat rather than a new car, or a new overcoat rather than a new rug, he almost never will consider the alternative of buying a steak dinner rather than having a prescription filled.

---

[4] Persons with chronic disorders (e.g., diabetes and glaucoma) are atypical in this respect. These people purchase medicine year after year and tend to seek the outlet with the lowest price. As a result, these maintenance-type drugs have a competitive element even though, as with other drugs, aggregate demand is fixed.

As one executive expresses it, a man buying a prescribed drug is purchasing something for which he would rather not make the expenditure. He would prefer a steak dinner, perhaps, to a bottle of pills, but he nevertheless buys the pills. It is a disagreeable, but necessary, purchase and so the pills are opted for rather than the steak dinner.

Thus, contrary to the usual pattern of making choices in the market place, the ordinary consumer of prescribed drugs assumes that there is no choice to be made; he buys regardless of price. This is indicative of a low-price elasticity of demand for drugs which in turn creates a tendency toward high prices.

SUBSTITUTIBILITY OF PRODUCTS

Substitutions Caused by Changes in Price and Income. The principle of substitutibility is a concept that is clearly related to price elasticity. When an individual first decides the products he will purchase with his income, he will not change the product mix he has selected unless there is a change in his income, the prices of the goods and/or the available product mix. For example, if an individual's income rises, he may alter his product choice from a Chevrolet to an Oldsmobile. The same result may occur if the prices of Oldsmobiles fall. In these two situations, alternate purchases are made *within* a commodity class when some other automobile has been substituted for the Chevrolet— each time for a different reason.

If everything remains the same (i.e., income level and merchandise availability) except prices of automobiles in general, there also can be substitutions *across* commodity classes. If automobile prices were to quadruple, individuals might decide to sell their automobiles and rent or purchase housing within walking distance of their major activities. Or, people might choose to purchase boats and commute via water where possible. Virtually every product can and will be substituted for another if the price of the originally preferred commodity rises sufficiently. This even applies to medical care. If office calls to physicians result in a per visit fee of $1,000, there probably will be a considerable reduction in the number of professional consultations made by patients.

Substitutions Resulting from Varied Product Mix. The main point concerning substitutibility as it relates to this study is that substitutions within merchandise classes may result from the availability of various product mixes from which selections can be made. If a person decides to purchase an automobile in a given price range, he has a choice of several products, e.g., standard Chevrolet, Ford, and Plymouth automobiles have little price differences. To make his selection from the assortment, the consumer considers such factors as body styles, interior colors, and design and finally settles upon his preference. This example is applicable to the overwhelming number of commodity classes from toothpaste to toys and up to and including nationally advertised headache remedies.

The idea of ease of substitution within commodity classes helps explain the price structure of the items in a given product group. Since the goods are competing with one another, the price structure will be arranged in some order of quality gradations that exist either in fact or in the consumers' minds.

Substitutibility in Proprietary Medicines—The substitution principle is apparent in the nonprescription medicine market. As far as the general buying public is concerned, there is a distinction between Anacin, Bayer's Aspirin, Excedrin, etc., and nonbrand name headache remedies. The brand name products are, or are thought to be, faster and/or more effective than ordinary aspirin. Hence, the branded products enjoy a higher selling price that nonbrand compounds in the headache remedy commodity class. The prospective purchaser has the choice of paying a relatively high price for the "better" (e.g., brand name) products or of paying a low amount for "inferior" items.

Substitutibility in Prescription Medicines—In the prescription drug field, product substitutibility is virtually nonexistent so far as the customer is concerned. He purchases the remedy his physician has selected. The patient rarely, if ever, thinks to ask the pharmacist or physician if there is a drug available with similar therapeutic characteristics that is less expensive than the one prescribed. Even if the patient did consult with the pharmacist, the druggist could not recommend an alternate because state laws do not allow the pharmacist to deviate from a prescription in any respect. Therefore, the substitutibility that exists within a product line of other commodity classes is absent from the product lines in the prescription drug commodity class.

The prescription buyer, then, must depend on his physician to prescribe a drug that is acceptable both therapeutically and economically. Two factors, however, prevent doctors from following this practice. First, physicians have many more areas of concern than drug prices; and further, there are a multitude of available drugs. For the majority of cases, it is an unjustifiable burden on the physician to provide the service of determining for his patient the least expensive of all appropriate drugs. Second, the practitioner ordinarily has used one or two branded drugs in a single generic category and is familiar with their therapeutic values and side effects. In this situation, the physician is unlikely to experiment with nonbranded or even other branded drugs of this generic class. He knows good results are obtained by using what he prescribed in the past and it is much easier on his overtaxed memory to specify the drug with which he is most familiar.

The end result is that high prices for prescription drugs, especially the newer ones, are to be expected. The combination of inelastic demand and low substitutibility dictate this conclusion.

Effect on Consumers

The preceding section suggests that one may expect prescription drug prices to be relatively elevated because of an inelastic demand for prescription drugs and because of a low order of substitutibility between the generally more expensive branded drugs and ordinarily lower cost nonbranded (generic) items with essentially the same properties. To this more or less natural tendency toward high drug prices must be added the results of free market barriers resulting from the actions of state legislatures and state pharmacy boards.

It is difficult to single out any one free market restriction that is solely responsible for elevated drug prices. In general, anything that limits competition tends to foster high prices.[5] The free market restrictions that most inhibit competition appear to be restrictions on the sale of nonprescription drugs in nondrug outlets, prohibition of the advertising of prescription drug prices and limitation of drugstore ownership to pharmacists. Other barriers[6] may have some price effect, but, if so, it is probably minimal.

ADVERTISING OF PRESCRIPTION DRUGS

More retail drug outlets prefer not to, and do not, advertise the prices of their prescription drugs. This statement emerges from conversations with several firms engaged in the retail sale of drugs. The two or three companies that advertise drug prices apparently do it only because they are compelled to do so for "competitive reasons."

[5] The writer is well aware of the complexity of the pricing decision. That entire books on price theory exist testifies to the numerous factors to be considered Besides the many economic approaches, businessmen will readily admit that pricing is neither easy nor precise. For these reasons the writer is loath to make categoric assortions regarding price structures, except where reliable statistics can be cited.

[6] Any device which tends to exclude a potential entrepreneur from an industry is called a "barrier to entry." Following this definition, arbitrary license denials and pharmacy ownership laws are barriers to entry and, accordingly, "administrative regulatory decisions" can properly be added to Professor Bain's list of entry barriers. See Joe S. Bain, *Industrial Organization* (New York: John Wiley & Sons, Inc., 1959), pp. 239–242.

Although this actual naming of prices is rare in advertising material, many firms try to project the image of low-cost prescriptions by publicizing discounted prices for other items, and, on the same page, mention something about the prescription department. Phrases such as "Price our prescriptions when you come in" quite often are seen when it is permitted by boards of pharmacy.

Chain stores that do not customarily advertise drug prices will modify that policy when the situation demands it. Gray Drug Stores, the largest drug chain in Ohio (154 stores) has resorted to price advertising to counter the competitive threat posed by Revco Drug Stores (60 stores).[7]

Another situation that often prompts a chain to modify its "no advertising of prescription drugs" policy is when the company is opening a new branch, especially if the store is in a city that is a new market area for the organization. The idea, more or less, is to acquaint the local population with the chain. The advertising is not expected to determine the eventual success or failure of the store. "If a new store is to be successful or unsuccessful, advertising doesn't affect the ultimate outcome. By advertising, a store which will prove to be profitable can be operating in the black in six months instead of the eighteen months to two years required without advertising," said one executive.

If the quote embodies correct reasoning, price advertising of drugs would be most useful to an expansion-minded independent. As a general rule, an independent retail druggist who has the desire and capacity to promote himself to chain status will not have the capital to sustain an unprofitable operation for eighteen months. From this standpoint, then, it seems unusual that independents generally oppose price advertising of prescription drugs, while chains, who could reduce the formation of new chains by attempting to have prescription drug price advertising outlawed, take a noncommital position.

One chain store executive interviewed indicated that although his company did not advertise the price of prescription drugs, his company would actually support legislation to permit such promotion, because as a matter of principle, unnecessary market restrictions are deleterious.[8] One who is suspicious of such altruism might suspect that the present advertising policy of the company is considered competitively wise for "image" reasons, as so many interviewees frankly stated was true in their cases.

Discounters do most of the price advertising of prescription drugs

[7] *NACDS Directory, 1964–65 Edition* (Washington: National Association of Chain Drug Stores, 1964), p. 117.

[8] As a qualification, the executive added that his company might at some future date want to change its advertising policy.

as court cases illustrate. It is likely that in many cases the advertising is designed to advance the general image that discounters cultivate of charging the lowest prices for commodities. Still, not all discounters emphasize prices of prescriptions in their promotions. Parkview Drugs, which operates the drug departments of about thirty discount operations, stresses the use of name brand drugs in its advertisements. Nevertheless, Parkview does discount the price of the drugs it sells and the knowledge of the savings that consumers can experience spreads very quickly.[9]

Prescription drug advertising is most apt to occur when a small and aggressive chain or discount operation is attempting to expand its activities as rapidly as possible. Sometimes such an approach is successful, as in the case of Revco which has grown to almost half the size of its chief competitor, Gray, in just a few years.

Since so few drug establishments engage in direct advertising of prescription drug prices, there is no evidence to indicate that these promotional efforts result in a lower price structure for prescription drugs. But as has already been indicated, the low price image is cultivated in standard advertisements. Keeping it in mind that chains and discounters do the bulk of price advertising (albeit not on prescriptions), it is interesting to compare prescription drug prices among chains, apothecaries, and neighborhood pharmacies. This information, exhibited in Table 12-2, indicates that the prescription drug prices of chains have consistently been well below those of apothecaries and neighborhood pharmacies. If these differences can be attributed to the indirect promotional efforts of the chains, then it also is possible that with the direct advertising of prescription drug prices, the average prescription prices of apothecaries and neighborhood pharmacies,[10] could be lowered.

Marketing experts would probably argue that advertising does not necessarily result in lower prices. Such an argument is appropriate, but is not entirely appropriate here. When advertising is informing the public rather than propogandizing, prices ought to be lowered. Most people do not realize that chains have lower prescription prices. If the public were aware of it, the prescription business of independents would suffer. At that point, the independents would lower their prices. This should result in a lower price structure.

The statistics presented in Table 12-2 might be also questioned

[9] Interview with Phillip Small, Chairman of the Board, Parkview Drugs, Inc. February 11, 1966.
[10] It should be noted that the statistics in Table 12-2 could well reflect economies of scale (associated with the large chain etablishments) instead of the benefits of advertising.

TABLE 12-2: Average Prescription Prices (Dollars)

Year	Apothecaries	Neighborhood Pharmacies	Chains
1960	3.42	3.19	3.09
1961	3.49	3.25	2.99
1962	3.62	3.22	3.08
1963	3.66	3.39	3.10

Source: *Chain Store Age*, October, 1964. Chain prices are from *Chain Store Age's* own survey; apothecary prices are from a survey conducted by the American College of Apothecaries, and neighborhood pharmacy prices are from the *Lilly Digest*, a survey limited almost exclusively to independents.

on the basis that neighborhood pharmacies and apothecaries fill more prescriptions from higher-priced drugs than do chains, so that average prescription prices have no meaning as to the differences in prices for comparable individual prescription drugs. But if prescription prices of independents are really as low as those of chains on individual items, resistance to price advertising of individual branded and generically named drugs should not be as adamant as it is. In view of the vigor of independents' opposition to prescription price advertising, one can only conclude that there *is* a price differential, and that chain drugstore prescription prices are lower than those of independents.

RESTRICTING THE SALE OF NONPRESCRIPTION DRUGS
TO DRUGSTORES

Chapter 6 indicates that, because of a number of lawsuits, the restriction of the sale of nonprescription drugs to pharmacies is not so widespread as in former years. Nevertheless, because of a singular court decision,[11] it is lawful in Wisconsin to sell Anacin or Bayer Aspirin in a supermarket but, at the same time, it is in violation of the law to sell nonbranded aspirin in the same supermarket.

Few organizations have had widespread operations where considerable restraints are placed on the sale of untrademarked nonprescription drugs. One company that has had a moderate amount of experience in this area is in favor of the limitation, for the understandable reason that the restriction results in a larger profit on the affected items than in states where the sale of untrademarked nonprescription drugs is not regulated.[12]

[11] *State* v. *Wakeen*, 263 Wis. 401, 57 N.W.2d 364 (1953).
[12] Confidential interview. The interviewee is the Director of Professional Services for a large company (headquartered in the midwest) that operates food stores and chain-type drugstores.

As was explained to the writer, in states where there are no limitations, a chain drugstore can easily underprice most independents and still make a substantial profit, but applying the technique to food retailers that sell untrademarked nonprescription drugs is another matter. Where food markets are allowed to sell all nonprescription drugs, they price the untrademarked products low enough to force chains to adopt a lower price structure than they prefer. In restrictive states this supermarket competition is absent and nonprescription drug prices are higher.

The restrictive rules device may provide a margin of survival for some independents, but these limitations simultaneously prevent healthy competition between drug chains and food chains and the correspondingly lower drug prices that would result.

LIMITING DRUGSTORE OWNERSHIP TO PHARMACISTS

For this restraint to result in elevated drug prices, it is necessary for pharmacists to lack financial backing or to be uninterested in adopting and improving mass merchandising techniques.

Pharmacists have complained that they are not able to obtain choice sites (shopping centers) on which to erect large drugstores. There probably is some truth to this grievance. For example, when a developer is searching for prospective businesses to occupy a shopping center, he must consider the number of consumers that will be attracted to the shopping center as a whole. A large department store and a large food chain considering the establishment of a branch at that location want assurances that all businesses in the shopping center will have a drawing capacity; otherwise, sales for the entire area will not reach their potential. For this reason, developers are reluctant to lease or sell space in a proposed shopping center even to a financially sound independent druggist if he is not generally known to consumers. Firms such as Walgreen's and Superx are preferred.

A more serious argument against limiting drugstore ownership to pharmacists is the tendency of independents to cling to the operational philosophy of high prices and low volume. That is, it generally is against their nature to adopt and refine new, superior sales techniques. Obviously, this does not apply to *all* pharmacists. Many of the most successful and innovative chain and discount store executives are pharmacists. Those chains and discounters have such a large exposure that promising managerial-type pharmacists can be observed (at the store level) and moved up in the organizational hierarchy. Still, many of the executives complain that too many of the pharmacists associated with the firms want only to fill prescriptions or, at most, manage one store.

It is intriguing to ponder why many pharmacists seem to have such limited ambitions. Two explanations of this apathy are offered. One reason for the anti-merchandising attitude exhibited by pharmacists is their exposure to the American Pharmaceutical Association (APhA) philosophy that merchandising is a sordid word and that pharmacists who indulge in such practices cannot have professional stature. According to APhA, the two categories are mutually exclusive. This attitude toward merchandising is exemplified by the following remarks of Dr. William S. Apple, Executive Director of APhA:

> When this decade of the sixties opened, it was heralded as the beginning of a time unit of great possible changes and opportunity. Some referred to it as the "sizzling sixties." . . . As far as pharmacy is concerned, these . . . years have been sizzling indeed. In fact, pharmacy has found itself not only in the frying pan and in the fire, but slowly rotated on a spit over the coals as well.
>
> *We have seen commercialists invade and use our profession* not for public health service, but for profit and as a "traffic builder." A whole collection of money-making angles have [sic] been exploited—closed-door pharmacies, over-65 club memberships, mail order prescription operations, trading stamps, leased discount units, and other such operations that offend both the spirit and principles of our profession.[13]

A second explanation for pharmacists' lack of enthusiasm in innovative merchandising is the nature of training they receive. Education in pharmacy is largely scientific, the bulk of the courses dealing with the chemical composition and therapeutic effects of drugs. The young men drawn into this profession are likely to have a personality profile closer to that of a research chemist than that of a salesman. Thus, education is, in a way, a managerial selection technique. Those who survive the curriculum and become pharmacists are not likely to have an inclination toward nonscientific pursuits involving a substantial amount of self-promotion.[14]

These two reasons for the limited entrepreneurial ambitions of pharmacists support the hypothesis that even if most pharmacists were

---

[13] William S. Apple, "Individual Practice of Pharmacy," *The Virginia Pharmacist*, Vol. 47, No. 1 (Jan. 1963), p. 13. An address delivered to the Annual Meeting of the Southern California Pharmaceutical Association, Anaheim, California, November 28, 1962.

[14] Persons who are aware of the high proportion of pharmacists in state legislatures relative to their total and relative to other nonlegal occupations will be dubious of the statement that pharmacists in general are not interested in self-promotion. Such a peculiarity is explained by the long-standing interest of pharmacists in state protective laws. Pharmacists (HARD) have been the major force behind fair trade legislation for almost forty years. In addition to this tradition of seeking legislative relief through fair trade and a host of other devices, pharmacists are constantly exhorted by their professional publications to become politically active.

financially situated so that they could open chain-type drugstores, their orientation is such that the vast majority would not care to do so and would not seek new and better ways of promoting their stores and products. It is on this basis that pharmacy ownership exclusively by pharmacists is objectionable from the economic standpoint.

THEORY OF MAXIMUM WANT SATISFACTION

Given the foregoing, one cannot conclude a priori that high drug prices are detrimental. If it is in the public interest to preserve neighborhood drugstores, and if high drug prices can accomplish it, then excessive drug prices may be tolerable. The crucial question is whether the interests of consumers are more vital than the preservation of small business. The theory of maximum want satisfaction indicates the interests of the consuming sector as viewed by economists.

To economists man is a hedonist. That is, his work is directed toward self-satisfaction. Though this theory may not be accurate in all respects, it explains how most people spend their income. According to the hedonistic theory, an individual considers all available products and services and then allocates his income among the goods in such a way as to achieve maximum satisfaction. In this case man is selfish. He spends his money so as to derive the maximum amount of pleasure from his spending.

Although there recently have been arguments advanced that extensive self-indulgence is socially reprehensible,[15] these academicians do not doubt that hedonism is an accurate reflection of the buying patterns of consumers. Those who do not condone this attitude of the consuming public would remove a part of available purchasing power through increased taxation and use the revenue to finance projects such as parks, schools, and hospitals that man is too selfish to adequately support voluntarily. Perhaps it is not too much of a distortion of this view to suppose that it could be extended to include preservation of "the American way of life" (small business) through the enactment of protectionist-type laws for the benefit of small retail druggists. Under this expanded view, small retail druggists are considered socially desirable to the extent that it is proper to require citizens to forego their self-indulgence (i.e., attaining maximum want satisfaction), in order to maintain such enterprises via higher prices.

It is intuitively evident that in any sector of the economy where demand is high and relatively inelastic and there is little opportunity for substitution, excessive prices are inimical to maximum want satis-

---

[15] John Kenneth Galbraith, *The Affluent Society* (Cambridge: The Riverside Press, 1958).

faction. The higher the prices of drugs, the more consumers will have to divert their incomes from other items that they want to purchase. The political determination to be made is whether maximum want satisfaction or protection of retail druggists is more important.

Problem of Resource Allocation

If higher prices to consumers were the only issue, free market restrictions in the retail drug industry might be more palatable since most consumers spend a relatively small proportion of their income on drugs. The restrictions, however, also result in certain rigidities in the pattern of resource allocation. The consequence is that resources remain in the retail drug industry that could better be employed elsewhere. That is, the investment of people and capital could be used more efficiently in other industries.

ALLOCATION OF LAND AND CAPITAL

Large stores generally can achieve a turnover of merchandise at a rapid pace and consequently obtain a greater utilization of their invested land and capital. Consider inventory. A drug department must carry a certain quantity of inventory so as to be able to fill the wide variety of prescriptions written. The amount of inventory required does not vary directly with volume, especially in prescription drugs. Hence, a neighborhood pharmacy that fills, say, twenty diverse prescriptions a day must maintain approximately the same level and type of stock as does a larger operation that sells, in the same day, hundreds of prescriptions. Thus, the larger store, with only a slightly larger inventory (and prescription area) is able to support a great many more sales.

In the absence of restrictions, chain and discount drug establishments flourish. Independent retailers must adopt the most efficient utilization of their land and capital to survive. Inevitably some cannot—as competition becomes more intensive the weaker, less competent entrepreneurs must fall by the wayside.

With entry constraints, there is a large number of small drugstores that, because of high mark-ups, do not have to function at peak efficiency to survive. This results in an enormous investment in prescription drugs, pharmacy equipment, other capital goods, and land. Because of this situation there is underemployment of the physical resources utilized in the drug industry, since the same pharmaceutical services could be provided with less resources if the restrictions did not exist. In addition, since small businesses do not operate on a large scale, they lose the economies of scale that are inherent in large multi-unit operations. By taking advantage of economies of scale,[16] underutilized resources can be eliminated and shifted to activities where they can be effectively exploited.

ALLOCATION OF LABOR

Highly skilled labor is not being used to maximum advantage when it is employed in a less exacting field. Pharmacists generally experience this condition and their position would worsen if free market restrictions in the drug industry were broadened.

A pharmacist spends five years in an educational institution acquiring a knowledge of drugs. Yet, when he begins to pursue his career, either as an independent druggist or working for one, he may well find that he is spending a large proportion of his time selling chocolates and shaving cream. Many pharmacists do not enjoy being engaged in such nonprofessional pursuits. Chains and discounters capitalize on this discontent by pointing out to pharmacists that enough prescriptions are sold in their establishments to permit full-time professionalism.[17] Thus, despite the anti-discounter attitude of their schools, many pharmacists prefer association with chain stores and discount operations.[18]

There are two restrictions that are especially contrary to an efficient allocation of the resource of labor. The first is the requirement that a pharmacist manage each drugstore. As has been previously discussed, certain factors indicate that the proportion of pharmacists with the inclination and ability to manage a firm is quite small. As a result, in those states that require management by a pharmacist, chains are forced to use druggists as administrators, regardless of their managerial capacity. One executive interviewed indicated that this requirement might not be so undesirable if it were not for the fact that there are several outstanding nonpharmacists that the company would like to make managers. The result often is that the best qualified individuals are confined to nonadministrative positions where they are not efficiently utilized, while frequently the unqualified are perforce assigned

---

[16] A more precise statement would be "by taking advantage of conditions where the elasticity of productivity is greater than unity." See Sidney Weintraub, *op. cit.*, pp. 54–57.

[17] Confidential interview. This inducement does not appeal to merchandising-oriented pharmacists employed by chains and discounters, but such men are quickly informed that they can advance in the organization if they demonstrate desire and ability.

[18] In a recent interview, Dr. Alvah G. Hall, Dean of the School of Pharmacy of the University of Southern California, was quoted as saying, "I've tried to discourage my students from going into discount pharmacies, but there are always some who want to make a million dollars in a hurry." Ed. Rosenthall, "Heeding Voice of Necessity," *Drug News Weekly*, February 14, 1966, p. 13.

to managerial functions. The chains readily indicate that they really prefer pharmacist-managers, but have difficulty in locating individuals with the right qualifications.

Another labor allocation problem is the requirement that compels each drugstore to employ two pharmacists. In addition to the fact that these laws or rules accentuate the shortage of pharmacists, many locations do not justify eighty to eighty-eight hours per week of prescription filling availability. In questioning operating personnel about the effects of the two-pharmacist requisite, the curious phenomena of "up-front" sales subsidizing the prescription department emerges at some locations. Apparently the logical thing to do is to eliminate the prescription department in those drug stores, but the fear persists that other sales would be sufficiently reduced to make the entire store unprofitable. In this case, then, the prescription department is not really being subsidized. Nevertheless, profits are needlessly lost, labor is needlessly misallocated, and perhaps drug prices are needlessly high.

Innovations in Merchandising Methods

Perhaps the most serious criticism of free market restrictions in the retail drug industry is that they virtually proscribe innovation.[19] As soon as someone utilizes a new method that has public acceptance (i.e., a successful innovation), a regulation or law appears that is designed to reduce the impact of the innovation and/or to eliminate it entirely, if possible.[20] Also, the litigation presented throughout this book clearly illustrates that many boards of pharmacy are oriented toward the past rather than toward the future.

Innovation and innovators are held in high regard by economists:

Competition is never "perfectly perfect." Somebody must try to peer into the future to decide whether there will be a demand for shoelaces or what will be the price of wheat. And in the world as we know it, there is a chance for a man with a brand new idea to invest in a revolutionary machine or a softer soft drink—to promote a new product or to find a way to lower the costs on an old one.
. . .
The innovator . . . is the man with vision, originality and daring.[21]

[19] Prescription drug price advertising, discount pharmacies, the sale of prescription drugs by mail, pharmacies located in food stores and general merchandise discount houses, union-operated pharmacies, and the sale of proprietary medicines are examples of innovation. Chapters 10 and 11 discussed the opposition to these new techniques.
[20] See Appendix I.
[21] Paul A. Samuelson, *Economics: An Introductory Analysis* (6th ed.; New York: McGraw-Hill, 1964), pp. 602–603.

If innovations are important, it seems imperative to suppress conditions that inhibit the creative climate. Yet in the retail drug industry new ideas are frequently declared illegal on the basis of being detrimental to the public health when public health is not at all involved.

Virtually every innovation springs from a public need or desire. When a new idea or technique fulfills those needs and desires, it is difficult to justify contrary legislation, so long as the public health is not adversely affected.

Viewing free market restrictions as a totality, the goal of state pharmacy boards appears to be to preserve the existing patterns and modes of retail drug distribution and to reclaim ground that has been lost in the courts. This static or noninnovative state is not viewed favorably today, when the emphasis is on economic growth and when dynamacism in all areas is mandatory.

If politicians come to the conclusions that the protection of independent retail druggists is more vital than low prices, efficient allocation of resources, and innovation, such a position cannot be challenged except by voters. The important point for legislators to keep in mind is that restrictive practices are to be weighed against innovation, resource allocation, and prices—not as an adjunct to or a part of measures to protect the public health.

CHAPTER THIRTEEN

Limitations on Managerial Decisions

The various restrictive pharmacy laws and regulations described in previous chapters place a number of restraints on the freedom of managerial activity. Many of the merchandising opportunities that become visible to drugstore executives are never acted upon for this reason. By reducing or eliminating alternative courses of action, a major advantage of private entrepreneurship—individual initiative—is lost.

Previous chapters have been devoted primarily to explaining the restrictions that exist in the retail drug industry. The purpose of this chapter is to enumerate some of the major managerial functions and decisions that are constrained by laws and negative attitudes of boards of pharmacy.

There are four major areas that are influenced by unfavorable laws, regulations, and pharmacy board attitudes. These are (1) the decision to enter a particular marketing area, (2) design of physical features of retail drug outlets, (3) advertising and promotional decisions, and (4) policy decisions concerning the operation of drugstores.

Entry Problems

Before a particular geographical market area is entered by a firm, there are a multitude of decisions to be made concerning the general area and the particular store location. Affirmative answers are required for the questions of favorable store location, reasonable price of real estate, ability of the firm to meet competition in prices and services, and so on. In some states another major factor must be added—the climate as propagated by state laws and pharmacy board officials. There are many facets to the problem of entry with respect to legal and regulatory conditions.

Some states have ownership laws that prevent a corporate proprietor from operating in the pharmacy field or which limit the amount of equity a corporate owner may have in its drugstores if it operates in that state. Some firms have decided to avoid states with ownership laws, thus helping the statutes accomplish their purpose. Others have resorted to fictitious corporations where pharmacists ostensibly own the specified percentage of stock, but in which the pharmacists have signed agreements that make their stock control nonexistent. Still other corporations have purchased, or have attempted to acquire, a drug corporation already doing business in the state and operate through the captive company.

Although it is possible to solve the entry problem in the states that have ownership laws, the simple and straightforward practice of building a store and opening it for business is denied. Moreover, attempting to subvert the law in order to gain entry may prove to be expensive beyond ordinary operational costs. So, the outside entrepreneurs must look very carefully before leaping—past experience in other states becomes worthless.

Entry into states without ownership laws may be even more difficult than acquiring operational permission from jurisdictions with ownership statutes. If there is an element of antagonism toward a chain, a board of pharmacy may decide—perhaps as the result of protests from pharmacists in the state—that it is expedient to deny the firm's application for a license on some spurious ground. This would not, perhaps, present much cause for entrepreneurial concern if it were not for the usual requirement that a store be completely ready for operation (including the employment of a pharmacist) before that outlet may be considered for a license. If the license is denied, the firm must resort to litigation, or be prepared to accept a minimum financial loss equal to the sum expended in readying the store for operation. Nevertheless, in such a situation, if the firm has sufficient determination and money, the courts will award a license, presuming that the Parkview case constitutes a precedent.

Despite legal precedent, however, it is not possible to determine in advance whether a license application will be denied. The experience of Osco in Massachusetts exemplifies this situation. Osco, desiring to avoid a Parkview situation, had some of its company officials talk to board officials to try to determine what their reaction would be to an Osco license application. Apparently, there was no indication that a permit would be denied so Osco proceeded to acquire and stock a store and employ a pharmacist. Unfortunately, the consultations either gave Osco a false impression or else the board changed its mind, because the license was denied.

Even when the board does not make an outright denial—or at least a refusal that is definitely not actionable—there may be many unexplained and arbitrary delays in granting the license, a move which some think is an attempt to convince outsiders that they are not wanted. For example, there may be a long lapse of time before receipt of a license application is acknowledged. Sometimes the request is lost in transit and a new one must be filed. Some time later, the application will be returned for corrections or additional information and may even require a second correction. In a few weeks the store inspector appears. More time is lost while certain minor deficiencies in the outlet are corrected and the store is re-inspected. Once the license is granted, clerical shortages suffered by the board of pharmacy may prevent immediate issuance of the permit and the U.S. mail has been accused of misplacing licenses after they have been signed and sealed.

Executives in the retail drug industry are reluctant to discuss and/or hypothesize as to the reasons for delays in license issuance, especially once their firm has been granted a permit. Renewal delays are rare and they prefer to keep it that way. Moreover, there is no evidence that such postponements, when they do exist, are intentional. Nevertheless, several licensing requests that have resulted in litigation, notably Superx in Michigan and Parkview in Massachusetts, have been deferred in one way or another for several months before they even reached the courts. Recognizing that the possibility of licensing delays and/or denials must be considered, it is not surprising that chain executives think twice, or several times, before giving the order to proceed in states known to be unfriendly to their firm or to chain stores in general.

There are other important aspects to the entry problem. Even if it is known that entry can be ultimately achieved, it may not be worthwhile. For example, a company's corporate image may be darkened in its entry efforts, especially if a court action is necessary to secure an operating permit. Superx experienced this problem in its battles with the Michigan Board of Pharmacy. There was widespread publicity that Superx had been disbursing amphetamines and barbiturates without prescriptions, an allegation not borne out by any evidence given in the courts. Superx did dispense amphetamines and barbiturates without a written prescription, a common practice in Michigan even though it was a violation of Michigan statutes. Superx and many other drugstores accepted telephoned orders from physicians. Yet it was intimated that Superx's action was unique and that no prescription had been received, orally or otherwise. Although the Superx case is unusual in several respects, a similar situation could arise again, and the great value of a favorable public image must be weighed against the anticipated profitability of stores in one state.

In addition to the damage to its corporate image, there are possible litigation expenses to be considered. Apparently companies will go to great lengths to prove that they refuse to be intimidated. Thus, most companies, feeling that they have to fight if it is forced upon them, consider the great financial burden that will arise if litigation ensues. To preclude the eventuality of an expensive court fight, companies sometimes do not attempt to enter a particular state. They do not wish to appear to have a lack of determination, so their reluctance to expend a large sum of money—which they would feel compelled to do if the litigation became necessary because of a license denial— automatically excludes them from contested territory.

Physical Features of Drugstores

One cause of license delays or denials is a firm's nonconformance to certain physical requirements for its drugstore. One example of these standards is the necessity of installing an outside entrance in those pharmacies that are part of a larger operation. This is designed to assure public access to drugstores contained in membership or "closed door" stores. Aside from the fact that the desire to serve only those people who have paid a membership fee is prevented, the freedom to locate the pharmacy in the most desirable location within the larger store is thwarted. Usually the drugstore will have to be placed at the front of the store, because the outside entrance requirement may be coupled with the provision that the passage be on a street. Sometimes the entrance requirement is not specified in advance; the interior design of the store then has to be changed after all equipment has been installed and the store has been stocked. In any event, the pharmacy location passes beyond the control of the entrepreneur.

Another imposition upon the freedom of action is the board of pharmacy's control over the size of the prescription department. Such rules generally require a certain percent of a store's total floor space to be allocated to the proposed drug department. By requiring 10 or 15 percent of total floor space to be included in the pharmacy, discount stores[1] frequently must forego a prescription department, except when it is permissible to enclose the pharmacy.[2] Thus, the manager is not permitted to use his judgment in determining, on the basis of expected

---

[1] This rule has also adversely affected the establishment of large drugstores.
[2] Some state laws require the drug department of a store to be completely enclosed. As such, the pharmacy is sometimes considered to be a separate entity and need not comply with statutory requirements.

number of customers, the size a prescription department should be. Instead, the decision is based on statutory requirements that depart from economic considerations since the percent rule specifies the space a pharmacy must occupy and treats as irrelevant the possible need for a different size pharmacy (smaller) than the one required.

Apparently, uncertainties as to what space is to be considered a part of the pharmacy and confusion as to other requirements have led entrepreneurs to the practice of submitting blueprints of a proposed building to the boards of pharmacy in advance of fixturing the store. Although this insures that the physical arrangement of the store will be acceptable to the officials, layout control is no longer in the hands of the owners. Moreover, this procedure allows the board of pharmacy to introduce other specifications concerning physical features that are not spelled out in the law or in board regulations.

In several states, then, if a chain desires to operate a drugstore, a substantial amount of its executive decision-making powers must be delegated to the board of pharmacy, whose members are generally independent retail druggists and, hence, are competitors of the chain.

Advertising Controls

How an establishment will be promoted is a major concern of an entrepreneur. Although the motivation of public health protection appears to be remote, boards of pharmacy or laws passed at the insistence of state pharmaceutical associations exert a strong influence on what may and may not be done in promoting drugstores.

The most common form of advertising is signs that are placed outside the building that houses a firm. These signs announce whose business it is and what type of merchandise is sold by the firm. In some states, the board of pharmacy attempts to specify the content of the signs. Once again, corporate policy will have to be reversed if outdoor signs do not please the officials. Pharmacy boards sometimes prohibit outdoor signs from announcing that the business is a drugstore or that there is a drug department in a large general merchandise store. Thus, a corporate owner may be required to change the outdoor signs he customarily uses to remove the word "drug" and it may be necessary or desirable to revamp entire advertising campaigns.

A further control, again unrelated to the preservation of public health, is the frequent ban on newspaper advertisements that infer that discounts are given on prescription drugs. Such a rule is particularly odious to a large chain operation that places local ads from a central office. Duplicate ads are made necessary, reducing the economy of scale inherent in one advertisement for all stores. More important philosophically, the right to promote products as owners prefer is diminished. Those who find it profitable to combine discounting with advertising that fact are prevented from using the technique.

Advertising men are very clever and can usually convey the discount message despite prohibitions to that effect. But the effort expended to break the spirit of the law while abiding by the letter results in an additional cost of doing business, which is to the detriment of the public in the long run.

Another advertising prerogative, in most fields, is conveying to the public the prices that various products command. This is a standard practice for luring customers into a store, the intent being to encourage the purchase of other items besides those that carry a special price. To prevent such public notice of prescription prices, as is the practice in many states, removes still another tool from the managerial decision-making kit. This method of boosting sales is somehow defined by boards of pharmacy as contrary to the public interest.

The opposition to advertisement of prescription prices seems to be motivated by financial considerations. Independents cannot or will not meet the prices of the larger operators, and advertisements that permit comparison pricing are distinctly uncomfortable to them. Another plausible reason for the opposition is a lack of enthusiasm for incurring advertising expenditures which may, at best, only maintain the level of sales. Finally, advertisements are expensive and the federal government takes a jaundiced view of independents pooling resources to advertise common prices. This smacks of price fixing, according to the government.

That advertising of prescription drug prices is strenuously opposed by independents is given credence by the experience of Gray Drug Stores in Ohio. Gray mounted an advertising campaign in the Dayton area, mainly to forestall competition in that area from Revco. Independents were so outraged that they demanded the resignation of a Gray employee who is on the Ohio Board of Pharmacy, charging him with a conflict of interest.[3] This occasion may partially explain the general lack of prescription price advertising by chains; their best business decision may be not to advertise prices if such promotion will incur the vengeful wrath of the independents.

Store Operations

In addition to the many other restrictions on managerial decisions, there are several devices that act as constraints on the operation of

[3] Max A. Myers, "Conflict of Interest and the Ohio State Board of Pharmacy," Paper Presented at the LAO Conference of the Ohio State Pharmaceutical Association, September 23–24, 1964, Lincoln Lodge Motor Hotel, Columbus, Ohio. Mr. Myers was, at that time, President of the Miami Valley (Dayton area) Pharmaceutical Association.

individual stores. One such operating restriction is the limitation on the number of hours that an employee-pharmacist may work each week. A manager is thus prevented from arranging the most advantageous work schedules for his employees. There might be some logic in this rule from a standpoint of public health if it were not for the fact that an owner-pharmacist may work as many hours as he chooses. Long hours may increase the possibility of errors in filling prescriptions, but an owner is no more immune to fatigue than an employee.

In conjunction with limitation of working hours is the rule that at least two full-time pharmacists must be employed by a pharmacy even though it might not be necessary if the store is not to be open long enough to require the services of two full-time pharmacists. Again, the requirement need not be met if the store is privately owned by a pharmacist. Such rules have the effect, and perhaps the intent, of increasing the cost of corporate operators as compared to independent owners.

A second operating restraint is the frequent statutory requirement that the drugstore manager be a pharmacist. Such a rule is a serious infringement on the unfettered conduct of business. Chain store executives view this as one of the most severe of all the managerial limitations. These same executives explain that they prefer pharmacist-managers, but think there should be no such requirement. The chains contend that demonstrably competent personnel should be given a chance to prove that they can manage a store, regardless of whether they are pharmacists.

The restrictiveness of the pharmacy-manager requirement is compounded for chains by the shortage of pharmacists and the peculiar drugstore economics that it engenders. Pharmacists, being in short supply, command approximately the same salary for a forty hour work week that a store manager does for a fifty-five hour period of employment. As a result, it takes a highly motivated pharmacist to consent to manage a store even when he perceives it to be a stepping stone to higher-paying jobs in the corporate hierarchy. In addition, according to drugstore executives, very few pharmacists are capable of managing a store because of their professional orientation. These conditions, coupled with the financial incentive for other employees (promotion to manager or assistant manager means a substantial salary increment for nonpharmacist personnel) to excel as drugstore managers, places a burden on the upper echelon of the corporate hierarchy. Not only must the executives contend with pharmacist-managers that are less than enthusiastic about possible administrative duties—they must also pacify their ambitious nonpharmacist employees who find their managerial ambitions thwarted.

Another unreasonable managerial restraint imposed by state pharmacy laws is the indirect control of business hours. This is accomplished through the requirement that the drug department be open at all times that the store is open for business. Since there is a substantial amount of money involved in the pay of pharmacists, it may be advisable to close the prescription department during certain hours when few prescriptions are filled. By refusing to allow this practice, the prescription department must be operated when it is not needed, or the business hours of the entire store must be reduced.

Proper inventory control can also be undermined by unrealistic laws. To demand that drug inventory be held at a certain percentage of a store's total inventory does nothing to further the preservation of public health and entails an unrealistic inventory of drugs. A requirement that a drugstore stock a certain dollar amount or a certain quantity of named drugs is a more reasonable demand. The intent of the percentage inventory requirement seems to be to make it difficult for larger (i.e., chain) stores to include a prescription department in their operations. The pharmacy boards' argument that without the rule an adequate supply of drugs would not be carried by a store does not carry weight. To attract and retain customers, drug outlets must be able to fill prescriptions. Since all drugstores want to keep their prescription customers, it seems likely that a sufficient line of drugs will be carried.

As is true of many situations, a method is available for circumventing the restrictive inventory rule. The only practical times to check the level of drug inventory is when a store is first opened or at the time the firm makes a regular inventory of its store. It is easy, however, for a firm to order and stock a large quantity of an expensive drug to meet the percentage rule for inspection purposes. Once the inspection has been completed, it is also easy for the store to let stocks decline or to return some drugs to the manufacturer. There is no evidence to indicate that this pattern has been followed, but the likelihood exists that it has been used. This is just one of the many counteractions that entrepreneurs find it necessary to perform in order to bypass a ridiculous operational rule.

The last restrictive store operation requirement to be considered is promotion schemes as distinct from advertising techniques. Many promotional programs are available and are used by those in the retail drug industry whenever possible. Examples are trading stamps given with purchases of prescriptions, a free prescription filled for every $100 of purchases, and senior citizens' plans.

The most restricted of the promotion schemes are those which give special discounts to certain classes of consumers, such as all patrons over a specified age (60 to 65 usually) and certain union members. The so-called senior citizen plans are particularly popular for very sound reasons. Use of this technique creates a public image for the participating pharmacies that their profits are being sacrificed for the benefit of older people with limited incomes and high medical expenses. Moreover, the younger relatives of the senior citizens are attracted by the generosity exhibited by such druggists and, as a result, total sales volume is pleasantly inflated.

A case could be presented in economic terms that such price discrimination in favor of special groups of consumers is not acceptable. Rather than stressing economic aspects, however, the standard argument advanced against such plans is that it is professionally unethical to promote the interests of one group of clients as opposed to other groups. Proponents of the price differential technique counter with the argument that physicians often accept lower than standard fees from their less advantaged patients. Nevertheless, this simple aim of increasing profits via attracting increased volume on nondiscriminatory priced items is prohibited in several states on ethical grounds, not on a rational economic or public health basis.

Reasons for Extent of Control

If the restrictive entry, advertising and operational practices just enumerated are so odious, why are they allowed to continue and, even in some instances, grow? Moreover, since it appears that the controls are poorly conceived, why do they persist? These questions arise when the limitations imposed on the retail drug distribution system by state boards of pharmacy and pharmacy legislation are analyzed. The answers are perhaps not quite so obvious.

It is true that there generally is a lack of public awareness about the managerial controls imposed on those engaged in the retail drug industry. Nevertheless, it is reasonable to expect that there would be a concerted opposition among those in the field whose self-interests are being injured. Despite this reasonable assumption, except when situations become crucial—such as a direct attack on the right to engage in and remain in a particular business activity—there is no organized dissenting voice. Some of course do fight, as the discussions of various litigations have indicated, but the majority accept the restrictions. From interviews with executives of retail drug outlets and a review of the industry literature, three reasons emerge for the acquiescence of chains to these many inhibitions.

A major axiom of those who tolerate the confinements is to avoid provoking trouble. The many restrictions and their resulting problems can be accommodated by a combination of undetected noncompliance and stoic resignation. As long as there is no immediate threat to retailers of excessive statutory managerial controls or perhaps denial of the right to function as a business enterprise, it is thought best to promote amiable relations with the pharmacy boards as much as possible. This mixed strategy has as its basis the extraordinary amount of power that a board of pharmacy has over the granting of licenses, to both pharmacists and pharmacies. Suspension or revocation of operational permits is a powerful weapon and it appears that the retailers most prudent course is a discreet mixture of subterfuge and cooperation.

Another powerful stimulus for compliance with pharmacy laws and regulations is the very high litigation cost that results from contesting the requirements. Individuals and corporations are forced to assess possible gains from the action against the legal expense involved and this places them at a tactical disadvantage. Boards of pharmacy draw upon the resources of state attorneys and, as an entity, incur no cash outlay. The members of the board, therefore, need not make the crucial judgement of cost as compared to chances for success, since there is no cost to them. As a result, a board will pursue a given case as far as state attorneys are willing to go.

The final explanation for the acceptance by chain store retailers of the extent and severity of control of managerial decisions by pharmacy boards is the apathy and/or hostility chains have toward state pharmaceutical organizations. As was pointed out in Chapter 3, these organizations exert a substantial amount of influence on the actions of the various boards of pharmacy. Yet, except in a few states, the leading chains have not exerted themselves to become active workers in the state associations. Such groups are beyond the control of the chains, but their presence could, doubtlessly, serve as a moderating influence on the associations' positions. The efforts along this line have met with conspicuous success in Ohio and Illinois. A chain store representative is a member of the board of pharmacy of each of these states, and it is important to note that restrictive rules and questionable actions are far less substantial in these states than in some others. To gain headway against managerial restrictions, the chains would be well-advised to participate in a professional dialogue with their independent counterparts at the state level. Frontal attacks in the legislatures only rigidify the chain and nonchain groups into uncompromising ideologies. Obtaining a voice on the inside apparently gets better results.

CHAPTER 14

Concluding Observations and Recommendations

In Chapter 2, a noted historian of the profession of pharmacy was quoted as saying that the "crassly commercial interest" no longer dominates the field of pharmacy. The results of this study show otherwise.

The preceding chapters include an analysis of several operating restrictions and delays or denials in issuing operating permits to various types of retail drug outlets. These tactics, which are attributable to many state boards of pharmacy, have been neither random events nor mere clerical oversights. Moreover, such actions by the agencies, although supposedly designed to protect the public health and welfare, actually are devised to enhance the competitive position of independent retail druggists. These conclusions are supported, first of all, by the realization that there is a conspicuous pattern to the license denials: few rejections have been experienced other than by large corporations. Most of the exceptions to this general statement merely reinforce the basic premise that the goal of boards of pharmacy and their supporters, is to narrow competition in the retail drug industry. For example, several licenses have been denied to smaller entrepreneurs who wished to operate pharmacies as a part of general merchandise stores that project a discount image.

Another reason to believe that there has been a conscious effort on the part of boards of pharmacy to refuse to license large chains and discounters is the many statements attributable to pharmacy leaders which assert that discount pharmacies and pharmacies located in supermarkets are to be damned to the everlasting fires. There can be no mistaking that these spokesmen for the profession, who, in effect, control the appointment of pharmacy board members, are adamantly opposed to discount and supermarket drug outlets. Further, the resolutions adopted by the American Pharmaceutical Association and the National Association of Retail Druggists state the opinions even more forcefully.

A third indicator of the economic purposes toward which the license denials and delays are directed is the restrictive rules and regulations adopted by the boards of pharmacy. These rules are, without question, intended to exclude as many chains and discounters as possible from the retail drug industry and to make operations difficult for those firms not excluded and/or those licensed because of a court order. The Massachusetts Board, in its relations with Osco Drugs, has even demonstrated that it refuses to be guided by the state's Supreme Judicial Court.

Finally, many courts have recognized and called attention to the economic orientation of the boards of pharmacy and have criticized the tactics and abuse of authority exhibited by the regulatory agencies. If an impartial interpretation of the true intent behind the boards' actions is to be found anywhere, it is in the opinions of the various benches that have ruled on litigation concerning license denials and operating restrictions.

The certainty that a comprehensive plan exists, in some states, to erect and maintain entry barriers and to enforce competition-reducing operating restrictions in the retail drug industry controlled the structure and objectives of this study. The purposes have largely been filled in the preceding substantive chapters; however, it seems appropriate to restate, in a summarized form, the responses to the issues originally posed.

Two objectives were to determine which pharmacy laws and regulations act as free market barriers and to indicate the prevalency of the restraints. Twenty-one different restrictions have been identified through the analysis of state laws and pertinent court decisions. The total number of restrictions present in the fifty-one jurisdictions included within the scope of this study is 204. It is significant that only fifty-five (27.4 percent) of the restrictions have been enacted as law and that 143 (73 percent) are rules and regulations promulgated by the boards of pharmacy. Hence, the pervasiveness of the restrictions arises primarily from the regulations enacted by the state licensing agencies.

Two additional aims were to gain an understanding of how these restrictions arise and why they have been perpetuated. It appears that the restraints are a combined result of the restrictionist philosophy of pharmacy owners, the changes in the methods of retail drug distribution following World War II, and the acquiescence of chain and discount drugstores to restrictive measures.

The fair trade edifice began to crumble shortly after the end of

World War II. At the same time, supermarkets began merchandising items (toiletries, proprietary medicines, and so forth) normally sold only by drugstores. Independent druggists retaliated by challenging, through the boards of pharmacy, the right of food stores and other outlets to sell high volume proprietary medicines such as Anacin, Alka-Seltzer, and Pepto-Bismol. This fight is still being waged, but the independents seem to have lost interest in the issue because of the *Loblaw* ruling in New York—a capstone to similar defeats experienced in several other states.

Concurrent with this activity to deprive nondrug outlets of the right to sell certain types of medications was the continuous promulgation of laws and regulations designed to combat various other competitive threats as they appeared. The restrictionist philosophy demanded that the changing distribution pattern be resisted.[1] Existing chain drugstores did not object—new entrants would create competition for them as well as for the independents. It was not until ownership laws were revived that chain drugstores began to roll out their artillery.

Two important factors have favored the continued growth of operational and licensing restrictions in the retail drug industry. One is the qualifications required, and the appointive processes of, members of the state boards of pharmacy. As the preceding chapters demonstrated, membership requirements are formulated to assure that pharmacy boards are composed of persons reflecting the views of the state pharmaceutical associations, which, in turn, are generally completely controlled by independent retail pharmacists. The normal and almost predictable result is that the boards concern themselves with protecting the interests of independent drugstores.

The other factor supporting the maintenance of the various restrictions is related to the first condition. This second factor is the apathy and/or hostility of chain drugstores toward the state pharmaceutical associations. Chain drugstores cannot dominate the state associations, but they could act as counterbalancing influences if they worked actively in the associations. Most chains, however, have refused to do so and have tried to ignore the associations. Two notable exceptions are Gray Drug Stores (Ohio) and Walgreen Drugs (Illinois). The existing regulatory conditions in Ohio and Illinois illustrate the benefits to be derived from striving to effect an accommodation with independents through the state pharmaceutical associations.

---

[1] The factors causing the shift of many drugstore items to other outlets are beyond the scope of this study, but it seems that the complementary forces of fair trade and a normally high retail price markup in the drug field made these items irresistible to food stores and other outlets that traditionally followed a lower markup policy.

The fifth purpose of this study was to isolate the economic and managerial consequences of free market restrictions. One important economic outgrowth suggested is that retail drug prices may be higher than they would be if the restrictions did not exist. If, all other things being equal, price competition produces lower prices, then there is no doubt that regulatory tactics which restrict competition result in retail drug prices that are too high. Two other economic consequences of the restrictions are a misallocation of manpower and capital resources—the restrictive canopy allows drugstores to survive that otherwise would have their resources shifted into other industries or to other sectors of the drug and health industries. Finally, the managerial consequences of restrictionism are simple, but devastating. A considerable portion of the entrepreneur's decision-making power is shifted from managers to boards of pharmacy, and the status quo is emphasized to the detriment of improvement and innovation.

Professional Status of Pharmacy

To pass judgement upon an occupation and to declare it to be professional or nonprofessional is always difficult. For the practitioners of a particular vocation, the opinions of the public at large and other professional bodies are most important. If a poll of these groups showed that pharmacists are regarded as professionals, most pharmacists probably would be satisfied.

But to provide consistent appraisal of various occupations, a set of objective criteria—against which each can be measured—is necessary. Pharmacy, as explained in Chapter 2, meets or exceeds several standards: rigorous academic training, a professional legal responsibility, professional personal relationships and professional ethical relationships.

In one very important area, however, pharmacy scores a very low rating. The critical failing is the weakness of the service motive as compared to the commercial (or profit-making) motive. Though surrounded by phrases such as "public health and safety," the practices of pharmacists as embodied in law and board of pharmacy regulations are intended to, and do, restrict competition—especially competition from drug chains and discounters.

Similarly, pharmacists have always emphasized the commercial rather than the professional. This is exemplified by the relative strength of the National Association of Retail Druggists (NARD) and the American Pharmaceutical Association (APhA). The former, strongly merchant oriented, has always been far more powerful than the latter, supposedly professionally oriented, organization.

Paradoxically, most employee pharmacists appear to be truly concerned with professionalism, much to the dismay of chain drugstore executives. These pharmacists seem to be uninterested in learning about merchandising, do not wish to sell "up front" merchandise, and have little interest in becoming executives. In short, employee-pharmacists seem to want only to fill prescriptions and to earn a good salary while doing so.

Viewed in the aggregate, then, pharmacy must be regarded as a profession as long as employee-pharmacists adhere to their currently held views. Such an appellation will, however, continue to be in danger until the employee-pharmacists seize control of pharmaceutical organizations and direct them into professional paths and/or until owner-pharmacists purge themselves of the merchant philosophy.

To predict the form and timing of the transition would be difficult in any event. With the advent of government financed health care for the aged and its unforseeable impact upon the retail drug industry, any reliable assessment of future changes in pharmacy is not, as yet, possible. Nevertheless, given the structure of the industry as it now exists, it is unlikely that significant changes will occur within the immediate future.

Concluding Observations

It would not be accurate to create the impression that the philosophy and activities of independent pharmacists compare unfavorably with those of other vocations requiring occupational licenses. This study has been confined to the retail drug industry, but there are indications that a similar state of affairs exists in other fields. Some examples are cited to show that restrictionism is not a trait unique to pharmacists.

New Jersey courts have declared advertising restrictions unconstitutional in two cases. One involved gas station signs and the other concerned price lists posted in barber shops.[2] Also in New Jersey, a statute declaring that used car dealers had to operate from buildings of a certain size was held to be unconstitutional.[3]

Barbers appear to practice restrictionism in Illinois and thirteen other states where there are minimum-price laws pertaining to haircuts. Also, the knowledge required to pass the licensing examination given by the state boards is too esoteric to be useful to a barber in

---

[2] *State* v. *Garrubo*, 124 N.J.L. 19, 10 A.2d 635 (Sup. Ct. 1940); *Regal Oil Co.* v. *State*, 123 N.J.L. 456, 10 A.2d 495 (Sup. Ct. 1939).

[3] *New Jersey Used Car Trade Ass'n* v. *Mazer*, 1 N.J. Super. 371, 61 A.2d 751 (1948).

his work. The examinations apparently are designed to act as entry barriers rather than tests of an individual's competence as a barber.[4]

The barbers' union (Journeymen Barbers, Hairdressers, and Cosmetologists) supports such restrictions. One of its vice-presidents has said:

We are particularly pleased to see the Barber Boards of 47 states giving heed to the law of supply and demand. Good schools and well-trained students are necessary for future progress of the barber profession, but too many schools and too many students . . . can stop progress and shatter the hopes of the future. . . . Operators of schools and colleges should put teaching and sufficient training ahead of accumulating dollars . . . This cannot be done if students do not have sufficient practice on the chair. Too many students mean [sic] too many poorly trained students and too many poorly trained students mean [sic] too many cut-rate barbers. The law of supply and demand must be heeded if we are to continue to hold our present price structure and go forward to make our profession what it should be.[5]

Another reason for the advocacy of licensing requirements by barbers (and taxicab) unions is that a strike cannot be broken by calling strikebreakers from the outside—a "scab" would need a license to work and he could be prohibited from acquiring one.[6]

Operating restrictions that apply to taxicabs exist in some cities, the primary one being an arbitrary limitation on the number of licenses granted. When this restriction exists (New York City), taxi fares are higher and the utilization of taxis as a mode of transportation is less than in cities (Washington, D.C.) where such restrictions do not exist.[7]

Recently, a group of New York City civil rights workers tried to convince the city that more taxis should be licensed to serve the mainly Negro Bedford-Stuyvesant section of New York City. This proposal was strongly denounced by fleet owners and independent taxi owners.[8]

Many states require plumbers to be licensed. The plumbers' union is usually represented on the examining boards. Since the union has endorsed licensing to exclude Negroes from the trade, color is often

[4] Simon Rottenberg, "The Economics of Occupational Licensing," in *Aspects of Labor Economics*, A Report of the National Bureau of Economic Research (Princeton: Princeton University Press, 1962), pp. 14–20.

[5] As quoted in *Ibid.*, p. 15.

[6] Sumner H. Slichter, *Union Policies and Industrial Management* (Washington: The Brookings Institution, 1941), p. 49.

[7] J. R. Meyer, J. F. Kain, and M. Wohl, *The Urban Transportation Problem* (Cambridge: Harvard University Press, 1965), pp. 353–357.

[8] *The New York Times*, May 4, 1966.

a factor used to determine competence.[9] This is a striking example of the opportunity for arbitrary use of power by licensing boards.

A New York City restaurant owner recently learned of licensing problems by first-hand experience. Philip Rosen, owner of Cafe Chambord for twenty-four years, was opening at a new location, or so he thought. Seven weeks after his application for a liquor license at his new location, he was still waiting for the permit to be issued. His losses average about $1,000 per week. Rosen's past record is unblemished and he is an outstanding restaurateur. His business was rated as a top New York restaurant by *Holiday*, a gourmet food magazine.[10]

A final example outside the health field:

Not many witnesses would be as frank as the representative of the California Embalmers' Association who appeared at a Committee hearing to advocate that the general educational prerequisite for an embalmer's license be increased from high school graduation to two years' college and that thoroughly educated, trained and experienced embalmers from other states be required to serve a one-year apprenticeship in California before becoming eligible for a license. When asked the reasons for these requests, he candidly said that it was to reduce the number of embalmers coming into the field because a surplus existed which was keeping compensation low, in his opinion.[11]

The last example of restrictionism comes from a health profession—pathologists. Pathologists are physicians who have specialized in the analysis of human tissue (including blood) to determine what disease or condition has caused a deviation (in tissue or blood) from the normal appearance and function of the item under analysis. Pathologists usually serve as diagnostic aides to other physicians and surgeons.

The U.S. Justice Department has filed an antitrust suit against the College of American Pathologists, alleging that the defendant and co-conspirators have conspired to and have monopolized interstate trade as it pertains to the commercial medical laboratories with which pathologists are usually associated. According to the complaint filed by the Justice Department, the goals of the illegal concerted action were to insure that (1) all commercial medical laboratories would be owned by and operated solely for the profit of pathologists, (2) all commercial

---

[9] Herbert R. Northrup, *Organized Labor and the Negro* (New York: Harper & Bros., 1944), pp. 23–24.

[10] *The Wall Street Journal*, April 26, 1966.

[11] California, Senate, *1956 Partial Report to the Legislature by the Senate Interim Committee on Licensing Businesses and Professions*, Sacramento, p. 9.

medical laboratories owned by chemists, biologists, physicists, or other nonpathologists would be forced out of business regardless of quality of service, (3) no commercial medical laboratory owned by a member of the College of American Pathologists would engage in price competition with other members, and (4) no medical laboratory owned by a member of the College of American Pathologists would compete on a basis of price in the purchase of goods and services from hospitals.[12]

To accomplish these goals, the College of American Pathologists has allegedly (1) induced pathologists to refuse to accept positions with or affiliate with commercial medical laboratories not owned by pathologists, (2) induced pathologists to refuse to accept salaried positions with hospitals operated for profit or which charge patients fees for laboratory services, unless the entire profit from the medical laboratory accrued to a pathologist, (3) agreed to attempt to establish a commercial boycott by all doctors of all commercial medical laboratories not owned by pathologists, (4) made price-fixing agreements by which the prices charged for the services of the laboratories are maintained at artificially high levels, and (5) made price-fixing agreements by which the prices paid for goods and services purchased by the laboratories from hospitals and other institutions are maintained at artificially low levels.[13]

From the restrictions practiced by this group of dissimilar trades, it appears, as previously indicated, that restrictionism may exist in a considerable number of occupational licensing activities. It is probable that pharmacists' activities are more visible because they are more numerous and because they are opposed by some strong drug chains and trade organizations.

Detailed studies of possible free market restrictions in other professions, occupations, and trades are needed, for if pharmacists are typical—and there is no reason to believe they are not—some explanation might be forthcoming for the rapid price rises that have occurred in recent years in the service sector of the economy. Further, additional inquiries should indicate whether restrictions derive from the several licensing boards, and, if so, whether a complete revision of occupational licensing is needed.

Moving from occupational licensing to the economics of health care, there are several subject areas of the latter that appear to justify extensive research. Some of these are (1) the distribution of and compensation for welfare prescriptions, where such prescriptions are filled by privately owned pharmacies, (2) the impact of medicare on the drug

---

[12] *Complaint, United States* v. *American College of Pathologists,* Civil No. 66 C 1253, No. D.Ill., filed June 3, 1966.

[13] *Ibid.*

industry, with particular reference to pricing and distribution channels, (3) the significance of Title XIX (medicaid) for welfare patients, medicare recipients, and the remainder of the drug-buying public, and (4) the equity of the competition between public and private sources of drugs. The last field suggested comprises out-patient dispensing by tax-supported hospitals and clinics and drugstores established by the Office of Economic Opportunity.

Recommendations

If it is the intent and desire of the general public that the nation's enterprises be conducted in accordance with the philosophy of maximum attainable competition, several changes in the state pharmacy laws are needed to preclude the future promulgation of restrictive regulations that act as free market barriers. The following recommendations should also serve to reduce the number and impact of current restrictions.

First, the state attorney general should be empowered and required to approve regulations promulgated by a pharmacy board before the provisions become effective. A board of pharmacy would be likely to exercise more restraint if it knew that its proposal would be scrutinized by the official charged with representing the board in litigation instituted under the regulation.

Second, the board should be required to hold, give prior public notice of, and make a record of hearings convened for the purpose of discussing proposed regulations. Such hearings are now held in some states, but notice is given only to pharmacists and no record of the hearing's proceedings is made. If the proposed regulations, after discussion, appear to be satisfactory to the board, the transcript of the hearings should be a part of the package forwarded to the attorney general for his inspection. In this way, the attorney general would be aware of any objections to the proposed rules.

The final procedural change should be a mandatory vote by all board members, via absentee ballot if necessary, on proposed regulations and on license applications where hearings are held to determine the eligibility of the petitioner for such permits.[14]

[14] In June, 1967, bills were pending to provide some control of the various licensing boards nominally reporting to the director of the California Department of Professional and Vocational Standards. The bills would (1) have the boards' inspectors report directly to the director of the Department, (2) place board secretaries on per diem rather than salary when secretaries are selected from board membership, (3) limit board members to two terms, (4) make the Department Director an ex officio member of the boards with voting rights, (5) require thirty days' notice to the public prior to board meetings, and (6) require the boards to submit reports deemed necessary by the Department Director. (Senate Bills 1454, 1241, 812, 817, 696, and 818 respectively.)

In addition to modifications of promulgation and voting procedures, changes also should be made in the statutory provisions controlling the selection and composition of the boards of pharmacy. Such amendments actually are much more important than the three proposed procedural modifications, for it is the board itself that is the crucial element in regulation of the retail drug industry.

First, the governor should be given exclusive appointive power (with perhaps confirmation by the upper house in the state legislature) over the membership of the pharmacy board. Lists that the various state laws permit to be proposed by the state pharmaceutical association, either on a compulsory or optional compliance basis, should be prohibited. The governor, being a political animal, is almost bound to submit to recommendations that result from the operation of the law. This does not eliminate, of course, the executive's right to solicit information concerning appropriate appointments. He must not, however, be compelled—by law or by the informal pressure of an optional list—to comply with or accept a proposed board membership list from any group.

Further, the governor should be allowed to remove board of pharmacy members at will. In the present situation, the boards are virtually independent of the state government. The only cause for removal of a member is malfeasance in office, a difficult charge to substantiate. The board would be more responsive to public opinion if the governor could eject board members in response to a public outcry.

The composition of the board should also be altered to eliminate domination by independent drugstore owners. Assuming that a five man board is the correct size, no more than three should be pharmacists. Two of these should represent the interests of retail pharmacy. One of the retail pharmacists should be an employee. The other pharmacist should represent other pharmaceutical interests such as hospital pharmacies, drug manufacturing firms, and pharmaceutical education or research establishments. The remaining two board members should be representatives of the public, the main requirement concerning their appointment being no connection with any segment of the drug industry.[15]

These revisions concerning the composition of pharmacy boards and their regulatory powers would substantially aid in combating the forces that restrict the right of any person or company to enter the legal occupation of drug retailing—a right guaranteed by our system of government, endorsed by the courts, and required to insure the maintenance of meaningful competition.

[15] As of May, 1967, there was a proposal before the Florida legislature that the licensing boards be brought under a director and that each licensing board be composed of three members of the profession and two public members.

Whatever the merit of the recommendations, they are not, in and of themselves, sufficient. Some effort must be made by employee pharmacists to incorporate themselves into the power structures of state pharmaceutical associations to mute the vociferous agitation of the associations for restrictive laws and regulations, for the state associations will always influence the boards of pharmacy. Similarly, drug chains must be induced to bring their countervailing power to bear if permanent changes are to be effected. Pharmaceutical associations exert constant pressure and chains must exert a constant pressure in the opposite direction if reasonable regulation is to be achieved in the retail drug industry.

The Role of the Federal Government

Those fearful of an expansion of the power of the federal government as well as those who propose more federal control to solve any problem will observe that recommendations which would result in an enlargement or contraction of federal influence have been avoided. There is ample justification for the absence of such proposals.

First, although it was not a focal point of this study, it appears that the federal government has sufficient power to police the quality of drugs that reach the consumer. Any failures of the FDA appear to result from a shortage of funds and manpower, rather than legislative mandate.

Second, if there is restraint of trade involved in the issues raised, present antitrust laws and their recent interpretations are strong enough to secure injunctions against conspiratorial tactics.

Third, the controversy is between two strong economic groups, and as a result, court actions to test the legality of the restrictions are not an unbearable burden for the parties in conflict. Also, lobbying before the state legislatures and public appeals are open avenues to both economic interest groups.

Fourth, the first three reasons convince the writer that federal action is not needed and therefore should not be sought as a solution.

Fifth, there is the issue of where to draw the line. If a federal agency is to regulate the licensure of pharmacists and the retail trade practices of pharmacists engaged in retail drug pursuits, should not a similar agency do the same for physicians, lawyers, accountants, engineers, and all other vocations requiring licensure? If not, which ones should be under federal jurisdiction and which ones should not?

Finally, and most important, there are many activities of state boards of pharmacy that are handled quite well with the existing relationship, and a change of federal-state balance of power could well have an overall detrimental effect. There appears to be a rather intimate relationship between each board of pharmacy and the pharmacists it regulates. This closeness is especially helpful in rooting out those that violate state and federal narcotic laws. In fact, federal agents rely largely upon the state regulatory bodies to maintain surveillance in this sphere so that federal agents can devote their time to illicit international distribution of drugs and their domestic termini. Other advantages of the close relationship between state boards and those they regulate could be cited, but the narcotics problem is a serious and growing problem and is the most striking argument for a continuance of state control of retail pharmacy.

The preceding discussion could be amplified, but it is not necessary. This study has emphasized many of the shortcomings in the regulation of retail pharmacy. The regulators need no assistance in calling attention to the many good things they accomplish.

Selected Provisions of the State Pharmacy Laws and Selected Rules and Regulations of the State Boards of Pharmacy

ALABAMA

EXCERPTS FROM LAWS RELATING TO PHARMACY[1]

Section 216. Appointees to be Active Pharmacists. Only registered pharmacists who have been licensed in this state for at least ten years and are actively engaged in retail pharmacy shall be eligible for appointment to the state board of pharmacy.

Section 217. Majority of Members to be Graduates in Pharmacy. At least a majority of the members of the board shall be graduates of a school or college of pharmacy, . . . but they shall not be connected with any school or college of pharmacy in a professional or executive capacity . . .

Section 218. Appointment by Governor . . . From a list of five eligible names submitted by the Alabama pharmaceutical association, the governor shall appoint a member of the board . . .

Section 223. Board to Make . . . Rules and Regulations. The board shall have [the] power to make by-laws, [and] rules and regulations for the proper performance of its duties . . . and to carry out the provisions of this chapter. . . .

Section 236. Administration of Medicines by Physicians, Dentists and Veterinarians, Patent and Proprietary Medicines Exempted; Wholesalers

[1] *Ala. Code* tit. 46, c. 12 (1958) and Supp. 1965.

and Manufacturers Exempted. Nothing herein contained shall be construed to prevent . . . the sale of patent or proprietary medicines or remedies, which do not contain opium or cocoa leaves, or any compound, manufacture, salt, derivative or preparation thereof, when sold at retail in original packages . . .

Section 257. Medical Doctors Owning and Operating Drug Stores. The provisions of this chapter shall not prevent any legally licensed medical doctor from owning or operating a drug store provided that said medical doctor fill only his own prescriptions and not do a general prescription business.

SELECTED RULES AND REGULATIONS OF THE ALABAMA STATE BOARD OF PHARMACY[2]

No. 4. . . . It is hereby promulgated that the term patent medicine as used in the [Act of 1923, H. 423 and the Act of 1931, S. 136] . . . shall not be interpreted to mean those packages of medical preparations which are advertised to the Physician under copyright names, or to those products recognized by the United States Pharmacopoeia or National Formulary (except those which have been classed as household remedies) or to those products or preparations which, from the nature of their composition, and known effects, should not be dispensed by any one except a licensed Pharmacist, or practicing Physician . . .

No. 17. No permit shall be issued to a non-registered owner who has only one full-time pharmacist employed.

Permits in the above-named category in force as of June 23, 1959, will continue to be renewed provided applicants are fully complying with the [the law in other respects] . . .

No. 18. . . . The practice of forwarding physician's prescriptions by mail or other carrier to be filled by pharmacists not licensed by or subject to the jurisdiction of the Alabama State Board of Pharmacy is proscribed and forbidden. The doing of any act in aid of this practice by any pharmacist, pharmacy, apothecary shop, drug store or employee of either, in the State of Alabama is prohibited. Without limiting the generality of the above, no person who is not registered as a pharmacist by the Alabama State Board of Pharmacy shall accept prescriptions from qualified medical practitioners or patients thereof and transfer, transmit or transport same to pharmacists or others at different locations either within or without the State of Alabama for compounding or dispensing.

No. 19. On or after September 23, 1963, all non-registered owners of pharmacies, drug stores, apothecaries, drug shops, or any such combination of such words or titles, shall have two or more full-time registered pharmacists in their employ at each drug store, apothecary, pharmacy, or other like establishments, so operated by such nonregistered owner or owners.

[2] Alabama State Board of Pharmacy, "Rules and Regulations." (Mimeographed.)

Permits in the above-named category in force as of September 23, 1963, will continue to be renewed provided applicants are fully complying with [the law in other respects] . . .

ALASKA

EXCERPTS FROM LAWS RELATING TO PHARMACY[3]

Article 1. Section 08.80.010. Creation and Membership of Board of Pharmacy. There is created the Board of Pharmacy, composed of five members, each of whom shall be a pharmacist licensed in the state who has been actively engaged in the practice of pharmacy in the state for a period of three years immediately preceding his appointment. . . .

Article 1. Section 08.80.020. Term of Office. Members of the board are appointed by the governor, and confirmed by the legislature . . .

Article 1. Section 08.80.030. Powers of the Board. The board may

. . .

    (4) do whatever is necessary and advisable to carry out the purposes of this chapter.

Article 1. Section 08.80.040. Duties of the Board. The board shall

. . .

    (6) issue a list of potentially dangerous medicinal ingredients or preparations that may be sold only under the direct supervision of a licensed pharmacist; the failure to include an ingredient or preparation in this list does not affect any law or regulation which prohibits or restricts the sale of the ingredient or preparation.

Article 3. Section 08.80.320. Pharmacist Required.

    (a) A pharmacy shall have a licensed pharmacist on duty during the hours that the pharmacy is open for business.

. . .

Article 3. Section 08.80.330. Licensed Pharmacist as Manager. If the owner of a pharmacy is not a licensed pharmacist, he shall place a licensed pharmacist, designated the manager, in full charge and control of the pharmacy. . . .

Article 4. Section 08.80.370. Vending Machine Sales Prohibited. No mechanical device or vending machine wherever located, may be used to dispense a drug, medicine or preparation containing poison.

Article 4. Section 08.80.390. Pharmacist Required in Hospitals and Clinics. A hospital or clinic which dispenses drugs for out-patient treatment shall have a licensed pharmacist in charge of the dispensary, except that prescriptions may be compounded and dispensed by or under the supervision of the prescribing physician.

[3] *Alaska Stat.* tit. 8, c. 80 (1962) and Supp. 1965.

ARIZONA

EXCERPTS FROM LAWS RELATING TO PHARMACY[4]

Article 1. Section 32-1902. Board of Pharmacy.
A. . . . No person shall be appointed to the board unless he has been registered as a licentiate in pharmacy in this state for at least ten years prior to the date of appointment. . . .
B. On or before January 15 of each year the secretary of the Arizona pharmaceutical association may submit to the governor a list of the names of at least seven of its members who have been nominated by the association . . . The governor shall make his appointments to the board from the nominees on the list or from others having the necessary qualifications.

Article 1. Section 32-1904. Powers and Duties.[5] The board may:
1. Make by-laws, rules and regulations necessary for the protection of the public appertaining to the practice of pharmacy and the lawful performance of its duties.

Article 1. Section 39-1921. Acts and Persons not Required to be Licensed. Nothing contained in this chapter shall be construed to prevent:
2. The sale of nonnarcotic or nonpoisonous patent or proprietary medicines when sold at retail in original packages . . .
. . .

Article 3. Section 32-1971. Pharmacy Operated by Hospital. A pharmacy operating in connection with a hospital shall comply with all the provisions of this chapter requiring registration of drug stores and pharmacies, with all regulations of the board of pharmacy, and in addition shall meet the following requirements:
1. In hospitals with one hundred beds or more, the pharmacy or drug dispensing room shall be under the supervision of a licentiate in pharmacy licensed in this state.
2. In hospitals of less than one hundred beds where the drug room is not under the supervision of a licentiate in pharmacy, the services of a registered licentiate in pharmacy in the community where the hospital is located or a pharmacists' inspector from the board of pharmacy shall be obtained periodically to consult with the hospital administrator relative to the labeling, storage and dispensing of drugs.
3. The licentiate in pharmacy shall, with the approval of the administrator of the hospital, initiate procedures to provide for the administrative and technical guidance in all matters pertaining to the handling and dispensing of drugs.

[4] *Ariz. Rev. Stat. Ann.* tit. 32, c. 18 (1956) and Supp. 1965.
[5] The prohibition of the vending of (1) drugs in original packages and (2) patent medicine except by a registered pharmacist was declared unconstitutional. *State* v. *Childs*, 32 Ariz. 222, 257 P. 366 (1927).

SELECTED RULES AND REGULATIONS OF THE
ARIZONA STATE BOARD OF PHARMACY[6]

No. I-13. Sale of Devices, Drugs, Medicinal Chemicals, Medicines, Poisons, require a prescription, but is of such nature, or the condition for which it is intended is of such nature, that oral directions, caution or warning should be given, in addition to the printed direction, caution or warning on the label, shall be dispensed under the supervision of a registered pharmacist in a licensed pharmacy, dispensary, or drug store.

Such drugs shall include, unless otherwise exempted by the Board of Pharmacy:

(1) Parenterals [injectibles].

(2) Any drug that is changed from prescription-only legend to over-the-counter status by the Federal Food and Drug Administration.

(3) Any drug bearing a warning or certain label.

No. I-8. Restriction on Mail Order Prescriptions. No person shall compound and dispense a prescription when a bona fide traditional physician-pharmacist-patient relationship does not exist. The traditional physician-pharmacist-patient relationship is that condition whereby the pharmacist knows either the physician, the patient, or both, and/or can readily and easily, in customary normal procedure check on factors concerning the prescription.

No. I-13. Sale of Devices, Drugs, Medicinal Chemicals, Medicines, Poisons, or Proprietary or Patent Medicines by Mechanical Devices or Vending Machines Prohibited. The use of any mechanical device or vending machine in connection with the sales of any device, drug, medicinal chemical, medicine, poison, or proprietary or patent medicine is unlawful.

No. II-5. It shall be unlawful for any person not a licentiate in pharmacy or for any firm, corporation or co-partnership to open, advertise, or conduct a place of business, pharmacy, dispensary, drug store, apothecary shop or store in which drugs, medicines or poisons are retailed, compounded, and disposed, unless such place of business has a registered pharmacist on duty during all business hours.

ARKANSAS

EXCERPTS FROM LAWS RELATING TO PHARMACY[7]

Section 72-1001. Definitions.

. . .

10. Proprietary medicines, when not otherwise limited, means remedies that a certain individual or individuals have the exclusive right to manufacture or sell.

. . .

---

[6] Arizona State Board of Pharmacy, *Rules and Regulations.* Phoenix, [1965].
[7] *Ark. Stat. of 1947 Ann.* tit. 72, c. 10 (1957) and Supp. 1965.

Section 72-1002. State Board of Pharmacy—Appointment—Qualifications—Terms—Vacancies. . . . The Governor shall appoint five (5) experienced pharmacists who shall have actively been engaged in the drug business for the last five (5) years immediately preceding their appointments . . .

Section 72-1004.1. Reasonable Rules and Regulations Authorized. The Arkansas State Board of Pharmacy shall have [the] authority to make reasonable rules and regulations, not inconsistent with law to carry out the purposes and intentions of this act and the pharmacy laws of this state which said Board deems necessary to preserve and protect the public health.

Section 72-1020. Exemptions from Act. . . . The provisions of this Act shall not apply to . . . the sales by wholesale druggists, wholesale or retail grocers, or other wholesale or retail dealers or manufacturers of proprietary medicines in original packages; nor to the sales of those drugs commonly known as "Grocer's drugs" in original packages when put up under the direction of a registered pharmacist of this or some other state.

SELECTED RULES AND REGULATIONS OF THE ARKANSAS STATE BOARD OF PHARMACY[8]

No. 20. The sale of any drugs or medicines, whether proprietary or legend, by means of a vending machine or any other mechanical device is hereby expressly prohibited.

No. 23. No person, firm or business establishment shall offer to the public, in any manner, their services as a "pick-up station" or intermediary for the purpose of having prescriptions filled or delivered, whether for profit or gratuitously. Nor may the owner of any Pharmacy or Drug Store authorize any person, firm or business establishment to act for them in this manner.

No. 24. Hereafter, no Registered Pharmacist, Licensed Practical Druggist or any person, firm or Corporation holding a Registered Pharmacy Permit shall advertise the name or price of tranquilizing drugs or antibiotics or other drugs which can be purchased and dispensed only by means of prescription from a Physician. . . .

No. 25. In any store, firm or place of business not devoted primarily to the operation of a licensed pharmacy, the prescription department shall be completely separated from the remainder of the building by some type of partition and said department shall be arranged or constructed so that it may be locked to prevent unauthorized persons from entering in the absence of the registered pharmacist.

[8] Arkansas State Board of Pharmacy, *Arkansas State Laws Pertaining to the Practice of Pharmacy and official Rules and Regulations of the Arkansas State Board of Pharmacy* (Little Rock, 1964), pp. 63–73.

No. 30. . . . All drug stores or pharmacies must have on duty an Arkansas Registered Pharmacist a minimum of 40 hours per week. The said 40 hours per week must be served by a single pharmacist and said requirement of 40 hours per week cannot be met by a combination of two or more pharmacists with less than 40 hours each. . . .

CALIFORNIA

EXCERPTS FROM LAWS RELATING TO PROFESSIONS[9]

Article 6. Section 651. Representation of Price or Fee at Discount. It is unlawful for any person licensed under this division or under any initiative act referred to in this division to offer for sale or to sell any commodity or to offer to sell or render or to render any service under the representation that the price or fee which is to be, or is, charged for such commodity or service, or both, is at a discount, or under the representation that the price or fee which is to be, or is, charged for such commodity or service, or both, is at a percentage or otherwise less than the average fee or price than regularly charged under like conditions by the person so licensed or by other persons for such commodity or service or commodity and service. The provisions of this section shall not be construed to modify or establish prices or fees or to modify or affect in any manner any other provision of this section.

Article 6. Section 654. Prohibited Arrangements Between Opticians or Pharmacists and Medical Licensees. No person licensed under Chapter 5 [i.e., physicians, etc.] . . . of this division may have any membership, proprietary interest or co-ownership . . . to whom patients, clients or customers are referred . . . Nor, after June 1, 1967, shall any person licensed under Chapter 5 of this division have any membership, proprietary interest, or co-ownership . . . with a pharmacy regulated by Chapter 9, . . . except that this shall not apply to a hospital pharmacy nor prohibit ownership in the building in which a pharmacy is located . . . .

EXCERPTS FROM LAWS RELATING TO PHARMACY[10]

Article 1. Section 4000. Board of Pharmacy; Administration and Enforcement. . . . The . . . State Board of Pharmacy . . . shall be appointed by the Governor.

Article 1. Section 4001. Board Members; Appointment; Qualifications. The Governor shall appoint seven competent registered pharmacists . . . to serve as members of the board. The Governor shall appoint one public member who shall not be a licentiate of the board or of any other board under this division . . .

[9] *Cal. Bus. and Prof. Code* div. 1, c. 1.
[10] *Id.* at div. 2, c. 9.

Article 1. Section 4003. Board Members; Teaching. No member of the board shall teach pharmacy in any of its branches, unless it be as a teacher in a public capacity and in a college of pharmacy. . . .

Article 1. Section 4008. Rules and Regulations; Subjects of Regulations. The board may make such rules and regulations, not inconsistent with the laws of this State as may be necessary for the protection of the public. . . .

Article 3. Section 4052. Exceptions in General.
   (a) Except as otherwise provided in Articles 7, 8, and 9 of this chapter, this chapter shall not apply to any packaged, bottled or nonbulk chemicals or drugs when identified by and sold under a trademark, trade name or other trade symbol printed, owned or registered in the United States Patent Office or as provided by the laws of the State of California, and labeled with directions for use and with the name and address of the manufacturer or distributor, if such chemical or drug meets with the requirements of the pure food and drug laws of the United States of America and of the State of California. . . .

   . . .

Article 4. Section 4080.5. Issuance of Permit to Medical Licensees Prohibited. The board shall not issue any new permit to conduct a pharmacy to a person who is licensed under Chapter 5 . . . of this division.

SELECTED RULES AND REGULATIONS OF THE CALIFORNIA STATE BOARD OF PHARMACY[11]

Article 2. Section 1714. Building Standards. Any new pharmacy, *or* any existing pharmacy which is being remodeled, must comply with the following provisions:
   (a) *Approval of Plans.* The pharmacy area, merchandising area, waiting area, storeroom, restroom, and all partitions, doors, windows, and fixtures shall be indicated on floor plans submitted to the Board of Pharmacy. Such plans shall be approved by the Board of Pharmacy prior to proceeding with new construction or remodeling.
   (b) *Compounding and Dispensing Area.* The area to be occupied by the prescription compounding and dispensing department of any pharmacy shall be not less than 240 sq. ft.

   . . .
   (d) *Separation of Pharmacy and Access.*
      (1) The pharmacy shall be separated from the merchandising area by a barrier with a minimum height of 5 ft. and of sufficient width which will render the narcotics or dangerous drugs . . . inaccessible to any person. The Board of Pharmacy

[11] *Cal. Admin. Code* tit. 16, c. 17.

may permit alternate types of separations if in its opinion they provide equivalent security. The only access to the pharmacy shall be by doors or gates which can be locked.*

(2) A permanent barrier or partition extending from door to ceiling shall be provided to separate the pharmacy, or the pharmacy and adjoining merchandising area, from the rest of the building or the outside. Such permanent barrier may consist of gates or doors, and may include required swinging exit doors. All such gates or doors shall be capable of being locked.*

. . .

(h) *Existing Pharmacies.* Existing pharmacies licensed by the Board of Pharmacy prior to the effective dates of these regulations, may have their use continued if they reasonably conform, to the intent of these regulations.

* *Note:* For requirements concerning separations based on operations of the pharmacy, see Section 1715, Security Standards.

Article 2. Section 1717. Pharmaceutical Practice.

. . .

(f) No licensee shall participate in any arrangement or agreement whereby prescriptions may be left at, picked up from, accepted by, or delivered to any store or shop not licensed as a retail pharmacy. Provided, however, that nothing in this section shall prohibit a licensee from picking up prescriptions, or delivering prescriptions, at the office or home of the prescriber, at the residence of the patient, or at the hospital in which a patient is confined, by means of an employer or by use of a common carrier.

(g) The compounding, filling, dispensing, furnishing or refilling of a prescription of a medical practitioner shall be as follows:

. . .

The typing of the label; the checking of the directions on the label with the directions on the prescription to determine accuracy; the selection of the drug or drugs from stock; the counting, measuring, mixing, pouring, compounding or preparation of the drug or drugs; the placing of the finished product into the proper container; the addition onto the prescription of the required notations, shall all be done by a registered pharmacist or a registered intern pharmacist under the immediate supervision of a registered pharmacist.

. . .

Article 8. Section 1755. Sale of Drugs, Medicines, and Chemicals by Mechanical Devices or Vending Machines Prohibited. The use of any mechanical device or vending machine in connection with the sales or disposition of drugs and/or medicines and/or chemicals is unlawful.

Article 8. Section 1756. Exemption for Mechanical Devices for Storage of Hospital Floor Stock. Section 1755 shall not apply to any mechanical device to be used for the furnishing of drugs and medicines for registered patients in any hospital licensed by the board or holding a permit from the board. Every device shall comply with all of the following provisions:

1. All drugs and medicines to be stocked in the device shall be packaged for use in the device by a registered pharmacist in the employ of the hospital and shall be packaged in the hospital in which the drug is to be administered.
2. The device shall be stocked with drugs and medicines only by a registered pharmacist in the employ of the hospital.
3. A registered pharmacist in the employ of the hospital shall be personally responsible for the inventory and stocking of drugs and medicines in the device and shall be personally responsible for the condition of the drugs and medicines stored in the device.
4. A registered pharmacist in the employ of the hospital shall be the only person having access to that portion, section, or part of the device in which the drugs or medicines are stored.
5. All containers of drugs or medicines to be stored in the device shall be correctly labeled as required by federal and state laws by a registered pharmacist in the employ of the hospital. The label shall include the method of administration of the drug or medicine.
6. At the time of the removal of any drug or medicine from the device, the device shall automatically make a written record showing the name and strength of the drug or medicine removed, the name of the patient for whom the drug or medicine was ordered, the name or registry number of the nurse and the name of the physician who ordered the drug or medicine, and that the permanent record be maintained in possession of the pharmacist.
7. A registered nurse, a physician and surgeon, or a registered pharmacist shall be the only persons authorized to remove any drug or medicine from the device and such removal by a registered nurse or a physician and surgeon shall be made only pursuant to a physician's chart order.
8. The device shall be used only for the furnishing of drugs or medicines for administration in the hospital to registered in-patients or emergency patients in the hospital.
9. Every hospital seeking approval to use such a device shall, prior to the actual use of the device register with the board and file a notice of intention to use the device, the name of the manufacturer of the device, a description of the device, the serial number of the device, the location of each device in the hospital, and the name of the registered pharmacist who is to be responsible for stocking the device.

   No such device shall be used until approval has been granted, and no change in the location of the device or in the registered pharmacist responsible for stocking the device shall be made without prior written notice to the board.

As used in this section, a "pharmacist in the employ of the hospital shall not include any pharmacist who is, or is employed by, any manufacturer, wholesaler, distributor, or itinerant vendor of drugs or medicines."

COLORADO

EXCERPTS FROM LAWS RELATING TO PHARMACY[12]

Article 1. Section 48-1-1. State Board of Pharmacy. The state board of pharmacy shall be composed of five registered pharmacists, having at least ten years' practical experience as dispensing pharmacists in this state. . . . All appointments shall be made by the governor from a list of eligible persons supplied by the Colorado Pharmaceutical Association, which list shall contain at least five names for each position to be filled. . . .

Article 1. Section 48-1-2. Officers—Powers and Duties.
(1)(a) The board has the power and it is its duty to:

. . .

(d) Make such rules and regulations not inconsistent with the laws of this state as may be necessary for the regulation of the practice of pharmacy and the lawful performance of its duties.

. . .

Article 1. Section 48-1-13. Compounding or Sale of Drugs.

. . .

(4) A proprietary or patent medicine may be sold by any proprietary or patent medicine dealer duly licensed by the board.

Article 1. Section 48-1-24. Definitions. Unless otherwise indicated by the context, the following words and phrases, when used in this chapter, shall mean:

. . .

(5) "Proprietary or patent medicine," a medicine in its unbroken, original package which is advertised, promoted, offered for sale or sold by or under the authority of the manufacturer, or primary distributor thereof, directly to the general public under a trade mark, trade name or other trade symbol privately owned, whether or not registered in the United States patent office, and the labeling of which bears: A statement specifying affections, symptoms or purposes for which the product is recommended; adequate directions for use and such warnings as are necessary for the protection of users; an accurate statement of the quantity of the contents in terms of weight, measure or numerical count; a statement of the active ingredients; the name and address of the manufacturer or primary distributor. Provided, that the term "proprietary

[12] *Colo. Rev. Stat. of 1958 Ann. c.* 48 (1963) and Supp. 1965.

or patent medicine" shall not apply to any medicine which may be dispensed only upon prescription, or is designated under any law of this state as a narcotic, hypnotic, habit-forming, dangerous or poisonous drug or medicine, nor to any therapeutic vitamin.

. . .

Article 2. Section 48-2-2. Employer Not To Require Or Permit Excess. No person, firm or corporation employing another person to sell, at retail, drugs and medicines, or to compound physicians' prescriptions shall require or permit said employee to perform work in any store, dispensary, pharmacy, laboratory, or office for more than an average of nine hours per day or for more than one hundred eight hours in any two consecutive weeks, nor more than thirteen days in such consecutive weeks. . . . The periods of rest to be taken by the employee shall be so apportioned that the employee shall be entitled either to two half-days or to one complete day of rest during each week.

SELECTED RULES AND REGULATIONS OF THE COLORADO STATE BOARD OF PHARMACY[13]

No. 61-4-2. Vending Machines Forbidden. No drug or medicine . . . shall be dispensed to the public by means of a vending machine.

No. 61-4-7. Pharmacy Must Be in Daily Charge of a Registered Pharmacist. Every licensed pharmacy must be in the continuous daily charge of a registered pharmacist. Being in charge means having direct control of the pharmaceutical affairs of said pharmacy. . . .

No. 61-11-14. Advertising of Prescription Drugs Prohibited. No pharmacy shall advertise, directly or indirectly, by any media whatsoever, any medicine which can be dispensed only upon prescription.

No. 61-11-15. Receiving of Prescriptions. Any written or oral prescription must be received in a pharmacy licensed by the State Board of Pharmacy for the purposes of compounding, dispensing, professional advice, or delivery; provided however, that a licensed pharmacy may designate a duly authorized agent to receive such prescriptions, bring them to the licensed pharmacy for compounding, and deliver them to the patient, only in those areas where pharmaceutical services are not available.

No. 64-9-2. Each of the following acts is an act in the compounding of a prescription and shall be performed only by a person authorized to compound the prescription:

1. Read and interpret the prescription . . .
2. To accurately measure or compound ingredients specified by [the] practitioner.
3. Read, interpret, and write adequate label directions . . .
4. Affix label in, or to, the container containing the medicine . . .

[13] Colorado State Board of Pharmacy, "Rules and Regulations." (Mimeographed.)

The above rules shall be equally applicable to any mechanical device used or intended to be used for prescription drugs which are sold exposed or offered for sale or disposition.

RULES OF PROFESSIONAL CONDUCT[14]

No. 5. A registered pharmacist or a pharmacy shall not promote or advertise for sale to the public, by any means, in any form or through any media, harmful or dangerous drugs, medicines, poisons, chemicals, or prescription items normally compounded, sold, or dispensed by a registered pharmacist in his professional capacity, nor shall the use of terms such as "Cut Rate" or "Discount," or any similar phrase or word in connection with professional services, be permitted to degrade the professional nature of pharmaceutical services . . .

No. 7. A registered pharmacist or pharmacy shall not . . . discriminate against anyone in the offering or performance of professional services. . . .

No. 9. A registered pharmacist or a pharmacy shall not participate in any plan, agreement, or arrangement which eliminates or affects detrimentally the traditional relationship of physician-patient-pharmacist and the freedom of choice inherent thereto.

No. 10. The independent judgment of a pharmacist is a public trust and his first allegiance is to the patient whom he serves. No pharmacist shall, except with a person licensed to practice pharmacy, directly or indirectly share compensation arising out of or incidental to his professional services—nor shall he accept professional employment from any persons who, for compensation, prescribe drugs used in the compounding or dispensing of prescriptions.

No. 13. A registered pharmacist or a pharmacy shall not operate a pharmacy which does not offer complete prescription service to the general public. A complete prescription service shall include the filling of ALL prescriptions, whether compounded or single items, narcotics, or other drugs—in any quantity which might reasonably be expected to be filled by other licensed pharmacies—and shall include an adequate inventory of all necessary pharmaceuticals and chemicals and shall provide that emergency services shall be available at all times. Non-profit hospital pharmacies shall be exempted from this regulation *only* where service is limited to in-patients.

CONNECTICUT

EXCERPTS FROM LAWS RELATING TO PHARMACY[15]

Section 20-163. Appointment and Term of Commissioners; Compensation. The commission shall . . . consist of five persons, each of whom shall

[14] Colorado State Board of Pharmacy, "Code of Professional Conduct." Adopted May 20, 1963. Effective August 20, 1963. (Mimeographed.)

[15] *Conn. Gen. Stat.* tit. 20, c. 382 (1958) and Supp. 1965.

be a licensed pharmacist of at least ten years' practical experience in the practice of pharmacy and, at the time of his appointment, shall be actively engaged in the practice of pharmacy in this state. The governor shall, annually, . . . appoint one commissioner, who may be selected from a list of six persons nominated by the Connecticut Pharmaceutical Association . . .

Section 20-164. Powers and Duties of Commission. Said commission may adopt regulations for the performance of its duties and for the conduct of the business of retailing or dispensing drugs, medicines and poisons . . .

Section 20-166. Sale of Drugs and Patent Medicines Permit. . . . in a store not a licensed pharmacy, proprietary and patent medicinal compounds or preparations put up separately in sealed containers and labeled and accompanied with directions for use and with the name and address of the manufacturer or distributor thereof may be sold in the original unbroken containers in which the article is offered to the public for consumption . . .

Section 20-169. Pharmacy to be in Charge of Registered Pharmacist. Each such licensed pharmacy shall be in the direct charge and management of a pharmacist . .

Section 20-175. Regulations Concerning Licenses; Causes for Suspension or Revocation. [The] . . . commission may make regulations concerning the licensing of any pharmacist or pharmacy and the suspension or revocation of any such license, or with reference to the conduct of such licensed pharmacist and the manner in which any such licensed pharmacy is conducted. Any license to practice pharmacy or to conduct any pharmacy may be suspended or revoked or reissued by said commission, and any of the following shall be sufficient cause for such suspension or revocation:

. . .

   (17) advertising to the general public of the sales price of any preparation which bears on its label "Caution, federal law prohibits dispensing without prescription" or words of similar import.

SELECTED RULES AND REGULATIONS OF THE CONNECTICUT STATE COMMISSION OF PHARMACY[16]

Section 20-175-6. Certain Security Safeguards in the Construction and Physical Set-Up of Pharmacies. In any building, store, firm or place of business not devoted primarily to the operation of a licensed pharmacy, the licensed pharmacy shall be completely separated from any other enterprises within the building, store, firm or place of business by partitions approved by the commission of pharmacy and the entire licensed pharmacy

---

[16] Connecticut Commission of Pharmacy, *Statutes and Regulations Governing the Practice of Pharmacy and the Sales of Drugs and Medicines* (Hartford, 1964), pp. 14–29.

shall be arranged or constructed so that the public will not have illegal access to any of the drugs, medicines and proprietary medicinal compounds. Such licensed pharmacy shall be constructed so that it may be locked to prevent unauthorized persons from entering during the absence of the registered pharmacist.

Section 20-175-6a. Pharmacy in Retail Establishment. On and after February 26, 1963, the portion of the premises occupied by a new pharmacy in a retail establishment, the principal business of which is not the operation of a pharmacy, (a) shall be separated by partitions from the other business operations, (b) shall be so arranged or constructed so that no unauthorized person will have access to any drug, medicine or poison, and (c) shall have direct public access from the outside.

Section 20-175-26. Pharmacist to be Present When Pharmacy Open for Business. No pharmacy shall at any time be open for business unless there is present therein and in charge thereof either a licensed pharmacist or an assistant licensed pharmacist.

Section 20-175-44. Sale of Patent or Proprietary Medicinal Compounds in Vending Machines. No patent or proprietary medicinal compounds, preparations or units put up in sealed or unsealed containers, labeled and accompanied with directions for use . . . shall be sold or offered or exposed for sale or dispensed by any means in any type of vending machines.

DELAWARE

EXCERPTS FROM LAWS RELATING TO PHARMACY[17]

Subchapter I. Section 2501. Appointment; Qualifications; Terms of Office; Vacancies; Oath.
  (a) The State Board of Pharmacy . . . shall consist of five persons . . . licensed . . . residents of this State and actively engaged in the practice of pharmacy . . . [and] appointed by the Governor . . .
  (b) Annually, . . . the Delaware Pharmaceutical Society shall submit to the Governor the names of five persons . . . and from this number the Governor shall appoint one member to fill the vacancy annually occurring . . .

Subchapter I. Section 2503. Seal; Powers; Record; Reports; Quorum.
  (a) The Board shall . . .
    (1) Adopt such rules and by-laws, not inconsistent with law, as may be necessary . . . for the discharge of the duties imposed under this chapter, or any laws of this state . . .
    . . .

[17] *Del. Code Ann.* tit. 24, c. 25 (1953) and Supp. 1965.

Subchapter II. Section 2521. Certificate Requirement; Exceptions.

. . .

   (d) Nothing in this section shall be construed to interfere with—

      . . .

      (3) The selling at retail of non-poisonous domestic remedies; or

      (4) The sale of patent or proprietary preparations . . .

   . . .

Subchapter III. Section 2541. Supervision and Control. The compounding, dispensing, and control of all drugs issued in hospitals shall be under the supervision of a registered pharmacist on a full-time or part-time basis. Hospitals unable to secure such services locally from either hospital or retail pharmacists, shall consult with the Board of Pharmacy. . . .

Subchapter IV. Section 2561. Prescription Department . . .

   (a) Except in stores in which a pharmacist is on duty at all times when the store is open for business, the owner of the business or the pharmacist making application for a permit to conduct a pharmacy must agree to place his entire stock of prescription drugs . . . in a room or adequately partitioned-off section . . . which room or section must be provided with a door or doors which can be locked when the store is without the attendance and supervision of a pharmacist.

   . . .

   (e) No permit shall be issued for the operation of a retail pharmacy unless the prescription department . . . shall consume at least 7½% of the total floor area of the store.

SELECTED RULES AND REGULATIONS OF THE DELAWARE STATE BOARD OF PHARMACY[18]

No. 18. . . . When any person, partnership, or corporation desires to open a pharmacy in a leased section of a large commercial operation, the Board shall require . . . that the leased section be partitioned off completely from floor to ceiling and that this section shall have an entrance from the street. Entrance from the internal portion shall be optional. This regulation is enacted to provide proper professional service as is found in operations which are pharmacies enTOTO and do not represent a small segment of a large commercial venture.

DISTRICT OF COLUMBIA

EXCERPTS FROM LAWS RELATING TO PHARMACY[19]

Section 2-607. Board of Pharmacy. . . . There shall be in and for the District of Columbia a Board of Pharmacy, consisting of five licensed phar-

---

[18] Delaware State Board of Pharmacy[1] "Rules and Regulations." (Mimeographed.)
[19] *District of Columbia Code* tit. 2, c. 6 (1961) and Supp. 1965.

macists, appointed by the Commissioners of said District, each of whom shall have been for the five years immediately preceding, and shall be during the term of his appointment actively engaged in the practice of pharmacy in said District. . . .

FLORIDA

EXCERPTS FROM LAWS RELATING TO PHARMACY[20]

Section 465.021. Scope.
  (1) This chapter . . . shall not be construed to prohibit the sale by merchants of home remedies, or of those preparations commonly known as patents or proprietary preparations where such are sold only in original or unbroken packages.

   . . .

Section 465.041. Board of Pharmacy . . .

   . . .
  (3) Only registered pharmacists who have been licensed in this state at least five years and are actively engaged in retail pharmacy shall be eligible for appointment to the . . . board of pharmacy.

   . . .
  (5) . . . the Florida state pharmaceutical association shall from among its membership, nominate three candidates . . . for the next occurring vacancy . . . and from among the nominees . . . the governor may make his appointment for the vacancy. . . .

   . . .

Section 465.14. Authority to Make Rules and Regulations. The Florida board of pharmacy is authorized to make such rules and regulations not inconsistent with law, as may be necessary to carry out the duties . . . conferred . . . by this chapter and as may be necessary to protect the health, safety and welfare of the public . . .

Section 465.23. Promoting Sale of Certain Drugs Prohibited.
  (1) It is declared that the unrestricted use of certain narcotics, central nervous system stimulants, tranquilizers, barbiturates and other hypnotic and somnifacient drugs, causing abnormal reactions that may interfere with the user's physical reflexes and judgments, may create hazardous circumstances which may cause accidents to the user and to others, thereby affecting the public health, safety and welfare. It is further declared to be in the public interest to limit the means of promoting the sale and use of these drugs. All provisions of this section shall be liberally construed to carry out these objectives and purposes.

[20] *Fla. Stat. Ann.* tit. 30, c. 465 ((1965).

(2) No pharmacist, owner or employee of a retail drug establishment shall use any communication media to promote or advertise the use or sale of any of the following:

(a) Narcotics;

(b) Central nervous system stimulants;

(c) Tranquilizers;

(d) Barbiturates;

(e) Other hypnotic and somnifacient drugs.

SELECTED RULES AND REGULATIONS OF THE FLORIDA STATE BOARD OF PHARMACY[21]

Section 280-1.11. Hospital or Clinic Dispensing. Pharmaceutical preparations which are administered to patients . . . shall only be taken from the original container, or from a container which has been prepared by a Florida registered pharmacist in accordance with existing laws, rules, and regulations affecting pharmacy in the State of Florida, and only single doses of such preparations shall be removed from said container, and then only after such has been prescribed for a specific patient by a person authorized by law to so prescribe and such order has been duly recorded upon the records of said institution. . .

Section 280-1.20. Code of Conduct. . . .

XI. Prescription Sub-Stations. No pharmacist, employer or employee of a retail drug establishment shall maintain a location, other than a pharmacy . . . from which to solicit, accept or disperse prescriptions.

. . .

XIII. Unrestricted Drug Service. No pharmacist or retail drug establishment permittee shall engage in a restricted, limited, partial or closed door service or operation to the public or to any group of persons not available to the entire public; provided, however, that this provision shall not apply to a hospital or institutional pharmacy prescription department.

. . .

GEORGIA

EXCERPTS FROM LAWS RELATING TO PHARMACY[22]

Section 84-1303. Number . . . of Members of Board; Eligibility . . . The Georgia State Board of Pharmacy shall consist of five members and shall be commissioned by the Governor . . . No person shall be eligible for appointment to membership on said Board who is not a licentiate . . . of this State, and who has not actually been engaged for a period of five years or more in the retail drug business. If any member . . . shall cease

[21] *Fla. Admin. Code* c. 280-1 (1965).
[22] *Ga. Code Ann.* tit. 84, c. 84-13 and c. 84–99 (1955) and Supp. 1965.

to be actually engaged in the retail drug business, his membership on said Board shall at once become vacant; and no person who has any official connection with any school or college of pharmacy shall be eligible to appointment, and if any member of said Board shall, after his appointment . . . become connected with any school or college of pharmacy, his membership on said Board shall immediately become vacant. . . .

Section 84-1304. Georgia Pharmaceutical Association to Elect Members of Board. The Georgia Pharmaceutical Association shall from its membership annually elect one member to fill the next vacancy occurring on the Board . . . When regularly submitted to him by the secretary of said Association, the Governor shall make the appointment to fill such vacancy . . .

Section 84-1309. Rules and Regulations to Carry Out This Chapter and Chapter 42-1. The Georgia Board of Pharmacy shall have the power and authority to adopt, enact, establish and maintain all such rules and regulations, not inconsistent with the laws and Constitution of this State and of the United States, as shall, in its judgment, be necessary for the carrying out of the purposes of this Chapter and Chapter 42-1 . . .

Section 84-1317. Who May Compound or Sell Drugs, etc. . . . This section [prohibiting the sale of drugs by other than licensed people] . . . shall not be construed to prohibit the sale by merchants of home remedies, . . . or the sale by merchants or preparations commonly known as patent or proprietary preparations when sold only in the original and unbroken packages . . . Provided, however, that no drugs shall be sold or dispensed by vending machines.

Section 84-1324. Exceptions of Persons and Poisons from Law Respecting Compounding and Sale of Poisons. This Chapter shall not be construed to prohibit the sale by merchants of home remedies, not poison, or the sale by merchants of preparations commonly known as patent or proprietary preparations when sold only in the original and unbroken packages . . .

Section 84-9961. Penalty for Sale or Dispensing Drugs by Use of Vending Machines. Any person, firm or corporation, or combination thereof, who shall sell or dispense drugs by the use of vending machine shall be guilty of a misdemeanor . . .

SELECTED RULES AND REGULATIONS OF THE GEORGIA STATE BOARD OF PHARMACY CONCERNING THE CHIEF INSPECTORS OFFICE[23]

No. II. . . . No business establishments, other than [pharmacies] . . . shall engage in the practice of accepting and receiving prescriptions and forwarding same to a Drug Store or Pharmacy to be filled and returned

[23] Georgia State Board of Pharmacy, *Rules of the Board* (Atlanta, n.d.).

to the forwarding agency, which, in turn, delivers the filled prescriptions to the patient or agent of the patient and collects the charge therefor. No attempt shall be made to eliminate the patient-pharmacist contact and prevent proper supervisory control over the dispensing of medicines essential to the proper practice of pharmacy. . . .

No. V. It is prohibited for any drug store, pharmacy, apothecary or other business establishment . . . to advertise for retail sale at a specific price any drugs or medication which can be dispensed or sold only by or on prescription . . . This Regulation is not intended to and should in no wise state or establish or restrict in any way the prices charged for such drugs . . . the advertising for retail sale at a specific price . . . will tend to induce certain individuals to delay in purchasing needed medication; such practice will tend to cause and lend its support to the substitution of drugs and medications; such practice will tend to induce the request for sale of such drugs and medications without proper authorization; such practice will tend to mislead the general public by inducing individuals to patronize such advertising establishments when the average citizen is unable and unqualified to read and interpret prescription orders or to determine the name of the needed medication. . . .

HAWAII

EXCERPTS FROM LAWS RELATING TO PHARMACY[24]

Section 71-1. Definitions. For the purposes of this chapter:

. . .

(c) *Patent Medicine.* "Patent medicine" means any packaged, bottled, or non-bulk chemical, drug or medicine, when identified by and sold under a trademark, trade name or other trade symbol privately owned or registered in the United States patent office, or registered as provided by the laws of the Territory, and which is labeled with directions for use, and bears the name and address of the manufacturer or distributor; provided such chemical, drug, or medicine meets the requirements of the pure food and drug laws of the United States . . .

Section 71-2. Board of Pharmacy; Appointment; Qualifications; Term. There shall be a board of pharmacy of five members who shall be nominated . . . and appointed by the governor . . .

The members of the board . . . shall have been licensed as pharmacists and actively engaged in the practice of pharmacy in this State for at least five years prior to their appointment. Three members of the board shall be residents of the city and county of Honolulu and two shall be residents of counties other than the city and county of Honolulu. . . .

---

[24] *Hawaii Rev. Laws of 1955* tit. 7, 71 (1963) and Supp. 1965.

Section 71-4. Meetings; Powers and Duties of Board.

. . .

(e) *Power to Regulate.* The board may make such rules and regulations, not inconsistent with law, as may be necessary to carry out the purpose of this chapter, which purpose is hereby declared to be the protection of the public health and safety. Such rules and regulations . . . when approved by the governor, shall have the force and effect of law.

. . .

SELECTED RULES AND REGULATIONS OF THE HAWAII STATE BOARD OF PHARMACY[25]

No. 1.5. Price Advertising. It shall be unlawful to advertise, cause to be advertised, conduct or otherwise participate in the advertising of the price of prescription drugs to the public.

IDAHO

EXCERPTS FROM LAWS RELATING TO PHARMACY[26]

Section 37-2205. Pharmacies—Determining Drug to be Poisonous or Habit-Forming-Hearing-Appeal. . . . Any drug or medical supply, packaged or bottled, when identified by and sold under a trade mark, trade name or other trade symbol privately owned or registered in the United States Patent Office, and meeting the requirements of the Federal Food, Drug and Cosmetic Act, and the administrator thereof, shall be deemed not poisonous, dangerous, habit-forming or harmful under the provisions of this act, unless so determined and designated by the board and the Idaho administrator of health. Whenever such determination and designation is made by the board and the Idaho administrator of health, all such poisonous, dangerous, habit-forming or harmful drugs shall be unavailable to the public and dispensed only by a licensed pharmacist. . . .

Section 54-1701. State Board of Pharmacy—Appointment—Term. There is hereby created a state board of pharmacy, consisting of four members, one of whom shall be the director of public health, . . . ex officio, and three of whom shall be appointed by the governor . . .

Section 54-1702. Qualifications of Appointive Members. Only a registered pharmacist who has been licensed in this state for at least five years and is at the time actively engaged in retail pharmacy therein shall be eligible for appointment . . .

In making appointments the governor shall give consideration to the recommendations of the board of directors of the Idaho State Pharmaceutical Association, Inc., who shall be privileged at any time of vacancy to

[25] Hawaii State Board of Pharmacy, "Rules and Regulations." (Mimeographed.)
[26] *Idaho Code Ann.* tit. 37, c. 22; tit. 54, c. 17 (1961).

submit to him a list of eligibles containing the names of at least three times the number to be appointed.

Section 54-1707. Powers and Duties of Board. The board of pharmacy shall have the . . . powers . . .

. . .

(3) With the consent of the director of public health, to make such regulations as are necessary and feasible to carry out its powers and duties under this act . . .

SELECTED RULES AND REGULATIONS OF THE IDAHO STATE BOARD OF PHARMACY[27]

No. 1-665-66. The dispensing of drugs or medical supplies by any mechanical device or vending machine shall be prohibited in the state of Idaho.

ILLINOIS

EXCERPTS FROM LAWS RELATING TO PHARMACY[28]

Section 55.4. Application of Act. Nothing contained in any section of this Act shall apply to, or in any manner interfere with;

. . .

(d) the sale of patent or proprietary medicines and household remedies when sold in original and unbroken packages only, if such patent or proprietary medicines and household remedies be properly and adequately labeled as to content and usage and generally considered and accepted as harmless and non-poisonous when used according to the directions on the label . . .

Section 55.7. Powers and Duties of Department. The Department [of Registration and Education] shall . . .

(9) *Rules and Regulations.* Formulate such rules and regulations, not inconsistent with law, as may be necessary to carry out the purposes and enforce the provisions of this Act.

(10) *Action and Report of Board of Pharmacy—Necessity for Exercise of Powers.* None of the [foregoing] . . . powers . . . shall be exercised by the Department [of Registration and Education], except upon action and report in writing of the Board of Pharmacy to take such action and to make such report for the profession of pharmacy involved herein.

Section 55.51. Creation of Board—Qualifications of Members. There is created in the Department of Registration and Education the State Board of Pharmacy. It shall consist of 7 members one of whom shall be a full time teacher of professional rank in the University of Illinois College of Pharmacy. Each member shall be a registered pharmacist in good stand-

[27] Idaho State Board of Pharmacy, "Rules and Regulations." (Mimegraphed.)
[28] *Ill. Ann. Stat.* c. 91 (1966).

ing in this State, and each member, except the full time teacher of professional rank in the University of Illinois College of Pharmacy, shall have at least 5 years' practical experience in the practice of pharmacy subsequent to the date of his registration as a registered pharmacist in the State of Illinois.

Section 55.53. Recommendations for Appointments—Notice of Vacancies. In making the appointment of members on the Board, the Director shall give due consideration to recommendations by the members of the profession of pharmacy and by pharmaceutical organizations therein. The Director shall notify the pharmaceutical organizations promptly of any vacancy of members on the Board.

SELECTED RULES AND REGULATIONS OF THE ILLINOIS STATE BOARD OF PHARMACY[29]

Rule V. Interpretation of the Term "Gross Immorality" Under Section 7(f)[30] of the Pharmacy Act of the State of Illinois.

. . .

(2j) Wilfully filling or offering to fill any prescription for a drug, medicine or therapeutic device, or wilfully dispensing or delivering the same on a prescription, if such prescription is received, directly or indirectly, through the United States Mail, and the drug, medicine, or therapeutic device prescribed therein is dispensed or delivered, directly or indirectly, through the United States Mail.

(2k) Wilfull professional association or connection with any person or place wilfully filling or offering to fill any prescription for a drug, medicine or therapeutic device, or the wilfully dispensing or delivering the same on a prescription, if such prescription is received, directly or indirectly, through the United States Mail and the drugs, medicine or therapeutic device prescribed therein is dispensed or delivered, directly or indirectly, through the United States Mail.

(2l) Wilfull advertising, soliciting or otherwise promoting the sale of a "dangerous drug" . . . to the patient or ultimate consumer, by the name (generic name, trade name or otherwise) of such "dangerous drug."

Rule VIII. Definition of the Term "Practice of Pharmacy" Under Section 3,[31] of the Illinois Pharmacy Practice Act. The term "Practice of Pharmacy" includes, but is not limited to: (1) the soliciting of filling prescriptions;

---

[29] Illinois State Board of Pharmacy, *Rules and Regulations for the Administration of the Illinois Pharmacy Practice Act* (Springfield: Department of Registration and Education, 1963), pp. 5–11.

[30] This section allows the suspension or revocation of a license if a person is found to be guilty of gross immorality.

[31] This section prohibits anyone, except pharmacists, from engaging in the practice of pharmacy.

(2) the filling of prescriptions; (3) the dispensing of any drug or medicine on a prescription; (4) the removal of any drug or medicine from one container into another container which other container is to be delivered to or for the ultimate patient, on a prescription, or to or for the ultimate consumer, without a prescription; and (5) the placing of directions for use or other required labeling information on a container of any drug or medicine which is to be delivered to or for the ultimate patient, on a prescription, to or for the ultimate consumer, without a prescription.

Rule IX. Unlawful Acts Under Section 5 of the Illinois Pharmacy Act.
. . .

6. It shall be unlawful for any person not authorized to engage in the practice of pharmacy in this State to supply to any patient in this State a drug, medicine, or therapeutic device on a prescription which was issued in this State and filled or refilled outside of this State.

INDIANA

EXCERPTS FROM LAWS RELATING TO PHARMACY[32]

Section 63-1101. Board of Pharmacy . . . The governor of Indiana shall appoint five (5) pharmacists . . . who shall constitute . . . the Indiana Board of Pharmacy . . . all of said appointments shall be made by the governor from pharmacists of recognized experience and ability, who are actually engaged in the retail drug business. No person in any manner connected with any school of pharmacy shall be eligible to serve on said board. . . .

Section 63-1114. Sales Prohibited—Exceptions. . . . nothing in this act shall apply to, nor in any manner interfere with, the business of a general merchant in selling any of the following articles, to wit: Medicines of secret composition, and which are advertised to the general public, and popularly known as patent or proprietary medicines, providing said medicines are not poisonous. . . .

Section 63-1214. Minimum Qualifications for Permit. To be eligible for . . . a permit to operate a drug store or pharmacy, a person shall establish, to the satisfaction of the board, the following minimum qualifications:

1. That such drug store or pharmacy is or will be engaged in the bona fide practice of pharmacy.
   . . .

3. A registered pharmacist shall be in personal attendance and on duty in the drug department of the drug store at all times when [the] drug department is open to the public and be responsible for the

[32] *Ind. Stat. Ann.* tit. 63, c. 11 and c. 12; tit. 35, c. 35 (1961) and Supp. 1965.

lawful conduct of such pharmacy. Provided, however, that no drug store may be operated without a registered pharmacist more than fourteen (14) hours of any one (1) calendar week . . .

. . .

6. That such drug store shall have and maintain at least ten percent (10%) of its total inventory of merchandise in prescription drugs. Prescription drugs means any drugs bearing the legend "Federal law prohibits dispensing without prescription," and drugs which can be sold only upon the prescription of a licensed physician, dentist or veterinarian.

Section 63-1223. Enforcement of Act—Rules and Regulations. The Indiana pharmacy board shall . . . possess all powers necessary to fulfill the duties prescribed in this act or other acts relating to said board. It may adopt rules and regulations for the efficient enforcement and carrying out of any of the provisions of this act or other such act as may confer power and duties upon the board.

Section 35-3339. Mechanical Device for Dispensing Dangerous Drugs Prohibited—Exceptions—Mechanical Device Defined—Inspection for Violation. On and after the effective date of this act it shall be illegal for any person to maintain, operate, or use any type of mechanical device in which any dangerous drug or narcotic drug is stored or held for the purpose of dispensing for such mechanical device said dangerous drug or narcotic drug: Provided, however, That such mechanical device may be used for the storage and dispensing of dangerous drugs when such mechanical device is located on the premises of any business or establishment holding a valid pharmacy permit issued by the Indiana Board of Pharmacy and where such mechanical device will be operated under the direct supervision and control of a registered pharmacist. . . .

SELECTED RULES AND REGULATIONS OF THE INDIANA BOARD OF PHARMACY[33]

Regulation 6. Section 2. All drugstores, pharmacies or apothecary shops shall be located in a room separate and apart from any area containing merchandise not offered for sale under the pharmacy permit and the drugstore, pharmacy or apothecary shop shall be considered to be in a suitable room where such room is stationary and has the following minimum safety, health and security features . . .

a. A complete enclosure extending from ground level to the ceiling on all sides and encompassing all the products which are to be sold or intended for sale or dispensed in connection with the pharmacy permit.

b. All entries and exits must be through a door or doors capable of being securely locked so as to prevent entry at times when the drugstore is closed.

[33] Indiana State Board of Pharmacy, "Rules and Regulations." (Mimeographed.)

Regulation 14. Section 1. Any person applying to the Board for a permit to open or establish a drugstore or pharmacy shall submit at the time of the qualifying inspection prior to the opening of the establishment, a physical inventory of the amount of merchandise in said establishment, and setting forth an inventory of "legend drugs," . . . which prescription drugs shall constitute a minimum of 10% of the total inventory of all merchandise.

Regulation 17. Section 2. Definition of "Practice of Pharmacy": The term "practice of pharmacy" or "practice of the profession of pharmacy" means and includes the compounding, filling, dispensing, exchanging, giving, offering for sale, or selling, drugs, medicines or poisons, pursuant to prescriptions or orders of physicians . . . or any other act, service, operation or transaction incidental to, or forming a part of, any of the foregoing acts, requiring, involving or employing the science or art of any branch of the pharmaceutical profession, study or training.

Regulation 17. Section 3. Definition of "Bona Fide Practice of Pharmacy": A drugstore or pharmacy is engaged in the bona fide practice of pharmacy . . . when such drug store or pharmacy has as its principal business purpose the sale and dispensing of drugs, medicines and health supplies intended for the general health, welfare and safety of the public without placing or advertising any department or departments on a more important level than the practice of pharmacy. . . .

Regulation 20. Section 1. The term "gross immorality" . . . shall also mean and include . . . the following . . .
 . . .

(b) The registered pharmacist or a pharmacy shall not advertise or promote in any way or through any media either by trademark or generic name articles or medical preparations for sale . . . which contain harmful, dangerous or so-called legend drugs or preparations and thereby create the unsafe and possibly harmful and dangerous effect upon the public and by such advertising and promotion encourage the sale or unnecessary or unneeded use of such articles . . . by the public. . . .

IOWA

EXCERPTS FROM LAWS RELATING TO PHARMACY[34]

Section 147.12. Examining Boards. . . . the governor shall appoint a board of examiners for each . . . profession. . . .

Section 147.16. Practice Requirement for Examiners. Each examiner shall be actively engaged in the practice of his profession and shall have been so engaged in this state for a period of five years just preceding his appointment . . .

[34] *Iowa Code Ann.* tit. 7, c. 147 and c. 155 (1949) and Supp. 1965.

Section 147.18. Disqualifications. No examiner shall be an officer or member of the instructional staff of any school in which any profession regulated by this title is taught, or be connected therewith in any manner . . .

Section 147.20. Nomination of Examiners. The regular state association or society or its managing board for each profession may submit each year to the governor a list of six persons . . . The governor in making an appointment to the board of examiners for such profession shall select one of the persons so named. . . .

Section 147.100. Renewal Fee. The secretary of the pharmacy examiners shall annually add two dollars and fifty cents to the renewal fee provided in this chapter for a person licensed to practice pharmacy. Such additional amount shall be considered as a part of the regular renewal fee and payment of the same shall be a prerequisite to the renewal of his license. The funds derived from the additional renewal fee collected under this section shall be paid to the state pharmacy association upon the order of its treasurer and secretary. Said funds shall be used by such association in the advancement of the art and science of pharmacy.

Section 155.2. Persons Not Engaged In. Neither section 155.1 nor section 155.6 shall be construed to include the following classes:

. . .

3. Persons who sell, offer or expose for sale proprietary medicines or domestic remedies which are not in themselves poisonous or in violation of the law relative to intoxicating liquors.

Section 155.3. Definitions. . . .

. . .

7. For the purpose of this chapter the term "proprietary medicines" or "domestic remedies" means and includes completely compounded packaged drugs, medicines and nonbulk chemicals which are not in themselves poisonous or in violation of the law relative to intoxicating liquors which are sold, offered, promoted and advertised by the manufacturer or primary distributor directly to the general public under a trademark, trade name, or other trade symbol privately owned, whether or not registered in the United States Patent Office, and the labeling of which bears (a) a statement specifying affections, symptoms or purposes for which the product is recommended, (b) adequate directions for use and such cautions as may be necessary for the protections of users, and (c) an accurate statement of the quantity of the contents in terms of weight, measure or numerical count, (d) a statement of the active ingredients, and (e) the name and address of the manufacturer or primary distributor: Provided, however, this definition shall not apply to the sale, or offering for sale, of any drug for use by man which is only advertised or promoted professionally to licensed physicians, dentists or veterinarians by the manufacturer or primary distributor, or the label of which

bears the statement "Caution: Federal law prohibits dispensing without prescription," or which sale is by law limited to dispensing by prescription.

. . .

Section 155.19 Rules and Regulations. The board shall adopt, amend, promulgate and enforce such reasonable rules, regulations and standards as may be designed to accomplish the purposes of this chapter, and as may be necessary for the provisions set forth herein.

SELECTED RULES AND REGULATIONS OF THE IOWA STATE BOARD OF PHARMACY EXAMINERS[35]

No. 8. Minimum Standards for the Practice of Pharmacy.
   1. Standards.
      1.1. . . . the phrase "fill the prescriptions" shall be deemed to include the following:
         1.1(1). Read and interpret the prescription . . .
         1.1(2). Accurately measure, or compound, ingredients specified by the practitioner.
         1.1(3). Read and interpret, and write, adequate label directions . . .
         1.1(4). Affix label in, or to the container containing the medication as prescribed for the patient.
      2.1. The above rules shall be equally applicable to any mechanical device used or intended to be used for prescription drugs which are sold, exposed or offered for sale or dispensed. . . .

Rules and Regulations Filed and Indexed January 31, 1962. . . .
   1. No pharmacist or retail pharmacy . . . shall advertise directly or indirectly, by any media affecting the public, any drug, medicine or device bearing the legend, "Caution: Federal law prohibits dispensing without prescription," or whose sale is restricted to a prescription by Iowa law. . . .

   . . .

   3. This rule is not intended to and should not in any way establish or restrict the price charged for such drugs, medicines or devices by retail sale.

RULES AND REGULATIONS OF OTHER DEPARTMENTS AFFECTING PHARMACY: HEALTH—HOSPITALS[36]

Regulation 25.
   A. Pharmacy Service:
      1. The pharmacy operating in connection with a hospital shall . . . comply with the provisions of the *pharmacy law* requiring regis-

---

[35] Iowa Board of Pharmacy, *Rules and Regulations of Board of Pharmacy With Laws, Rules and Regulation of Other Departments Affecting Pharmacy; Opinions of the Attorney General; Board of Pharmacy Report* (Des Moines, 1964), p. 68.
   [36] *Id.* at 69–70.

tration of drugstores and pharmacies, and the regulations of the Iowa state board of pharmacy examiners.

2. In all hospitals with a pharmacy or drug room, this service shall be under the complete supervision of a pharmacist licensed to practice in the state of Iowa.

Section 9. Drug Storage and Handling.

. . .

9.10. A qualified nurse or responsible person shall dispense and administer all medications. The nurse shall be held responsible for all medications.

. . .

9.13. A pharmacy operating in connection with a nursing home shall comply with the provisions of the Pharmacy Law requiring *registration of drug stores and pharmacies* and the regulations of the Iowa State Board of Pharmacy Examiners.

In all nursing homes with a pharmacy or drug supply, this service shall be under the *complete* supervision of a pharmacist licensed to practice in the State of Iowa.

OPINION OF THE ATTORNEY GENERAL, JUNE 1, 1962[37]

Health: Pharmacy Examiners Board. The operators of a mail-order pharmacy business, located in a foreign state, without a license to practice pharmacy in the State of Iowa are in violation of [the Iowa Pharmacy Laws] . . .

KANSAS

EXCERPTS FROM LAWS RELATING TO PHARMACY[38]

Article 16. Section 65-1626. . . . *[State Pharmacy Act]; Definitions.* For the purpose of this act:

. . .

(b) The term "domestic remedies and medicines in unbroken packages" means and includes completely compounded packaged drugs, medicines, medical and dental supplies and nonbulk chemicals labeled with directions for use, identified by and sold under a trade mark, trade name, or other trade symbol, privately owned or registered in the United States patent office, which are sold or offered for sale to the general public.

. . .

Article 16. Section 65-1630. Rules and Regulations. The board may adopt and promulgate such reasonable rules and regulations, not inconsistent with law, as may be necessary to carry out the purposes and enforce the provisions of this act . . .

[37] *Id.* at 71.
[38] *Kan. Stat. Ann.* c. 65 and c. 74 (1964) and Supp. 1965.

Article 15, Section 74-1603. State Board of Pharmacy; Creation; Membership. There is hereby created a state board of pharmacy which shall consist of five members . . .

Article 15. Section 74-1604. . . . [State Board of Pharmacy]; Appointment; Terms; Vacancies; Qualifications. The governor shall appoint . . . [as] provided for in [the following] . . . section . . . the members of said board . . .

No person shall be eligible for appointment as a member of the board unless (1) he has been registered as a pharmacist in Kansas for at least five years and (2) he has been . . . actively employed in the practice of pharmacy in Kansas for at least five years immediately preceding the date of his appointment.

Article 15. Section 74-1605. . . . [Board of Pharmacy]; Nominations Submitted By State Pharmaceutical Association; Oaths. On or before April of each year, commencing in the year 1954, the state pharmaceutical association shall nominate from among its membership ten (10) candidates who shall meet the requirements herein provided for the vacancies which occur prior to April 1 of the next succeeding year on the said board of pharmacy, and from among the nominees when legally submitted and certified by the president and the secretary of the state pharmaceutical association, the governor shall make his appointment for the vacancy or vacancies. . . .

SELECTED RULES AND REGULATIONS OF THE KANSAS STATE BOARD OF PHARMACY[39]

No. 68-2-17. Advertising. (c) No pharmacy or pharmacist shall advertise directly or indirectly in such a way or manner as to cause or suggest that the patient purchase drugs in excess of the quantity prescribed or authorized. (Authorized by K.S.A. 65-1630, Eff. January 1, 1966.)

No. 68-2-20. Prescription, Putting Up, Filling and Refilling. The terms putting up of prescription and Prescription [sic] shall be filled or refilled, shall be deemed to include any and all of the following:
   (1) Read and interpret the prescription of a duly licensed prescriber, whether transmitted to the pharmacist by writing or orally.
   (2) Accurately count, measure, or compound, ingredients specified by the prescriber.
   (3) Read and interpret, and write, adequate label directions as are necessary to assure the patient's understanding of the prescriber's intentions.
   (4) Affix lable in, or to the container the medication as prescribed for the patient.
(Authorized by K.S.A. [sic] 65-1630, Eff. January 1, 1966.)

[39] Kansas State Board of Pharmacy, *Kansas Pharmacy Law, Rules and Regulations* (n.p., 1963), pp. 22–36. (Regulations 68-2-17 and 68-2-20 are a mimeographed insert to page 22.)

No. 68-6-11. Separate Entrance. Every place of business for which a pharmacy permit is issued, shall have a separate outer entrance and shall be so constructed that it may be completely closed when not open for business, in charge of a pharmacist. (Authorized by Ch. 290, Sec. 16, Laws of Kansas, 1953; compiled October 23, 1953.)

No. 68-6-16. Branches, Agents and Pick Up Stations. No pharmacy nor pharmacist, shall have, participate in, or permit an arrangement, branch, connection or affiliation whereby prescriptions are advertised, solicited, accepted, collected, or picked up, from or at any location other than a pharmacy for which a drug store permit in good standing has been issued by the Board. (Authorized by Ch. 290, Sec. 16, Laws of Kansas, 1953; Compiled March 26, 1958.)

No. 68-6-17. Advertising. (a) No pharmacy nor pharmacist, shall advertise in any manner, the names of any drug, medicine, or other item, which may not otherwise by dispensed except upon prescription issued by a duly licensed practitioner: *PROVIDED,* that nothing in this regulation shall prohibit the furnishing of professional information to qualified practitioners. (b) No pharmacy nor pharmacist shall advertise either directly or indirectly, or by inference, or implication, to purport professional superiority in any manner. (Authorized by Ch. 290, Sec. 16, Laws of Kansas, 1953; compiled March 26, 1958).

No. 68-9-14. Institutions; Mechanical Drug Distributing Device; Filling. Any mechanical device now or hereafter used in institutions, public or private, or wherever pre-packaged drugs are distributed for the use of patients in such institutions, shall have such drugs physically packaged and placed in the machine prior to distribution, only by a pharmacist duly certified to practice by the state of Kansas. (Authorized by Ch. 290, Sec. 16, Laws of Kansas, 1953; compiled October, 20, 1962.)

KENTUCKY

EXCERPTS FROM LAWS RELATING TO PHARMACY[40]

Section 315.040. Exceptions to Chapter.
    (1) Nothing in this chapter shall apply to the sales of usual nonpoisonous domestic remedies, harmless drugs or medicines or patent or proprietary medicine in the original package by any store.
   . . .

Section 315.130. Portion of Fees to be Turned Over to Association. The board shall each year turn over to the [Kentucky pharmaceutical] association, for the advancement of the art and science of pharmacy, out of the annual renewal fees collected by it, two dollars for each licensed pharma-

[40] *Ky. Rev. Stat. Ann.* tit. 26, c. 315 (1963) and Supp. 1965.

cist and assistant pharmacist who has paid his renewal fee during the year.

Section 315.150. Kentucky Board of Pharmacy: Members; Appointment; Term; Vacancy; Oath; Quorum.
   (1) The Kentucky Board of Pharmacy shall consist of five members.
   (2) . . . at its regular annual meeting the [Kentucky pharmaceutical] association shall select and submit to the Governor one list of five persons and one list of three persons, each of whom has had at least five years' experience in compounding and dispensing physicians' prescriptions in this State. The Governor shall . . . appoint one person from each list so submitted. . .
   . . .

LOUISIANA

EXCERPTS FROM LAWS RELATING TO PHARMACY[41]

Section 1172. Louisiana Board of Pharmacy; Appointment; Qualifications of Members. The Louisiana Board of Pharmacy . . . shall consist of nineteen members to be appointed by the governor as follows: two members shall be chosen from each congressional district . . . and three shall be chosen from the state at large.

Each member of the board shall be a licensed pharmacist who has been licensed in this state for at least five years and who is actively engaged in the practice of pharmacy and not connected with any school or college of pharmacy in a professional or executive capacity.

Section 1178. Powers and Duties of the Board.
   A. The board shall:
      (1) Make necessary rules and regulations to carry out the purposes and enforce the provisions of this Chapter . . .
      . . .

Section 1204. Exceptions. . . . . The provisions of this Chapter do not apply to storekeepers and other vendors dealing in and selling commonly used remedies and household drugs in original packages as purchased from a manufacturer or wholesaler, or to the manufacture or sale at wholesale or retail of packaged, bottle or non-bulk chemicals, drugs, medicines, medical and dental supplies, cosmetics and dietary foods when identified by and sold under a trademark, trade name, or other trade symbol, privately owned or registered in the United States Patent Office, sold or offered for sale to the general public, if such articles meet the requirements of the Federal Food, Drug and Cosmetic Act.

For the purpose of this Section, "commonly used remedies and household drugs" means only simple remedies which are not deleterious or habit

[41] *La. Rev. State* tit 37, c. 14 (1964).

forming and the usage and use of which are generally known and understood by people who are without medical knowledge.

SELECTED RULES AND REGULATIONS OF THE LOUISIANA STATE BOARD OF PHARMACY[42]

Section 5. . . .

(A) *Area of Prescription Department.* The area devoted to the prescription department and laboratory shall not be less than ten per cent of the main floor area of the pharmacy or drug store . . .

Section 10. No person, firm or corporation shall sell, dispense, distribute or otherwise dispose of, nor permit the sale, dispensing, distribution or other disposition of, any drugs or medicines by means of an electrically or mechanically operated device, (whether for compensation or not) including, without limitation, vending machines, coin operated machines of all kinds, prescription drug dispensing machines, and all other devices of a similar nature, the intention of this regulation being to protect the health, safety and welfare of the public by insuring that drugs and medicines, particularly those of a potent or dangerous nature, as well as those bearing the Federal caution label, shall be sold, dispensed, distributed or otherwise disposed of other than by mechanical, electrical or other automatic means. This regulation shall be applicable uniformly throughout the State of Louisiana, in pharmacies, hospitals. clinics, stores and otherwise.

Section 20. No permit to operate a pharmacy shall be granted or renewed unless evidence satisfactory to the Louisiana Board of Pharmacy shows that a registered pharmacist will be on duty at all times during normal hours, totaling a minimum or 40 hours per week. No part time pharmacies will be permitted to operate.

Section 22. Under no circumstances shall the name, trademark or slogan of any pharmacy include any reference, directly or indirectly, to prescription prices, by use of the words "DISCOUNT," "WHOLESALE," "CUT-RATE," "PRICED-RIGHT," or otherwise . . . No advertising copy or material of any kind (including, but not limited to radio, television, newspapers, hand bills, novelties, signs, etc., used by or in connection with any pharmacy) shall include any reference to prescription prices, directly or indirectly, by use of the words quoted above, or otherwise, such as by saying "LET US PRICE YOUR PRESCRIPTION," "WE WON'T BE UNDERSOLD," etc. The spirit of this regulation shall not be violated by means of advertising copy or materials which are placed separately but in close relationship so as to state or create the impression that discount or reduced prices on over-the-counter items indicate, directly or indirectly, similar low or reduced prices on prescription items.

[42] Louisiana Board of Pharmacy, *Louisiana Pharmacy Law, Barbiturate and Central Nervous Stimulant Law of Louisiana, Ethical Pharmacist Certificate Law of Louisiana, Rules and Regulations, Code of Ethics* (n.p., 1962), pp. 22–23.

CODE OF ETHICS[43]

Preamble. Pursuant to the authority granted by Louisiana Act 272 of 1956, . . . the following Code of Ethics is hereby adopted by the Louisiana Board of Pharmacy . . . in the interest of promoting the public health, safety and welfare.

Section 2. Definition of "Practice of Pharmacy": The term "practice of pharmacy" or "practice of the profession of pharmacy" means and includes the compounding, filling, dispensing, exchanging, giving, offering for sale, or selling, drugs, medicines or poisons, pursuant to prescriptions or orders of physicians . . . [and] other practitioners, or any other act, service, operation or transaction incidental to or forming a part of any of the foregoing acts, requiring, involving or employing the science or art of any branch of the pharmaceutical profession, study or training.

Section 5. Refusal, Revocation, or Suspension of Certificates: The Louisiana Board of Pharmacy . . . may refuse to issue, . . . renew, or may revoke or suspend, . . . any license, certificate, or permit . . . where the Louisiana Board of Pharmacy finds that the applicant or holder thereof has been convicted . . . of . . .

. . .

    (K) Advertising by means of signs, newspaper, radio, television, handbills, or in any other manner, the price of any drug, medicine, or prescription item, normally compounded, sold, or dispensed by a Registered Pharmacist . . . or using with reference to such drugs and medicines, the term "cut-rate" or any similar word or phrase tending to degrade the professional nature of pharmaceutical services. Advertising in any manner, whatsoever, of drugs, medicines or prescription items normally compounded, dispensed, or sold by a Registered Pharmacist . . . shall be limited to the experience, integrity, skill or other professional qualifications of the pharmacy or pharmacist. Any other reference to such drugs, medicines, or prescription items, or to the prescription department, shall be considered unethical.

    (L) Having, participating in, or permitting, an arrangement, branch, connection, or affiliation whereby prescriptions are advertised, solicited, accepted, or collected from, or at, a location other than a pharmacy for which a permit . . . has been issued . . . By way of extension, and not limitation, it shall be unethical to have, participate in, or permit, any such arrangement, branch, connection, or affiliation with, any grocery store, dry cleaning establishment, sundries store, department store, or similar establishment. However, this prohibition shall not prevent any bona fide transaction whereby a prescription is picked up at the residence or office of an individual, to be filled, compounded, or dispensed, for the use of said individual or a member of his family.

[43] *Id.* at 25–26.

MAINE

EXCERPTS FROM LAWS RELATING TO PHARMACY[44]

Subchapter I. Section 2801. Registration Required; Exceptions. . . . This
section shall not apply to . . . nonpoisonous patent or proprietary medicines when sold in original and unbroken packages . . .

*Subchapter II. Section 2851. Nomination and Appointment; Tenure; Va-
cancies; Compensation; Expenses.* A Board of Commissioners of the Profession of Pharmacy . . . shall consist of 5 pharmacists all of whom shall
be . . . actively engaged in the practice of their profession, [and] who
shall be appointed . . . by the Governor . . . The board shall have power:
  1. *Rules and Regulations.* To make such rules and regulations, not
     inconsistent with the laws of this State, as may be necessary for
     the regulation and practice of the profession of pharmacy and the
     lawful performance of its duties;
  . . .
  4. *Enforcement.* . . . The Maine Pharmaceutical Association may, at
     its annual meeting each year, nominate 6 members of said associa-
     tion, whose names shall be forthwith certified by the president and
     secretary of said association to the Governor, and members of said
     board, appointed during any year, shall be selected from the persons
     whose names are so certified for said year, unless in the opinion
     of the Governor said persons are manifestly unsuitable or
     incompetent.

*SELECTED RULES AND REGULATIONS OF THE
MAINE STATE BOARD OF PHARMACY*[45]

Unprofessional Conduct. Good and sufficient causes for the discontinuance
of or refusal to renew any registration of a pharmacist . . . and for the
refusal to grant or renew, or for the revocation of a license to conduct
a pharmacy . . . shall include but shall not be limited to the following
acts herein defined as unprofessional conduct in the practice of pharmacy.
  . . .
  6. To enter into an agreement or an arrangement which in any way
     tends to limit the free choice of the public in the selection of a
     pharmacist or a pharmacy to provide pharmaceutical services.
  . . .
  16. To solicit, collect, accept, or dispense prescriptions for drugs, medi-
      cines and poisons at any location or establishment other than the
      licensed pharmacy at which the prescriptions are to be filled or

[44] *Maine Rev. Stat. Ann.* tit. 32, c. 41 (1965).
[45] Maine Board of the Commissioners of the Profession of Pharmacy, *Laws
Relating to Apothecaries, Title 32, 22 and the Rules and Regulations* (n.p., 1964),
pp. 32–36.

compounded. Provided, however, that this section shall not be construed as to prohibit the collection of the prescription or the delivery of the prescribed drugs, medicines or poisons at the residence, office, or place of employment of the person for whom the prescription is issued.

Rule. No. 21. It shall be unlawful for any pharmacy, pharmacist or other licensee of the Maine State Board of Pharmacy who furnishes drugs directly to the consumer to advertise directly or indirectly by any public media whatsoever any drug, medicine or appliance bearing the legend: "Caution: Federal law prohibits dispensing without prescription"; or any drug media or appliance whose sale is restricted to prescription dispensation by any state or federal law. . . .

Rule. No. 24. . . . In order to be eligible for a permit to operate under the Pharmacy Law, . . . [an] apothecary store shall be properly identified . . . by name and signs common to an apothecary store. The entrances and exits to such a store shall not include any openings from any other adjacent business establishments; nor shall any apothecary store be conducted as an adjunct of, or subsidiary to, any other form of business establishment.

CODE OF ETHICS[46]

Preamble. . . . this Code of Ethics has been adopted by the membership of the Maine Pharmaceutical Association and endorsed by the Maine Commission of Pharmacy.

Chapter 3. The Duties of Pharmacist[s] Toward Each Other and Pharmacy.

. . .

9. The pharmacist shall not use advertising matter or make statements on circulars, letters in the windows or in the store, of a character tending to deceive or mislead the public. Specifically, he shall not use the phrase "cut-rate" or other signs which tend to degrade or ridicule the profession of pharmacy before the public.

. . .

11. The pharmacist shall not advertise definite fixed prices, in the sale of drugs and medicines where professional services and materials are variable.

MARYLAND

EXCERPTS FROM LAWS RELATING TO PHARMACY[47]

Section 257. Board of Pharmacy—Composition, Qualifications, Terms of Office and Vacancies. The Governor shall appoint five persons to be Commissioners of Pharmacy, said Commissioners . . . shall . . . have had

[46] *Id.* at 37–41.
[47] *Md. Ann. Code* art. 27 (1957) and art. 43 (1965).

at least five years' active pharmaceutical experience in compounding . . . prescriptions, and of whom at least four are actively engaged in the practice of pharmacy. None of said Commissioners shall be connected with any school of pharmacy either as teacher, instructor, or member of the board of trustees. . . . In the case of any vacancy or vacancies, . . . the Governor shall appoint a successor from a list of pharmacists of three times the number of vacancies to be filled, said list to be submitted by the Maryland Pharmaceutical Association. . . .

Section 266A. . . . [State Board of Pharmacy]—Suspension and Revocation of Pharmacists' Licenses.

    (a) *Power of Board; Notice; Hearing.* The Board of Pharmacy is hereby granted power and authority either to reprimand a pharmacist or assistant pharmacist or to suspend or revoke his license for any reason as hereinafter set forth . . .

    . . .

    (c) *Grounds.* The Board's power either to reprimand a pharmacist or assistant pharmacist or to suspend or revoke his license shall be for any of the following causes:

        . . .

        (4) Upon proof satisfactory to the Board of Pharmacy that a pharmacist or assistant pharmacist is guilty of grossly unprofessional conduct. The following acts on the part of a pharmacist or assistant pharmacist are hereby declared to constitute grossly unprofessional conduct:

            . . .

            (iii) The association by a pharmacist either as a partner co-owner, or employee of a pharmacy, wholly or substantially owned by physician, dentist, veterinarian, or other medical practitioner or group thereof; but this paragraph shall not be construed or applied to have any retroactive effect or to apply to any such association existing on June 1, 1963, for such period as that association remains in continuous existence.

            (iv) The advertising to the public by any means, in any form or through any media, the prices for prescriptions, dangerous or nonproprietary drugs, or fees for services relating thereto or any reference to the price of said drugs or prescriptions whether specifically or as a percentile of prevailing prices, or by the use of the terms "cut-rate," "discount," "bargain" or terms of similar connotation.

    . . .

Section 268. . . . [Board of Pharmacy]—Permit to Establish Pharmacy.

    . . .

  (b) *Issuance on Proof of Certain Facts; Refusal; Display; Term.* On evidence satisfactory to the said Maryland Board of Pharmacy;

    . . .

(c) that said pharmacy will be constantly under the personal and immediate supervision of a registered pharmacist, a permit shall be issued to such persons . . . as the said Maryland Board of Pharmacy shall deem qualified to conduct such pharmacy;

(d) that the said pharmacy shall not engage in a restricted, limited, partial or closed-door service or operation to the public or to any group of persons but must be available to the entire public, provided however, this provision shall not apply to a hospital pharmacy;

. . .

(f) the said pharmacy shall not offer professional services under terms and conditions which tend to interfere with or impair the free and complete exercise of professional judgment skill or enter into any agreement which denies the patient the right of free choice of pharmacists; and

(g) that said pharmacy shall not violate any of the provisions of Section 266A (c) (4) of this article. . . .

. . .

Section 271. Application to Sales by General Merchants. Nothing in this subtitle shall be so construed as to prevent, or in any way make unlawful, or interfere with, the sale or display by general merchants, of any proprietary or patent medicines; or the sale by such general merchants of commonly used household or domestic remedies, in original, unopened packages, or farm remedies or ingredients for spraying solutions, in bulk or otherwise, provided the said household or domestic remedies are clearly labeled with the ordinary name of the article or articles contained therein and the name of the manufacturer or distributor thereof, or the sale by such general merchants of doses of household or domestic remedies to be consumed upon the premises.

Section 272. Sale of Drugs, Medicines, etc., by Vending Machine. It shall be unlawful for any person, copartnership, association or corporation to sell, distribute, vend or otherwise dispose of any drug, medicine or pharmaceutical or medical preparation by means of a vending machine, automatically operated coin machine, or other similar device; provided, however, that, whenever the State Board of Health determines that a specified commodity is not deleterious or injurious to public health and safety and the dispensing of such specified commodity from such a machine or device is approved by such Board and a permit issued by it for the dispensing of such specified commodity from such a machine or device, the provisions of this section shall not be applicable as to such permitted and approved specified commodity. Any person, copartnership, association or corporation that shall violate this section shall, upon conviction, be deemed guilty of a misdemeanor and fined not more than one hundred dollars ($100.00) for each offense, and each and every day such violation continues shall constitute a separate and distinct offense.

Section 307. Definition of Dangerous Drugs. The term "dangerous drugs" . . . shall mean . . . any drug intended for use by man which . . . is not safe for use except under the supervision of a practitioner licensed by law to administer such drugs.

Section 311. Applicability of Subtitle; Advertising Drugs.

. . .

   (b) *Advertising.* No pharmacist or pharmacy shall be permitted to advertise through any media other than a professional or trade publication any dangerous drug by either its "trade name" or by its generic or formulary name.

. . .

Section 313. Penalty. Any person, firm or corporation who violates any of the provisions of this sub-title [Sections 307–313], or refuses, neglects or fails to comply with the provisions and requirements hereof, shall be deemed guilty of a misdemeanor and upon conviction thereof shall, for the first offense, be fined not more than $250.00, for the second or subsequent offense not more than $500.00.

MASSACHUSETTS

EXCERPTS FROM LAWS RELATING TO PHARMACY[48]

Section 22. Board of Registration in Pharmacy, Appointment, etc. There shall be a board of registration in pharmacy . . . who . . . shall have had ten consecutive years of practical experience in the compounding and dispensing of physicians' prescriptions, and shall actually be engaged in the drug business. . . . One member shall annually in January be appointed by the governor . . .

Section 35. Application of Certain Laws Restricted. Sections thirty and thirty-six A to forty-one, inclusive, of this chapter, sections twenty-nine to thirty G, inclusive, of chapter one hundred thirty-eight and section two of chapter two hundred and seventy shall [not prohibit the sale] . . . of patent and proprietary medicines . . .

Section 39. . . . Board to Be Satisfied as to Management, etc. The board may . . . register a store for the transaction of the retail drug business . . . but no such registration shall be made . . . in the case of a corporation unless it shall appear to the satisfaction of the board that the management of the drug business in such store is in the hands of a registered pharmacist.

Section 42A. Rules and Regulations; Revocation or Suspension of License, etc.; Hearings; Rules, etc., to Form Part of Application for License, etc. The board may make such rules and regulations as it deems necessary

[48] *Mass. Ann. Laws* tit. 2, c. 13 (1966) and tit. 16, c. 112 (1965) and Supp. 1965.

to enable it to properly enforce the provisions of law relating to the retail drug business and pharmacy, and regarding any other matter within its jurisdiction . . .

SELECTED RULES AND REGULATIONS OF THE MASSACHUSETTS STATE BOARD OF PHARMACY[49]

Rule 17.

(a) Drug stores must have a registered pharmacist on the premises during the entire time the store is open. The presence of a registered-assistant pharmacist will fulfill this requirement during the temporary absence of a registered pharmacist, which absence shall not be more than six hours in any one period of twenty-four consecutive hours.

. . .

CODE OF PROFESSIONAL CONDUCT[50]

No. 2. A registered pharmacist must be on duty at all times when the pharmacy is open for business.

No. 16. The registered pharmacist or pharmacy shall not advertise or promote in any way, or through any media, either by trade-name or by generic name, articles or medical preparations for sale or for the compounding, filling or refilling of prescriptions which contain harmful, dangerous or so-called legend drugs or preparations and thereby create the unsafe and possible harmful and dangerous effect upon the public and by such advertising and promotion encourage the sale or unnecessary or unneeded use of such articles or medical preparations by the public. Such advertising or promotion is considered a fraud upon and deceit of the public and is therefore, unethical and an act of malpractice, because a practitioner's prescription is required before such drugs may be acquired by the public.

No. 20. The registered pharmacist or pharmacy shall not advertise by any means, in any from or through or by any media, harmful or dangerous drugs, medicines, or prescription items, normally compounded, sold or dispensed by a registered pharmacist in his professional capacity, by use of the terms "cut-rate" or "discount" or any similar phrase or word which would tend to degrade the professional nature of pharmaceutical services . . .

No. 21. The registered pharmacist or pharmacy shall not participate in any plan, arrangement, or agreement which eliminates or affects detrimentally the patient-pharmacist-prescriber relationship, such as mail order prescription business, since such a plan, arrangement or agreement is detrimental to the public health, public welfare and safety of the public and is therefore unethical.

[49] Massachusetts Board of Registration in Pharmacy, *Pharmacy Laws and Rules and Regulations* (Boston, 1965), p. 31.

[50] Massachusetts Board of Registration in Pharmacy, "Code of Professional Conduct," September 29, 1961. (Mimeographed.)

No. 23. No pharmacy or pharmacist, shall have, participate in, or permit an arrangement, branch, connection or affiliation whereby prescriptions are advertised, solicited, accepted, collected, or picked up from or at any location other than a pharmacy for which a drug store permit in good standing has been issued by the board.

No. 24. A pharmacy being established, remodelled [sic] or moving to a new location shall not . . . maintain a prescription department in the pharmacy which is less than 20% of the total floor area of the pharmacy or retail drug store . . .

No. 29. No new application for a pharmacy will be approved by the Board and a pharmacy now licensed by the Board will be denied a renewal thereof, if an assurance is not received by and given to the Board . . . that the pharmacy does not and will not engage in the practice of customarily refusing to compound or dispense prescriptions which may reasonably be expected to be compounded or dispensed for the general public in a pharmacy by pharmacists. Such an assurance shall be considered essential to prevent the restricted practice or closed-door operation of the pharmacy and such practice shall be deemed as a practice or operation against the best interest of the public health and public well-being.

MICHIGAN

EXCERPTS FROM LAWS RELATING TO PHARMACY[51]

Section 14.757 (2). Board of Pharmacy; Membership, Appointment; Term, Vacancies; Removal; Compensation; Eligibility. Section 2. (1). The board shall consist of 5 members appointed by the governor with the advice and consent of the senate . . . The members . . . shall be registered pharmacists, licensed in this state at least 10 years, actively engaged in the practice of pharmacy . . .

Section 14.757 (6). Powers of Board. Section 6. The board shall:

. . .

- (g) Make such bylaws, decisions, rules and regulations, not inconsistent with law . . . a may be necessary to carry out the purposes and enforce the provisions of this act.
- (h) Adopt rule of professional conduct, not including rules relating to price determination. The rules shall be appropriate to the establishment and maintenance of a high standard of integrity and dignity in the profession.

Section 14.757 (14). Supervision of Pharmacies, Revocation or Suspension of License. Section 14. Every pharmacy when open for business shall be under the personal supervision of a duly licensed and registered pharmacist.

[51] *Mich. Stat. Ann.* tit. 14, c. 126 (1956) and Supp. 1965.

A registered pharmacist may not simultaneously have personal supervision of more than 1 pharmacy. The board may revoke or suspend any license or certificate issued under this act for violation of the provisions of this section.

Section 14.757 (15). Revocation or Suspension of License or Certificate; Grounds. Section 15. The board shall have the power to withhold, revoke or suspend any license or any certificate of registration issued under this act after giving reasonable notice and an opportunity to be heard to any person who shall have:

. . .

(4) Failed to comply with the rules of professional conduct.

(5) Promoted to the public in any manner a drug which may only be dispensed pursuant to a prescription.

(6) Employed the mail to sell, distribute, or deliver a drug which requires a prescription when the prescription for such an article has been received by mail.

Section 14.757 (29). Drugs and Poisons Exempt. Section 29. . . . . this act shall not apply:

. . .

(c) To the manufacture and sale of proprietary medicines except those proprietary medicines which are poisonous, deleterious or habit forming.

. . .

Section 14.771. Ownership of Pharmacies and Drug Stores; Exception as to Store Selling only Patent Medicines. Section 1. Every pharmacy, drug store or apothecary shop shall be owned by a registered pharmacist and no partnership or corporation shall own a drug store, pharmacy or apothecary shop unless at least 25 percent of all stock is held by registered pharmacists, except that any corporation, organized and existing under the laws of the state of Michigan, or any other state of the United States, authorized to do business in the state of Michigan and empowered by its charter to own and conduct pharmacies, drug stores or apothecary shops and which, at the time of passage of this act, owns and conducts a drug store or stores, pharmacy or pharmacies, apothecary shop or shops in the state of Michigan may continue to own and conduct the same and may establish and own additional pharmacies, drug stores or apothecary shops in accordance with provisions of this article: Provided, That any such corporation which shall not continue to own at least 1 of the pharmacies, drug stores or apothecary shops theretofore owned by it, or ceases to be actively engaged in the practice of pharmacy in the state of Michigan, shall not be permitted thereafter to own a drug store, pharmacy or apothecary shop: And provided further, That any person not a registered pharmacist who at the time of the passage of this act owns a pharmacy, drug store or apothecary shop in the state of Michigan, may continue to own and conduct the same in accordance with existing laws and regulations:

And provided further, That the administrator, executor or trustee of the estate of any deceased owner of a pharmacy, drug store or apothecary shop, or the widow, heirs or next of kin of such deceased owner, may continue to own and conduct such pharmacy, drug store or apothecary shop in accordance with existing laws and regulations: Provided further, That this act shall not apply to stores or shops in which patent or proprietary medicines and ordinary domestic or household remedies . . . are the only drugs and medicines sold at retail.

Section 14.772. Penalty. Section 2. Any individual firm or corporation violating the provisions of this act shall be deemed guilty of a misdemeanor and upon conviction shall be subject to a fine of not less than five hundred [500] dollars and cost of prosecution.

SELECTED RULES AND REGULATIONS OF THE MICHIGAN STATE BOARD OF PHARMACY[52]

R 338.482. 12. Housing of Pharmacy.

. . .

(c) All pharmacies which occupy less than the entire premises owned, leased, used or controlled by the licensee, shall be permanently enclosed by partition from floor to ceiling. . . .

R 338.486. 16. Pharmaceutical Services in Hospitals.

(a) Hospital pharmacies shall be licensed and are subject to and shall be conducted in accordance with all existing statutes, rules and regulations of this state and of the United States.

(b) The control of all drugs issued in hospitals shall be under the supervision of a registered pharmacist on a basis which is adequate to provide the pharmaceutical services the institution requires.

(c) No drug shall be compounded or dispensed except by a pharmacist or a physician or a pharmacy intern working under the immediate supervision of a pharmacist, and all orders for prescription drugs shall be interpreted by a pharmacist or physician before said drugs are administered. This shall be done, either by filling the prescription or by issuing a separate written order for its procurement from floor stock, drawn in such manner as to avoid error.

(d) The hospital, upon recommendation of the pharmacist in charge and the therapeutics committee, or a comparable committee of the medical staff, shall adopt written policies and procedures for the safe handling of drugs by hospital personnel, which shall be available to the Michigan board of pharmacy.

R 338.490. 20. Rules of Professional Conduct. The statement of principles expressed in the code of ethics of the American Pharmaceutical Association are hereby adopted as a guide to the conduct of the pharmacist . . . In addition, the following rules are adopted as appropriate to the establish-

[52] Michigan State Board of Pharmacy, *Michigan Laws Relating to Pharmacy* (Lansing, 1964), pp. 42–47.

ment and maintenance of a high standard of integrity and dignity in the profession of pharmacy.

. . .

3. A pharmacist is privileged by law to practice the profession of pharmacy and in so practicing he has a responsibility to make his professional services available to the public;

   (a) Without discriminating in any manner between patients, groups of patients or by compromising the kind or extent of professional services or facilities made available; and

   (b) without requiring an individual to be a member of any organization, or to pay or contribute any enrollment, membership, or participation fee as a condition for obtaining professional services; and

   (c) by offering complete pharmaceutical service, compounding or dispensing all prescriptions which may reasonably be expected to be compounded or dispensed by pharmacists . . .

MINNESOTA

EXCERPTS FROM LAWS RELATING TO PHARMACY[53]

Section 151.02. State Board of Pharmacy Formed. The Minnesota state board of pharmacy shall consist of five pharmacists actively engaged in the practice of pharmacy in this state, each of whom shall have had at least five consecutive years of practical experience as a pharmacist immediately preceding his appointment.

Section 151.03. Appointment of Members. The members of the state board of pharmacy shall be appointed by the governor . . .

Section 151.04. Recommended Names. The Minnesota state pharmaceutical association shall recommend five names for each appointment to be made, from which list the governor may select.

Section 151.06. Powers and Duties. . . .

. . .

(10) . . . it shall be the duty of the board to make and publish uniform rules and regulations not inconsistent herewith for carrying out and enforcing the provisions of this chapter.

Section 151.26. Exceptions. . . . Nothing in this chapter shall apply to or interfere with the manufacture, wholesaling, vending, or retailing of non-habit forming harmless proprietary medicines when labeled in accordance with the requirements of the state or federal food and drug act . . .

Section 151.28. Board May Turn Over Funds for Advancement of Science of Pharmacy. The board may each year turn over to the Minnesota state

[53] *Minn. Stat. Ann.* c. 151 (1946) and Supp. 1965.

pharmaceutical association for the advancement of the science and art of pharmacy, out of the annual fees collected by it, such sum as it may deem advisable, not to exceed $1.00 for each pharmacist and assistant pharmacist who shall have paid his renewal fee during such year. . . .

SELECTED RULES AND REGULATIONS OF THE MINNESOTA STATE BOARD PHARMACY[54]

No. 12. No license shall be issued for a pharmacy which is kept open more than 56 hours per week, unless at least two registered pharmacists are employed in such pharmacy or drug store on a schedule that will assure the presence of one registered pharmacist at all times. This regulation shall not apply when the owner of a pharmacy is a registered pharmacist and is continuously and personally in charge of such pharmacy.

No. 14. The Board of Pharmacy of the State of Minnesota shall hereafter refuse to grant licenses for the operation of pharmacies or drug stores in the State of Minnesota to individuals who are not registered pharmacists in the State of Minnesota and to corporations which are not owned and controlled by pharmacists registered in the State of Minnesota, unless the issuance of licenses to other individuals or corporations is a necessity from the standpoint of public health and welfare. All sales of the corporate stock of a corporation to which a license to conduct a pharmacy has been issued, shall be reported to the Board of Pharmacy forthwith upon forms furnished by the Secretary thereof. A sale of such stock resulting in a change in the control of such corporation constitutes a change of ownership within the meaning of this regulation.

Provided, however, that this regulation shall not affect pharmacies or drug stores for which licenses have already been issued and which are in actual operation at the time of adoption of this regulation.

No. 15. Hereafter applications to conduct pharmacies or drug stores in open market places, super stores, or super markets, self-service stores and other similar establishments shall be denied.

No. 16. That the issuance of a license to the widow of pharmacist be not refused on the ground that she is not a registered pharmacist, provided assurances will be given that when the pharmacy is disposed of by the widow of the registered pharmacist owner it will be sold only to a registered pharmacist or a corporation or partnership controlled by registered pharmacists of this State.

No. 17. No pharmacy shall be licensed hereafter unless (1) the space which it occupies has an entrance which affords the public direct access from the street, (2) the space which it occupies is separated from the remainder of the building in which it is located by walls extended from the floor to the ceiling, which walls may contain doors to the interior of the building which may be closed and locked when the pharmacy is not in charge

[54] Minnesota State Board of Pharmacy, "Rules and Regulations." (Mimeographed)

of a registered pharmacist, and (3) the space which it occupies contains not less than 400 square feet. . . . This regulation shall not apply to any pharmacy which has been granted a license prior to the effective date hereof.

No. 18. Hereafter the Board . . . shall refuse to . . . grant a license to any pharmacy which . . . sells . . . merchandise in any manner . . . similar to the manner in which merchandise is sold in super markets . . . using one or more checkout counters, unless there is provided . . . a drug area . . . which drug area shall include within it the prescription department . . . Any sale of drugs . . . must be made and completed in its entirety within the drug area by or under the personal supervision of a pharmacist or of an assistant pharmacist in the temporary absence of the pharmacist.

No. 19. (a) No registered pharmacy or other registered store shall display or offer for sale, drugs, medicines, chemicals or poisons in any manner designed to permit the purchaser to serve himself. (b) No pharmacist or other person employed in a store . . . or a pharmacy, shall sell to any person any drug, medicine, chemical or poison to which such person has served himself.

No. 20. Hereafter no pharmacist or pharmacy shall solicit by advertising of any kind the sale or distribution of drugs by prescription by any mail order plan of any form. The mail order sale of drugs by prescription is prohibited whenever such sale has been solicited by advertising of any kind by any person or persons. No pharmacist or pharmacy shall accept or fill a prescription which has been received by mail and that has been written by a practitioner not licensed to practice his profession in this state.

No. 21. No pharmacist or pharmacy shall advertise in any manner, prices, percentiles of prices or discounts for prescriptions and drugs requiring a prescription.

No. 22. It shall be deemed unlawful to distribute, dispense or vend any drug by automatic or vending machine.

MISSISSIPPI

EXCERPTS FROM LAWS RELATING TO PHARMACY[55]

Section 8851. State Board of Pharmacy. The State Board of Pharmacy . . . is . . . to consist of five practicing pharmacists, each of whom has had not less than five years of practical experience as retail pharmacists . . . Four members of this State Board of Pharmacy shall be appointed by the Governor from a list of twenty-one names submitted to him by the Mississippi State Pharmaceutical Association . . . The fifth member

[55] *Miss. Code of 1942 Ann.* tit. 32, c. 9 (1957).

of the State Board of Pharmacy shall be the secretary and executive officer of the said board and shall be nominated by the Mississippi State Pharmaceutical Association and appointed by the Governor . . .

Section 8852. By-Laws and Regulations. The State Board of Pharmacy shall have the power:

    (a) To make such by-laws and regulations, not inconsistent with the laws of this State, as may be necessary for the protection of the public . . .

    . . .

Section 8864. Penalty Without License—Minimum Qualifications and Operational Procedures.

    . . .

    (b) To be eligible for the issuance of a permit by the Mississippi State Board of Pharmacy to operate a drug or prescription department in a store, the applicant shall establish to the satisfaction of the . . . Board . . . evidence of the following minimum qualifications and operational procedures:

    (1) That such store is or will be engaged in the bona fide practice of Pharmacy and shall be open to the general public.

    . . .

    (4) That such store has maintained at all times during the 12 months period immediately preceding the permit application date, at least ten pecent (10%) of its total inventory in prescription drugs, based on cost; and has allotted at least ten percent (10%) of such store's selling area for a drug and prescription department; provided, however, if any applicant [has not been in business for the preceding 12 months he shall sign an affidavit certifying that he will comply with the above] . . . further provided, nothing in . . . this subsection shall apply to any store operating under a permit issued . . . prior to March 1, 1962.

    . . .

Section 8877. Sale of Patent Medicines Not Affected. . . . nothing in this chapter shall be construed to prohibit the sale of patent or proprietary medicines sold by dealers, merchants or agents not licensed throughout the state.

SELECTED RULES AND REGULATIONS OF THE MISSISSIPPI STATE BOARD OF PHARMACY[56]

Article I.

    1. *Adoption by the Board of a code of ethics:*

    (a) Code of ethics of the American Pharmaceutical Association adopted by the Board of Pharmacy October 20, 1964 as a statement of principles by the profession for the self-government of its members.

[56] Mississippi State Board of Pharmacy, "Rules and Regulations." (Mimeographed.)

(b) Maintenance and promotion of the physician-pharmacist relationship in the interest of public health and safety.

(c) To insure that no one member of the profession of pharmacy violates the high ethical tradition of the profession.

. . .

4. *Permits to new stores:*

(a) Before a new permit is issued, each pharmacy, apothecary and/or drug store shall comply with the following: If a person, association or holding company owns or controls store operations in one building or under one roof and provisions are made by door, passageway, window or other means for customers to pass and be served directly from one store operation to the other, then the entire area of all such store operations shall be deemed by the Board as one selling area under the provisions of the Mississippi Code Section 8864—paragraph (4) of section (b) requiring that the drug and prescription department shall consist of at least ten percent (10%) of the store selling area.

. . .

Article II.

2. Regulate the clandestine traffic in prescription drugs through unauthorized channels such as industrial and utility firms, mail order outfits, private schools and colleges, orphanages and home [sic] for alcoholics (not equitable that retail pharmacist must observe the laws in regard to legend drugs while no effort is being made to prevent others from trafficking in dangerous drugs).

. . .

Article III.

1. Except in an emergency, no person shall by himself or through another, procure or attempt to procure for himself or another, from or at any location other than a pharmacy which is registered with and has a permit from the Mississippi State Board of Pharmacy, prescriptions to be compounded or dispensed. The participating in or facilitating of such prohibited practices by a pharmacist shall constitute malpractice in pharmacy. For purposes of this regulation the term "person" includes individual, partnership, corporation, association, and agency.

(a) The phrase "except in an emergency" allows the usual prescription pickup and delivery—such exceptions to be cancelled, if abused, by the Board in its discretion.

(b) The phrase "procure or attempt to procure" prohibits not only receipt of prescription documents as a regular course of business, but also prohibits advertising mail order pharmaceutical services and soliciting prescriptions by mail.

(c) The phrase "prescriptions to be compounded or dispensed" only eliminates traffic in prescription documents and NOT in compounded and dispensed prescriptions.

(d) The phrase "participation in" declares such activity on the part of a pharmacist to be malpractice. On this basis, the State Board of Pharmacy may take appropriate action under the substance and procedure for revocation and suspension of registration for malpractice.

(e) The phrase "by himself or through another" precludes the use of an agent or independent contractor and the term "person" includes individuals and business organizations other than pharmacists.

(f) The State Board of Pharmacy of Mississippi is specific in its registrations and the issuing of permits and therefore underscores the intrastate limitations of such terms and precludes any misconceptions.

Article IV.

1. *Store Permit cancelled for cause:*

(a) There being no established prices on prescription drugs, the advertising of a *discount* and/or the use of any *word or words* that would indicate to the public that such prices are lower or cheaper at such store constitute false and misleading advertising and is hereby prohibited. Such advertising is hereby prohibited through any type advertising media.

. . .

2. *Unprofessional conduct and possible loss of license:*

(a) No pharmacist shall accept professional employment from any person who for compensation, prescribes drugs used in compounding and dispensing prescriptions.

(b) A registered pharmacist shall no operate a pharmacy which does offer complete prescription service to the general public. (Complete prescription service shall include the filling of all prescriptions, in any quantity which might reasonably be expected to be filled by any other licensed pharmacy and shall include an adequate supply of all pharmaceuticals and shall make emergency service available at all times).

(c) Any pharmacist, either owner, partner or employee having knowledge of and/or condones by willfully and knowingly advertisers [sic] or sells [sic] any commodity below the stipulated price set forth by contract signed by both producer and retail buyer is guilty of *unprofessional* conduct and is hereby subject to Rules and Regulations governing such activities.

MISSOURI

EXCERPTS FROM LAWS RELATING TO PHARMACY[57]

Section 338.010. Licensed Pharmacists to Conduct Drug Stores—Exceptions.
. . . nothing in this section shall be so construed as to apply to the sale

[57] *Mo. Ann. Stat.* tit. 22, c. 338 (1960) and Supp. 1965.

of patent and proprietary medicines, and the ordinary household remedies and such drugs or medicines as are normally sold by those engaged in the sale of general merchandise . . .

Section 338.110. Board of Pharmacy.
1. The board of pharmacy shall consist of five persons not connected
   .   with any school of pharmacy, licensed as pharmacists and actively engaged in the practice of pharmacy within this state . . .
2. Annually the Missouri pharmaceutical association may submit to the governor the names of five persons licensed as pharmacists within the state, and from this number, or from others, the governor . . . shall appoint one member to fill the vacancy annually occurring . . .

Section 338.140. Board of Pharmacy—Powers—Duties.
1. The board of pharmacy . . . shall have [the] power to adopt . . . rules and bylaws not inconsistent with law as may be necessary for the . . . discharge of the duties imposed under this chapter . . .
   . . .

SELECTED RULES AND REGULATIONS OF THE MISSOURI STATE BOARD OF PHARMACY[58]

Volume III. Drug Stores.
1. A pharmacist is permitted to sign the application for a drug store permit of only the store in which he is employed as the Chief Pharmacist in Charge, and he shall be full-time regularly employed. No part-time pharmacist employee is eligible to sign a drug store permit application.
   . . .

MONTANA

EXCERPTS FROM LAWS RELATING TO PHARMACY[59]

Section 66-1503. Montana State Board of Pharmacy—Qualifications of Members—Term and Appointment. The Montana state board of pharmacy shall consist of three (3) pharmacists . . . each of whom shall have had at least five (5) consecutive years of practical experience as a pharmacist immediately preceding his appointment . . .

. . . The members of the board shall be appointed by the governor from the list hereinafter subscribed . . . Vacancies shall be filled by appointment by the governor for the unexpired term. Any member of the board who, during his incumbency, ceases to be actively engaged in the practice of pharmacy in this state, shall be automatically disqualified from membership upon the board, and such disqualification shall result in a vacancy which may be filled as provided. . . . The Montana State Pharmaceutical Association shall annually submit to the governor the names of

[58] Missouri State Board of Pharmacy, *Laws of the State of Missouri Relating to Pharmacies and Pharmacists* (n.p., 1962), p. 35.
[59] *Mont. Rev. Code* tit. 66, c. 15 (1962) and Supp. 1965.

five (5) persons, qualified as prescribed herein, for each appointment to be made, from which list the governor shall appoint a member or members of the board as heretofore prescribed.

Section 66-1504. Montana State Board of Pharmacy—Powers of Board.

. . .

(b) *Powers and Duties of Board of Pharmacy.* The Montana state board of pharmacy shall have power, and it shall be its duty:

. . .

(11) . . . to make and publish uniform rules and regulations not inconsistent herewith, for carrying out and enforcing the provisions of the act.

Section 66-1508. Store License—Certified Pharmacy License—Suspension or Revocation.

(a) The state board of pharmacy shall . . . license stores other than a pharmacy wherein may be sold ordinary household or medicinal drugs prepared in sealed packages or bottles by a manufacturer, qualified under the laws of the state wherein such manufacturer resides . . . nothing herein shall be construed to prevent any vendor from selling any patent or proprietary medicine in the original package when plainly labeled . . .

SELECTED RULES AND REGULATIONS OF THE MONTANA STATE BOARD OF PHARMACY[60]

No. 1–55. Regulations Governing the Issuing and Operation of Pharmacy or Drug Store Licenses Pursuant to the Laws of the State of Montana.

. . .

12. No license shall be issued for a pharmacy which is kept open more than 56 hours per week, unless at least two registered pharmacists are employed in such pharmacy or drug store on a schedule that will assure the presence of one registered pharmacist at all times. This regulation shall not apply when the owner of a pharmacy is a registered pharmacist and is *continuously and personally in charge of such pharmacy.*

13. The Montana State Board of Pharmacy shall after March 21st, 1955, refuse to grant licenses for the operation of pharmacies or drug stores in the State of Montana unless it is plainly shown that,

. . .

1. The owner of a pharmacy or drug store is a registered pharmacist in good standing in the State of Montana.
2. The manager or supervisor of the pharmacy or drug store is a registered pharmacist in good standing in the State of Montana.
3. If the applicant be a partnership each active member must be a registered pharmacist in good standing in the State of Montana; or

[60] Montana State Board of Pharmacy, *Montana Pharmacy Laws* (Billings, nd.), pp. 23–29.

4. If the applicant be a corporation its president and one other of its officers must be registered pharmacists in good standing in the State of Montana and that they will be actively and regularly engaged and employed in, and responsible for the management, supervision and operation of each of such pharmacy or drug store.

Nothing contained in this regulation shall affect pharmacies or drug stores for which licenses have been issued and which are in actual operation at the time of the adoption of this regulation.

14. Hereafter applications for licenses to conduct pharmacies or drug stores and other similar establishments shall be denied. (. . . adopted . . . March 21st, 1955.)

No. 2–55. Minimum Requirements for the Protection of the Public Health, Safety and Welfare Pertaining to the Space, Equipment and Requirements of Pharmacies Including Their Compounding Department or Departments.

. . .

b. Pharmacies shall occupy space (approximately 400 sq. ft.),
   1. With an entrance which affords the public direct access from the street.
   2. Which is separated from the remainder of the building in which it is located by walls extended from the floor to the ceiling, but such walls may contain doors or windows to the building interior which may be closed and locked when the pharmacy is not in charge of a registered pharmacist.

No. 2–56. Prohibitions Against Dispensing or Vending Medications From Automatic or Vending Machines. In the best interest, safety and protection of Public Health, it shall be deemed unlawful to distribute, dispense or vend any drugs or medicine by automatic or vending machines. (Regulation adopted October 26th, 1956.)

No. 104. Hospital Regulation. Hospitals not employing registered pharmacists may not compound prescriptions and may only furnish patients in the hospital such medication, which are prepared by a manufacturer, on physicians' orders.

It shall be unlawful for any hospital to furnish any outgoing patient with any medication, unless such hospital employs a registered pharmacist and then such medication must be properly labeled as required by law. (. . . adopted April 4th, 1954.)

NEBRASKA

EXCERPTS FROM LAWS RELATING TO PHARMACY[61]

Section 71-111. Board of Examiners; Appointment. For the purpose of giving examinations to applicants for license to practice the professions

[61] *Neb. Rev. Stat. of 1948* c. 71, art. 1 (1958) and Supp: 1965.

for which license is required by this act, the Department of Health shall appoint a board of examiners for each of said professions.

Section 71-114. Examiner; Qualifications; Third Term Prohibited. Every examiner shall be and have been actively engaged in the practice of his profession in the State of Nebraska, under a license issued in this state, for a period of five years just preceding his appointment . . .

Section 71-117. Examiners; State Associations Shall Recommend. The regular state association or society, or its managing board, for each profession may submit each year to the Department of Health a list of five persons of recognized ability in such profession who have the qualifications prescribed for examiners for that particular profession; *Provided,* each member of the Board of Examiners in Pharmacy shall be the recipient of a diploma of graduation from an accredited school or college of pharmacy. If such a list is submitted, the department, in making an appointment to the board of examiners for such profession, shall appoint one of the persons so named.

Section 71-119. Board of Examiners; Vacancy; How Filled. Any vacancy in the membership of a board of examiners caused by death, resignation, removal, or otherwise, shall be filled for the period of the unexpired term in the same manner as original appointments are made; *Provided,* the Department of Health shall select from the last list submitted.

Section 71-1, 143. Pharmacy; Practice; Persons Excepted . . .
[Section] 71-1, 147 shall not be construed to include the following classes:
    . . .
    (3) persons who sell, offer or expose for sale, patent or proprietary medicines . . .
    . . .

Section 71-1, 147, 09. Pharmacy; Rules and Regulations; Promulgation; Minimum Requirements and Standards. The Department of Health, upon the recommendation of the Board of Examiners in Pharmacy, is hereby granted authority to promulgate rules and regulations for the enforcement of this act . . .

NEVADA

EXCERPTS FROM LAWS RELATING TO PHARMACY[62]

Section 639.020. State Board of Pharmacy: Creation; Members and Their Qualifications.
    1. The state board of pharmacy consisting of five members appointed by the governor is hereby created.
    2. Appointees shall be competent registered pharmacists actively engaged in the practice of pharmacy in this state, residing in different

[62] *Nev. Rev. Stat.* tit. 54, c. 639 (1965).

parts of the state, and shall have at least 10 years' experience as registered pharmacists in this state.

Section 639.070. General Powers and Duties of Board. The board shall have power:

1. To make such bylaws and regulations, not inconsistent with the laws of this state, as may be necessary for the protection of the public . . .

   . . .

Section 639.215. Rules of Professional Conduct for Pharmacists.

4. Nothing contained in NRS 639.213 [in which it is declared that parmacy is a profession] and this section shall be construed as authorizing the board to adopt rules of professional conduct relating to prices or fees or to advertising and promotion of commodities or services.

SELECTED RULES AND REGULATIONS OF THE NEVADA STATE BOARD OF PHARMACY[63]

No. 5.01. The following acts or practices . . . are declared to be, specifically but not by way of limitation, unprofessional conduct and contrary to the public interest:

. . .

(h) Advertising to the public any prescription or legend drug which may be dispensed only on the legal prescription of a licensed practitioner by the use of its official or trade name, or by referring to its physiological [sic] or therapeutic effect.

. . .

(m) Aiding or abetting any person not licensed to practice pharmacy in this state.

NEW HAMPSHIRE

EXCERPTS FROM LAWS RELATING TO PHARMACY[64]

Section 318:1. Definitions.

XI. Proprietary remedies, when not otherwise limited, means remedies that a certain individual or individuals have the exclusive right to manufacture or sell.

. . .

Section 318:2. Appointment. There shall be a commission of pharmacy and practical chemistry consisting of three members, one to be appointed each year by the governor, with the advice and consent of the council . . . Vacancies shall be filled in like manner . . .

[63] Nevada State Board of Pharmacy, Rules and Regulations (Reno, 1964), pp. 45–57.

[64] *N.H. Rev. Stat. Ann.* tit. 30, c. 318 (1955) and Supp. 1965.

Section 318:3. Eligibility. The members shall have been registered pharmacists in this state for at least ten years, and at the time of their appointment shall be engaged in conducting a retail pharmacy.

Section 318:32. Rules and Regulations. The board may make and promulgate necessary rules and regulations . . . for the enforcement of this chapter and the carrying out of the intent and purposes herein expressed. . . .

SELECTED RULES AND REGULATIONS OF THE NEW HAMPSHIRE COMMISSION OF PHARMACY[65]

May 24–25, 1939. . . . Pharmacy permits granted to persons not registered in New Hampshire shall employ not less than two registered pharmacists at all times.

June 12, 1947. Vending Machines. It shall be unlawful to distribute through vending machines, or any automatic device not requiring individual attention of a person responsible for each individual sale of any drug or medicine, official or proprietary [sic], surgical supplies or device used in the prevention of disease of men.

The board passed the above regulation after considering the automatic vending machine dispensing of drugs, medicines, surgical supplies and devices. Without proper supervision of a responsible person to insure the drugs, medicines, surgical supplies or devices would meet proper qualifications to insure potency and therapeutic value, adequate sanitation, sterility, adulteration or contamination [sic]. To protect the public health and welfare of the people of the state against such risks as would be involved in the distribution of drugs, medicines, surgical supplies and devices in automatic machines or mechanical distribution of the item, the board passed unanimously for immediate effect the above regulation.

January 5, 1966. Amendment to that part of the regulation of May 24–25, 1939 relative to the floor space primarily devoted to the compounding of prescriptions. The words 75 square feet shall be changed to read 200 square feet.

NEW JERSEY

EXCERPTS FROM LAWS RELATING TO PHARMACY[66]

Section 45:14-1. Board of Pharmacy of the State of New Jersey; Membership; Appointments; Terms of Office. The board of pharmacy of the state of New Jersey . . . shall consist of five members, to be appointed . . . as hereinafter directed, by the governor, each of whom shall be a citizen of and an able and skilled registered pharmacist in this state, shall have

---

[65] New Hampshire Commission of Pharmacy, "Rules and Regulations." (Mimeographed.)

[66] *N.J. Stat. Ann.* tit. 45, subtit. 1, c. 14 (1963) and Supp. 1965.

been registered as a pharmacist in this state for at least five years prior to his appointment, shall be actually engaged in conducting a pharmacy at the time of his appointment and shall continue in the practice of pharmacy during the term of his office. No member shall be a teacher or instructor in any college of pharmacy . . . the New Jersey Pharmaceutical Association may annually send to the governor the names of three registered pharmacists . . . one of whom the governor may appoint to fill any vacancy occurring in the board.

Section 45:14-3. Officers of Board; By-laws and Rules; Meetings; Examination; General Powers and Duties of Board. The board . . . may make by-laws and rules for the proper fulfillment of its duties under this Chapter. . . .

Section 45:14-12. Refusal of Examination; Supervision or Revocation of Certificate; Person Deemed Unregistered During Suspension or Revocation; Hearing; Court Review. . . . the board may refuse an application for examination or may suspend or revoke the certificate of a registered pharmacist or a registered assistant pharmacist upon proof satisfactory to the board that such registered pharmacist or such registered assistant pharmacist is guilty of grossly unprofessional conduct and the following acts are hereby declared to constitute grossly unprofessional conduct for the purpose of this act:

. . .

  c. The promotion, direct or indirect, by any means, in any form and through any media of the prices for prescription drugs and narcotics or fees or for services relating thereto or any reference to the price of said drugs or prescriptions whether specifically or as a percentile of prevailing prices or by the use of the terms "cut rate," "discount," "bargain" or terms of similar connotation . . .

. . .

  e. Fostering the interest of one group of patients at the expense of another which compromises the quality or extent of professional services or facilities made available.

. . .

Section 45:14-29. Application of Provisions of Chapter Limited. . . . nothing in this chapter shall be construed to apply to or in any manner interfere with . . . the making and vending of nonpoisonous patent or proprietary medicines . . .

Section 45:14-33. Permit; Application; Fee; Display; Prerequisities. . . . No permit shall be issued [to a pharmacy] unless it appears to the satisfaction of the board that:

  a. The management of the pharmacy is in personal and continuous charge of a pharmacist registered in accordance with the laws of this State.

. . .

e. The said pharmacy shall not offer professional services under terms and conditions which tend to interfere with or impair the free and complete exercise of professional judgment and skill or enter into any agreement which denies the patient the right of free choice of pharmacies.

Section 45:14-36.1. Rules and Regulations by Board of Pharmacy. The Board of Pharmacy may promulgate rules and regulations setting up minimum requirements regarding adequate facilities for the safe storage of narcotic drugs; equipment for the prescription departments in pharmacies and drug stores; stock of drugs, pharmaceuticals and chemicals in prescription departments of pharmacies and drug stores; size and other space requirements of prescription departments; and other facilities necessary in the compounding of prescriptions; and may promulgate rules and regulations governing sanitation, orderliness and cleanliness in the pharmacy or drug store.

SELECTED RULES AND REGULATIONS OF THE NEW JERSEY STATE BOARD OF PHARMACY[67]

No. 45:14-36.1 (1). Area of Prescription Department. The area devoted to the prescription department and laboratory shall not be less than ten percent of the main floor area of the pharmacy or drug store, and in no instances shall it be less than fifty square feet. If the main floor area exceeds twelve hundred square feet, the minimum area of the prescription department shall not be less than one hundred and twenty square feet. After July 1, 1963 no permit will be granted for the operation of a new pharmacy, including pharmacies at new locations, unless the prescription department occupies exclusively a minimum of one hundred and fifty square feet.

NEW MEXICO

EXCERPTS FROM LAWS RELATING TO PHARMACY[68]

Section 67-9-2. Board of Pharmacy—Appointment—Oath—Organization—Officers—Compensation—Power and Duties of the Board. The Governor shall appoint five (5) persons, by and with the consent of the Senate, all of whom shall have been residents of the State and actively engaged in the drug business for three (3) or more years, and of at least eight (8) years' practical experience as druggists or pharmacists . . . The State Pharmaceutical Association of New Mexico shall annually submit to the Governor a list containing the names of five (5) persons . . . and each member of said Board . . . appointed by the Governor shall be appointed . . . from the names on said list. Any vacancy occurring on said Board shall likewise be filled . . . from the last annual list of names . . . submitted . . .

---

[67] New Jersey Board of Pharmacy, *New Jersey Pharmacy Laws, Regulations and Excerpts of Narcotic Drug Laws* (Newark, 1965), p. 18.

[68] *N.M. Stat. Ann.* c. 67, art. 9 (1961) and Supp. 1965.

. . . The Board of Pharmacy shall have the power to make bylaws and rules and regulations necessary for the protection of the public in the field of pharmacy . . .

Section 67-9-15. Restrictions on Use of Designated Terms—Emergency Drugs Dispensed by Physicians, Dentists or Veterinarians. . . . nothing in this act . . . shall be construed to prevent . . . the sale of nonnarcotic, nonpoisonous, or nondangerous patent or proprietary medicines by nonregistered persons or stores, when sold in original packages.

SELECTED RULES AND REGULATIONS OF THE NEW MEXICO STATE BOARD OF PHARMACY[69]

Regulation No. 19 (Revised). Hospital and Related Institutions Licensure (Effective November 5, 1964). All hospitals and related institutions must be licensed by the New Mexico State Board of Pharmacy and observe the following rules and regulations:

Hospitals and related institutions having over 75 bed capacity shall employ a registered pharmacist on a full time basis. Pharmacist will be responsible to the State Board of Pharmacy for the proper labeling, dispensing and control of drugs. No drugs shall be furnished out-patients unless hospital has an established pharmacy.

Hospitals and related institutions having less than 75 bed capacity, but more than 25 bed capacity shall be required to obtain the services of a registered pharmacist on a part-time or consultative basis.

Hospitals and nursing homes or related institutions having less than 24 bed capacity shall abide by the following rules and regulations: [none given]

Regulation No. 23. Prescription Room Requirements. Any new pharmacy, any existing pharmacy which is being remodeled, or any pharmacy which is moving from one location to another must meet the following requirements:

The area to be occupied by the prescription department and the area devoted to the sale of restricted drugs . . . shall not be less than 240 square feet. . . .

Regulation No. 26. (February 4, 1964). It shall be illegal for any pharmacy not licensed in the State of New Mexico, where patient-physician-pharmacist relationship is lost, to sell drugs on prescription written by physicians licensed in New Mexico.

Regulation No. 27. (June 16, 1964). The use of any mechanical device or vending machine in connection with the sales of any device, drug, medicinal chemical, medicine, poison, or proprietary or patent medicine is unlawful.

[69] New Mexico State Board of Pharmacy, *New Mexico Pharmacy Laws and Rules and Regulations* (n.p., 1962), pp. 41–46. (Regulations 19, 26, and 27 are contained in a mimeographed insert to the basic document.)

NEW YORK

EXCERPTS FROM LAWS RELATING TO PHARMACY[70]

Section 6802. State Board of Pharmacy.

1. *Membership.* The state board of pharmacy shall consist of nine examiners, four of whom shall be residents of the city of New York.
2. *Nominations.* At each annual meeting of the [New York State Pharmaceutical] association, nine licensed pharmacists shall be nominated by ballot, whose names shall be submitted to the [New York State Education] department in writing under the seal of the [New York State Pharmaceutical] association by the president and secretary thereof, promptly after the adjournment of such meeting.
3. *Appointments.* From the number thus submitted or from other licensed pharmacists of the state, the regents may appoint three persons to succeed the members whose terms of office expire on the following July thirty-first. . . .
4. *Examiners.* No person shall be appointed as an examiner unless he is a licensed pharmacist, and has legally practiced as such for at least ten years in this state. . . . The board shall make such rules approved by the regents not inconsistent with law, as may be necessary for the proper performance of its duties . . .

Section 6804. Revocation of Licenses and Certificates of Registration; Misdemeanors.

1. . . . Any license or certificate may be revoked or suspended . . .

. . .

   d. Upon proof that the holder . . . has advertised definite fixed prices for the compounding and/or dispensing of prescriptions;

. . .

   h. Upon proof that the holder thereof has been guilty of unprofessional conduct as defined by the regents.

   i. . . . The board of regents may promulgate rules, when necessary, to define and clarify the provisions of this subdivision. . . .

Section 6805. Registration and Operation of Establishments.

. . .

2. *Pharmacies.* . . . Every pharmacy shall be, at all times when open for business, under the personal supervision and management of a duly licensed and registered pharmacist . . .

Section 6807. Working Hours. No apprentice or employee in any pharmacy or drug store in a city having a population of over one million inhabitants, shall be required or permitted to work more than fifty-four hours a week. Nothing in this subdivision prohibits working six hours overtime any week for the purpose of making a shorter succeeding week, provided, however,

---

[70] *N.Y. Education Law* tit. 7, art. 137.

that the aggregate number of hours in any such two weeks shall not exceed one hundred eight hours.

Section 6816. Construction of Article.

. . .

2. Except as to the labeling of poison and to adultering, misbranding and substituting, . . . [this article] shall not apply:

. . .

c. To the sale of proprietary medicines except those proprietary medicines which are poisonous, deleterious and/or habit forming.

. . .

SELECTED REGULATIONS OF THE COMMISSIONER OF EDUCATION[71]

Article I. Section 57. Unprofessional Conduct. Unprofessional conduct . . . shall include but shall not be limited to . . .

. . .

3. Advertising of any character in respect to prescription prices, which includes or contains any fixed price or discount whatsoever or any reference thereto by the owner or owners of a pharmacy or pharmacies.

SELECTED RULES OF THE NEW YORK STATE BOARD OF PHARMACY[72]

No. 4. Care and Conduct of Pharmacy, Drug Store, Manufacturer/Wholesaler Establishment and Registered Store.[73]

. . .

b. . . . . [Each] pharmacy or drug store, if operated as a department of a general merchandising establishment, department store or discount house shall be permanently enclosed by a partition at least 9 feet 6 inches in height in which case the partition shall be from floor to ceiling . . .

NORTH CAROLINA

EXCERPTS FROM LAWS RELATING TO PHARMACY[74]

Section 99-55. Board of Pharmacy; Election; Terms; Vacancies. The Board of Pharmacy shall consist of five persons licensed as pharmacists within this State, who shall be elected and commissioned by the Governor as hereinafter provided. . . . The North Carolina Pharmaceutical Association shall annually elect a resident pharmacist from its number to fill the vacancy annually occurring in said Board, and the pharmacist so elected shall be commissioned by the Governor and shall hold office for the term of

[71] New York State Board of Pharmacy, *Pharmacy, Handbook 11 on Professional Education* (Albany: New York State Education Department, 1963), p. 88.

[72] *Id.* at 91–94.

[73] Part "e" and "f" of Rule 4 were promulgated on February 27, 1964, and included as mimeographed inserts to the basic document.

[74] *N.C. Gen. Stat.* div. 12, c. 90, art. 4 (1965).

five years and until his successor has been duly elected and qualified. In case of death, resignation, or removal from the State of any member of said Board of Pharmacy, the said Board shall elect in his place a pharmacist who is a member of said North Carolina Pharmaceutical Association, who shall be commissioned by the Governor as a member of the said Board of Pharmacy for the remainder of the term. . . .

Section 90-57. Powers of Board; Reports; Quorum; Records. The Board of Pharmacy . . . shall have the power and authority to define and designate non-poisonous domestic remedies, to adopt such rules, regulations, and by-laws, not inconsistent with this article, as may be necessary for the regulation of its proceedings and for the discharge of the duties imposed under this article . . .

Section 90-71. Selling Drugs Without License Prohibited; Drug Trade Regulated. . . . Nothing in this section shall be construed to interfere with . . . the selling at retail of nonpoisonous domestic remedies, nor with the sale of patent or proprietary preparations which do not contain poisonous ingredients, nor, except in cities and towns wherein there is located an established drugstore, and except in the counties of Bertie, Cabarrus, Cleveland, Cumberland, Duplin, Forsyth, Gaston, Guilford, Halifax Harnett, Henderson, Iredell, Mecklenburg, Montgomery, Moore, New Hanover, Orange, Pender, Richmond, Robeson, Rockingham, Rowan, Scotland and Wilson, shall this section be construed to interfere with the sale of paregoric, Godfrey's Cordial, aspirin, alum, borax, bicarbonate of soda, calomel tablets, castor oil, compound cathartic pills, copperas, cough remedies which contain no poison or narcotic drugs, cream of tartar, distilled extract witch hazel, epsom salts, harlem oil, gum asafetida, gum camphor, glycerin, peroxide of hydrogen, petroleum jelly, salt-petre, spirit of turpentine, spirit of camphor, sweet oil, and sulphate of quinine . . .

SELECTED RULES AND REGULATIONS OF THE NORTH CAROLINA STATE BOARD OF PHARMACY[75]

Article 2. Section 7. Nonpoisonous Domestic Remedies. "Nonpoisonous domestic remedies" means:

Alum	Distilled Extract of	Peroxide of Hydrogen
Aromatic Spirit of Ammonia	Witch Hazel	Petroleum Jelly
Aspirin Tablets	Epsom Salt	Saltpeter
Borax	Harlem Oil	Senna Leaves
Bicarbonate of Soda	Iodine 2%	Spirit Turpentine
Calomel Tablets	Gum Asafoetida	Spirit Camphor
Castor Oil	Gum Camphor	Sweet Oil
Compound Cathartic Pills	Glycerin	Sulphur
Copperas	Milk of Magnesia	Sulfate of
Cream of Tartar	Mineral Oil	Quinine

[75] North Carolina Board of Pharmacy, *Pharmacy Laws of North Carolina Including Rules and Regulations of North Carolina Board of Pharmacy* (Chapel Hill, 1966), p. 49.

Cough remedies which contain no poisonous or narcotic drugs. Exempt narcotic preparations, provided the dealer is registered under the Harrison Narcotic Law.

Article 2. Section 8. Patent or Proprietary Preparation. "Patent or proprietary preparation" means a medicinal preparation which is intended for use in the cure, mitigation, treatment or prevention of disease in man or other animal pursuant to self-diagnosis; when the same is identified by and sold under a trademark, trade name or other trade symbol, privately owned or registered with the United States Patent Office; which preparation is sold in the original and unopened package of the manufacturer or primary distributor; which preparation in itself is not poisonous as defined in Article 2, Section 6 of the Rules and Regulations of the Board of Pharmacy; which preparation is sold or offered for sale and is advertised for sale to the general public by the manufacturer or primary distributor; which preparation meets all of the requirements of the Federal Food, Drug and Cosmetic Act and the North Carolina Food, Drug and Cosmetic Act and regulations promulgated under either of these; and the labeling of which preparation does not contain the legend, "Caution: Federal Law prohibits dispensing without prescription" or any other legend or statement of like import.

NORTH DAKOTA

EXCERPTS FROM LAWS RELATING TO PHARMACY[76]

Section 34-15-02. Exemptions. The provisions of this chapter shall not apply to the following:

. . .

3. The keeping for sale and sale by general dealers of proprietary medicines in original packages and such simple household remedies as from time to time may be approved for such sale by the board;
4. Registered or copyrighted proprietary medicines;
5. The manufacture of proprietary remedies or the sale of the same in original packages by other than pharmacists.

Section 43-15-03. Board of Pharmacy—Appointment—Qualifications. The state board of pharmacy shall consist of five members appointed by the governor upon the recommendation of the North Dakota pharmaceutical association. The persons appointed shall be registered pharmacists and members of such association.

Section 43-15-05. Compensation of Board—Disposition of Fees. . . . Any moneys remaining after the payment of the per diem and expenses herein provided for shall be held by the treasurer of the board as a special fund

---

[76] *N.D. Century Code Ann.* tit. 43, c. 43-15 (1960) and Supp. 1965.

to meet the expenses of the board and of the reports and annual meeting of the North Dakota pharmaceutical association, and such other necessary expenses as may be incurred by the association.

Section 43-15-10. Powers of Board. . . . the board shall have the . . . [power,] in order to protect the public health, welfare, and safety:

. . .

2. To prescribe rules and regulations not inconsistent with this chapter governing and cancellation or suspension of a certificate or registration;

. . .

Section 43-15-30. Registered Pharmacist Member of North Dakota Pharmaceutical Association. Registration as a pharmacist by the board entitles the person so registered to a one year membership in the North Dakota pharmaceutical association.

Section 43-15-35. Requirements for Permit to Operate Pharmacy. The board shall issue a permit to operate a pharmacy, or a renewal permit, upon satisfactory proof that:

. . .

5. The applicant for such permit . . . is a registered pharmacist in good standing or is a partnership, each active member of which is a registered pharmacist in good standing, or a corporation or association, the majority stock in which is owned by registered pharmacists in good standing, actively and regularly employed in and responsible for the management, supervision, and operation of such pharmacy . . .

. . .

The provision of subsection 5 of this section shall not apply to the holder of a permit on July 1st, 1963, if otherwise qualified to conduct the pharmacy, provided that any such permit holder who shall discontinue operations under such permit or fail to renew such permit upon expiration shall not thereafter be exempt from the provisions of such subsection as to such discontinue on lapsed permit. The provisions of subsection 5 of this section shall not apply to hospital pharmacies furnishing services only to patients in such hospital.

Section 12. Sale by Vending Machines Prohibited: Evidence: Destruction.[77] The offering for sale, distribution or other disposition by means of a vending machine or other automatic machine of drugs, medicines or devices for the prevention of disease is expressly prohibited. Possession of such machines by a person, firm, or corporation in his place of business shall be prima facie evidence of sale. Any such machine shall be destroyed on order of a magistrate when found in violation hereof, and the possessor shall be guilty of a misdemeanor.

[77] North Dakota State Board of Pharmacy, *North Dakota Board of Pharmacy By-Laws, Rules and Regulations* (Bismark, 1965), p. 100.

SELECTED RULES AND REGULATIONS OF THE
NORTH DAKOTA STATE BOARD OF PHARMACY.[78]

No. 13. Who Can Own a Drug Store; Privilege of Selling Drugs. The Board of Pharmacy of the State of North Dakota shall hereafter refuse to grant a license for the operation of pharmacies or drug stores in the State of North Dakota to individuals who are not registered pharmacists in the State of North Dakota or to corporations, which are not owned and controlled by pharmacists registered in the State of North Dakota, unless the issuance of licenses to other individuals or corporations is a necessity from the standpoint of public health and welfare. . . .

OHIO

EXCERPTS FROM LAWS RELATING TO PHARMACY[79]

Section 4729.01. State Board of Pharmacy. There shall be a state board of pharmacy, consisting of five members, who shall be appointed by the governor with the advice and consent of the senate. The Ohio state pharmaceutical association may annually submit to the governor the names of five registered pharmacists, and from the names submitted or from others, at his discretion, the governor each year shall appoint one member of the board for a term of five years.

Section 4729.26. Rules and Regulations for Enforcement. The state board of pharmacy is empowered to make such rules and regulations, . . . not inconsistent with the law, pertaining to the practice of pharmacy as may be necessary to carry out the purpose of and enforce sections 4729.01 to 4729.35, inclusive, of the Revised Code.

Section 4729.27. Retail Drug Store Must Be Conducted by Legally Registered Pharmacist. A person not a registered pharmacist, who owns, manages, or conducts a retail drug store as defined in section 4729.02 of the Revised Code, shall have in his employ, in full and actual charge of such retail drug store, a pharmacist registered under the laws of this state. Any registered pharmacist, who owns, manages, or conducts a retail drug store shall be personally in full and actual charge of such retail drug store, or shall have in his employ in full and actual charge of such retail drug store, a pharmacist registered under the laws of this state.

Section 4729.29 Exceptions to Certain Provisions. Sections 4729.26, 4729.27, and 4729.28 of the Revised Code shall not apply to . . . the making or vending of proprietary medicines by a retail dealer, in original packages when labeled as required by the Federal Food, Drug and Cosmetic Act . . .

[78] *Id.* at 49–63.
[79] *Ohio Rev. Code Ann.* tit. 47, c. 4729 (1953) and Supp. 1965.

SELECTED REGULATIONS OF THE
OHIO STATE BOARD OF PHARMACY[80]

Rule B-9. Only a practitioner duly licensed in this state, or a pharmacist who is registered in this state and who is employed in a pharmacy under the supervision of this state board of pharmacy shall compound, fill, dispense or distribute prescriptions or dangerous drugs to the citizens of this state, unless either the physician or the patient involved in the physician-pharmacist-patient relationship resides within an area of thirty-mile radius of the pharmacy not under the supervision of this board of pharmacy.

Rule B-10. No pharmacist or owner of any pharmacy shall fill and dispense prescriptions obtained from a place which offers to the public, in any manner, its services as a "pick up station" or intermediary for the purpose of having prescriptions filled or delivered unless such place has a legally registered pharmacist in full and actual charge of such services.

Rule C-3.[81] The term dispensing as used in the Pharmacy Practices Act . . . consists of all activities and procedures between the receipt of the prescription order and the final, finished prescription medication ready for delivery to the patient.

Dispensing shall include but not be limited to drug selection from an original container, and packaging with appropriate labeling pursuant to the order of a licensed practitioner.

Rule C-6. No drug or medicine or device . . . shall be sold, or offered for sale or dispensed by means of any mechanical device unless such device is approved by the Board of Pharmacy.

OKLAHOMA

EXCERPTS FROM LAWS RELATING TO PHARMACY[82]

Section 353.1. Definitions . . . .

. . .

(8) "Patent or Proprietary Medicines" means and includes packaged medicines, drugs, medical and dental supplies, and bottled or non-bulk chemicals identified by and sold under a trademark, trade name or other trade symbol, privately owned or registered in the United States Patent Office, which are sold or offered for sale to the general public, if such articles or preparations meet the requirements of the Federal Food, Drug and Cosmetic Act.

. . .

[80] Ohio State Board of Pharmacy, *Drug Laws of Ohio* (Columbus, 1964), pp. 153–172. Rules C-2 through C-10 were included as mimeographed inserts to the basic documents. Rules C-2 through C-10 became effective April 1, 1965.
[81] This rule is no longer in force. See Chapter 10.
[82] *Okla. Stat. Ann.* tit. 59, c. 8 and c. 16 (1963) and Supp. 1965.

Section 353.3. Board of Pharmacy—Qualifications and Appointment of Members. The Board of Pharmacy shall consist of five (5) persons who have been registered no less than five (5) years, who are members of the pharmaceutical association and actively engaged in the practice of retail pharmacy within this State for a period of not less than five (5) years, who shall be appointed by the Governor, by and with the advice and consent of the Senate, from a list of names elected by vote of the members of the pharmaceutical association, voting to be done by mail ballot . . .

Section 353.4 Submission of Names to Fill Vacancies—Tenure. Annually the Secretary of the Oklahoma Pharmaceutical Association shall submit to the Governor names of the ten (10) persons who have been elected as provided in the foregoing section, and from this list the Governor shall appoint one member to fill the vacancy annually occuring on the Board of Pharmacy and the vacancies occurring from other causes shall be filled in like manner. . . .

Section 353.7. Powers and Duties of Board. The State Board of Pharmacy shall have the powers and it shall also be its duty:

. . .

(1) To adopt and establish rules of professional conduct appropriate to the establishment and maintenance of a high standard of integrity and dignity in the profession of pharmacy, and such rules shall be subject to amendment or repeal by the Board as the need may arise. Every person who practices pharmacy in this State shall be governed and controlled by the rules of professional conduct adopted by the Board, and the Board shall cause these rules to be printed as part of the application blanks for registration and renewal thereof, and each applicant shall subscribe thereto when making an application.

. . .

(n) To make and publish uniform rules and regulations such as may be necessary for carrying out and enforcing the provisions of this Act and such as in its discretion may be necessary to protect the health, safety and welfare of the public . . .

Section 353.11. Annual Renewal of Registration—Cancellation of Certificates —Payments to Oklahoma Pharmaceutical Association—Reports. . . . the State Board of Pharmacy shall each year turn over to the Oklahoma Pharmaceutical Association for the advancement of the profession of pharmacy, out of the annual fees collected by it, the sum of Two Dollars and fifty cents ($2.50) for each pharmacist or assistant pharmacist who shall have paid his renewal fee during such year. . . .

Section 353.13. Retailing, Compounding or Dispensing of Drugs by Other than a Registered Pharmacist or Assistant Unlawful—Store Management —Communities of 500 Population or Less . . . . it shall be unlawful for any person to institute, conduct or manage a pharmacy for the retailing,

compounding or dispensing of drugs, medicines or pharmaceutical preparations unless such person shall be a registered pharmacist, or shall place
in charge of said pharmacy a registered pharmacist . . .

Section 353.18. Regulation of the Sale of Drugs and Chemicals—Penalty
. . . .

. . .

(d) . . . nothing in this Act shall be construed to prevent the sale of
patent or proprietary medicines in original packages by any
merchant or dealer . . . .

Section 353.24. Unlawful Acts. It shall be unlawful for any person, firm or
corporation:

. . .

(d) To engage in any "mail order" prescription business in which
prescriptions are solicited and received through the mails for dispensing, or in which prescriptions are dispensed and delivered by
mail to customers other than those personally known to the
pharmacist in charge of a pharmacy and under circumstances
clearly dictating that such method of delivery is in the best interests of the health and welfare of the customer.

(e) To enter into any arrangement whereby prescription orders are
received, or prescriptions delivered at a place other than the
pharmacy in which they are compounded and dispensed. However,
nothing in this section shall prevent a pharmacist or his employee
from personally receiving a prescription or delivering a legally
filled prescription at a residence, office or place of employment of
the patient for whom the prescription was written.

Section 353.26. Revocation or Suspension of Licenses, Certificates or Permits.
The Board of Pharmacy is specifically granted the power to revoke or
suspend any certificate, license or permit issued pursuant to this Act to any
holder . . . who:

. . .

(e) conducts himself in a manner likely to lower public esteem for
the profession of pharmacy,

. . .

(g) exercises conduct and habits inconsistent with the rules of professional conduct established by the Board. . . .

*Section 736.1. Service, Commodity or Material Requiring Examination of
Prescription Prohibited—Hearing Aids and Trusses Expected.* No person,
firm, or corporation, or any professional group regulated and defined by
the Statutes of Oklahoma, shall advertise the price of any service, commodity or material which requires a prior examination and/or prescription
by and/or from a person licensed to practice a healing art in this State
as defined by Title 59, Oklahoma Statutes 1951, to determine the proper
service, commodity, or material to be rendered or delivered to the user

or consumer thereof for the purpose of the correction or relief of any abnormalities or deformities of the human. Provided this Act shall not prohibit the advertisement of hearing aids, and/or trusses.

SELECTED RULES AND REGULATIONS OF THE OKLAHOMA STATE BOARD OF PHARMACY[83]

Physical Requirements for Pharmacies.
1. The prescription department shall occupy at least 1570 of the floor space occupied by [the] Pharmacy, Drug Store or Drug Department and in no case less than 125 square feet.

. . .

OREGON

EXCERPTS FROM LAWS RELATING TO PHARMACY[84]

Section 689.120. Pharmacies . . . to be Under Supervision of Registered Pharmacist. No proprietor of a pharmacy shall:
(1) Fail to place in charge of such pharmacy a registered pharmacist.

. . .

Section 689.130. Registered Pharmacist to be in Charge of Drug Business. No person shall . . . conduct [a drug store] . . . unless the place of business is at all times in active personal charge of a registered pharmacist or in temporary charge of a registered assistant pharmacist.

Section 689.160. Exemptions from Application of Laws Relating to Preparation and Sale of Drugs.

. . .

(2) ORS 453.010 to 453.160, 689.010 to 689.640 and 689.990 shall not prevent:

. . .

(b) The sale of patent or proprietary medicines or remedies by shopkeepers not druggists as provided in ORS 689.330 and 689.340.

. . .

Section 689.510. The State Board of Pharmacy; Membership; Terms; Vacancies.
(1) There is established the State Board of Pharmacy, consisting of five members appointed by the Governor . . .

. . .

Section 689.530. Qualification of Board Members.
(1) Only registered pharmacists who have been licensed in this state for at least five years and are actively and continuously engaged in

---

[83] Oklahoma State Board of Pharmacy, *Oklahoma State Laws Relating to the Practice of Pharmacy* (Oklahoma City, 1964), pp. 31–35.

[84] *Ore. Rev. Stat.* tit. 52, c. 689; tit. 36, c. 453 (1953) and Supp. 1965.

the retail drug business are eligible for appointment to the board. They remain eligible to serve only while actively engaged in retail pharmacy in this state.

. . .

Section 689.540 Nominating Candidates for Board Membership. On or before May 1 of each year, the State Pharmaceutical Association may, from among its members, nominate five candidates for the next occurring vacancy on the board. From among these nominees when regularly submitted and certified by the president and secretary of the association, or from others having the necessary qualifications, the Governor shall make appointments for vacancies.

Section 689.620. Powers of Board. The State Board of Pharmacy may:
(1) Make such bylaws and regulations, not inconsistent with the laws of this state, as may be necessary for the protection of the public, appertaining to the practice of pharmacy and the lawful performance of its duties.

Section 453.310. Dispensing of Drugs by Automatic Vending Devices Prohibited.
(1) No drugs shall be dispensed to the public by means of automatic vending machines.
(2) As used in this section:
    (a) "Drugs" includes all medicine and preparations recognized in the United States Pharmacopoeia or National Formulary for internal or external use, and any substance or mixture of substances intended to be used for the cure, mitigation or prevention of disease of either man or animals.
    (b) "Automatic vending machine" means any mechanical device or contrivance whereby the purchaser is able to secure drugs without the aid or assistance of another party.

SELECTED RULES OF THE OREGON STATE BOARD OF PHARMACY[85]

No. 50-060. Restrictions on Advertising. It shall be unlawful for any pharmacy, pharmacist or licensee of the Oregon Board of Pharmacy, who furnishes drugs to the ultimate consumer to advertise, directly or indirectly, by any media affecting the public, any drug, medicine or appliance bearing the legend, "Caution: Federal Law prohibits dispensing without prescription" or whose sale is restricted to a prescription by Oregon law. Nothing in this regulation shall prohibit the furnishing of professional information to medical practitioners.

No. 50-065. Advertising in Mail Order Catalogs. Mail order catalogs mailed out generally to a trade area including Oregon, must bear an asterisk

[85] Oregon State Board of Pharmacy, "Rules and Regulations." (Mimeographed.)

before all items the advertising of which is prohibited or sale restricted in Oregon, with a footnote reading, "This item is not for sale in Oregon" of a type the same size as the type listing the items.

PENNSYLVANIA

EXCERPTS FROM LAWS RELATING TO PHARMACY[86]

Section 390-4. Licensing of Pharmacists.
  (a) The State Board of Pharmacy shall license any person to conduct a pharmacy who . . .
      (4) Has insured that a pharmacist duly registered in Pennsylvania shall be in charge of said pharmacy at all times that the pharmacy is open;
  (j) The board . . . shall have the power to promulgate rules and regulations governing standards of practice and operation of pharmacies including, but not limited to, rules and regulations governing the method of advertising, promotion and standards for filling and refilling prescriptions, such regulations to be designed to insure methods of operation and conduct which protect the public health, safety and welfare and prevent practices or operations which may tend to lower professional standards of conduct.

Section 390-5. Revocation and Suspension.
  (a) The board shall have the power to revoke or suspend the license of any pharmacist upon proof satisfactory to it that:
      . . .
      (9) He is guilty of grossly unprofessional conduct. The following acts . . . are hereby declared to constitute grossly unprofessional conduct of a pharmacist.
          . . .
          (ii) The advertising to the public of prices for prescriptions, dangerous or non-proprietary drugs, or any reference to the price of said drugs or prescriptions either specifically or as a percentile of prevailing prices;
          . . .
          (xii) To accept employment as a pharmacist, or share or receive compensation in any form arising out of, or incidental to, his professional activities from any medical practitioner or any other person or corporation in which one or more medical practitioners have a proprietary or beneficial interest sufficient to permit them to exercise supervision or control over the pharmacist in his professional responsibilities and duties;
          . . .

[86] *Pa. Stat. Ann.* tit. 63, c. 9 (1959) and Supp. 1965.

Section 390–6. Board of Pharmacy.

. . .

  (b) The board shall consist of the Superintendent of Public Instruction, ex officio, and five members who shall be . . . registered as pharmacists in Pennsylvania for a period of at least ten years previous to their appointment, and must at the time of appointment be engaged in the practice of pharmacy.
  (c) The Governor shall . . . appoint [the board] . . . A list of at least six [qualified] persons . . . may be submitted to the Governor by the executive committee of the Pennsylvania Pharmaceutical Association.

Section 390-8. Unlawful Acts. It shall be unlawful for:

. . .

  (2) . . . [anything] herein [to] prevent any person from selling or distributing at retail household remedies or proprietary medicines when the same are offered for sale or sold in the original packages which have been put up ready for sale to consumers, provided household remedies or proprietary medicines shall not include any narcotic drug, dangerous drug, or non-proprietary drug under the Drug, Device, and Cosmetic Act.

. . .

  (11) Any pharmacist or owner of a pharmacy [to advertise or promote] . . . dangerous drugs, narcotics or drugs containing either by name or prices therefor to the general public.

. . .

  (14) Any person to advertise the filling or refilling of prescriptions for any consumer or patient in Pennsylvania if said person is not licensed under this act or the said prescription is not filled or refilled in a pharmacy licensed by the board.

. . .

SELECTED RULES AND REGULATIONS OF THE PENNSYLVANIA STATE BOARD OF PHARMACY[87]

Requirements for Application for Registration and Permit to Conduct a Pharmacy. . . . No registration shall be issued to a Pharmacy that is not open to the public. Non-profit hospitals chartered in the Commonwealth of Pennsylvania shall be exempt from this requirement.

No permit shall be issued to a proposed Pharmacy that does not offer a complete prescription service. This shall include the filling of all prescriptions whether compounded or single items, narcotics or other drugs in any quantity which may be reasonably expected to be filled by other licensed pharmacists.

A registered Pharmacy shall have a segregated prescription department of not less than 15% of the available pharmacy area. . . . Such areas shall

[87] Pennsylvania State Board of Pharmacy, "Rules and Regulations." (Mineographed.)

not include waiting counters or display space attached to waiting counter. . . .

The Pharmacy must be a self contained unit properly separated from the rest of the building by permanent non-transparent walls with at least one direct entrance onto a public thorough-fare and the other doorway from the pharmacy to the rest of the building shall be of average size. The walls shall be of such material as to emphasize the safety of the pharmacy and shall be of such construction as to reasonably guarantee against unlawful ingress and egress. The entrances shall be so constructed as to constitute an adequate safeguard during those hours when the Pharmacy is not open to the public.

Requirements and Regulations on Standards of Practice.

. . .

 (3) The pharmacist has the responsibility to make his professional service available:

  (a) without discriminating in any manner between individuals or groups of individuals by compromising the kind or extent of professional services or facilities made available except that a pharmacist practicing in a hospital or similar institution shall not be required to extend pharmaceutical services to other than registered in-patients of that hospital or institution.

  (b) without requiring an individual to be a member of any organization, or to pay or contribute any enrollment, membership or participation fee as a condition for obtaining professional services.

  (c) offering complete pharmaceutical service by compounding or dispensing all prescriptions which may reasonably be expected to be compounded or dispensed by pharmacists.

 . . .

 (4) No pharmacist or pharmacy owner or pharmacy manager shall enter into any arrangement to accept prescriptions which have been solicited or collected by agents or others not licensed as pharmacists at places not licensed as pharmacies.

 (5) No pharmacist or pharmacy shall promote to the public in any manner a drug which can be dispensed only pursuant to a prescription.

 (6) No pharmacist or pharmacy shall dispose of professional services under conditions or terms which tend to interfere with or impair the free and complete exercise of professional judgement and skill or tend to cause a deterioration of the quality of pharmaceutical service or enter into any arrangement which denies the patient the right of free choice of pharmacist.

 . . .

 (10) No pharmacist or pharmacy shall use the terms "cut rate," "discount," "bargain" or "buy for less" or terms of similar connotation in conjunction with the offering of pharmaceutical service.

 . . .

RHODE ISLAND

EXCERPTS FROM LAWS RELATING TO PHARMACY[88]

Section 5-19-2. Board of Pharmacy—Composition. Within the department of health, there shall be a board of pharmacy . . . consisting of three (3) persons, each of whom shall be . . . a registered pharmacist of at least ten (10) years experience in the practice of retail pharmacy in this state.

Section 5-19-3. Appointment of Board Members. The members of said board shall be appointed by the director of health with the approval of the governor . . .

Section 5-19-6. Examination and Registration of Applicants—Rules and Regulations . . . . Said board is authorized and empowered to make such rules and regulations consistent with the provisions of this chapter and subject to the approval of the director of health as it may deem necessary or expedient for the practice of pharmacy.

Section 5-19-14. Place of Business of Pharmacist. . . . No registered pharmacist shall be the proprietor of more than one place of business, unless he shall keep, at each place of business of which he is the proprietor, at all times when open, a registered pharmacist or a registered assistant pharmacist. No registered pharmacist doing business or employed in any other state, shall be permitted to open shop in his state, unless he shall keep, at all times when open, a registered pharmacist or a registered assistant pharmacist in each shop operated in this state.

Section 5-19-20. Store License—Supervision by Pharmacist. . . . If a person co-partnership or corporation conduct [sic] and maintain [sic] more than one . . . shop or store, he or it shall employ at least one (1) registered pharmacist and shall have a separate registered pharmacist or registered assistant pharmacist at each such shop or store at all times when open.

Section 5-19-36. Persons and Substances Exempt. Nothing in this chapter . . . shall . . . interfere with the making and dealing with the proprietary medicines, popularly called patent medicines, or the ordinary household remedies and drugs . . .

SELECTED RULES AND REGULATIONS OF THE
RHODE ISLAND STATE BOARD OF PHARMACY[89]

No. 11. Advertising. No registered pharmacist and/or licensed pharmacy shall include, or permit or cause to be included, in any newspaper, radio

[88] *R.I. Gen. Laws* tit. 5, c. 19 (1956) and Supp. 1965.
[89] Rhode Island State Board of Pharmacy, "Rules and Regulations." (Mimeographed.)

or television broadcast. display sign, personal solicitation or other manner of advertising, any written or spoken words or statements of a character tending directly or indirectly to deceive or mislead the public, or which makes or sets forth any promises, guarantees, offers, inducements, representations, statements, or rewards of a character tending directly or indirectly to attract to such registered pharmacist and/or licensed pharmacy a demand for pharmaceutical services for the compounding or dispensing of drugs, medicines and poisons upon the prescriptions of a practitioner authorized by law to administer such drugs, medicines, and poisons . . .

No advertisement or public announcement of any kind shall be issued in the name of a licensed pharmacy unless such advertisement or public announcement shall include the name of the registered pharmacist to whom the license to conduct the pharmacy is issued and the number of the license issued for such pharmacy by the board of pharmacy.

No. 12. Prescription Room Area. Any new pharmacy or any existing pharmacy which is to be remodeled or which is to be moved to a new location must comply with the following requirements for the prescription room area:

> That portion or part of the entire licensed pharmacy which is to be occupied by the prescription compounding and dispensing department, including that portion or part thereof utilized for the sale of restricted drugs, shall be not less than ten per cent (10%) of the total floor area . . .
>
> . . .

No. 13. Unprofessional Conduct. Good and sufficient cause for the discontinuance of or refusal to renew any registration of a pharmacist or an assistant pharmacist, and for the refusal to grant or renew or for the revocation of a license to conduct a pharmacy . . . shall include but shall not be limited to the following acts herein defined as unprofessional conduct in the practice of pharmacy:

> . . .
> 6. To enter into an agreement or an arrangement which in any way tends to limit the free choice of the public in the selection of a pharmacist or a pharmacy to provide pharmaceutical services.
>
> . . .
> 16. To solicit, collect, accept, or dispense prescriptions for drugs, medicines and poisons at any location or establishment other than the licensed pharmacy at which the prescriptions are to be filled or compounded. Provided, however, that this section shall not be construed as to prohibit the collection of the prescription or the delivery of the prescribed drugs, medicines or poisons at the residence, office, or place of employment of the person for whom the prescription is issued.
>
> . . .

SOUTH CAROLINA

EXCERPTS FROM LAWS RELATING TO PHARMACY[90]

Section 56–1301. Board of Pharmaceutical Examiners; Election; Terms and Vacancies. The Pharmaceutical Association of the State of South Carolina shall elect six pharmacists doing business within this State who shall be commissioned by the Governor and shall constitute the Board of Pharmaceutical Examiners of the State . . . The Association shall annually elect one member of said Board to fill the vacancy annually recurring. In the case of the death, resignation or removal from the State of any member of the Board, the president of the Association shall appoint in his place a pharmacist, who shall be commissioned by the Governor, to serve for the remainder of the unexpired term.

Section 56–1302. Name of Board; Meetings, Officers and Rules. . . . The Board . . . may . . . adopt any rules or regulations for the conduct of its business and needful for the proper discharge of the business of the Board provided such rules and regulations shall not conflict with any of the provisions of this chapter.

Section 56-1311.1. Additional Regulatory Powers of the Board. The Board shall also regulate the practice of pharmacy, the operation of drugstores and phamacies and the compounding, dispensing, and sale of drugs, medicines, poisons and physicians' prescriptions and, in so doing, shall make, publish, supervise and enforce rules and regulations for the practice of pharmacy . . . But nothing herein shall be construed to authorize the Board to make regulations concerning the prices of goods or medicines sold by drugstores or pharmacies, the hours that such businesses may be operated or the hours of work of employees of such businesses.

Section 56-1316. Chapter Not Applicable to Certain Preparations. Nothing in this chapter shall apply to the . . . sale, at . . . retail, of packaged, bottled or nonbulk chemicals, drugs, medicines, medical and dental supplies, cosmetics and dietary foods when identified by and sold under a trademark, trade name or other trade symbol privately owned or registered in the United States Patent Office, sold or offered for sale to the general public, if such articles meet the requirements of the Federal Food, Drug and Cosmetic Act. . . .

SELECTED RULES AND REGULATIONS OF THE SOUTH CAROLINA STATE BOARD OF PHARMACEUTICAL EXAMINERS[91]

No. 31. Automatic Dispensing Machines. Machines used for the automatic dispensing of drugs must be maintained by and under the direct and immediate supervision of a registered pharmacist.

[90] *S.C. Code* tit. 56, c. 22 (1962) and Supp. 1965.
[91] South Carolina Board of Pharmacy, *Laws, Rules and Regulations* (n.p., 1965), pp. 9–19.

No. 37. Access to Prescription Services. Any pharmacy within this State engaged in the retail practice of pharmacy shall be accessible to the general public. If a pharmacy is part or parcel of a restrictive sales organization, a separate entrance to the prescription department shall be made available to the general public. . . . the meaning of this regulation shall be that pharmaceutical services shall be provided for the general public in all cases.

SOUTH DAKOTA

EXCERPTS FROM LAWS RELATING TO PHARMACY[92]

Section 27.1002. South Dakota Pharmaceutical Association: Membership; Purpose; Annual Meeting; Annual Report and Recommendation of Names for State Board of Pharmacy. The registered pharmacists of this state shall constitute an association under the name and title of the South Dakota Pharmaceutical Association, the purpose of which shall be to improve the science and art of pharmacy and restrict the sale of medicines to regularly educated and qualified persons. The Association shall hold an annual meeting at such time and place as may be determined by it, and it shall report annually to the Governor, recommending the names of at least three members who shall be practicing pharmacists doing a retail business in this state and otherwise qualified to be appointed as members of the State Board of Pharmacy.

Section 27.1003. State Board of Pharmacy: Membership, Terms: Appointments. The State Board of Pharmacy shall consist of three members . . . On or before the first day of October of each year, or whenever a vacancy shall occur on such Board, the Governor shall appoint a licentiate in pharmacy who shall be a member of the South Dakota Pharmaceutical Association as a member of such Board or to fill a vacancy therein.

Section 27.1004. Officers of State Board: Qualifications; Duties; Funds; Certificates of Registration. The Secretary and treasurer of the South Dakota Pharmaceutical Association shall be respectively the secretary and treasurer of the Board of Pharmacy and they shall each give such bonds as the Association may require. . . .

Section 27.1013. Conducting Pharmacy: Persons Authorized; Prohibitions; Exceptions, Physicians, Veterinarians, Patent Medicines; License for Sale of Patent Medicines Required; Definitions. It shall be unlawful for any person other than a registered pharmacist to retail, compound, or dispense drugs, medicines, or poisons or to open or conduct any pharmacy or store for retailing, compounding, or dispensing drugs, medicines, or poisons . . .

Nothing in this chapter shall apply to . . . the business of any physician . . . or . . . veterinarian . . . or prevent him from supplying to his patients such articles as may seem to him proper . . .

[92] *S.D. Code of 1939* tit. 27, c. 27.10 and Supp. 1965.

Nothing in this chapter shall be construed to prevent the sale of any patent or proprietary medicines in the original packages by persons other than pharmacists. . . . For the purpose of this section, patent or proprietary medicines shall be construed to include any medicine or drug which is prepared or compounded in proprietary form and sold at retail in the original packages and where the sale thereof is unregulated under the laws of this state.

Section 27.1014. Ownership of Pharmacies: Requirements; Limitations; Partnerships, Corporations; Vested Rights. Every pharmacy as defined by the laws of this state shall be owned by a licensed pharmacist and no partnership shall own a pharmacy unless all the partners are licensed pharmacists, except that any corporation organized and existing under the laws of this state or any other state in the United States and authorized to do business in this state and empowered by its charter to own and conduct pharmacies and which on the first day of July, 1931, still owned and conducted a registered pharmacy or pharmacies in this state, may continue to own and conduct such pharmacy and may establish and own additional pharmacies in accordance with the laws of this state; but any such corporation which shall not continue to own at least one of the pharmacies heretofore owned by it or which ceases to be actively engaged in the practice of pharmacy shall not be permitted thereafter to own a pharmacy, and except that any person, not a licensed pharmacist, who on the first day of July, 1931, owned a registered pharmacy in this state may continue to own and conduct such pharmacy in accordance with the laws of this state, and except that the administrator, executor, or trustee of the estate of any deceased owner of a registered pharmacy or the widows, heirs or next of kin of such deceased owner may continue to own and conduct such registered pharmacy in accordance with the laws of this state.

SELECTED RULES AND REGULATIONS OF THE
SOUTH DAKOTA STATE BOARD OF PHARMACY[93]

Section E. Restricted Professional Practices.

. . .

13. No pharmacist or pharmacy shall solicit by advertising of any kind the sale or distribution of drugs by prescription by any mail order plan of any form. The mail order sale of drugs by prescription is prohibited whenever such sale has been solicited by advertising of any kind by any person or persons.
14. No pharmacist or pharmacy shall advertise in any manner, prices, percentiles of prices or discounts for prescriptions and drugs requiring a prescription.

[93] South Dakota State Board of Pharmacy, *South Dakota Pharmacy Law-Chapter 27.10; Rules and Regulations of the South Dakota State Board of Pharmacy Pertaining Thereto* (n.p.: South Dakota Pharmaceutical Association, 1964), pp. 11–35.

Section F. Pharmacy Registration.

. . .

11. Whenever a pharmacist permitee has been granted full and complete authority to be in active management of a pharmacy by affidavit of non-pharmacist individuals or by affidavit of a non-pharmacist officer of a corporation, and where the pharmacy regularly registered by the State Board of Pharmacy on the renewal application of such pharmacist permitee includes—(a) a space or unrestricted floor area where general merchandise is sold, or offered for sale, and (b) a restricted floor area where only packaged drugs, medicines and poisons are displayed and offered for sale, and (c) a prescription department, such pharmacist manager shall require his non-pharmacist employer to maintain on the premises of such pharmacy opaque facilities of plywood, wallboard or similar material not less than three-eights inches in thickness and not less than eight feet high for closing and isolating such restricted drug area and prescription department from any unrestricted floor area where general merchandise is sold, or offered for sale, and opaque materials of such size and shape that they can be used conveniently to cover all signs designating such places of business as a pharmacy. . . .

12. Facilities for closing and isolating any restricted drug area and prescription department from unrestricted floor areas where general merchandise is sold, or offered for sale, shall not be required in any pharmacy which is owned and managed by pharmacists registered under the laws of this state and within which a pharmacist or pharmacy interne is on duty and in charge at all times when such pharmacy is open to the public.

. . .

Section H. Anti-Self-Service Regulations.

1. Every pharmacist conducting a retail pharmacy in this state shall segregate the sales display of packaged drugs, medicines and poisons from any sales display of general merchandise.

2. No pharmacist conducting a retail pharmacy in this state shall openly display any packaged drug, medicine or poison within an unrestricted floor area where general merchandise is openly displayed or offered for sale by the methods of self-service and unregulated check-out counter.

3. No packaged drug, medicine or poison shall be openly displayed for sale, within any pharmacy in this state, in a manner where the buyer may pick up and examine the package, unless such packaged drug, medicine or poison is displayed within a RESTRICTED DRUG AREA adjoining the prescription department of such pharmacy and within which restricted area no articles of general merchandise are similarly displayed.

4. All sales from such restricted drug area must be completed by a registered pharmacist, or by trained personnel over sixteen years

of age, who are acting under the direction and supervision of such registered pharmacist.

5. Every person selling or making delivery of any item from such restricted drug area shall be instructed by his pharmacist supervisor:

   (a) not to sell or deliver any item from the restricted drug area to any child under six years of age or to permit such children within restricted drug area unless they are under constant supervision of an adult person; and

   (b) not to sell or deliver any item which if applied externally, or taken internally may impair the normal functions of any tissues or organ of the body, unless the buyer is a reasonable adult person who has been warned to keep such item out of the reach of small children; and

   (c) not to sell or deliver any item, the labeling of which warns against unsafe dosage, or methods or duration of administration or application, in such manner and form, as are necessary for the protection of users, unless the buyer has been warned to use ONLY as directed on the label; and

   (d) not to sell or deliver any item, the labeling of which bears any WARNING or CAUTION against use in pathological conditions, or by children where its use may be dangerous to health, unless the seller is satisfied, after inquiry, that the buyer is not trying such item for self-medication for the first time, and that the buyer understands the proper use thereof and is a proper person to be entrusted with such item. If the buyer has not used such item before he shall be referred to the pharmacist supervisor for sale and delivery; and

   (e) not to sell or deliver any item, the labeling of which bears the statement "Warning—May be habit forming", unless the seller has been authorized by his pharmacist supervisor to complete such sale; and

   (f) not to sell or deliver any exempt-narcotic preparation unless the seller has been authorized to complete such sales and a record including the buyer's name and address, the kind of preparation and the quantity sold and the date of sale, has been entered in the pharmacy's Exempt-Narcotic Register; and

   (g) not to sell or deliver any ethyl alcohol rubbing compound until the pharmacist supervisor has signed his name on the label; and

   (h) not to sell or deliver any item without prescription, the labeling of which bears the statement "Caution: Federal law prohibits dispensing without prescription" and:

   (i) not to sell or deliver any poison to any minor person between the ages of six and sixteen years, or to any person known to be of unsound mind, except upon the written or telephoned order of a responsible adult person known to the seller; and

   (j) not to sell or deliver any poison until the seller shall have satisfied himself, after inquiry, that the buyer understands the poisonous nature of the item and that such poison is to be used for legitimate purposes, and if Schedule "A" poison, not until the buyer has signed his name in the pharmacy's Poison Register.

6. Such restricted drug area, shall, at all times when the pharmacy is open to the public, be under the VISION and SUPERVISION of a registered pharmacist or pharmacy interne.

7. The registered pharmacist in charge of a pharmacy shall be responsible to the public for every act of selling or delivering any drug, medicine or poison from a restricted drug area in such pharmacy.

8. No person, firm or corporation shall hereafter carry on, conduct, or transact business under a name which contains as a part thereof the words "self-service drugs", "self-service drug", "self-serivce drug store" or "self-service pharmacy", or in any manner by advertisement, circular, poster or sign, indicate to the public that drugs and medicines are being displayed and offered for sale by the methods of self-service.

Section I. Household Remedies.

. . .

8. No licensed dealer in selected household remedies shall openly display any household remedy within an unrestricted floor area where general merchandise is openly displayed or offered for retail sale by methods of self-service and unregulated [sic] check-out counter.

9. Every licensed dealer in selected household remedies shall segregate his sales display of household remedies from any sales display of general merchandise either:

    (a) in a manner where the buyer *cannot* pick up and examine the package, such as within a glass showcase or within a wall cabinet behind a counter and from which the buyer is not permitted to serve himself. Such showcases or wall cabinets must be equipped with doors which shall be closed and locked whenever a registered dealer in selected household remedies is not on duty in, and in charge of, the retail place of business where household remedies are sold at retail; or,

    (b) in a manner where the buyer *may* pick up and examine the package but within a RESTRICTED HOUSEHOLD REMEDY AREA where no general merchandise is displayed and which restricted area is separated from the remainder of the retail store by walls of solid construction not less than eight feet in height and such restricted household remedy area is controlled by doors which shall be closed and locked whenever a registered dealer in selected household remedies is not on duty in, and in charge of, such restricted household remedy area.

10. No retail sale or delivery of any household remedy shall be made by any person other than a registered dealer in selected household remedies, or by trained personnel over sixteen years of age; while

acting under the immediate VISION AND SUPERVISION of such registered dealer in selected household remedies.

11. No dealer in household remedies or his agent shall sell or deliver—

   (a) any household remedy to any child under six years of age (Where a restricted household remedy area is maintained, no children under six years of age shall be permitted within such area unless under the constant supervision of an adult person.) or,

   (b) any household remedy which if applied externally or taken internally may impair the normal functions of any tissues or organ of the body, unless the person to whom sold and delivered is a responsible adult person who has been warned at the time of sale and delivery to keep such household remedy out of the reach of small children, or

   (c) any household remedy which could be fatal to human life in doses of sixty (60) grains or less, to any minor person between the ages of six and sixteen years, or to any person known to be of unsound mind, except upon the written or telephoned order of a responsible adult person known to such registered dealer in household remedies, or

   (d) any household remedy the labeling of which warns against unsafe dosage, or methods or duration of administration or application, in such manner and form as are necessary for the protection of users, unless the person to whom sold or delivered is a responsible adult person who has been warned at the time of sale and delivery to use ONLY as directed on the label, or

   (e) any household remedy *intended for human use*, the labeling of which bears any WARNING or CAUTION against use in pathological conditions or by children where its use may be dangerous to health, unless the seller is satisfied, after inquiry, that the buyer is not trying such household remedy for self-medication for the first time and that the buyer understands all of the warning and caution statements and the proper use thereof and is a proper person to be entrusted with such household remedy. Where the buyer has not used such household remedy before, sale and delivery MUST BE REFUSED by such household remedy dealer pending a physician's examination.

12. No registered dealer in selected household remedies shall sell or deliver, or permit to be sold or delivered under his supervision, any United States Pharmacopoeia or National Formulary drug or medicine other than those specifically named in his certified list of registration.

13. Every licensed dealer in selected household remedies shall keep on file in his retail place of business "A Limited COURSE OF STUDY On The Retailing And Medicinal USES OF HOUSEHOLD REMEDIES" as published and furnished by the South Dakota State Board of Pharmacy.

14. The displaying of any household remedy contrary to regulations (8) and (9), or the selling or delivering of any household remedy contrary to regulations (11) and (12) shall be evidence that such person is incompetent or disqualified to perform the duties of a registered dealer in selected household remedies and shall be grounds for the revocation of such person's certificate of registration.

Section K. Patent and Proprietary Medicines.

1. Licenses for the retail sale of patent and proprietary medicines may be procured from the State Board of Pharmacy by persons other than pharmacists who are of good moral character over twenty-one years of age and conducting a retail place of business.

2. Application for a license to sell patent and proprietary medicines shall be made upon a form prescribed by the State Board of Pharmacy. Application blanks are available from the office of the secretary of the State Board of Pharmacy.

3. Licenses to sell patent and proprietary medicines are issued for the year commencing July first and ending June thirtieth.

4. The fee for such license is $3.00 annually. No rebates are given for periods of less than one year.

5. The license shall apply to the location for which the same is issued and shall be posted in a conspicuous place at such location.

6. Patent and proprietary medicines may be sold only in the original packages.

7. Patent or proprietary medicines shall be construed to include any medicine or drug which is prepared or compounded in proprietary form and sold at retail in the original package and where the sale thereof is unregulated under the laws of this state. Any medicine or drug is prepared or compounded in proprietary form when, and only when, that medicine or drug, its name, its formula and its process of manufacture meet the following requirements:

   (a) The NAME of the medicine must be a TRADE-NAME which is the sole property of the producer and which will distinguish the medicine from any other product which is manufactured or produced.

   (b) The name of the medicine must not contain as a part of the title, under which it is marketed, any United States Pharmacopeia or National Formulary official name or synonym.

   (c) The owner must have the exclusive right to make and sell.

   (d) The medicine must not be identical in composition with any United States Pharmacopeia or National Formulary drug or medicine irrespective of whatever name or trademark the same may be called or known.

   (e) The medicine must be either: (1) patented as to name and composition, or (2) made by a secret formula, or (3) the maker must have some exclusive process of manufacture by which exceptional virtues are imparted to his product as distinguished from other preparations of the same sort.

8. The Board of Pharmacy hereby exempts from regulated display and regulated sale by pharmacists:
   (a) Any medicine in the original package intended for use by man which is prepared or compounded in proprietary form and advertised directly to the public for self-medication and which medicine is neither an exempt-narcotic or barbiturate preparation; and
   (b) Any medicine in the original package intended for veterinary use which is prepared or compounded in proprietary form and which medicine is NOT labeled with the word "POISON" for shipment in interstate commerce.
9. The Board of Pharmacy hereby designates for unregulated display and unregulated sale by persons other than pharmacists who are licensed to sell patent or proprietary medicines as provided in SDC 27.1013, all medicines in the original package which the Board of Pharmacy has exempted from regulated display and regulated sale by pharmacists.

. . .

TENNESSEE

EXCERPTS FROM LAWS RELATING TO PHARMACY[94]

Section 63-1001. State Board of Pharmacy—Appointment and Terms of Members—Regulation of Practice—Definition of Terms. There shall exist . . . a state board of pharmacy . . . No person shall be eligible for appointment to the state board of pharmacy unless he shall have been a registered pharmacist under this or some other law of this state for a period of at least ten (10) years, and during the terms of his incumbency shall be actively engaged in conducting a retail pharmacy. The governor shall appoint the members of said board . . .

The Tennessee Pharmaceutical Association, Incorporated, shall annually from among its members recommend five (5) duly qualified persons from whom the governor shall be requested to make appointments . . . all vacancies occurring other than by expiration of term shall [also] be filled . . . by the governor from the nominees of this state pharmaceutical association as of that year.

Section 63-1002. Powers of Board—Meetings and Records. The board shall have power and authority to adopt such rules, regulations and/or bylaws not inconsistent with the laws of the state as are necessary for the regulation of its proceedings and the discharge of its duties . . .

Section 63-1010. Pharmacist Required for Sale of Medicines—Penalty. It shall be unlawful for any person, firm or corporation owning any pharmacy, apothecary shop, retail drug or chemical store to open its door for business, or at any time during business hours to permit the same to

[94] *Tenn. Code Ann.* tit. 63, c. 10; tit. 52, c. 12 (1955) and Supp. 1965.

remain open, except during the presence and under the personal supervision at all times of a registered pharmacist . . . provided, temporary absence of a registered pharmacist shall not be considered a violation of this chapter, if during his absence . . . no prescription shall be compounded or sold, medicine dispensed, poisons sold, and a sign is conspicuously displayed . . . containing the words, "pharmacist not on duty." . . .

Nothing in this chapter shall be construed to prevent the sale of patent or proprietary medicines in original single packages by any merchant or dealer. A proprietary or patent medicine is a medicine hereby defined as a medicine in its unbroken, original package which is advertised, promoted, offered for sale or sold by or under the authority of the manufacturer, or primary distributor thereof, directly to the general public under a trade mark, trade name or other trade symbol privately owned, whether or not registered in the United States patent office, and labeling of which bears (a) a statement specifying affections, symptoms or purposes for which the product is recommended; (b) adequate directions for use and such warnings as are necessary for the protection of users; (c) an accurate statement of the quantity of the contents in terms of weight, measure or numerical count; (d) a statement of the active ingredients; (e) the name and address of the manufacturer or primary distributor thereof; provided, however, that the term "proprietary or patent medicine" shall not apply to any medicine which may be dispensed only upon prescription, or is designated under any law of this state as a narcotic, hypnotic, habit forming, dangerous or poisonous drug or medicine, nor to any therapeutic vitamin. . . .

Section 52-1204. Selling, Bartering, Giving Away or Obtaining Barbital Unlawful—Exception . . . . it shall . . . be unlawful for any person to have [a] . . . prescription filled by mail . . . . the preceding sentence shall not apply to any person or firm whose mail order business is not more than fifteen per cent (15%) of his or its total volume of business.

Section 52-1206. Possession Without Prescription Unlawful. It shall be unlawful for any person to receive by mail or otherwise . . . and [legend] drug . . . without the same having been . . . dispensed by a duly licensed, registered pharmacist in this state . . . The provisions of this section shall not apply to any person or firm where mail order business is not more than fifteen per cent (15%) of his or its total volume of business.

TEXAS

EXCERPTS FROM LAWS RELATING TO PHARMACY[95]

Section 1. Membership; Qualifications; Terms; Vacancies; Oath. The State Board of Pharmacy shall be composed of six (6) members to be appointed by the Governor, each of whom shall have been a registered pharmacist

---

[95] *Tex. Civil Stat. Ann.* tit. 71, c. 8. art. 4542a (1960) and Supp. 1965.

in this state under the provisions of law for a period of five (5) years next preceding the appointment, and who continues to be actively engaged in the practice of pharmacy while serving the term for which he is appointed; and shall at the time of such appointment be in good standing and engaged in retail pharmacy and who is not a member of the faculty of any college or school of pharmacy . . .

Section 4. Officers of Board; Salary; Bonds; By-Laws and Regulations . . . The Board shall have the power to make by-laws and regulations, not inconsistent with the law, for the proper performance of its duties . . .

Section 8. Distribution of Drugs or Medicines, Except in Original Packages, Unlawful; Exceptions . . . . nothing contained in this Act shall be construed . . . to prevent the sale by persons, firms, joint stock companies, partnerships or corporations, other than registered pharmacists, of patent or proprietary medicines, or remedies and medicaments generally in use and which are harmless if used according to instructions as contained upon the printed label . . .

Section 17. Permits for Stores or Factories.

. . .

(d) The State Board of Pharmacy may, in its discretion, refuse to issue a permit to any applicant, and may cancel, revoke or suspend . . . any permit . . . for any of the following reasons:

. . .

(3) That the applicant [or licensee] . . . has in any manner advertised his selling price for any drug or drugs which bear the legend "Caution: Federal law prohibits dispensing without prescription."

. . .

SELECTED RULES AND REGULATIONS OF THE TEXAS STATE BOARD OF PHARMACY[96]

No. V. Regulations Governing Pharmacies.

. . .

(i) *Advertisement.*

(1) To clarify the provisions of Section 17(d)(3) of Article 4542a, the Texas State Board of Pharmacy hereby declares the following: It shall be deemed a violation of Section 17(d)(3) of Article 4542a for any pharmacist or pharmacy . . . to disseminate, personally or acting through agents or employees, by the use of any media of communication, the selling price for any drug or drugs which bear the legend "Caution: Federal law prohibits dispensing without a prescription" to members of the general public . . .

. . .

[96] Texas State Board of Pharmacy, *The Texas Pharmacy Law; Rules and Regulations* (Austin, 1963), pp. 16–26.

(j) *Vending Machines for Drugs Prohibited.* The sale of any drug or drug product bearing the legend "CAUTION: Federal law prohibits dispensing without a prescription" by vending machines or any other automatic device is prohibited in this state unless the vending maching or any other automatic device is stocked with legend item pharmaceuticals by a pharmacist duly licensed with the Texas State Board of Pharmacy.

. . .

UTAH

EXCERPTS FROM LAWS RELATING TO PHARMACY[97]

Section 58-1-5. Exercise of Departmental Functions by Director—Assistance of Representative Committees for Professions, Trades, or Occupations— Number and Qualifications of Members. The functions of the department of registration shall be exercised by the director of registration under the supervision of the commission of the department of business regulation and, when so provided, in collaboration with and with the assistance of representative committees of the several professions, trades and occupations as follows:

. . .

    (15) For pharmacists, a committee of five pharmacists to be designated as Utah state board of pharmacy.

. . .

Section 58-1-6. Committees—Appointment—Qualifications—Terms—Per Diem. The director of registration shall designate the members of the said representative committees provided for in 58-1-5. In designating members of such committees he shall give due consideration to recommendations by members of the respective professions, trades and occupations and by organizations therein. Each member of a committee must have had a license to practice in this state for a period of five years immediately prior to his appointment and be in good standing in the profession, trade or occupation for which appointed. The names of all persons so designated shall be submitted to the governor for confirmation or rejection . . .

Section 58-1-13. Action by Committee Prerequisite to Exercise of Certain Functions. The following functions and duties shall be exercised or performed by the department of registration but only upon the action and report in writing of the appropriate representative committee:

. . .

    (7) Promulgating and enforcing such rules and regulations as may be advocated by the representative committee of the several professions, trades and occupations for the protection or best interest of the public, provided such representative committees are authorized

[97] *Utah Code Ann.* tit. 58, c. 1, c. 12b and c. 17 (1963) and Supp. 1965.

by law to make and initiate such rules and regulations, and provided further, that such rules and regulations shall be approved by the department of registration.

Section 58-12b-1. Board of Pharmacy—Rules and Regulations—Promulgation. The board of pharmacy may make and initiate rules and regulations, not inconsistent with the laws of this state, as may be necessary for the protection of the public . . .

Section 58-17-14.5 Articles Which May Be Sold by Grocers, Dealers, and Others Without Restrictions . . . . all packaged drugs, medicines, medical supplies, bottled or nonbulk chemicals when identified by and sold under a trade-mark, trade name or other trade symbol privately owned or registered in the United States patent office, or as provided by the laws of the state of Utah, and labeled with directions for use and with the name and address of the manufacturer or distributor, provided such articles meet with the requirements of the Federal Food, Drug and Cosmetic Act and the food and drug laws of the state of Utah, may be sold by grocers, dealers and other vendors generally without restriction.

SELECTED REGULATIONS OF THE
UTAH STATE BOARD OF PHARMACY[98]

No. VI. Mechanical Device. Drugs may not be sold or dispensed by or through any mechanical device or vending machine.

No. VII. Requirements of Licensing.

. . .

  (c) No license will be issued to any pharmacy which is owned by a physician, group of physicians, clinic, or any other group of medical practitioners, which group of practitioners is authorized by law to prescribe drugs or medicines. Neither will a license be issued to operate a pharmacy in any building owend by or jointely occupied by any of the above mentioned practitioners, unless:

    1. Said pharmacy has a separate entrance which will allow ingress or egress of the general public.

    2. Said pharmacy (room or area) is rented not on a "Percentage of income" basis, but on a flat fee which shall be comparable to other similar rented locations in similar areas. Neither will a license be issued to a pharmacist who owns such a "clinic" building in which office space and facilities are rented to practitioners of medicine, the rental fee of which is based in any way on the number of prescriptions or on the volume of prescription business originating from said medical tenants.

. . .

[98] Utah State Board of Pharmacy, "Rules and Regulations." (Mimeographed.)

VERMONT

EXCERPTS FROM LAWS RELATING TO PHARMACY[99]

Subchapter 1. Section 1896. Exceptions. This chapter shall not apply to the
. . . sale of patent or proprietary medicines other than those containing
a narcotic drug . . .

Subchapter 2. Section 1931. Qualifications; Term of Office; Compensation.
The state board of pharmacy shall consist of five resident pharmacists,
each of whom shall have had at least five years practical experience in
the practice of pharmacy . . . Annually in the month of January, the
governor shall appoint a member of the board, and all vacancies on the
board shall be filled by the governor. . . .

Subchapter 2. Section 1935. Powers of Board. The board shall have the
power and is hereby authorized:

  . . .

  (8) to make and publish uniform rules and regulations not incon-
      sistent herewith in carrying out and enforcing the provisions of
      this chapter;

  . . .

Subchapter 4. Section 2016. Management. Each . . . registered pharmacy
shall be under the direct charge, management and supervision of a pharmacist duly licensed in accordance with the provisions of this chapter.

VIRGINIA

EXCERPTS FROM LAWS RELATING TO PHARMACY[100]

Article 1. Section 54-399. Legislative Finding; Definitions.

  . . .

  (17) The term *"proprietary medicine"* means completely compounded,
       originally packaged drugs or medicines which do not contain any
       dangerous drugs as defined in this chapter and are not dangerous
       to health when used according to the recommendations on the
       label, and the label or labeling of which conforms to the require-
       ments of the Virginia Dangerous Drug Law and all applicable
       provisions regarding dosage and does not contain the statement:
       "Caution: Federal Law Prohibits Dispensing Without Prescrip-
       tion."

  . . .

*Article 2. Section 54-405. Appointment and Qualifications of Members;
Terms and Vacancies.* The Board shall consist of five members, each of

[99] *Vt. Stat. Ann.* tit. 26, c. 29 (1959) and Supp. 1965.
[100] *Va. Code of 1950 tit.* 54, c. 15 (1958) and Supp. 1965.

whom shall be a registered pharmacist . . . to be appointed by the Governor . . .

Article 2. Section 54-406. Nominations by Virginia Pharmaceutical Association. Each appointment on the Board may be made from a list of at least five names for each vacancy sent to the Governor by the Virginia Pharmaceutical Association. . . . The Governor shall notify the Association promptly of any vacancy other than by expiration and like nominations may be made for filling of the vacancy. In no case shall the Governor be bound to make any appointment from among the nominees of the Association.

Article 2. Section 54-416. By-Laws, Rules and Regulations. The Board may . . . make such rules and regulations, not inconsistent with the laws of the State, as may be necessary for the lawful exercise of its powers.

Article 9. Section 54-478. Supervision of Pharmacist. . . . every . . . pharmacy shall be under the personal supervision of a pharmacist, except that during the temporary absence of the pharmacist, a registered assistant pharmacist may act in place of the pharmacist. . . .

Article 9. Section 54-479. Temporary Permit in Absence of Pharmacist. The Board of Pharmacy may, in its discretion, issue permits to such pharmacies as may be temporarily not under the supervision of a pharmacist to remain open for business for a period not to exceed ten days, but such pharmacy may not during such period . . . compound or dispense physicians' prescriptions. Pharmacies desiring such permit must make application to the Board, setting forth the circumstances upon which their applications are based.

SELECTED RULES AND REGULATIONS OF THE. .
VIRGINIA STATE BOARD OF PHARMACY[101]

Regulation 5. Registration of Pharmacies.
. . .
10. (1) From the effective date of this regulation, no pharmacy shall be issued a permit . . . unless:
    (a) The space which it occupies has an entrance which affords the public direct access from the street.
    (b) The space which it occupies is separated from the remainder of the building in which it is located by solid and durable walls extended from the floor to the ceiling which walls may contain doors to the interior of the remainder of the building, which must be closed and locked when the remainder of the building is closed to the public.
    (2) This regulation shall not apply to:
    (a) Any person who has been granted a permit to operate a pharmacy prior to the effective date hereof.

[101] Virginia Board of Pharmacy, *Rules and Regulations* (Richmond, 1966), pp. 5–14.

(b) To any hospital or similar institution . . .

(c) To any person identified in its firm name directly to the public as a "pharmacy" or "drug store" or other such terms permitted by Section 54-477, Code of Virginia, 1950, as amended.

(3) This regulation shall become effective January 1, 1963.

Regulation 6. One-Pharmacist Pharmacies.

. . .

3. . . . It will be lawful for the pharmacist-in-charge . . . to be temporarily absent from the pharmacy without the necessity of closing the merchandising section of the store, but . . . during such temporary absences as are regarded as necessary, the prescription room or partitioned-off section must be completely locked up . . . until the return of the pharmacist to duty, and a conspicuous sign with letters not less than three inches in height, reading "DRUG AND PRESCRIPTION DEPARTMENT TEMPORARILY CLOSED" or "PHARMACIST TEMPORARILY ABSENT" must be posted in the front section of the store where the public may see it.

4. "Temporary Absence," as applied to one-pharmacist stores, is defined to mean not more than a total of one-fourth the number of hours the pharmacy is open for business daily.

Regulation 11. Revocation of Certificates and Permits. When the holder of any certificate or permit . . . shall become . . . unfit . . . by reason of . . . unprofessional conduct . . . and repeated violations of law or the rules and regulations of the Board, . . . the Board shall, after notice to such holder, and after an opportunity has been given to him to be heard, revoke and annul the certificate or permit . . .

. . .

2. *Unprofessional Conduct.* Unprofessional conduct . . . shall include, but [shall] not be limited to, the following acts:

. . .

(b) The promotion to the public in any manner of a narcotic containing drug, or a drug which may only be dispensed pursuant to a prescription order . . .

. . .

(f) Discriminating in any manner between patients or groups of patients by fostering the interest of one at the expense of another . . .

. . .

Regulation 21. Vending Machines for Drugs Prohibited. The sale of any drug, or drug product by vending machine, or any other automatic device, is prohibited in this State.

Regulation 24. The Filling of Prescriptions. The compounding, refilling or dispensing of drugs pursuant to a prescription . . . shall include, but [shall] not be limited to, the following acts, which shall be performed by a pharmacist, or a student extern or pharmacy intern . . .:

. . .

3. . . . The preparation of the label . . . and the placement of the label and any accessory labels to the container.
4. . . . This regulation shall not apply to . . . the use of approved automatic dispensing systems.

WASHINGTON

EXCERPTS FROM LAWS RELATING TO PHARMACY[102]

Section 43.69.010. Board Created—Members—Qualifications—Terms—Oath —Removal. There shall be a state board of pharmacy consisting of three members to be appointed by the governor by and with the advice and consent of the senate.

Each member . . . at the time of his appointment shall have been a duly registered pharmacist under the laws of this state for a period of at least five consecutive years immediately preceding his appointment and shall at all times during his incumbency continue to be a duly licensed pharmacist. . . .

Section 43.69.030. Powers and Duties. The board shall:
(9) Regulate the distribution of drugs, nostrums, and the practice of pharmacy for the protection and promotion of the public health, safety and welfare by promulgating rules and regulations. Violation of any such rules shall constitute grounds for refusal, suspension or revocation of licenses to practice pharmacy.

Section 18.64.250. Unlawful Practices-Penalty for Violations-Exceptions. . . . nothing in this chapter or chapter 43.69 RCW shall operate in any manner to interfere with . . . selling proprietary medicine or medicines placed in sealed packages . . .

SELECTED RULES AND REGULATIONS OF THE WASHINGTON STATE BOARD OF PHARMACY[103]

No. 17. Drug Vending Machines. The use of any mechanical device or vending machine in the sale or dispensing of drugs, medicines or poisons . . . is prohibited.

No. 40A. Relating to Drugs by Prescription by Mail Order:
WHEREAS, the purpose of regulating the practice of pharmacy and the sale of drugs is the protection of the public health; and WHEREAS,

---

[102] *Wash. Rev. Code Ann.* tit. 18, c. 18.64 (1964); tit. 43, c. 43.69 (1965).
[103] Washington State Board of Pharmacy, *Statutes, Rules and Regulations Governing the Practice of Pharmacy; The Sale and Dispensing of Drugs, Poisons, Narcotics, and Medicines* (Olympia: State Printing Plant, 1964), pp. 42–57.

the sale and distribution of drugs by prescription is safeguarded by a direct, constant, and professional contact between the physician, patient, and pharmacist; and WHEREAS, RCW 18.64.250 prohibits any person from advertising in Washington in any manner drugs or names of like import, without having pharmacists licensed by Washington employed; and WHEREAS, mail solicitation of drugs by prescription impairs this profesional personal contact, tends to lead to falsification, forgery, and fraudulent prescription, and in many instances violates RCW 18.64.250; Now, HEREFORE, we adopt the following regulation: Hereafter no person shall solicit by advertising of any kind the sale or distribution of drugs by prescription by any mail order plan of any form. The mail order sale of drugs by prescription is prohibited whenever such sale has been solicited by advertising of any kind by any person or persons.

The term "person" is defined as "individual, partnership, corporation, association, and agency."

Adopted at a meeting of the Washington State Board of Pharmacy regularly called on October 20, 1960 as provided in RCW 43.69.020 and in accordance with the provisions of the administrative procedures act of 1959.

Effective date: November 20, 1960.

No. 41A. Relating to Drugs by Prescription by Mail Order:

WHEREAS, the purpose of regulating the practice of pharmacy and the sale of drugs is the protection of the public health; and WHEREAS, the advertising of price, percentiles of prices or discounts of prescription drugs requiring a prescription can mislead the public and may invite the use of substandard pharmaceuticals;

Now THEREFORE, we adopt the following regulation:

No person shall advertise in any manner, prices, percentiles of prices or discounts for prescription and drugs requiring a prescription.

The term "person" is defined as "individual, partnership, corporation, association, and agency."

Adopted at a meeting of the Washington State Board of Pharmacy regularly called on October 20, 1960 as provided in RCW 43.69.020 and in accordance with the provisions of the administrative procedures act of 1959.

Effective date November 20, 1960.

No. 43. Full Disclosure in Drug Advertisements.

WHEREAS, the purpose of regulating the practice of pharmacy and the sale of drugs is the protection of the public health; and, WHEREAS, the advertising of prescription or legend drugs tends to create a demand for a product which may not serve the best interest of the public and may result in an interference with necessary discretion of the physician: THEREFORE, no person shall advertise legend or prescription drugs unless the advertisement shall include:

(1) the ingredients of the product listed in the same order as is found on the label of the product.

(2) A brief summary relating to side effects, contraindications, and limitations as to the effectiveness of the drug.

(3) Length of time the drug has been produced for sale to the public.

(4) If the proprietary name and established or brand name of the drug differ, then both names must be stated with equal prominence.

(5) If the drug contains any habit forming ingredient that fact must be stated in type of size at least as large as the largest type or style used in the advertisement relating to that drug.

In no event shall any of the above required information be printed or displayed in type or style less than one-half in size to the largest type or style used in the portion of the advertisement refering to any legend or prescription drug.

Adopted at a public meeting of the Washington State Board of Pharmacy regularly called on the 20th day of March 1964 as provided in RCW 43.69.030 and pursuant to RCW 69.04.016. and 69.04.710.

No. 44. Misleading Advertising of Drug Prices.

WHEREAS, it is unlawful for any person or group of persons to conspire to fix or determine the prices of prescription or legend drugs, and,

WHEREAS, each pharmacy or pharmacy's owner is free to determine the price for which he chooses to sell his services and products, and,

WHEREAS, no established price for prescription or legend drugs exists,

THEREFORE, no person shall advertise in any manner discounts or percentiles of prices for prescription or legend drugs except discounts or percentiles from a pharmacy's or pharmacy's owners established regular prices, provided that a list of the established regular prices be available to the public in the pharmacy, and there shall be a duplicate list filed with the State Board of Pharmacy.

Adopted at a public meeting of the Washington State Board of Pharmacy regularly called on the 20th day of March 1964 as provided in RCW 43.69.030 and pursuant to RCW 69.04.016 and 69.04.710.

WEST VIRGINIA

EXCERPTS FROM LAWS RELATING TO PHARMACY[104]

Section 2895.[2]. Board of Pharmacy; Appointment, Qualifications and Terms of Members; Powers and Duties Generally. . . . the "West Virginia Board of Pharmacy" . . . shall consist of five practicing pharmacists, who shall be appointed by the governor by and with the advice and consent of the senate. Each member of the board, at the time of his appointment, shall be a . . . registered pharmacist of this State, and actively engaged in the practice of pharmacy. . . .

[104] *W. Va. Code of 1931* Ann. c. 16, art. 5 and Supp. 1965.

The board . . . shall have the authority to . . . adopt rules of professional conduct appropriate to the establishment and maintenance of high standards of integrity and dignity in a profession.

Section 2906(1).[14]. Pharmacies or Drug Stores to be Registered; Permit to operate; Fees; Registered Pharmacist to Conduct Business. . . . Every [pharmacy] . . . shall be in direct charge of a registered pharmacist . . .

Section 2906(6).[19]. Rules and Regulations of the Board of Pharmacy; Revocation of Permits; Employment of Field Agents, Chemists, Clerical and Other Qualified Personnel. The board of pharmacy shall make such rules and regulations, not inconsistent with law, as necessary, to carry out the purposes and enforce the provisions of this article . . .

Section 2906(8).[21]. Limitations of Article. The provisions of this article shall not apply to the sale of patent or proprietary medicines, nor to such ordinary drugs and dyestuffs as are usually sold in a country store. . . .

SELECTED RULES AND REGULATIONS OF THE WEST VIRGINIA STATE BOARD OF PHARMACY[105]

Article 13. Sale of Drugs by Mechanical Devices; Gratuities; Sharing Compensation.
   (1) *Sale of Drugs and Medicines by Mechanical Devices or Vending Machines Prohibited.* The use of any mechanical device or vending machine in connection with the sales or disposition of drugs and/or medicines is unlawful.

   . . .

Article 14. Rules of Professional Conduct.

   . . .

   3. *Refusal of Prescriptions.* It is the duty of a pharmacist to make his professional services available to the public. Every pharmacy offering pharmaceutical services to the general public shall provide complete pharmaceutical service, including the compounding or dispensing of all prescription orders which may be reasonably expected to be compounded or dispensed by pharmacists. No pharmacist shall refuse to accept and fill . . . any prescription order presented to him unless there is a valid reason for his inability to fill such prescription order.

   . . .

   8. *Promotion of Drugs.* No pharmacist or pharmacy shall promote to the public by any means a narcotic drug or other drug which may only be dispensed pursuant to a prescription order, which promotion

[105] West Virginia State Board of Pharmacy, *Statutes, Rules and Regulations Governing the Practice of Pharmacy and the Sale and Dispensing of Drugs, Poisons, Narcotics and Medicine* (n.p., 1966), pp. 41–63.

tends to cause such drugs to be used in excess of the requirements established in a legitimate physician-patient relationship.

. . .

12. *Place of Practice.* No pharmacist shall maintain a place of practice or location from which to solicit, accept or dispense prescriptions other than a pharmacy for which a permit has been issued by the West Virginia Board of Pharmacy.

. . .

WISCONSIN

EXCERPTS FROM LAWS RELATING TO PHARMACY[106]

Section 151.01. Board.
 (1) The state board of pharmacy consists of 5 resident pharmacists, at the time of appointment actually engaged in practice, appointed by the governor . . .

. . .

 (4) The board may adopt by-laws, rules and regulations . . .

Section 151.02. Registration. . . .

. . .

 (9) No drug store, pharmacy, apothecary shop, or any similar place of business, shall be opened or kept open for the transaction of business until it has been registered with and a permit therefore has been issued by the state board of pharmacy. This section shall not be construed to apply to any store or stores opened for the sale of proprietary or so-called patent medicines which conform to state and federal laws. . . .

. . .

Section 151.04. Practice.

. . .

 (2) No person shall sell . . . drugs . . . unless he be a registered pharmacist . . .
 (3) This shall not interfere . . . with the sale of proprietary medicines in sealed packages, labeled to comply with the federal and state pure food and drug law, with directions for using, and the name and location of the manufacturer . . .

. . .

SELECTED RULES AND REGULATIONS OF THE WISCONSIN STATE BOARD OF PHARMACY[107]

Phar. 1.03. Other Retail Enterprises. It is the policy of the board to discourage establishment of a drug department as an adjunct of larger, unrelated business enterprises.

[106] *Wis. Stat.* tit. 15, c. 151 (1957).
[107] *Wis. Admin. Code* Phar. 1.03—1.05 (March 1964).

Phar. 1.04. Prescription Department.

   (1) *Area of Prescription Department.* The area devoted to the sale of drugs shall be equal to not less than 15% of the main floor area of the store, and in no instance shall it be less than 120 square feet.

  . . .

Phar. 1.05. Professional Coverage. No pharmacy shall at any time be open for business unless there is present therein and in charge thereof a licensed pharmacist . . . The language "in charge" in section 151.04(2), Wis. Stats., shall mean the physical presence of the pharmacist on the premises. He shall be permitted momentary or brief necessary absence for a meal period during which time he must be immediately available to the pharmacy, and provided no drugs are sold or prescriptions compounded or dispensed during his absence. A meal period shall be construed as meaning a period at mid-day and/or during the evening hours in which a meal is normally consumed. In no instance shall such period exceed 60 minutes. . . .

Phar. 1.11. Drugs, Exempted Narcotic Preparations and Poisons. . . . Self-service display of drugs . . . is strictly prohibited. These items may be sold only by persons authorized to do so by the board of pharmacy under Ch. 151, Wis. Stats. . . .

Phar. 1.14. Vending of Drugs by Mechanism Prohibited. No person, firm or corporation shall purchase or rent or have in his or its possession or under his or its control any slot machine, vending machine or other mechanism or means so designed and constructed as to contain and hold any drugs of any kind and to release the same upon the deposit therein of a coin or any other thing of value. The sale or distribution of any drugs by any manner or device by means of such slot machine, vending machine or other mechanism is prohibited.

Phar. 1.17. Advertising Availability of Dangerous Drugs by Name Prohibited. No pharmacist, proprietor or manager of any pharmacy shall advertise in any manner the availability of dangerous drugs by name.

Phar. 1.18. Advertising Prices of Prescription Medication Prohibited. No pharmacist, proprietor or manager of any pharmacy shall advertise in any manner prices to be changed for prescription medication, either specifically or as a percentile of prevailing prices.

WYOMING

EXCERPTS FROM LAWS RELATING TO PHARMACY[108]

Section 33-307. Board of Pharmacy Created; Designation; Composition; Organization; Qualifications, Compensation, etc., of Members; Disposition of Funds; Secretary's Bond; Powers and Duties Generally. . . . Hereafter,

[108] *Wyo. Stat.* 1957 tit. 33, c. 22.

only registered pharmacists who have been licensed in this state for at least five years and are actively engaged in retail pharmacy shall be eligible for appointment to the . . . board of pharmacy.

The governor shall nominate, and by and with the advice and consent of the senate, shall appoint three persons from among such registered pharmacists in the state, as have had five years practical experience in the dispensing of physicians' prescriptions or are graduates of a school or college of pharmacy generally recognized at the time of graduation.

No member so appointed shall be connected with any school or college of pharmacy in a professional or executive capacity. . . . Any member of the board who during his incumbency, ceases to be actively engaged in the practice of pharmacy in this state, shall be automatically disqualified from membership. . . .

Except as otherwise provided in this act. . . . the board of pharmacy shall have the power, and it shall be its duty:

. . .

(9) . . . to make and publish rules and regulations not inconsistent herewith, for carrying out the provisions of this act.

Section 33-321. Exemptions.

. . .

(c) Nothing in this act shall apply to the . . . sale by any method at retail of economic poisons, packaged drugs, medicines, medical and dental supplies, bottled or non-bulk chemicals, cosmetics and dietary foods when identified by, and sold under a trade mark, trade name or other trade symbol, privately owned or registered in the United States patent office, sold or offered for sale to the general public, if such articles meet the requirements of the Federal Food, Drug and Cosmetic Act.

Physician Ownership Bill Introduced by Senator Hart

89TH CONGRESS
1ST SESSION

S. 2568

IN THE SENATE OF THE UNITED STATES

SEPTEMBER 28, 1965

Mr. HART introduced the following bill; which was read twice and referred to the
Committee on the Judiciary

A BILL

To strengthen the antitrust laws by prohibiting the payment to or
receipt by persons licensed to engage in the practice of medicine,
of profit, rebates, refunds, commissions, discounts, rentals or
other valuable considerations in connection with the supplying to
patients drugs, devices, or other products prescribed by such
licensees.

1   *Be it enacted by the Senate and House of Representatives*

2   *of the United States of America in Congress assembled,* That this

3   Act may be cited as the "Medical Restraint of Trade Act."

4   FINDINGS OF FACT

5   SEC. 2. The Congress finds and declares that the payment to

6   and receipt by persons licensed to engage in the practice of medi-

7   cine, of profit in connection with the furnishing to patients of

8   drugs, devices, or other products prescribed for consumption or

1   use by patients tends to lessen competition and substantially to

2   restrain and to monopolize trade and commerce and constitutes

3   a burden upon interstate commerce in such products.

5   SEC. 3. As used in this Act—

6   (a) The term "person" shall mean any natural person, firm,

7   corporation, or association of any kind;

8   (b) The term "licensee" shall mean any person licensed by

9   any State, any governmental division thereof, or any association

10 or society authorized under any State law to issue such a license,

11 to engage in the practice of medicine;

12 of the rendition by such licensee of professional service to or for

13 rendered in the practice of his profession by the licensee;

14 (d) The term "profit" shall mean any markup above actual

15 cost of the product to the licensee, discount, refund, rebate, com-

16 mission, rental for space leased from a licensee based in whole or

17 in part on a percentage of income from drugs or devices sold or

18 furnished by the tenant or unreasonably high rental in lieu thereof,

19 or other valuable consideration; and

20 (e) The term "drug or device" shall mean drug or device as

21 defined in the Federal Food, Drug, and Cosmetic Act, as amended

22 (21 U.S.C. 321), and other products prescribed by a licensee for

23 consumption or use by man.

1   PROHIBITION OF MEDICAL RESTRAINTS OF TRADE

2   SEC. 4. (a) It shall be unlawful—

3   (1) for any person to pay, offer to pay, or allow, directly

4   or indirectly, to any licensee, or for a licensee to knowingly re-

5   ceive directly or indirectly, any profit for or in connection with

6   the referral of patients of the licensee to such person for the

7   furnishing of any drug or device; or

8   (2) for any licensee to accept or receive directly or indi-

9   directly from any person any profit on or resulting from the

10   sale, rental, furnishing, or supplying by such licensee of any

11   drug or device to such person in connection with or as a result

12   of the rendition by such licensee of professional service to or for

13   such person, except that nothing herein shall apply to a li-

14   censee furnishing to his patient such drug or device when an

15   emergency exists or shall apply to the administration of a unit

16   dose of a drug in any form to a patient by the licensee or by a

17   nurse or assistant under direction of the licensee.

18   (b) Every person, firm, corporation, or association who shall

19   violate this Act shall be deemed guilty of a misdemeanor, and,

20   on conviction thereof, shall be punished by fine not exceeding

21        $5,000, or by imprisonment not exceeding one year, or both

22   said punishments, in the discretion of the court.

1   (c) The several district courts of the United States are in-

2   vested with jurisdiction to prevent and restrain violations of this

3   Act; and it shall be the duty of the several district attorneys of the

4   United States, in their respective districts, under the direction of

5   the Attorney General, to institute proceedings in equity to prevent

6   and restrain such violations. Such proceeding may be by way of

7   complaint setting forth the case and praying that such violations

8   shall be enjoined or otherwise prohibited. When the parties com-

9   plained of shall have been duly notified of such complaint the

10   court shall proceed, as soon as may be, to the hearing and de-

11   termination of the case.

Revised Physician Ownership Bill Introduced by Senator Hart

A BILL

To strengthen the antitrust laws by prohibiting the sale by licensed practitioners of drugs, or devices, prescribed by such practitioners and the knowing receipt of rebates, refunds, discounts or commissions in connection with the supplying to patients of such products, with certain exceptions, and for other purposes.

Be it enacted by the Senate and House of Representatives of the United States of America in Congress assembled, That this Act may be cited as "Medical Restraint of Trade Act."

Findings Of Fact

Sec. 2. The Congress finds and declares that the sale of drugs, or devices, directly or indirectly, or the knowing receipt or rebates, refunds, discounts, or commissions by practitioners in connection with the supplying of such products to patients tends to lessen competition and substantially to restrain and to monopolize trade and commerce and constitutes a burden on interstate commerce in such products.

Definitions

Sec. 3. As used in this Act—

(a) The term "practitioner" shall mean any person licensed by any State, District of Columbia or any Territory of the United States, any governmental division thereof, or any association or society authorized under any law of any State, District of Columbia or any Territory of the United States, to issue such a license qualifying such person to administer drugs, or devices in the practice of medicine in the diagnosis, cure, mitigation, treatment or prevention of disease in man or to affect the structure or any function of the body of man.

(b) The term "drug" shall mean (1) articles recognized in the official United States Pharmacopoeia, official Homeoepathic Pharmacopoeia of the United States, or official National Formulary, or any supplement to any of them; and (2) articles intended for use in the diagnosis, cure, mitigation, treatment or prevention of disease in man; and (3) articles intended to affect the structure or any function of the body of man; and (4) articles intended for use as a component of any article specified in clause (1), (2) or (3) of this paragraph; but does not include devices or their components.

(c) The term "device" shall mean instruments, apparatus, and contrivances, intended (1) for use in the diagnosis, cure, mitigation, treatment or prevention of disease in man; or (2) to affect the structure or any function of the body of man.

(d) The term "community pharmacy" shall mean an office, pharmacy, drugstore or other establishment which engages in the sale of drugs or devices.

(e) The term "optical dispensary" shall mean an office, shop, or other establishment which engages in the sale at retail or wholesale of optical devices which affect any function of the human eye.

(f) The term "leasehold interest" shall mean rental for space leased from a practitioner or practitioners by a community pharmacy or optical dispensary based in whole or in part on a percentage of income from drugs or devices sold or furnished by the tenant or an unreasonably high rental for such space in lieu of such percentage of income.

Prohibitions

Sec. 4. It shall be unlawful for a practitioner directly or indirectly to: (a) sell drugs or devices; or (b) own a legal, beneficial, or lease-hold interest in a community pharmacy or optical dispensary, except that nothing herein shall apply (1) to a practitioner furnishing a patient any drug or device in an emergency; or (2) to the administration of a unit dose of a drug in any form to a patient by or under the supervision of a practitioner; or (3) to the sale of drugs by hospitals, nursing homes, or sanitariums to patients confined therein; or (4) where there is no community pharmacy or optical dispensary reasonably available as a source of such drugs or devices in the trading area of the practitioner's place of practice or the patient's place of actual residence, taking into account the needs and reasonable convenience of the patient.

Sec. 5. It shall be unlawful for a practitioner directly or indirectly to knowingly receive from a community pharmacy or optical dispensary or a community pharmacy or optical dispensary to knowingly pay to a practitioner any rebate, refund, discount, commission, or other valuable consideration on income received or resulting from the sale or furnishing to patients of drugs or devices by such community pharmacy or optical dispensary.

Sec. 6. It shall be unlawful (a) for a drug company to give or sell to practitioners any legal or beneficial interest in the company with the intent or for the purpose of inducing those practitioners to prescribe to their patients the drugs of the company; or (b) for a practitioner to acquire or own a legal or beneficial interest in any drug company with the intent or for the purpose of prescribing its drugs to his patients and thereby gain financial benefits for himself; or (c) for a drug company to pay to a practitioner or a practitioner to receive from a drug company any rebate, discount, refund, or commission in connection with the prescribing of the company's drugs by the practitioner.

As used in this section a "drug company" shall mean any person, partnership, firm, or corporation which manufactures drugs, or buys drugs from another and processes or packages them, and sells the drugs under its labels or trade names.

Jurisdiction Of Courts;
Duty Of District Attorneys

Sec. 7. The several district courts of the United States are invested with jurisdiction to prevent and restrain violations of this Act; and it shall be the duty of the several district attorneys of the United States, in their respective districts under the direction of the Attorney General, to institute proceedings in equity to prevent and restrain such violations. Such proceeding may be by way of complaint setting forth the case and praying that such violations shall be enjoined or otherwise prohibited. When the parties complained of shall have been duly notified of such complaint the court shall proceed, as soon as may be, to the hearing and determination of the case.

Suits By Person Injured;
Limitation Of Actions

Sec. 8. Any person, firm or corporation who shall be injured in his business or property by reason of anything forbidden in this Act may sue therefore in any district court of the United States in the districts in which the defendant resides or is found, without respect to the amount in controversy and shall recover threefold the damages by him sustained, and the cost of suit, including a reasonable attorney's fee.

Any action to enforce any cause of action under this section shall be forever barred unless commenced within three years after the cause of action arose.

Effective Date Of Act

Sec. 9. This Act shall take effect on the first day of the sixth month beginning after the date of enactment of this Act.

Bibliography

Books

ANDREWS, P. W. S. and FRANK A. FRIDAY. *Fair Trade: Resale Price Maintenance Re-examined*. New York: St. Martin's Press, 1961.

ARTHUR, WILLIAM R. *The Law of Drugs and Druggists*. 4th ed. St. Paul, Minnesota: West Publishing Co., 1955.

BAIN, JOE S. *Industrial Organization*. New York: John Wiley & Sons, Inc., 1959.

BOWE, WILLIAM J. *Estate Planning and Taxation: Chartered Life Underwriter Edition*. 2nd ed. Buffalo, New York: Dennis and Co., Inc., 1965.

GALBRAITH, JOHN KENNETH. *The Affluent Society*. Cambridge: The Riverside Press, 1958.

HAYNES, WILLIAM. *The American Chemical Industry—A History*. 6 vols. New York: D. Van Nostrand, Inc., 1954.

KREMERS, EDWARD and GEORGE URDANG. *History of Pharmacy*. 3rd ed. Revised by Glenn Sonnedecker. Philadelphia: J. B. Lippincott Co., 1963.

LaWALL, CHARLES H. *Four Thousand Years of Pharmacy*. Philadelphia: J. B. Lippincott Co., 1927.

LEBHAR, GODFREY M. *Chain Stores in America, 1859–1962*. 3rd ed. New York: Chain Store Publishing Corp., 1963.

MEYER, J. R., J. F. KAIN, and M. WOHL. *The Urban Transportation Problem*. Cambridge: Harvard University Press, 1965.

NACDS Directory, 1964–65 Edition. Washington: National Association of Chain Drug Stores, 1964.

NORTHRUP, HERBERT R. *Organized Labor and the Negro*. New York: Harper & Bros., 1944.

OLSEN, PAUL CRANDALL. *Marketing Drug Products*. New Brunswick, N.J.: Rutgers University Press, 1948.

PETTIT, WILLIAM. *Manual of Pharmaceutical Law*. 2nd ed. New York: MacMillan Co., 1957.

SAMUELSON, PAUL A. *Economics: An Introductory Analysis*. 6th ed. New York: McGraw-Hill, 1964.

SLICHTER, SUMNER H. *Union Policies and Industrial Management*. Washington: The Brookings Institution, 1941.

SMITH, ADAM. *The Wealth of Nations*. Edited by Edwin Cannan. New York: Random House, n.d.

WEINTRAUB, SIDNEY. *Intermediate Price Theory*. Philadelphia: Chilton Books, 1964.

WILCOX, CLAIR. *Public Policies Toward Business*. 2nd ed. Homewood, Ill.: Richard D. Irwin, Inc., 1960.

Reports

ALDERFER, HAROLD F. *Professional Licensing in Pennsylvania*. Philadelphia: Fels Institute of Local and State Government of the University of Pennsylvania, March 1962.

BUTTERFIELD, CHARLES JR. *Legislation Affecting Pharmacy Introduced in State Legislatures During the Year 1965*, October 9, 1965. Report Submitted by the Legislative Committee of the National Council of State Pharmaceutical Association Executives to the Council. (Mimeographed.)

California. Department of Professional and Vocational Standards. California Board of Pharmacy. *Hearings Re Changes in Rules and Regulations of Proposed Section 1769*, Vol. II. Hearing held in Los Angeles on February 21, 1962.

California. Senate. *1956 Partial Report to the Legislature by the Senate Interim Committee on Licensing Businesses and Professions*. Sacramento, 1956.

CHAPMAN, W. O. and O. P. FIELD. *Indiana Licensing Law*. Bloomington: Bureau of Government Research, Department of Government, Indiana University, 1953.

The Great Atlantic and Pacific Tea Company Annual Report for the Fiscal Year Ended February 26, 1966. New York: The Great Atlantic and Pacific Tea Co., 1966.

Kroger Annual Report, 1965. Cincinnati, Ohio: The Kroger Co., 1965.

Massachusetts. *Report of the Special Commission Established to Make an Investigation and Study Relative to Establishing and Regulating a New Category of Over-the-Counter Proprietary Preparations Used for Self-Treatment to Be Known as "Potentially Harmful" Drugs*. House Document No. 3075. January 1966.

Minnesota. *Report of the Interim Commission on Sale of Home Remedies*. March 1965.

New York. *Annual Report of the Joint Legislative Committee on Imitation Food Products and Problems*. Legislative Document No. 34, March 30, 1957.

New York. *Annual Report of the Joint Legislative Committee on Imitation Food Products and Problems*. Legislative Document No. 56, March 31, 1958.

North Carolina Board of Pharmacy. *Eighty-Fourth Annual Report*. Chapel Hill: North Carolina Board of Pharmacy, 1965.

Proceedings of the National Association of Boards of Pharmacy. Chicago, 1951, 1961, and 1965.

Safeway Stores, Incorporated—Annual Report, 1965. Oakland, California: Safeway Stores, Inc., 1966.

U.S. Bureau of the Census, Census of Business, 1963. *Retail Trade: Sales Size, BC63-RS2. Vol. I.* Washington: U.S. Government Printing Office, 1964.

U.S. Senate. Committee on the Judiciary. Subcommittee on Antitrust and Monopoly. *Hearings, Physician Ownership in Pharmacies and Drug Companies.* 88th Cong., 2d Sess., 1964. Washington: U.S. Government Printing Office, 1965.

U.S. Senate. Committee on the Judiciary. Subcommittee on Antitrust and Monopoly. *Report, Physician Ownership in Pharmacies and Drug Companies.* 89th Cong., 1st Sess., 1965. Washington: U.S. Government Printing Office, 1965.

WALLER, HERMAN S. and SIDNEY WALLER. *Pharmacy Ownership Legislation.* A Report Prepared for the National Association of Retail Druggists. Chicago: National Association of Retail Druggists, *ca.* 1964.

Legal Documents

Only those cases which have not been decided are listed below. Refer to the Index for decided cases (even though an appeal may be pending).

Only those statutes cited in the text are listed below. See the footnotes following Appendix I for the statutes and regulations cited in Appendix I.

Transcript of Superior Court Proceedings. Vol. II. *Cohen v. Board of Registration in Pharmacy.* Superior Court No. 79683 in Equity. January 4–5, 1965.

Massachusetts Board of Registration in Pharmacy. *Application of Osco Drug of New England, Inc. for Registration of a Store for the Transaction of Retail Drug Business at 97 River Street, Dorchester.* March 1, 1966.

Massachusetts Board of Registration in Pharmacy. *In the Matter of: Camille J. LeFrancois—Osco Drug of New England, Inc.* Hearing held on July 13, 1965, at 14 Beacon St., Boston, Massachusetts.

Massachusetts Board of Registration in Pharmacy. *In the Matter of: Osco Drug of New England, Inc.* Hearing held on October 19, 1965, at 14 Beacon St., Boston, Massachusetts.

Mich. Admin. Code. R338.485.15(b) and (d) (Supp. 37).

Michigan Board of Pharmacy. *In the Matter of the Application of Superx Drugs for: Pharmacy License.* Proceedings held at the Board office on September 29, 1965.

Michigan Board of Pharmacy. *In Re Application of Superx Drugs Corporation.* December 16, 1965.

Minnesota State Board of Pharmacy. *In the Matter of: Application for Licenses to Operate Pharmacies or Drug Stores, Snyder Drug Stores, Inc.* Transcript of hearing held on July 20, 1962 at the Board office.

Minnesota State Board of Pharmacy. "Minutes of the 379th Meeting."
  July 20, 1962 (in the files of the Board).
Nev. Rev. Stat. tit. 54, c. 639, s. 639.270.
N.J. Stat. Ann. tit. 45, subtit. 1, c. 14, s.45:14-12.
Pa. Stat. S.9377a-1 and s.9377a-2 (Supp. 1928).
Rhode Island Session Laws of 1870. C.856, s. 8.
Petition for Writ of Certiorari. Snyder's Drug Stores, Inc. v. *Minnesota
  State Bd. of Pharmacy.* Fourth Judicial Dist. Ct. Minn. Filed August
  17, 1962.
Order for Writ of Certiorari. Snyder's Drug Stores, Inc. v. *Minnesota State
  Bd. of Pharmacy.* No. 579593. Fourth Judicial Dist. Ct. Minn. August
  17, 1962.
Writ of Certiorari. Snyder's Drug Stores, Inc. v. *Minnesota State Bd. of
  Pharmacy.* No. 579593. Fourth Judicial Dist. Ct. Minn. August 17,
  1962.
Brief for Plaintiff. Supermarkets Gen. Corp. v. *Sills.* Super. Ct. N.J.
Trial Brief for Plaintiff. Supermarkets Gen. Corp. v. *Sills.* Super. Ct. N.J.
Appendix to Brief for Plaintiff. Vol. I and II. *Superx Drugs Corp.* v. *State
  Bd. of Pharmacy.* State Supreme Court File No. 50087.
Compaint. United States v. *American College of Pathologists.* Civil No.
  66 C 1253. No. D. Ill. Filed June 3, 1966.
Indictment. United States v. *Northern Cal. Pharmaceutical Ass'n.* Criminal
  No. 37653, D. No. Cal.
Va. Code of 1950. tit. 59, c. 1.1, s. 59.8.2 (1958).

Articles and Periodicals

American Druggist, January 5, 1953 through July 1967.
APPLE, WILLIAMS. "Individual Practice of Pharmacy," *The Virginia Phar-
  macist,* Vol. 47, No. 1 (Jan. 1963), pp. 13–16, 20–21.
BACHMAN, JULES. "Economics of Proprietary Drugs," *Annals of the New
  York Academy of Sciences,* Vol. 120, Art. 2 (July 14, 1965), pp.
  881–882.
BROWN, FRANCIS G. "The Pharmaceutical Industry," in *Development of
  Modern Industry.* Edited by Glover and Cornell. 3rd ed. New York:
  Prentice-Hall, 1957.
COLLINS, BETTY N. "Does New York State Have a Kangaroo Court?," *Al-
  bany Law Review,* Vol. 23 (May 1959), pp. 315–335.
COWEN, D. L. "The New Jersey Pharmaceutical Association," *New Jersey
  Journal of Pharmacy.* Vol. 18, No. 12 (Dec. 1945), pp. 16–17.
The Detroit Free Press, March 2, 1963.
"The Donovan-Carlino Bill," *The New York State Pharmacist,* August 1953,
  p. 15.
Drug News Weekly, January 24, 1962 through July 1967.
Drug Topics, August 10, 1953 through July 1967.
EILER, LEE E. "Pharmacy, by Pharmacists, in Pharmacies," *The Kentucky
  Pharmacist,* Vol. 26, No. 7 (July 1963), pp. 10–12, 17.

EDMONDSON, J. RICHARD and WILLIAM F. WEIGEL. "Recent Developments in the Law Relating to the Retail Sale of Drugs," *Food Drug Cosmetic Law Journal*, Vol. 20, No. 8 (Aug. 1965), pp. 469–476.

"Four Drug Classes Are Needed," *APhA Newsletter*, Vol. 3, No. 7 (March 28, 1964), p. 2.

"Friends of the Grocers," *The Brooklyn Pharmacist*, April 1965, pp. 3–4.

GESOALDE, NICHOLAS S. "Executive Secretary's Page," *New York State Pharmacist*, Vol. 39, No. 4 (April 1964), p. 7.

GRUZ, NATHAN I. "Professional Licensing Legislation," *The Maryland Pharmacist*, Vol. 39, No. 12 (Sept. 1964), pp. 746, 748, 750, 752–753.

HANSON, ARTHUR B. "Antitrust Looks at Profession of Pharmacy," *Journal of the American Pharmaceutical Association*, Vol. NS1, No. 11 (Nov. 1961), pp. 680–682.

HERZOG, SOL A. " 'Twixt Supermarket and Courts—Whither Pharmacy,' " *Journal of the American Pharmaceutical Association*, Vol. XIV, No. 12 (Dec. 1953), pp. 764–770.

"H. F. 1869 Defeated by State Senate as Legislature Adjourns," *Minnesota Pharmacist*, Vol. 19, No. 8 (May 1965), p. 11.

"Ill. Forces Spiegel to Shut Down Its Rx Mail-Order Plan," *APhA Newsletter*, Vol. 1, No. 3 (Feb. 10, 1962), pp. 1, 3.

KEEFER, CHESTER S. "Summary and Conclusions," *Annals of the New York Academy of Sciences*, Vol. 120, Art. 2 (July 14, 1965), pp. 1002–1005.

Lansing State Journal (Lansing, Mich.), September 19, 22, 26, 1962.

LEAKE, CHAUNCEY D. "The History of Self-Medication," *Annals of the New York Academy of Sciences*, Vol. 120, Art. 2 (July 14, 1965), pp. 815–832.

The Lowell Sun (Lowell, Mass.), January 28, 1965.

MAHLER, DAVID. "What the Census Shows . . . and What It Fails to Show," *Chain Store Age—Drug Executives Edition*, February 1966.

MANDELL, H. GEORGE. "Therapeutic Range and Extent of Use of Home Remedies," *Annals of the New York Academy of Sciences*, Vol. 120, Art. 2 (July 14, 1965), p. 910.

National Clearinghouse for Poison Control Centers Bulletin, May–June 1966, pp. 1–10. Published by the Public Health Service of the Department of Health, Education and Welfare.

New York Times, May 4, 1966.

"Resale Price-Fixing Under the Fair Trade Laws," *Business Week*, August 28, 1937, pp. 37–44.

ROTTENBERG, SIMON. "The Economics of Occupational Licensing," in *Aspects of Labor Economics*, A Report of the National Bureau of Economic Research. Princeton: Princeton University Press, 1962.

SALONGER, MATTHEW L. "The Jersey Proprietary Case," *The New York State Pharmacist*, Vol. 28, No. 8 (Aug. 1953), pp. 16, 30.

SCOTT, MILDRED. "Arizona's AntiTrust Complaint," *The Arizona Pharmacist*, Vol. 43, No. 1 (Jan. 1963), p. 6.

"State Regulation of Drugs: Who May Sell 'Patent and Proprietary' Medicines," *The Yale Law Journal*, Vol. 63 (Feb. 1954), pp. 550–559.

Times Union (Albany, N.Y.), April 8, 1964.

"Too Many Pharmacies," *The Brooklyn Pharmacist,* March 1965, p. 11.

"The Veto Message," *New York State Pharmacist,* Vol. 39, No. 4 (April 1964), p. 13.

The Wall Street Journal, April 26, 1966.

WEIGEL, WILLIAM F. "State Legislation Restricting the Sale of Drugs," *Food Drug Cosmetic Law Journal,* Vol. 13, No. 1 (Jan. 1958).

WEISS, E. B. "Is the Traditional Pharmacist as Dead as the Dodo?," *Advertising Age,* April 8, 1963, pp. 100, 102.

"White Cross Drops Suit Against ACPA," *Allegheny County Pharmacist,* November 1964, p. 7.

WILSON, JOSEPH G. "How Professional Is Engineering?," *Mechanical Engineering,* Vol. 86, No. 6 (June 1964), p. 19.

Worcester Telegram (Worcester, Mass.), April 13, 1965.

Personal Interviews

CRAIG T. ALLEN, JR., Secretary and Treasurer, Osco Drug, Inc., Melrose Park, Illinois. January 13, 1966.

WILLIAM S. APPLE, Executive Director, American Pharmaceutical Association, Washington, D.C. January 26, 1966.

FRANCIS BALASSONE, Secretary, Maryland Board of Pharmacy, Baltimore, Maryland. February 9, 1966.

HINTON F. BEVIS, Secretary, Flordia Board of Pharmacy, Tallahassee, Florida. April 14, 1966.

BENJAMIN BROWN, Attorney, Boston, Massachusetts. March 31, 1966.

J. B. CARSON, Secretary, Virginia Board of Pharmacy, Richmond, Virginia. June 15, 1966.

CECIL L. CLIFTON, Joint Secretary, Georgia Examining Boards, Atlanta, Georgia. April 14, 1966.

JAMES D. COPE, Executive Vice President (then Secretary), The Proprietary Association, Washington, D.C. November 3, 1966.

PAUL H. CREWS, Secretary, State Pharmacy Examiners, Des Moines, Iowa. January 10, 1966.

CLIFFORD DAVID, Attorney, Smith, Kline & French Laboratories, Philadelphia, Pennsylvania. February 4, 1966.

GEORGE E. DEWOLF, Attorney and Insurance Manager, Osco Drug, Inc., Melrose Park, Illinois. January 13, 1966.

EDWARD DILLON, JR., Attorney, Little Rock, Arkansas. January 3, 1966.

JACK ECKERD, President, Eckerd Drugs of Florida, Inc., Clearwater, Florida. April 19, 1966.

C. B. ERICKSON, Law Department, Star Markets, Inc., Cambridge, Massachusetts. April 25, 1966.

GLENN T. EVANS, Regional Vice President-Operations, Superx Drugs, Inc., Cincinnati, Ohio. December 30, 1966.

ARNOLD FAUDMAN, President, Arnold Drugs, Inc., Mount Clemens, Michigan. February 17, 1966.

BENJAMIN FELSTEN, Staff Assistant to the Executive Vice President, Food Fair, Inc., Philadelphia, Pennsylvania. December 8, 1965.

ARTHUR L. FERGUSON, Law Department, Kroger Co., Cincinnati, Ohio. December 30, 1965. Also telephone conversation, December 1966.

ARTHUR A. FORCIER, Chief of Pharmacy Section, Rhode Island State Board of Pharmacy, Providence, Rhode Island. March 30, 1966.

GRANT C. GENTRY, General Counsel, Osco Drug, Inc., Melrose Park, Illinois. January 13, 1966.

GORDON GRIFFITH, President, Ray and Derick, Inc., Northumberland, Pennsylvania. December 3, 1965.

KENNETH S. GRISWOLD, Secretary, New York State Board of Pharmacy, Albany, New York. March 29, 1966.

PAUL G. GRUSSING, Secretary, Minnesota State Board of Pharmacy, St. Paul, Minnesota. January 10, 1966.

JAMES F. HOGE, ROGERS, HAGE & HILLS, Attorneys, New York, New York. March 29, 1966.

JACK KELLY, Legal Counsel, Pharmaceutical Manufacturers Association, Washington, D.C. January 24, 1966.

JOHN P. KERN, Director of Professional Services, Gray Drug Stores, Inc., Cleveland, Ohio. February 18, 1966.

EVAN M. KJELLENBERG, Law Department, Kroger Co., Cincinnati, Ohio. December 30, 1965.

ROBERT KLEGAN, Vice President of Drug Operations, National Tea Co., Chicago, Illinois. January 14, 1966.

DAVID J. KRIGSTEIN, Secretary, Delaware State Board of Pharmacy, Wilmington, Delaware. February 9, 1966.

ALBERT LERNER, Head of Drug and Non-Food Division, Penn Fruit, Inc., Philadelphia, Pennsylvania. November 19, 1965.

JOSEPH A. MARCUS, President, GEM International, Inc., St. Louis, Missouri. January 21, 1966. (Telephone Conversation.)

H. C. McALLISTER, Secretary, North Carolina Board of Pharmacy, Chapel Hill, North Carolina. April 12, 1966.

MRS. VERNA McHUGHES, Assistant to the Secretary, Arkansas State Board of Pharmacy, Little Rock, Arkansas. January 4, 1966.

FRED MEHAFFY, Secretary, National Association of Boards of Pharmacy, Chicago, Illinois. February 15, 1966.

JAMES H. MERRITT, Executive Vice President, National Association of Chain Drug Stores, Washington, D.C. December 31, 1965.

JEROME D. PITKOW, President, Crown-Shop Rite Drugs, Inc., Cranford, New Jersey. May 19, 1966.

DONALD E. PRESCOTT, Assistant to the Executive Director, American Pharmaceutical Association, Washington, D.C. October 19, 1965.

PAUL A. PUMPIAN, Secretary, Wisconsin Board of Pharmacy, Milwaukee, Wisconsin. January 12, 1966.

BERNARD, W. RICHLIN, President, Bernie's Drug Concessions, Inc., Philadelphia, Pennsylvania. November 23, 1965.

HAROLD ROSENWALD, Attorney, Boston, Massachusetts. March 31, 1966.

WILLARD SIMMONS, Secretary, National Association of Retail Druggists, Chicago, Illinois. February 15, 1965.

JACK SKYLES, Vice President in charge of Chicago-Osco stores, Osco Drug, Inc., Chicago, Illinois. January 13, 1966.

DAVID SMALL, President, Parkview Drugs, Inc., Kansas City, Missouri. February 11, 1966.

PHILLIP SMALL, Chairman of the Board, Parkview Drugs, Inc., Kansas City, Missouri. February 11, 1966.

W. G. SMITH, Secretary-Manager, Arkansas Pharmaceutical Association, Little Rock, Arkansas. January 4, 1966.

STANLEY W. STEPHENS, Vice President of Administration and Merchandising, Superx Drugs, Inc., Cincinnati, Ohio. December 30, 1965.

JOHN P. STREET, Director of Professional Services, Osco Drug, Inc., Melrose Park, Illinois. February 16, 1966.

EDWARD P. TARLOSKI, Secretary, New Jersey Board of Pharmacy, Newark, New Jersey. March 28, 1966.

LLOYD W. TRACY, Secretary, Missouri Board of Pharmacy, Jefferson City, Missouri. January 7, 1966.

H. M. TROWERN, JR., Vice President, Brewer Pharmacal Engineering Corp., Upper Darby, Pennsylvania. November 19, 1965; May 26, 1966; and June 10, 1966.

ROBERT T. WALKER, Secretary, Tennessee State Board of Pharmacy, Nashville, Tennessee. February 7, 1966.

SIDNEY WALLER, Counsel, National Association of Retail Druggists, Chicago, Illinois. February 15, 1966.

ALLAN G. WEATHERWAX, Secretary, Michigan Board of Pharmacy, Lansing, Michigan. January 15, 1966.

WILLIAM F. WEIGEL, ROGERS, HOGE & HILLS, New York, New York. March 29, 1966.

JEROME WILLITS, Health and Beauty Aids Merchandiser, Food Fair, Inc., Philadelphia, Pennsylvania. December 8, 1965.

THOMAS D. WYATT, Secretary, South Carolina Board of Pharmacy, Columbia, South Carolina. April 13, 1966.

Unpublished Material

BELLOWS, CHARLES. Letter to Alf Bergerud, dated October 11, 1962.

BERGERUD, ALF L. Letter to F. Marion Fletcher, dated August 11, 1966.

CAPEN, PHILAN DONALD. "An Economic Analysis of the Pharmaceutical Industry." Unpublished MBA Thesis, University of Pennsylvania, 1959.

CULLEN, FREDERICK J. "A Statement on the New Jersey Declaratory Judgement Action." July 16, 1954. In the file "Pharmacy Laws and Legislation" of the American Pharmaceutical Association, Washington, D.C. (Typewritten.)

EVANS, ROBERT L. Letter to Floyd N. Heffron, dated March 30, 1962.

FERGUSON, ARTHUR L. Letter to F. Marion Fletcher, dated August 3, 1966.

HARROD, LESLIE D. "The Need for Modern Pharmacy Laws." An address before the House of Delegates of the American Pharmaceutical Association, August 29, 1947. In the files of the American Pharmaceutical Association. (Mimeographed.)

HUGHES, GEORGE DAVID. "Has the Struggle for Differential Advantage Changed the Distribution of Drugs?" Unpublished MBA Thesis, University of Pennsylvania, 1959.

HUGHES, JAMES JOSEPH, JR. "The Pharmaceutical Industry, 1953–1957." Unpublished MBA Thesis, University of Pennsylvania, 1959.

LOUD, THEODORE EWALD. "The Independent Pharmacy's Need for Resale Price Maintenance." Unpublished MBA Thesis, University of Pennsylvania, 1960.

McALLISTER, H. C. Letter to Herbert R. Northrup, dated November 22, 1965.

MERRITT, JAMES H. Letter to F. Marion Fletcher, dated March 29, 1966.

MYERS, MAX A. "Conflict of Interest and the Ohio State Board of Pharmacy." Paper presented at the LAO Conference of the Ohio State Pharmaceutical Association, September 23–24, 1964, Lincoln Lodge Motor Hotel, Columbus, Ohio.

New York State AFL-CIO. "Memorandum in Opposition to New York Ownership Bills Introduced in 1965 in N. Y. Legislature." (Mimeographed.)

Oregon University Bureau of Municipal Research and Service. "Licensing of Businesses and Occupations by Oregon Counties." Information Bulletin No. 141. Eugene, Oregon, March, 1964. (Mimeographed.)

The Proprietary Association. "A Brief Look at the History of the Proprietary Association." (Mimeographed.)

WALSH, LAWRENCE E. Letter to John J. McMillan, dated May 3, 1960.

Index